CW00663068

?

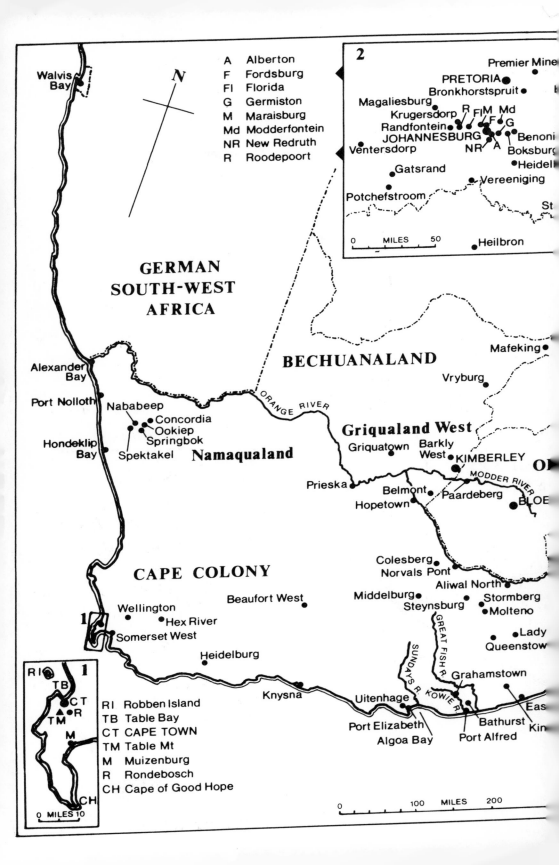

FOREWORD
by Dr. John Rowe

Gold, diamonds and copper have been the main incentives luring Cornish people to South Africa for nearly two centuries. Ironically, however, as Richard Dawe's researches reveal the first of the three was copper, up at O'okiep inland from Namaqualand's Skeleton Coast. There, first prospecting began with ventures promoted by the Dutch Governor, Simon van der Stel, in the late 1680s, but it was little more than mere 'fossicking' until some Cornish miners came in during the late 1830s.

These, however, were not the first Cornish on the South African scene for some came out from Cornwall when the British Government promoted settlement in the Eastern Cape in 1820, including 'birds of passage' like the Oslers who found the farming potential of the aptly named Zuurveld not to their liking, and William Cock, a man gifted with entrepreneurial talents who made good in business activities and some notoriety in provincial politics. Diamond discoveries instituted a major influx of miners in the late 1860s, although there had been mutterings of gold discoveries, even of mythical mines associated with King Solomon and of the golden 'Empire' of Monomotopa long before the first Dutch settlement of the Cape in 1652. Furthermore, in October 1854 traces of gold in the Witwatersrand were discovered by a young Boer, Pieter Jacob Marais, back from the California diggings – almost thirty years before the great rush started.

Mines were the 'pull' factors bringing about the migration of so many Cornish folk to South Africa. The 'push' factors which drove so many from their homeland – the catastrophic decline of copper mining, wayward fluctuations in tin prices, economic depression accompanied by social distress partially alleviated in numerous cases by remittances sent home by emigrants – all these are effectively recounted and analysed in this work. Nor is the cost in blood ignored. On the quartz reefs of the Rand pneumatic drills came to be known as widow-makers, with many phthisis victims dying aged less than thirty. Mining accidents, also, took a toll.

And, too, human conflict – warfare. When the British Government annexed the Cape in 1814, it acquired a colonial community of Boers already at odds with what they regarded as an exploiting metropolitan 'Old World' government, and one, too, involved in a series of conflicts with indigenous native tribes destined to last over a century; those natives, furthermore, being pushed against their frontiers by the imperial Zulu power of Shaka and his successors. Regular and volunteer soldiers from Cornwall were to fight, suffer and die in such battles as Isandlwana, Majuba, Magersfontein, Spion Kop and Paardeburg.

Less and ambiguous renown emanated from the notorious Jameson raid with many Cornish miners leaving the Rand convinced that they should have no part in a conflict between millionaire 'Randlords' and Kruger's government.

That last episode, however, stressed the fact that so many of the Cornish miners on the Rand were and regarded themselves as 'birds of passage'. With increasing talk about the 'African disease' emigration to and, certainly, any lengthy sojourning in Rand mines came to be regarded as a gamble with mortal illness, and a large proportion of those who came out never lived to see their homeland again.

Not all, nevertheless, were miners. Like Cock in the earlier days of the century in the Eastern cape many engaged in trade and merchanting. From an extensive range of Cornish and South African newspapers has, not surprisingly, come much information on Cornish journalists, newspaper owners and proprietors. Various other professions emerge; religion brought out that stormy Anglican bishop, John Williams Colenso, besides a fair sprinkling of humble local preachers among early established Cornish Methodist denominations. Offsetting early Zuurveld disillusionment were sugar planters in Natal, but the typical tenant of yeoman farmer of the Old Country was unused to the extensive acreage of so many veld pastoral holding. There were many prominent figures associated with mining, among whom Francis Oats and Lewis Michell, right hand men of Cecil Rhodes, demand mention. Among more exotic characters, Transvaal's equivalent of America's Far West 'Lawman' Deadwood Dick, Llewellyn May who assumed Boer 'nationality' by taking the name Frederick de Witt Tossel and claimed close acquaintance with Oom Paul Kruger.

Hailing from Redruth Arthur H. James became known by 'Cousin Jacks' on the Rand as 'Cyanide James'. The process of extracting gold from quartz using cyanide was the subject of prolonged and costly litigation, reminiscent of the conflict of Boulton and Watt with the Hornblowers and Trevithick in Cornwall a century earlier. While the introduction of the process ensured the survival of gold mining on the Rand at a critical time, the actual discoverers of the process ended their days comparatively poor men.

Such was also the lot of numerous Cornishmen who toiled in African diamond and gold diggings. They were numerous, but it is difficult to hazard an estimate particularly since so many were relatively transient 'birds of passage'. Nor should it be forgotten that there were times when South Africa had not alluring but repelling features. Anglo-Boer antipathies were at times acute; there were racist attitudes which too often bedevilled industrial and social relationships.

Cornish immigrants brought to the South African diamond and gold fields mining, technological and managerial skills. It seems certain that they came out in greatest numbers in the quarter century before the outbreak of the first World war. For this and later years Richard Dawe has drawn upon numerous records and reports of Cornish Associations and societies in South Africa which maintained, in good times and bad, close links with their homeland. These are sources to gladden the hearts of family historians on both sides of the Atlantic and 'Down Under' Oceania as well.

With passing years some of these organisations have lapsed; bonds with Cornwall may have loosened when the Afrikaaner National Government severed connection with the British Commonwealth and attempted to enforce apartheid. On the whole the Cornish element in South Africa eschewed racism, but the decline of the Old Country associations was a dark aspect of that unhappy era of South African history. Somewhat ironically during those times in segregated Soweto black folk were still speaking English with, it was said, a most remarkedly Cornish brogue.

Last but far from least a religious heritage. To South Africa as to mining regions elsewhere the Cornish brought a Christian faith, predominantly with some Protestant Methodist denominational traits, different from the fundamentalist Dutch Reformed Church of the Boer Afrikanders. Nevertheless it was two Cornish Anglicans whose careers presented the outstanding challenge to Afrikander racism. Bishop John William Colenso's scepticism of Old Testament historical authenticity could be regarded as condemning nationalist Boer religious commemoration of Dingaan's Day as heretical, but even more serious was his pro-Zulu stance in the war with Cetewayo. Later, during the Second Boer War and its aftermath the 'pro-Boer' humanitarian activities of Emily Hobhouse, daughter of the Rector of St. Ive, helped the reconciliation of Boer and Briton in the earlier decades of the twentieth century.

It is disappointing that Richard Attenborough's film about Gandhi omitted the role played by Cornishman William Hosken who supported Gandhi when he was in South Africa. Similarly the BBC television series on Rhodes did not portray the parts played by Francis Oats, Lewis Michell and other Cornishmen in the Rhodes story. Fortunately Richard Dawe has given us an insight into the parts played by these and many other Cornish pioneers.

November 1997

John Rowe.

Dedication for
my brother
Ian James Dawe
1946 – 96

*'The only true history of a country
is to be found in its newspapers'*

Lord Macaulay

NOTE: Newspapers from South Africa and Cornwall
were studied extensively in the preparation of this
book and referenced in notes at the end of each
chapter. In some cases the spellings of surnames used
by these newspapers may contain inaccuracies.

AUTHOR'S PREFACE

This book is the end result of many years research and although much was done in isolation it would be remiss of me not to pay tribute to a number of people and institutions without whom the book would never have been completed.

Initial inspiration came some thirty years ago from the late A.L. Rowse when in Cornwall at my home town – Launceston – following the publication of his book *The Cornish in America* he concluded a lecture by suggesting that not only was the story of the Cornish emigration overseas to be the biggest and most significant of Cornish themes but he hoped that others would follow him to give a complete picture of the Cornish diaspora. They did. A.C. Todd and John Rowe, like Rowse, completed the picture of the Cornish diaspora on the American continent whilst Philip Payton has covered the continent of Australia. My aim was to follow in this tradition and tell the story of the Cornish emigration to the continent of Africa namely South Africa.

Much of the material used for this study is extracted from my earlier works, *The Effect Chinese Labour had on the Cornish Miner in South Africa* (M.A. thesis October 1984) and *The Role and Influence of the Cornish in South Africa 1886-1925* (M.A. dissertation November 1986). I should therefore like to thank my former tutor Norman Levy at Middlesex University not only for his help and advice but for making my studies stimulating and rewarding. During that time I received generous help and advice from Gillian Burke, John Rowe, Hugh Miners, Claire Leith and especially Philip Payton who, from the very start, showed a genuine interest in my work and has not hesitated to give me full support In particular I was fortunate to meet Norman Hannan and thank him for the genuine interest, enthusiasm and encouragement he has given me over many years.

I would also like to thank Dr. B.A. Austin, Claire Bowden-Dan, Jory Bennett, K. Hilary Borkett, Phyllis Ferguason, Mrs. M.V. Hall, Bunny Henwood, Frank Maguire-Tresidder and the late Paul Smales. I would like to thank Staff at the British Library, the Collindale Newspaper Library, Camborne Library, the Institute of Commonwealth Studies, Launceston Library, Middlesex University, Redruth Library, Royal Commonwealth Society, Royal Cornwall Library (Truro) and staff at the Cornwall Record Office and Institute of Cornish Studies for making facilities available to me.

Special thanks go to Roger Ballard-Tremeer, Counsellor at the South African Embassy, who not only provided me with access to the Embassy library but showed personal interest in the project. Thanks also go to Roger van Eeghen of De Beers, who gave me access to material at the De Beers London Office.

In South Africa I owe debt to a number of people (nearly all of Cornish descent, the majority of whom I have never met in person) who responded magnificently to my letters for help – by supplying me with their family history and in some cases family photographs. The generosity of Graham Dickason, Carol Botha, Ken Sara, V.N. Kendall, Gerald Reed, Richard Skewes, Vera Kirby, June Melville, Daniel Freemantle Tregonning, Harry and Thalia Wroth, Iris Morshead, Margaret Marsh, Christine Higgo-Hartwig, Shelagh O'Byrne-Spencer, Olive Bennetts, Stephanie McFadzean, Rodney Trudgeon, A.H. Giddy, Shelia Mitchell, Ada Grassman, Barbara Paynter, Joy Nelson, Darrell Hall, Peter Hitchins, Janet Lee and Don Henwood was overwhelming. I would like to thank the Editors of the *Diamond Fields Advertiser*, the Johannesburg *Star* and the *Settler Magazine* and in particular, staff at the Killie Campbell Africana Library (Durban), Africana Museum & Public Library (Johannesburg), Albany Museum & 1820 Settlers Memorial Museum (Grahamstown), Africana Library (Kimberley), Municipal Library (Krugersdorp), the Treverton Trust and St. Stithians College. My thanks also go to the O'okiep Copper Company.

Above all I am indebted to Lambert Truran, who in some ways is co-author of this book. From our first meeting in Cornwall, in 1987, he has not failed in his help and advice. More importantly, having lived in Southern Africa from 1948 until 1991, he was able to assist in carrying out valuable research on my behalf, providing me with much information and giving me the benefit of his experience, having been closely involved with the Cornish community in Southern Africa. I hope this book measures up to his expectations.

I owe much to my friend and teaching colleague Keith Kilkenny who not only carried out the only proof-reading of the book, but as a Yorkshireman helped with non-partisan but critical judgments. His help and encouragement I value most deeply.

I must also thank Catherine Gilbert and Bev de Schoolmeester for typing much of my early work and more recently as I have come to grips with modern technology I have to thank two people who have helped me along this complicated path, namely Paul Sutton and Paul Hodge, good friends and a pleasure to work with. I am indebted to Mrs Pat Phillipps for further proof-reading and Roger Penhallurick for providing the excellent map of South Africa inside the covers.

I owe much to the late Len Truran who first agreed to publish my work until illness prevented him from doing so. However, I owe more to Charles Thurlow, my present publisher, who was prepared to have confidence in my efforts as well as giving valuable advice and assistance which has finally enabled this to see the light of day. I am indeed most grateful.

Finally my thanks go to my wife Ann for her moral support and enduring patience over these past years.

Contents

LIST OF ILLUSTRATIONS

INTRODUCTION

CORNWALL

Cornishmen from the beginning have always dug for wealth... tinners, copper-seekers, quarriers, slate-breakers, clay-workers, farmers: an earthy people with an earthy knowledge... Those who desire to understand the Cornish and their country, must use their imagination and travel back in time.[1]

Daphne Du Maurier.

Sadly, Cornwall today is remembered by some people only for its spectacular coastline, its clotted cream, pasties and piskies. Its history appears to be a tangled web of myth and legend. At one end of the spectrum lies all things Celtic – of King Arthur, Mark and Tristan – while at the other, shrouded in mist, lurk the smugglers and wreckers. The modern fictional writings of Daphne Du Maurier and Winston Graham have somewhat confused the issue, by creating a romantic Cornwall which really exists only within the pages of *Jamaica Inn* and the *Poldark* books.

Such is the persistence of the myth-making that today Cornwall can boast of a Poldark Mine (in reality the old Wheal Roots/Wendron Consols Mine, near Helston) and at Delabole a Poldark Inn, which, like the Jamaica Inn on Bodmin Moor, is little more than a tourist attraction. Somewhere amidst all this lies the great tract of Cornish history, still largely unknown to many people – including the Cornish.[2]

It was Cornwall's mineral wealth – vast resources of copper and tin that played the major role in the county's history. By the early nineteenth century the Cornish mines were producing three-quarters of all the copper and nearly half the tin used in the world. Cornwall's thriving copper industry was centred on the St. Day-Gwennap district, (with the Consolidated and United Mines) and the Camborne-Redruth district (with the Dolcoath and Carn Brea Mines). Later new copper mines were opened up in mid-Cornwall, the most productive being Fowey Consols near St. Blazey whilst in East Cornwall, in the Liskeard area, the mines of South Caradon and Phoenix United were two of the last great copper mines to survive. The richest copper mine of all – Devon Great Consols – lay just over the Cornish border near Tavistock. The Cornish tin mines were centred on the Camborne-Redruth area with mines such as the Basset Mines, Tincroft & Cook's Kitchen and of course Dolcoath and South Crofty and the St. Just-Penwith area, with mines such as Levant, Botallack, Ding Dong, Geevor and Giew.

Cornwall also led the world in mining machinery and expertise in deep level hard rock mining. Not only was Cornish mining equipment soon being exported world-wide – one of Harvey's engines (now a national monument in the Netherlands) was used by the Dutch to drain the Haarlem Meer – but so too were Cornish engineers. As early as 1816 Richard Trevithick, Henry Vivian, Thomas Trevarthen and William Ball set out from Cornwall on the South Sea whaler *The Asp,* to inspect Trevithick's own engines which had been supplied a few years earlier to pump water from the silver mines of Peru. In 1818, however, the *Royal Cornwall Gazette* reported:

> It appears from letters just received by a person in this country from South America that the Cornishmen who went out to that country... for the purpose of erecting Steam Engines on the silver mines of Pascoe in Peru have not met with that encouragement which they were fully given to expect.[3]

Trevithick was unfortunate, in that his engines were destroyed in a rebellion in 1820. He eventually returned to England in 1827 to die penniless in Dartford, Kent in 1833.

In Cornwall the rapid growth of the mining industry – 75 mines employing 16,000 workers in 1800, rising to 200 mines employing 30,000 in 1837, with 300 mines employing over 100,000 workers by 1860 – saw a rise in Cornwall's population, from 200,000 to 350,000 over roughly the same period.

At the beginning of the nineteenth century and with the disappearance of Anglesey from the world's copper markets, outside competition was for many years non-existent.[4] Cornwall had been unrivalled as the main source of copper ore in the world. From 1820 onwards, however, as vast quantities of copper were discovered first in Chile and then Michigan, U.S.A. and South Australia, competition led to a relative depression in the Cornish copper industry. The result was the first wave of large scale emigration, as Cornishmen went off to work in the mines of the very countries which were competing with Cornwall. The 1849 California Gold Rush encouraged even more to emigrate, and with the complete collapse of the Cornish copper industry in the 1860's miners, faced with the economic reality of unemployment and starvation left in their droves – 'an estimated 7,300 miners emigrating in the first eighteen months after the 1866 crash'.[5]

Within a decade the same fate, precipitated by wild speculation in the financial tin market, was to cripple the Cornish tin industry. Until 1872 the Malayan States and Cornwall had between them produced the world's supply of tin. The discovery of alluvial tin deposits in eastern Australia, combined with the opening of the Suez Canal in 1869 precluded any recovery of the Cornish tin industry as the price of tin continued to be disastrously low. Hundreds of Cornish mines were closed down and abandoned or, to use the Cornish expression, became knacked bals. What followed was a steady migration of 'young Cornishmen carrying unique skills and knowledge to every mining camp in the North American continent and to Australia.'[6]

Cornwall saw a migration of its male work force unequalled to that in any other county in England. To determine the exact number of those who emigrated from Cornwall is, as A.C. Todd claims, 'almost impossible to calculate with any accuracy without a searching survey of the county parish by parish'.[7] A further difficulty pointed out by John Rowe is that British records of emigration did not differentiate the Cornish from those who emigrated from the shires.[8] A final complication is the actual type of migration undertaken by the Cornish miner. Gillian Burke has identified two kinds, that of the 'single roving miner' who travelled between the mining camps of the world and Cornwall and 'emigration pure and simple'.[9] The waves of the sea which had long battered the Cornish coast were now to be matched by the waves of emigration that were to de-populate Cornwall's mining communities, so that today a great number of people overseas feel that they have their roots in Cornwall.

The first edition of the *Cornish Post & Mining News*, 14th September 1889, reminded its readers that:

> *There is scarcely a mine, be it in the auriferous plains of equatorial Africa, or the snow clad silver yielding reefs of N. America, from the lead mines of Nevada, Colorado and Montana and the gold laden creeks of California away down to the Southern States, to Mexico and the Argentina Republic, from Chile to far away Tasmania and back again to the diamond diggings of Natal and the Transvaal where a Cornishman may not be found.*[10]

This was no romantic fantasising on the part of a provincial newspaper – it was plain fact.[11] Cornish miners were to be found in all of the places cited by the *Post,* and more – such as India, West Africa and many parts of Europe, as letters and correspondence to the *Post* and other Cornish newspapers at that time bear witness. The now traditional saying 'wherever in the wide world a deep hole has been dug for minerals you will find in it a Cornishman'[12] was almost literally true. However, there is little doubt, in the case of the Cornish miner, as to the main areas of migration – North, Central and South America, Australia and South Africa. It has been estimated that in the second half of the 19th century some 170,000 Cornishmen and women left Cornwall with their families[13] and there is no doubt that the greatest number went to the American continent. Here, says Rowe, 'all estimates of their numbers are pure conjectures, but it is hardly likely that first-generation Cousin Jacks and Jennies have exceeded a hundred thousand'.[14] The second area to which Cornish emigrants went en masse was Australia, and Philip Payton has calculated that the total number just for South Australia was '16,000 or even higher with some 30,000 people of Cornish birth or direct descent in the

Colony at the turn of the century'.[15] The third area – South Africa – probably attracted no more than 10,000 Cornish.[16] Rowse considers:

> *The story of the Cornish emigration overseas is the most important in the history of our Cornish people. It has been a very individual factor in the building up of new and young nations.*[17]

South Africa in particular was to become more important to Cornwall than any other part of the world where the Cornish settled.

The relationship between Cornwall and South Africa is more than just special. In his autobiography *A Cornish Childhood*, Rowse claims that, 'there is something very pathetic and moving in that close connection between our Cornish villages and South Africa'; he proceeds to wax lyrical about 'that teeming ant-heap of the Rand, the raw horror of Jo'burg and the gaunt visaged men, yellow-faced who returned home to Cornwall to gasp their last breath'.[18] The sentiments expressed by Rowse can perhaps only be understood when it is realised that two of his uncles, who were miners, did not return from South Africa; they lie together in the same cemetery in Johannesburg.

The Cornish newspapers would often highlight the importance of South Africa to Cornwall, by giving news from South Africa prominence over local and national affairs, such as:

> *the connection between Cornwall and the Transvaal is so intimate that I make no apology for occasionally discussing the situation on the Rand.*[19]

or:

> *When the button is pressed in Africa, the bell rings in Cornwall... a change in thought and action in South Africa affects the little Western county which has contributed so much of the labour and enterprise to... the land of gold and diamonds.*[20]

and even more to the point:

> *– we are living on South Africa.*[21]

Travel writers found it irresistible to mention South Africa in relation to Cornwall at the expense of other areas, so that it appeared Cornish miners went only to South Africa. In 1897 Arthur H. Norway wrote of the population of Cornwall having been

> *drained off from Camborne or Redruth to toil for foreign taskmasters at Johannesburg or Kimberley... their bodies are sweltering in the heat of an African mine.*[22]

A decade later C. Lewis Hind, on leaving Cornwall on the Penzance to Paddington mail train, described the scene at Camborne and Redruth stations which was enacted every Friday throughout the year when the Cornish miners left home to catch the South African boat from Southampton and remarked:

Johannesburg is but a suburb of Cornwall.[23]

The only major study of the Cornish in South Africa has been written by a South African who admits to having 'only a limited first hand knowledge of Cornwall'.[24] However, its value lies in the detailed examination of some 48 cemeteries in South Africa, resulting in the alphabetical listing of over 1,400 Cornishmen and women who emigrated from Cornwall and who died in South Africa during the period 1820-1940. Such a list has been invaluable and all credit goes to Graham Dickason. G. Burke and P. Richardson have looked closely at the link between miners' phthisis (pronounced tysis) in Cornwall and the Transvaal,[25] while Burke herself has looked at the migration of Cornish miners to South Africa in the wider context of the *Cornish Diaspora.*[26] Henry Blackwell and Norman Hannan have individually produced intimate studies at the more personal level of what South Africa meant to their own family history,[27] whilst A.K. Hamilton Jenkin in *The Cornish Miner* somewhat frustrates the reader by appearing unwilling to put names to the Cornishmen in South Africa. For example he describes the Ferreira Deep gold mine as being:

almost entirely manned with Dolcoath tributers superintended by a captain who was himself a Camborne man, one of an old Dolcoath family.[28]

Although the name of the captain may have been obvious in 1927, when Jenkin's book was first published, today we are left wondering as to his identity. The present study attempts to give answers to questions such as these.[29]

Finally, as Payton points out emigration became a central theme in nineteenth century Cornish history;[30] therefore it is hoped that this study will be read in conjunction with the works of Rowse, Rowe, Todd, Payton, Burke and others, in order to understand more fully the subject of the Cornish Migration and the general impact of the Cornish overseas. As one newspaper, *The Tribune Review*, of Butte City, U.S.A. commented:

The history of Cornwall is an interesting volume which contains much relating to the past achievements of a people who, in their isolation, kept proud pace in the world's progression, yet if properly compiled, the history of Cornwall across the sea would be equally as interesting.[31]

Notes – Introduction

1. Daphne Du Maurier, *VANISHING CORNWALL* (LONDON 1972) p.14-15

2. For Cornwall's early history see Charles Woolf, *AN INTRODUCTION TO THE ARCHAEOLOGY OF CORNWALL* (TRURO 1970)

3. *ROYAL CORNWALL GAZETTE*, 10th OCTOBER 1818

4. D.B. Barton, *A HISTORY OF COPPER MINING IN CORNWALL AND DEVON 3rd EDITION* (TRURO 1978) p.45 Open Cast mining of copper at Parys Mountain, Anglesey in the 1760s halted Cornwall's dominance of world copper production for some twenty years. See J.R. Harris *THE COPPER KING A BIOGRAPHY OF THOMAS WILLIAMS OF LLANIDAN (LIVERPOOL 1964)*

5. D.B. Barton, p.79. By 1874 only two major copper mines survived – both in East Cornwall – South Caradon and Marke Valley. Both had been abandoned by 1890. Devon Great Consols mine closed in 1903.

6. A.K. Hamilton Jenkin, THE *CORNISH MINER* (3rd EDITION NEWTON ABBOT 1972) p.237

7. A.C. Todd, THE *CORNISH MINER IN AMERICA* (TRURO 1967) p.19

8. John Rowe, THE *HARD ROCK MEN* (LIVERPOOL 1974) p.113

9. S. Marks & P Richardson, *INTERNATIONAL LABOUR MIGRATION HISTORICAL CORNISH DIASPORA OF THE NINETEENTH CENTURY* p.62 See also Rowe, *HARD ROCK MEN* p.295

10. *THE CORNISH POST & MINING NEWS (C.P.M.N.)* 14th SEPTEMBER 1889

11. Perhaps the *POST* should have more correctly stated that the diamonds were dug at Kimberley in Cape Colony, and that it was mainly gold which was dug in the Transvaal.

12. Claude Berry, *PORTRAIT OF CORNWALL* (LONDON 1963) p.109 This saying appears elsewhere in similar form e.g. 'where a hole is sunk in the ground, no matter what corner of the globe, you will be sure to find a Cornishman at the bottom of it, searching for metal' Halliday, *A HISTORY OF CORNWALL* p.298

13. Graham B. Dickason, *CORNISH IMMIGRANTS TO SOUTH AFRICA* (CAPE TOWN 1978) p.13 Leonard Courtney, in a lecture given at Truro in June 1897, estimated that by the end of the century 230,000 Cornishmen would have departed from the county. See Todd, *CORNISH MINER IN AMERICA* p.19 William Hosken at the 3rd Annual Cornish Banquet in Johannesburg, reckoned 180,000 had left Cornwall since 1861, see *CORNISHMAN*, 18th JUNE 1908.

14. Rowe, HARD *ROCK MEN* p.295 *Cousin Jacks and Jennies* were the nicknames given to Cornish men and women. The term Cousin Jack apparently originated in the U.S.A., where it was said that every Cornish miner had a cousin back in Cornwall who would be coming out after a job Rowe also points out in his preface that aware of the profanity of many Cornish – it was a corruption of cussing Jack. I myself had a letter from a South African-Cornish woman who described herself as a *Cousin Ginny*.

15. Philip J. Payton THE *CORNISH MINER IN AUSTRALIA* (KERNOW 1984) p.12

16. I am indebted to Graham Dickason who in a letter to me stated that 'at the peak of a period when Cornishmen could be identified as such, numbers were never greater than 10,000 persons, and which must be seen against a European descended population, largely agrarian, no greater than 1 million'. In comparison the population of Cornwall at the end of the nineteenth century was approximately one third of a million.

17. Philip Payton, *THE CORNISH FARMER IN AUSTRALIA* (REDRUTH 1987) p. VII Forward by A.L. Rowse

18. A.L. Rowse, A *CORNISH CHILDHOOD* (LONDON 1942) p.34

19. *C.P.M.N., 26th* JANUARY 1905

20. *IBID., 20th* DECEMBER 1906

21. *THE CORNUBIAN AND REDRUTH TIMES,* (CORNUBIAN) 31st JANUARY 1902

22. Arthur H. Norway, *HIGHWAYS AND BYWAYS IN DEVON & CORNWALL* (LONDON 1897) p.317. Norway was born in Wadebridge but had spent most of his life in the employment of the General Post Office at St. Martins Le Grande, London. He was also for a short time Secretary of the Post Office in Ireland. His most important book was his *History of the Post Office Packet Service* (1895). Norway died in 1938. Perhaps less well known is the fact that his son was Nevil Shute, the author of *A Town Like Alice, On the Beach, Slide Rule* and many other successful novels. His full name was Nevil Shute Norway.

23. C. Lewis Hind, DAYS *IN CORNWALL (2nd Ed. LONDON* 1907) p.352

24. Dickason, *CORNISH IMMIGRANTS TO SOUTH AFRICA p.113*

25. G. Burke & P. Richardson, THE *PROFITS OF DEATH: A COMPARATIVE STUDY OF MINERS' PHTHISIS IN CORNWALL AND THE TRANSVAAL 1876-1914. JOURNAL OF SOUTH AFRICAN STUDIES VOL 4 No 2* APRIL 1978

26. Marks & Richardson, INTERNATIONAL *LABOUR MIGRATION HISTORICAL PERSPECTIVES* p.57-75

27. Henry Cecil Blackwell, FROM *A DARK STREAM* (KERNOW 1986) and Norman Hannan, TRAVELS *AND HEARTACHES OF A MINING FAMILY* (ROMFORD 1984)

28. Jenkin, *CORNISH MINER* p.331

29. The captain was J. Harry Johns – see Chapter 4 Land of Gold 1870-99.

30. Payton, *CORNISH IN AUSTRALIA* p.8

31. *CORNUBIAN,* 16th AUGUST 1909. Interestingly D.B. Barton advertised *The Cornish Miner Overseas* as a forthcoming book but it was never published.

CHAPTER ONE

CORNISH PIONEERS OF THE CAPE AND NATAL 1820-1899

*I am enamoured. This beautiful country has written itself on
my heart and if I was to die today I am confident that the words
South Africa would be found on my heart strings.*[1]

Richard Lander

Cornish explorer Richard Lander from Truro arrived in Cape Town 13th July 1823 after a stormy and hazardous voyage of nearly five months and based his opinion above on a stay of less than a year during which he journeyed from one extremity of the colony to the other.[2]

Whether his views were shared by the Cornish men and women who had reached the Cape before him perhaps will never be known. It is unlikely, however, that the Cornish convicts en route to the penal colony of Australia would have expressed similar sentiments, as South Africa for them was but the last stage on a long, tedious and dangerous voyage, which they were making through no choice of their own.[3]

Cape Colony (South Africa) was originally Dutch but was occupied by the British during the Napoleonic Wars before being ceded to Britain on 13th August 1814. The colony was of prime strategic value to Britain, being virtually half way between the staging islands of St Helena and Mauritius en route to India. The main role of the British garrison stationed at the Cape was to stop the indigenous natives from crossing the Great Fish river, which had been declared the Colony's eastern boundary in 1812. Lord Charles Somerset, the Governor of the Colony, appealed for immigrants. There had already been five so-called Kaffir Wars between 1779-1819 and Somerset hoped that a sufficient number of settlers would provide the necessary strength to defend themselves, unaided by troops. If the settlers also owned their land they would be more than ready to defend it.

The official circular setting out the conditions of the emigration scheme stated that the settlers to the colony would be placed on the South-East coast of Africa about 600 miles, or a nine-day coach journey from Cape Town, in the province called by the Dutch *Zuureveld* and situated between the Sundays and Great Fish rivers. So that the settlers would arrive at the beginning of the planting season, the transport ships were scheduled not to leave the country until after November.

Four thousand settlers were eventually selected from all over Britain during which time the *Royal Cornwall Gazette* commented on how talk centred on the mania of emigration.[4] However, less than a dozen Cornishmen and their families took advantage of the Government assisted scheme and emigrated to South Africa.

The leader of the small Cornish party was Benjamin Osler, and he and the other members of the party, came mainly from the Falmouth/Penryn district.[5] They were transported in two ships, one being the *Nautilus* which left London on 19th December 1819 and the other the *Weymouth* which sailed from Portsmouth for the Cape on 7th January 1820. The Cornish party was settled in an area twelve miles south of the town of Bathurst and north east of the Kowie river. The actual location Osler named Pendennis probably after Pendennis Point, Falmouth. Little is known about the early Cornish settlers but it soon became obvious that life in the new settlement was far from easy. A combination of lack of finance and lack of farming experience – John Bridgeman being the only farmer in the group – linked with bad luck in the shape of alternate droughts and floods, cattle stolen by raiding tribesmen or contracting disease, were all factors leading to the breaking up of the group Within two years Osler and part of his family had returned to Cornwall while others in the group dispersed to different parts of the Colony (One famous Osler descendant was the legendary South African rugby full back, Bennie Osler). As Dickason rightly points out:

> *The few that did remain at Pendennis were to become so insignificant numerically that from then on their story melts with that of the settlement itself, conversely reflecting their great adaptability and absorption into the new country.*[6]

Perhaps mention should be made here that Donald Woods, the once banned South African journalist claims that his great-great grandfather Frederick was one of the original settlers, and was said to have come from Cornwall.[7] A distinguished Cornishman who played a prominent role in the early history of South Africa has been described as perhaps the most enterprising of all the 1820 settlers.[8] He was William Cock, a wealthy printer from Penryn who travelled on board the *Weymouth* with his wife Elizabeth and three children, William (age 4) John (age 2) and Loveday (age 3 months).

In his diary[9] Cock tells how the *Weymouth* nearly did battle with a Cuban slave vessel on the outward journey and when his party eventually arrived at Cape Town, having been four months at sea, it was not without tragedy. Twenty children had died on board from measles, one of them Cock's own son John. On reaching Algoa Bay, the party settled near the Kowie river. Cock purchased some oxen and after an abortive attempt to go into business with a partner, he secured a Government contract to supply meat to the troops. In 1826, following a trip to Cape Town, he purchased a fast schooner and began to move cargo between Algoa

Bay and Table Bay. Cock's business expanded and he obtained a Government contract to trade with Mauritius.

After a visit home to Cornwall in 1836 Cock returned to South Africa where he resumed his business for a while from Cape Town. Before leaving Cornwall he had in his head a notion to build a port at the mouth of the Kowie river and set about putting that plan into action. It was to be anything but easy for as Cock noted if he could have foreseen the trouble, labour and anxiety that awaited him in connection with the opening of the Kowie, he would have remained in Cape Town.10

The story of how Cock put into action his most enterprising scheme is told in Eric Turpin's *Basketwork Harbour*. It is therefore sufficient to relate that Cock, without advice of engineers or other experts, and with his own capital – an estimated £7000 – succeeded in changing the course of the Kowie river. This was done by 300 Hottentot labourers who drove in rows of stakes interlaced with wattle basketwork. The building of a concrete breakwater, wharves and warehouses, plus a railway, completed in 1843 South Africa's first man made port. Named Port Francis it was later renamed Port Alfred after Queen Victoria's second son who visited the colony in 1860, although Cock's granddaughter Harriet11 deputised for the Prince in the actual naming ceremony. Cock naturally became Chairman of the Kowie Harbour Company and founded his own shipping company – the Kowie Navigation Company – building up a modest fleet of ships. It was not all success, however, especially when his iron schooner, the *British Settler,* carrying South Africa's first export of wool, sank off St. Helena with all hands.

In 1849 the Cape nearly erupted when the British Government decided to impose a convict settlement on the Colony. Although sympathetic to the colonists' views, as the Government's representative the Governor of the Cape Sir Harry Smith could hardly head a revolt. Cock now a member of the Legislative Council was the only one to take the Governor's side for, as he explained at a public meeting at Grahamstown organised by the Anti-Convict Association, although "all that he possessed, the labour of the last 30 years, was at stake" he was only prepared to take "proper means in order to obtain the revocation of the Order in Council, converting the Cape of Good Hope into a Penal Settlement".12 Although cheered on that occasion Cock quickly became unpopular. On the arrival of the convict ship *Neptune* at Table Bay in October 1849 a pledge was taken by the colonists to boycott the ship. Shops closed and all kinds of work stopped – anyone not signing the pledge being classed as a traitor and banks and markets were closed against them. Smith wisely forbade the convicts to disembark. Unfortunately Cock's diary ends at this point so we are denied Cock's own words, but his actions speak for themselves. Ignoring the threat of the pledge he personally supplied the *Neptune* with necessary victuals on the humanitarian grounds that the convicts had no say in the dispute; he also refused to resign from the Council. Fortunately the episode ended in the colonists' favour when the British Government reversed its decision and the *Neptune* sailed on to Australia in February 1850. Credit at home in helping the Government change its mind goes to another Cornishman, Sir William Molesworth (1810-55) the radical M.P. for the City of London and a future Secretary of State for the Colonies.

William Cock has been described as:

> *A determined fellow with pluck and perseverance against every difficulty and discouragement*[13] and as a man of *great ability and strength of character,*[14]

which the building of Port Alfred and the Convict Episode testify. With the latter event over, Cock once more became a respected member of the Colony, being elected to the Legislative Assembly for Albany in 1854 and later to the Upper House where he represented the Eastern division 1856-57 and 1865-68. At the 50th Jubilee of British Settlers celebrated at Grahamstown in 1870, the Rev. Henry Hare Dugmore, himself an original settler, gave a lecture in which he singled out Cock as a man who

> *deserved success for perseverance in the face... of multiplied discouragements.*[15]

Sadly it was not to be; Cock's dream of a permanent port faded as quickly as the river silted up, preventing large ships from docking. William Cock died on the 11th February 1876 at Port Alfred less than three months after the death of his wife Elizabeth. Despite heavy rain on the day of the funeral the *Grahamstown Journal* reported:

> *everyone at Port Alfred joined in a tribute of respect to the departed worthy.*[16]

A few days later the paper referred to Cock as the:

> *Unsullied Patriot, the Good Citizen, the unfailing friend and the staunch and unwavering advocate of the Eastern Province.*[17]

Today Cocks Castle still stands above the west bank of the Kowie river as a lasting monument whilst beside the river itself only the ruins of the old Custom House remain as a memory of one Cornishman's inspiration and vision.

From 1836 onwards many Cornish folk, helped by assisted passages, went to settle in Australia – many Cornish miners heading to the copper fields of South Australia at the same time as copper mines were closing in Cornwall. One Cornish family, which had originally intended to emigrate to Australia but was unable to secure a passage, settled for South Africa instead. Thus it was on 2nd February 1850 the Higgo family from Penzance arrived in Cape Town on board the *Gletana*. Such was the relief and joy of the people of Cape Town on hearing the news brought by the *Gletana* that the convict ship *Neptune* was at last to leave, that the Higgo family on arrival found themselves garlanded and presented with special gifts.

The Higgo family consisted of John and Mary Ann Higgo and their six sons and four daughters. Two more daughters were born shortly afterwards. As skilled

The Higgovale granite quarry just below Table Mountain. John Higgo is standing on the right foreground.

stonemasons the Higgo men found no problem obtaining work with the Colony's Permanent Works Department. At first the family lived at Penzance Cottage in Swellendam, their main task being to build bridges in the area. Their four sons, – Henry, James, William and George – moved back to Cape Town to work a quarry just below Table Mountain at Kloof Nek. The land upon which they built their homes (and the Quarry) became known as Higgovale. In its heyday at the turn of the century the quarry employed some 120 men, many of them Cornish. The granite produced by the Higgos went towards the construction of a number of Cape Town's finest buildings such as Cape Times Building, the Old Mutual Building in Darling Street, the Palmerston, Criterion and Royal Hotels and the Standard Bank, Adderly Street as well as the Diocesan College at nearby Rondebosch. Many of the streets in Cape Town today still have the kerbstones that originally came from the Higgo quarry.

A fascinating insight into the life of the Higgo family has been faithfully recorded by a Higgo descendant Christine Higgo-Hartwig. When the Quarry was doing well William Higgo's house, aptly named Granite House, had cooks, housekeepers, a governess and a tutor for the education of the children, while at Kloof House, the home of Arthur Higgo (a son of William) there was a refreshment stall to supply walkers and day trippers with milk, ginger beer or lemonade. The methods used by the Higgo women to feed and look after their families were reminiscent of those practised in Cornwall. Milk was usually set out in large basins covered by wet cloths before the cream was skimmed off – butter was churned by hand and large outside ovens were used in which bakings were large. Vegetables were home grown but Malay vendors carrying balancing baskets on a long shoulder pole and the horse-drawn fish cart heralding its irregular coming by the wailing of a horn plus the catching of fish called snoek were new experiences.

There is no doubt that the Higgo family had laid down foundations as firm as the granite which supports several of Cape Town's old buildings and many South Africans bearing the name Higgo can look back with admiration to their Cornish ancestors. Stone from Higgovale was also used when improvements were made to Cape Town Docks. The Harbour Engineer in Chief to the Cape Government was Cornishman Sir John Coode of Bodmin. He was responsible for the construction of the Cape Town breakwater and the design of the Table Bay Harbour. He inspected William Cock's harbour at Port Alfred and in 1871 supervised the development of Durban's harbour. Coode's expertise was sought world-wide, from harbour building in New Zealand to breakwater construction in Columbia, South America. His remuneration whilst in the Cape was very lucrative for he was paid 30,000 guineas on top of his travelling and hotel expenses.[18]

A number of Cornishmen arrived at the Cape in order to undertake religious work before Osler and Cock arrived with their groups. In March 1820 the Rev. Davies of Penzance gave

> *a variety of interesting and pleasing details of the manners of the natives*
> *of South Africa amongst whom he had been a missionary.*[19]

George Glover (1832-1919) also from Penzance was a Priest at the Cape in 1855 whilst William Hayle Rogers (1835-1920) from Helston was a priest and Boston Frederick Carlyon (1815-1897) from Truro was the Rector of Stellenbosch (1850-62). Among other Cornishmen who featured in Cape Colony's early life was Robert Carne (1844-1919) who was a monumental mason at Wynberg. Carne had married a Penzance woman and their daughter Helen (named after her mother) married John James (1860-1929) a builder from Cornwall, who had also settled at Wynberg. John Grenfell Moyle of Marazion was often at the Cape in his capacity as Military Surgeon while his son Richard stayed to become a teacher. The most prominent Cornishman in the educational life and work of Cape Colony during the last quarter of the nineteenth century was without a doubt James Gill from East Looe. Having graduated from Christ's Hospital School he went to the Cape as Professor of Classics in 1861. Gill was considered to be one of the best classical scholars in South Africa in his lifetime, and when he died at Muizenburg in 1904 it was reported that he had been possessed of brilliant intellectual gifts.[20]

Another well-known Cornishman who landed at the Cape and who became a leader in the field of commerce was Samson Rickard Stuttaford from Helston. In 1857 aged only 24 Stuttaford opened a haberdasher's shop at Cape Town, from which was to grow one of South Africa's major departmental store groups. With the help of his brother William, Stuttaford supplied goods to the Royal party when Prince Alfred visited the Colony in 1867 and was thus able to put *By Appointment* in all his advertisements. By 1872 Stuttaford & Co. had moved from their original premises in Darling St. to occupy a prime site at the corner of Adderly St. and Hout St. It cost them £10,000 – a very large sum then. Within a few years Samson Rickard Stuttaford was in a position to return to England to organise the buying and shipping from London for his stores, visiting South Africa about twice a year.

The last major influx of Cornish to make their mark on Cape Colony's early history was a group of Cornish miners. It has been generally assumed that the first Cornish miners arrived in South Africa in 1852 to work in the copper mines of Namaqualand, Western Cape. However, according to the *Cornubian* magazine the official organ of the old Cornish Association of the Transvaal, Cornish miners had actually arrived some sixteen years earlier:

> In 1836 Captain Alexander, soldier and explorer landed just south of the
> Orange River on a bay to which he gave his name... The buildings which
> housed the hundred or so Cornish miners who adventured with him were
> also found, littered with fragments of English crockery and other
> evidences of prolonged occupation. These almost forgotten men were
> probably the first group of Cornish people to come to South Africa.[21]

Mining for copper in the area later became centred on the townships of O'okiep, Springbok and Concordia further south. Most of Namaqualand is remote desert and therefore transport over rough terrain became a major problem for the Cape Copper Mining Company in 1862. At first mule trains were used to take the copper ore to the coast at Hondeklip Bay where it went to Swansea in South Wales for smelting. The O'okiep Mine was said to be raising more and richer ore than Devon Great Consols,[22] but due to the heavy transport costs the mine was less profitable. The Cape Copper Mining Company's consulting engineers, John Taylor & Sons, sent out one of their Cornish engineers to carry out a feasibility study on the possibility of a railway line being built.

The engineer was Richard Thomas Hall (1823-89) which was a good choice, for he already had experience of similar transport problems at his home in Cornwall at Devoran. In the nineteenth century, before it silted up, Devoran, situated on the River Fal at Restronguet Creek, was a very busy port, as well as being a terminus for the early horse-drawn *Redruth & Chacewater Railway* or *Tramroad* – of which Hall had been Superintendent Engineer in 1849. Hall left Cornwall for South Africa leaving behind his wife Elizabeth née Penrose (1823-1912) and nine children. Thanks to D.D. Hall, (a great-grandson of Richard Thomas Hall) an excellent account has been compiled entitled *The Story of a South African Pioneer and His Family*. It is a first class model for anyone who might attempt a comprehensive family history and genealogy. It also contains a number of fascinating letters which Richard Thomas Hall, the subject of the account, wrote to his wife while making his first journey to South Africa.23 On leaving Cornwall 8th May 1865 Hall wrote:

> *We left Falmouth on Monday morning at 3 o'clock with a head wind and heavy seas against us – by 4 o'clock I was sick.*24

After a couple of days suffering from sea sickness he recovered and was able to describe his fellow passengers to his wife and "the pleasures of a voyage at sea, not that it had much in its favour... the monotony is very tedious". Hall arrived at Cape Town on 5th June, his first impression being that it was a queer place, certainly picturesque. It is obvious from his letters that he missed his family, but he set about carrying out his assignment. From Cape Town he sailed up the coast to Hondeklip Bay, which Hall described as a wretched place. He then rode on horseback, to Springbok a distance of some seventy three miles. Describing the surrounding countryside he wrote:

> *About 25 miles from the Bay we come to the foot of a mountain and from this point to near Springbok the road is of a mountainous character – in some cases very steep indeed – nothing like it in Cornwall.*25

Other letters told of the people he met – the kindly Captain Clemes at the O'okiep Mine, the Curate at Springbok who was not respected – by white or black, and at Port Nolloth "Mr. Dreyer, a very respectable young africaner – that's a new name for you – it means one who was born in the colony of white parents". Hall had plenty of new experiences to relate to his wife such as sleeping out in the veldt, being able to pluck lemons straight from the tree and eating them skin & all without making a wry face and eating pickled oysters before dinner then a nice bit of broiled goat on the grid. It appears that he was not completely cut off from Cornwall either for as well as writing him letters his wife sent copies of the *West Briton* newspaper.

His last letter from O'okiep to his wife was dated 6th October 1865 and informed her that he was planning to travel overland to Cape Town, calculating that the journey by cart and six horses and in company with two others would take 14 or 15 days. He made it safely home to Cornwall but was soon on his way back to South Africa in November 1868. His proposed scheme – that of building a 2ft 6in gauge railway line from O'okiep to Port Nolloth – had not only been accepted but he had been given the task of constructing it.

The preserved loco Clara at O'okiep in 1980 (photograph by K. Brown).

The ninety-two mile railway between O'okiep and Port Nolloth was finally completed in 1876. South African travel writer, Lawrence Green, considered it one of the finest engineering feats South Africa had known at that time.[26] Richard Thomas Hall meanwhile had already moved with most of his family to Cape Town being employed by the Cape Government railways to undertake new surveys. One of his sons, Dickon, having begun his career in the railway workshops at Port Nolloth became a fitter in the Cape Railways before being Locomotive Superintendent at Beaufort West. Later, in 1891, he was appointed the first President of the Railway Institute in Bloemfontein, a position he held until 1895. Another son Henry completed an apprenticeship with the Cornish engineering firm Tangyes of Birmingham before joining his family at the Cape in 1870. Having also worked on the O'okiep – Port Nolloth railway he became an engineer helping in the construction of a number of railway lines in the Cape, including one running through the Hex River Pass.

With the large number of Cornish miners going to Namaqualand it was perhaps not surprising that a Cornish way of life was to develop in this remote copper region of South Africa. Dickason mentions the irrepressible Cornish organising their picnics, wrestling and carol singing.[27] It appears the Cornish were responsible for the introduction of cricket into the area, with the first multi-racial cricket tours taking place up and down Hall's railway line.[28] Also attributed to them was the Cornish fondness for tea,[29] and both Dickason and Green testify to the number of Cornish expressions still to be found in the area. Dickason on his visit recalls being served in a Namaqualand hotel by a charming elderly coloured waitress whose grandfather had come from Gwennap in 1861.[30] Green on the other hand met Jack Meadows:

> *The Cornishman who ran the line for more than thirty years. Travellers called it the 'one man railway' at that period for the service had been reduced to one train a week each way, and Jack Meadows was playing many parts. He sold me my ticket, saw the freight into the van, blew his whistle and then climbed on board as conductor (in addition to these duties Jack Meadows became harbour-master on arrival at Port Nolloth).*[31]

The Cornish also brought Methodism to the region, and an account in the *West Briton* in 1883 tells of how the Namaqualand Cornish raised £700 by means of a three day bazaar for the building of a new chapel designed to seat 300 people.

Nicholas Edward Moffet from Tuckingmill, one time organist of the Wesleyan Church was for thirty-four years Sunday School Superintendent and organist at Port Nolloth, as well as being manager of the railway. J. Jones, from neighbouring Camborne, had been for nineteen years local preacher and Sunday School Superintendent at Nababeep. In 1918 both men received long service certificates in connection with their Sunday School work.[32] Another Cornishman who was a local preacher and pioneer Methodist, responsible for churches being erected at Port Nolloth and O'okiep, was Charles Rowe from Hayle.[33]

Perhaps the most prominent Cornish mining family at Namaqualand was that of Kitto. William Kitto senior had been one of the first managers of the Cape Copper Company and his son, William Frank Kitto, was Superintendent of the Company for six years from 1892. Having begun work as a lad in the Cornish mines he eventually ended up as Superintendent of a mine on the Isle of Man. His son, also William Frank, arrived in Namaqualand in 1907 but with the death of his father replaced him on the Isle of Man.[34]

The majority of miners at Namaqualand copper mines were Cornish, evidence for which is easily found by a visit to the local cemeteries. Here lie dozens of Cornish who were never to return to Cornwall again – men like James Thomas of Gwennap (who was Inspector of Explosives), John Wadge from Gunnislake and

The O'okiep copper mine in about 1880 shows an early beam pumping engine supplied by Harveys of Hayle in 1874. Water pumped from the shaft is used for a water wheel, behind the engine house and other machinery.

A later 50 inch Cornish beam pumping engine made by Harvey's of Hayle which worked from 1885 until 1919 when the Cape Copper Co. closed the mine. The engine is now preserved as a national monument. (Photo by J. Porter, Kew Bridge Steam Museum 1997).

Thomas James Rodda of St. Just (who had been in charge of operations at Specktakel Mine in 1871). Not all these were miners, and not all have been recorded by Dickason. For example at O'okiep sadly can be found the graves of some very young Cornish. Richard and Jane Paul's 15 year old son died 27th May 1880 followed the next day by their daughter Elizabeth. Their other daughter Emily had already died in infancy. James Isaac, son of James and Mary Isaac of Perranzabuloe, died 10th May 1881, aged 11 years but perhaps the most poignant gravestone in the O'okiep cemetery belongs to 16 year old William Trevithick who was accidentally killed in 1877.

Recent research on the Namaqualand district which is of Cornish interest is by Kenneth Brown. He covers the industrial story of the O'okiep Copper Mine from its opening in 1852 through to its closure in 1919 and eventual reopening as a museum in the late 1960's with help in research from the Cornish *Trevithick Society. A* fascinating insight into the types of Cornish engines used in the mines – one being a Harvey 50 inch pumping engine – the mining methods which were based on the old Cornish *tut and tribute* system[35] and of course the route and construction of Hall's unique railway – provides the subject for an article in *The Journal of the Trevithick Society.*[36] However, Hall's railway was finally closed in 1941, the rails being eventually sold for scrap metal and Port Nolloth which "had echoed to the wild songs of a horde of thirsty Cornish miners; sorrowfully… watched them depart generations later as the mines closed down".[37] Yet some Cornish remained. Green, on another visit to Port Nolloth, was shown around by William Carstins, of whom he wrote:

His father had been the port superintendent in the early days, his sons were brought up there. Port Nolloth without a member of the Cornish family of Carstins would be like London without a Cockney.[38]

William Carstins must have been one of the unluckiest Cornishmen in South Africa. In 1925 Green had watched Carstins and his son Jack work a diamond claim six miles south of Port Nolloth and thought the washing of gravel a dreary and unprofitable business.[39] Carstins many years later told Green how Jack had picked out a diamond – the first in Namaqualand – but he had dissuaded the family from going north to Alexander Bay thus preventing them from perhaps discovering the vast wealth that lay there and which is worked on a large scale today. If it was any consolation many another Cornish man or woman also missed out on discovering a fortune. Hugh Lanion Hall, a younger son of Richard Thomas Hall, and one of his sisters used to ride their horses to Alexander Bay and along the coast:

little thinking then that we were riding over thousands of pounds worth of diamonds. Many of the miners from the O'okiep Mine, when their contracts were up would get a couple of donkeys to carry their swag and a Hottentot guide, and would tramp all the way to Kimberley across the desert, where the only water was in little fountains known only to the Hottentots. They went to look for diamonds, leaving the world's richest diamond coast behind them.[40]

In Cornwall, between Redruth and Camborne, at Barncoose next to Maynes Garage, used to be found *O'okiep House* while in Broad Lane Illogan was a house named *Port Nolloth* – just two reminders of the time when Cornwall had much stronger links with Namaqualand. Today there is little remaining of the Cornish in Namaqualand apart from the mine machinery and engine houses at O'okiep while on a map Dicks Cutting is but a name reminding us of Hall's railway, now long gone. Perhaps the real memorial is the fact that all the railways in Africa, south of the Sahara have a 3ft 6in gauge which was adopted by the Colonial Select Committee in 1872 on the advice of Richard Thomas Hall.

A number of Dutch colonists in the Cape had begun to resent living under British rule which they felt was not only unfair but interfered with their way of life. Such was the dissatisfaction that hundreds of Boers or Voortrekkers left their farms and began in 1836 what has become known as the *Great Trek*. One party of Boers, led by Piet Retief from Grahamstown was massacred by a force of Zulus on 6th February 1838. By the end of the year the Boers took their revenge. Led by Andries Pretorius they dug in at Blood River forming their wagons into a laager defence. The Boers then made a covenant with God for his assistance in the forthcoming battle. What followed led many to believe that the hand of God had truly intervened, for some 3000 Zulus were killed whereas, unbelievably, not one Boer was killed. From thereafter the day of the Battle (16th December 1838) was celebrated as Dingaans Day or The Day of the Covenant and became a symbolic date in the Afrikaaner calendar.[41]

Many years later when it was decided to have a permanent memorial to remember the victory at Blood River the work went to Percy Ley, a Cornish firm of stonemasons at Pretoria. In shape the monument resembles a Voortrekker wagon and the photograph overleaf shows Austin Reed with the foreman Cyril Woodley who worked on the stone monument. Both men were Cornish and had served their apprenticeships at the De Lank Quarries situated in the parish of St. Breward in North Cornwall. Percy Ley was the company also responsible for the construction of Pretoria's Union buildings which were built between 1910-13 at a cost of over £1 million.

Natal was annexed by the British on 12th December 1843 and there were various emigration schemes to encourage settlers to the new colony, the most notable being that of Joseph C. Byrne. Between 1849-51 some 4,500 British people took advantage of the free assisted passage and promise of land in Natal, for a down payment of £10. A number of Byrne's ships called at Plymouth and it

The monument to commemorate the Battle of Blood River 1838.

Part of monument sculpted by Cornish stonemasons Austin Reed and Cyril Woodley in 1938.

has been calculated that in all 235 persons embarked at Plymouth over the three years.[42] Amongst these were a number of Cornish families.

Paul Henwood was persuaded by his brother John to accompany him, his wife Harriet, their two young children (William and Rebecca) and to emigrate from his home in Tideford, East Cornwall to South Africa in 1849. The Henwoods sailed on the *Henry Tanner* and after a sixteen week voyage arrived in Durban on 15th October although not without tragedy as little Rebecca had died at sea. Misfortune also greeted them on arrival; first the weather prevented an easy disembarkation and then it turned out that the land allocated to them was totally unsuitable for cultivation. To earn a living the twenty one year old Paul began trading and was one of the first Cornishmen to trade in the two Boer Republics of the Orange Free State and the Transvaal. Henwood described his first visit to Pietermaritzburg:

> *a bleak, windy, dusty day in the winter of 1850 – the houses were few and scattered and the streets with open water sluits and lined with Syringa trees, were ill-kept and seemed deserted.*[44]

It was here, however, that he met and married his wife Mary Jane Coulson, 6th May 1854. An unidentified newspaper cutting describes how Henwood met one farmer who was later to become the President of the Boer Republics. :

> *To the bearded farmer who came to meet him he said "Mr. Kruger, my name is Paul Henwood. I am travelling on the Rand selling hardware. Is there anything you need?"*
> *And so Oom Paul became one of the early customers of Henwoods.*[45]

The ambition of Paul Henwood was to establish his own trading stores and this was achieved when he opened the first real Hardware Store in Durban and Henwoods was thus founded in 1856. When the building was rebuilt in 1860 it earned the distinction of being the first double storey store in Durban. Henwood's business now began to expand rapidly, a Henwoods Store was opened in Pietermaritzburg in 1862 and Johannesburg in 1886 (see Chapter 4). Like fellow Cornishman Samson Rickard Stuttaford, Paul Henwood returned to England from where he organised his business affairs, only visiting South Africa roughly every two years. In 1872 Paul sent out to Durban his nephew John Roseveare to start a drapery business under the name Henwood & Roseveare.

When Paul Henwood died in 1907 The *Natal Witness* commented:

> *one of the earliest of the Natal colonists whose life and work was distinguished throughout by high ideals successful enterprise and the best qualities of the commercial Pioneer... he was one of the oldest Natal Colonialists living in England... he was held in the greatest esteem by South Africans of all classes.*[46]

Whilst Paul Henwood had set himself up as a trader, John Henwood had showed his versatility by the number of jobs to which he put his hand. Born at St. Germans in Cornwall 1812 John had already run an engineering business over the border in Devon before coming to South Africa. In South Africa John was a transport rider, trader, butcher, hotel manager and farmer before returning to engineering once more. He was so skilled with his hands that his Zulu helpers called him John *Tshetsha* meaning the Quick One. It was John who made the barrels that enabled the first salt meat to be packed and exported from Natal to Madagascar. It was for his love of horses, though, that John Henwood will perhaps be best remembered:

> *He performed several record rides. On his wife's bay 'Eagle', he rode*
> *from Durban to Maritzburg in five and three quarter hours and at the age*
> *of seventy-two rode from Pinetown to Rosetta in one day – a matter of*
> *eighty-two miles.*[51]

John Henwood was, not surprisingly, a keen race horse competitor and he and his son William won a number of prizes. In 1902 William's horse Chaos won the Durban July Handicap, the first South African bred horse to do so. John Henwood died on 13th December 1886 at his home in Pinetown and is buried with his wife in St. John's Churchyard, Pinetown (Their six children – William, John, Mary, James, George and Isabella all remained in South Africa).

Following in the wake of large Cornish families like the Cocks, Higgos and Henwoods no fewer than thirty-seven members of the Acutt family were to leave Britain to settle in Natal. All the South African Acutts are descended from Robert Acutt (1781-1849) a Supervisor of Excise in Cornwall and Devon, and Juliana Cotton (d.1855), who were married at Stratton in North Cornwall on 12th January 1805. Three of their sons – Robert, William and Richard – became prominent figures in the early history of Durban. William was the first Acutt to reach South Africa embarking at Durban in May 1850 from the Byrne ship *Edward*. Gaining experience with a Durban firm of general merchants William set up a successful retail business and served on Durban Town Council on at least three occasions. Robert became a leading figure in the auctioneering and real estate business – Acutts Arcade and Acutt Street in Durban being named after him. Richard, the third son, was not only a successful sugar planter but was also the first person to export arrowroot from South Africa. His farm was named Trenance after the Cotton family home in Cornwall.[48]

Natal's economy was based on the wattle, tea and most of all the sugar industries in which a Cornish connection was prominent. One of the largest sugar estates in Natal, a few miles from Durban, was named Mt. Edgecumbe (Mount Edgecumbe in East Cornwall overlooks the River Tamar to Plymouth). There was also a Cornubia Sugar Factory in Natal. Two Cornish families in particular were closely connected to Natal's lucrative sugar industry, namely Blamey and Polkinghorne.

John and Elizabeth Blamey and four children left their home town Penryn on the *King William* for Natal on the 25th October 1849. The Blamey's settled on the cotton lands at Mount Moreland (Natal) and at first carried out mixed farming to provide an income which was obtained by regularly sending butter, bacon, ham and mealies to Durban to be sold. By 1854 Blamey could afford a horse and in

1863, like many Cornish settlers in Natal at that time, turned to growing sugar, which was even more profitable. Within two years their sugar was being crushed in their own mill and they were able to return to Cornwall for a visit in 1872, having an interest in an estate called Duduran, in Kenwyn Parish. Unfortunately after returning to Natal, John Blamey died at Verulum the following year in a riding accident. Elizabeth Blamey survived her husband until 1896 when she died on the 6th August aged 84. The *Cornishman* reported:

> *many young men in the colony today are indebted to her for kind and sound advice from which they have profited* 49

Two of John Blamey's sons James Roach Blamey (1842-1906) and John Cardell Blamey (1844-1888) were themselves successful sugar planters, whilst a third son Alfred (1852-1928) was a farmer and transport businessman. A fourth son Leonard, died young. Of Blamey's three daughters, Margaret (1846-1850) died at sea, Sarah (1850-1889) married Thomas Metcalf a manager of a sugar estate, whilst Ellen (1854-1943) married Marshall Campbell, who became a prominent and wealthy sugar farmer. He was also responsible for making a donation which was used in creating the Killie Campbell Library at Durban.50

John Trevenyan Polkinghorne left his home town Penzance in 1850 under the Byrne Emigration Scheme with his wife Mary, and her brother John William Ackerman, who was also his close friend. The ship they sailed on, *The British Tar*, was wrecked at Durban the day after they landed in September 1850. Polkinghorne and Ackerman had been allocated land near Umblanga but by 1854 the Polkinghornes had moved to Verulum, calling their estate Penare. Polkinghorne first made his money by taking part in the Zululand cattle trade and gained a reputation as an astute and successful trader. He then turned to farming. Although unsuccessful at growing first cotton and then coffee, he finally made his fortune when he turned to sugar. Polkinghorne was to become a public figure in Natal, first as a Magistrate for Verulum and then as J.P. for the Colony. In 1860 he entered the Legislative Council as representative for Victoria County division. By 1879 he was Colonial Treasurer for Natal thus being the first colonist to fill an executive post in Natal and it was said that his grasp of fiscal matters always ensured an attentive audience for his Budget speeches. When Natal obtained self government status in 1893 Polkinghorne was appointed President of the new Legislative Council in recognition of his public service to the Colony. With sugar becoming a staple crop, South Africa was faced with its first major labour shortage. Intensive farming on vast plantations could only be profitable with a large and cheap labour force and the Colony turned to India to solve its problems. Polkinghorne himself became Chairman of the Indian Immigration Trust Board and another link with Cornwall was that the first indentured Indian labourers arrived on 16th November 1860 on board the *Truro*. Within ten years, some 5,000 Indians were working on the sugar plantations of Natal, the number having risen to 30,000 by the end of the century. Many Indian workers, after serving their period of indenture (a contract was usually for five years), stayed on in Natal to work on the railways and in agriculture – much of the fruit and vegetables sold in Durban and Pietermaritzburg being a result of their labour. Some Indians had reached Natal on their own accord and became established as traders – often referred to as Passengers or Arabs. However, the exploitation of the Indian migrant worker and the increased racial discrimination which was becoming more and more written into South African Law was to become a major issue after the Boer War.

Polkinghorne died aged 80 on 28th September 1901, just after he had attended a procession on the occasion of the visit to Natal of the then Duke and Duchess of Cornwall. His wife Mary had died three years earlier. Their four sons John, Trevenor, James and Edward, (a manager of the Natal Bank at Heidelberg), remained in South Africa. The *Natal Witness* wrote:

> *the Colony thus loses one of its ablest public men, who was a link with the past and a landmark of the present.*[51]

A street in Durban was named after him.

Another Cornish family who sailed on *The British Tar* was that of Harvey. The Rev. Francis Harvey the 12th son of John Harvey, a foundry owner at Pool near Redruth, was a prominent Cornish folklorist, lecturer and temperance worker. He arrived in Durban with his wife Anna and their three children Mary, Thomas and John where they were among a party of Wesleyans who settled in the Verulum district (30 miles north of Durban). The Harvey family lived at Hayle House which is still standing, although its name has been removed. Both John and Thomas Harvey were to become prominent Natal Pioneers. John married Sally Richards Adams in 1863. Of their nine children, one, Morgan (called after his grandmother's maiden name), was a Pioneer of the Barberton goldfields in the Eastern Transvaal. Thomas went into partnership with M.B.W. Greenacre from Norfolk to establish the firm of Harvey Greenacre in March 1869. It became Durban's premier department store and Harvey Greenacre became a household name in Natal and further afield for over a century. Thomas eventually returned to England first to London as a buyer and then entered politics to become M.P. for Mid-Hertfordshire. Thomas Harvey was a strong Methodist and supporter of Gladstone (no liquor was sold at Harvey Greenacre stores). He later became Chairman of the South African section of the London Chamber of Commerce.

Trevean House in Bellour, Durban, built in 1880 is today a listed building and a reminder of the debt owed by Natal to two Cornish brothers from Falmouth. Charles Hitchens left Cornwall in 1874 to join his brother, Captain James Francis Hitchens, in the shipping business, the African Boating Company Ltd at the Point, Durban. Charles became a member of Durban's Town Council in 1882, serving for two years. In 1893 he was elected as a member of the Legislative Assembly for Alfred County and later was elected Senator. Having already had experience as a member of the Natal Harbour Board he entered the government in 1906 as Minister of Railways and Harbours and with the Union of South Africa in 1910 he was to remain a member of the Senate until his death on the 30th April 1914, at Trevean House. Charles had married Annie Athalie Steele; their children were Francis St. James (1880-1940 a lawyer), Harry Cyril (1882-1961 Pioneer sugar farmer), Charles Vivian Steele (1884-1946 who lived at Umfolozi in Zululand) and Athalie Stella (1901-02). James Hitchens, who married Fanny Jones, died in June 1910 being described as a businessman and gentleman.[52]

One Cornishman who had the unique distinction of serving as the first and last military head of the Civil Service in Natal was Major David Erskine (1816-1903) from Restormel, near Lostwithiel. Having had a long military career, mainly serving in India and Australia he was appointed Colonial Secretary for Natal in 1858. Although not well-liked – Frances Colenso (see later) described him as a gentleman, though a cipher as a public servant,[53] one of his achievements was to bring the Natal Volunteers up to a high standard of discipline. He left Natal in 1875, becoming Resident Magistrate for Walvis Bay 1878-80 before retiring to England to live at the Isle of Wight, where he died in 1903.

One of Erskine's sons, St. Vincent William (1846-1904) was a treasury clerk in Natal in March 1868 but left to accompany the German explorer Karl Mauch who had planned to travel north in Africa from the Transvaal to Egypt. However, the two men had an apparent disagreement and Erskine set out to explore the Limpopo river tracing its course to the Indian Ocean, which he reached on the 5th September 1868. From there he made his way back, and despite almost dying from fever and dysentery, reached Natal to return to his civil service post in 1869. His reputation as an explorer was enough for the Secretary of Native Affairs, Theophilus Shepstone, to commission him to return to the Limpopo region once more as Ambassador. During 1871-74 Erskine made a number of journeys exploring and making contact with the various Chiefs, sometimes as a surveyor, at others solely as trader and hunter. It was as a surveyor in 1876 that he began mapping the Griqualand East area, but in 1878 he was lucky to escape with his life during the Griqua uprising. He was with his wife Mary, besieged at Kokstad, when a powder magazine exploded killing eight Europeans and injuring Erskine and several others. He survived, however, ending his days as a mining and civil engineer at Johannesburg – but it is for his exploration of South East Africa that he is best remembered. In Durban a seaside boulevard is named Erskine Terrace, and a southern suburb of the city is called Wentworth, the name of the Erskine family seat on the Isle of Wight.

St. Vincent had married a daughter of the Natal advocate and politician D.A. Buchanan; a second daughter married Erskine's brother – Stuart Townsend

Erskine. He was also an explorer, and surveyed a route from Delagoa Bay to Swaziland for McCorkindales Glasgow & South Africa Company in 1869 or 1870. Another brother, Robert Henry Erskine, was a member of the Natal Carbineers but was killed in action during the Langalibalele Rebellion in 1873.

The Langalibalele Rebellion was a sad and tragic episode in Natal's early history involving a small tribe – the Hlubi, led by their Chief Langalibalele – coming to grief through the laws of Natal. No native was allowed to own a gun and the Hlubi, who had come into Natal seeking protection and refuge from a neighbouring tribe the Mpande, were ordered to hand over their guns. Unfortunately many of the Hlubi had worked at the diamond mines and had been paid for their labour with guns so handing them over was tantamount to handing over their wages. The Hlubi, rather than comply with the law tried to leave Natal for Basutoland. They were met by a well armed force of men led by Major Durnford, the size of which easily outnumbered the entire Hlubi. The confrontation resulted in a panic and three white soldiers, one of whom was Erskine, were killed. This in turn was followed by an appalling act of revenge as the white force went on the rampage and butchered hundreds of Hlubi including women and children. Langalibalele was captured and tragedy turned to farce as the old Chief underwent a mock trial. With virtually no defence he was sentenced to imprisonment on Robben Island. Only one man was prepared to champion the Hlubi cause and he was a Cornishman, John William Colenso.

Born on the 14th January 1814 during a storm in St. Austell, Colenso was to cause more than one storm in South Africa as Bishop of Natal. Branded as a traitor, a heretic and a rationalist devil[54] Colenso was without a doubt the most controversial Cornishman to go to South Africa. Although his father had been involved in tin workings in the Pentewan Valley, Colenso first went into teaching, where his flair for mathematics enabled him to write much needed text books on the subject. Then, persuaded by his wife Frances (née Bunyon), he entered the church. On 30th November 1853, aged 39, he became a Bishop and within two weeks set out on a preliminary visit to Natal:

> On Thursday evening December 15th 1853 I sailed from Plymouth in company with the Bishop of Cape Town.

With these words Colenso began his diary of his visit to Natal, a diary from which later in 1855 he was able to publish the contents entitled *Ten Weeks in Natal.* His speedy and pleasant voyage took only thirty-five days: a great contrast to many of the voyages undertaken by the Cornish at that time. On arrival in Natal he wrote comparing the scenery with that of Devonshire and Cornwall and his Cornishness was very evident in his writing as when describing the death of a cockroach by ants he noted how the ants pulled one and all together. He did not remain long in Durban, which he described as little more than a large collection of

1864.
FROM A PHOTOGRAPH BY J.E. MAYALL.

John William Colenso 1814-1883.

cottages interspersed with green foliage,[55] but very much like John Wesley travelled all over the country on horseback, often in the company of Theophilus Shepstone, the Secretary of State for Native Affairs. The two men formed a friendship that later led Mrs Colenso to remark that Shepstone was perhaps one of his dearest friends in either hemisphere.[56] Just before he returned home Colenso met two other Cornish ministers at Maritzburg;they were Messrs Pearse and Thomas.[57] Colenso returned to England where he set about raising funds – a task at which he was highly successful – and he was able to finance the return of his family to Natal the following year, taking with him a large missionary team. Colenso set up his headquarters at Bishopstowe, overlooked by Natal's own Table Mountain six miles outside of Pietermaritzburg, with a mission station nearby which the Zulus called *Ekukanyeni* – meaning home of light. A school was built in which two of his daughters, Harriet and Frances Ellen, taught. All the Colensos became, like Shepstone, fluent in the Zulu language but it was Colenso himself who wrote and published an English-Zulu dictionary, a Zulu grammar and who translated the New Testament into Zulu, all on his own printing press at Bishopstowe. Such was Colenso's standing and respect amongst the Zulu people that they called him *Sokululeka* – the father who brings light and *Sobantu* – the father of his people. Due to the later prejudice and hatred toward the Colensos, their many achievements in the Mission between 1855-62, including a rapid and extensive church building programme, have gone largely unrecognised

Marianne Churchill, a member of a wealthy merchant family in early Natal described Colenso:

a fine looking man, tall and commanding in appearance a fine, intellectual brow and piercing eyes. There is a benevolent smile occasionally relieves the otherwise stern aspect, but a look of anxiety and care have already taken a firm hold...

but rather perceptively added:

I do not think our good Bishop will repose on a bed of roses. In the pulpit his much liked, simple practical sermons distinguished by their clear intelligence and feeling delivery attract a crowded church.[59]

How right she was! On his first visit Colenso had upset his fellow missionaries by refusing to condemn the native practice of polygamy. He had also come to the conclusion that much that had been written in the Old Testament was little more than myth rather than fact and therefore was not to be believed. He expressed his unorthodox views in two theological works, *Romans* (in 1861) and the longer *Pentateuch*, covering several volumes (in 1862-63). No less than 41 Bishops condemned him and he was called, amongst other things a liar, irresponsible and the antichrist. Following a trial at Cape Town, which he did not attend on the grounds that it was illegal, Colenso was deposed as Bishop of Natal by Robert Grey, the Archbishop of Cape Town. Colenso went to England and appealed to the Crown Court which found that Grey had no legal jurisdiction over Colenso and so his virtual excommunication of Colenso was declared invalid. Joseph Churchill, who had admired Colenso for his boldness and candour, thought Grey to have been tyrannical and unprincipled.[60] When Colenso returned to Natal from England, however, he found his churches locked against him and when he eventually obtained access to St. Peters in Pietermaritzburg he found even the bell ropes had gone missing. Friends ignored him whilst Grey consecrated W.K. Macronie as a rival Bishop. It was all to no avail for Colenso had the courage of his convictions and stood firm, keeping his post as Bishop of Natal and being loyally supported by people such as Charles Darwin, Charles Dickens, Thomas Huxley, Rajah Brooke and fellow Cornishman Leonard Courtney, amongst many. Colenso's own capacity to raise a much needed fighting fund helped to finance the legal battles that followed. The religious controversy eased slightly with Grey's death in 1872 but by then Colenso was about to cause another storm.

The following year saw the Langalibalele Rebellion and with it the ending of the friendship between Colenso and Shepstone which had lasted some twenty years. Colenso's support of the Hlubi people was seen as mischievous and he and Shepstone went to England, each to put forward a different case. Colenso won and Langalibalele was given a reprieve being released from Robben Island but he had to remain at the Cape at a special reserve, in exile. Victory for Colenso also resulted in the recall of the popular Governor, Sir. Benjamin Pine, who had conducted the mock trial of Chief Langalibalele. Such was the anger at this of many people in Natal, that when Colenso returned, the shopkeepers of Durban closed early in protest. For Mrs Colenso to suggest in one of her letters that somehow they – the Colensos – were out of harmony with society was an understatement.

Colenso's most enthusiastic supporters were members of his own family, especially his wife Frances and eldest daughter Harriet. She accompanied her father on his visits to Langalibalele at the Cape and later wrote a number of books and tracts in his support. She carried on his work to such an extent she earned from the Zulus the title *his Staff*. The Hlubi tribe, which during their Chief's exile was virtually based at Bishopstowe, came mainly under the care of Harriet who they regarded as their patron saint.[61]

Colenso became even further estranged from Shepstone over the latter's policy to annex the Transvaal in 1877, and his handling of the Zulu War 1879 (see next chapter). As Frances Colenso wrote:

> As to Mr. Shepstone, as soon as John found the line he was taking he said in this case 'it must be war to the knife between us' and he has not been to his house since, though of course they salute in public. The split between these two has been an immense puzzle to the world around. I don't suppose they, or perhaps Mr. S. himself, can understand a man's sacrificing his own private friendships and public supporters on account of a question of wide general interest, of justice and humanity[62]

Colenso has been called a man of considerable personality, deeply sincere, extremely opinionated and as stubborn as a mule by one author[63] and a man of outstanding integrity by another.[64] Henry Rider Haggard, later Sir Rider Haggard and the author of *King Solomon's Mines* and *She*, considered Colenso "a very strange man, you cannot but admire, with his intellect written on his face"[65] and described him as "tall, able and agreeable but one who was desperately at loggerheads with everybody",[66] but thought his unpopularity amongst many colonists was not on account of religious matters, but because "he was so strong and, as they considered, so intemperate an advocate of the rights of natives".[67] Rider Haggard found himself more or less in sympathy with Colenso.

Bishop John Colenso died on 23rd June 1883, and was buried in front of the altar of St. Peter's Cathedral, Pietermaritzburg. His life had indeed been a stormy one – from the religious controversy and his calm stand against oppressive dogma to his steadfast belief that the native was to be treated on equal terms. He was not afraid to make his unpopular views known, being ready to criticise if necessary the church, his good friend Shepstone and hence the Colonial Government's policy and even the British Government over its heavy handed and unnecessary action as regards the Boers and Zulu. As Garibaldi once wrote to him:

I know as you know the hostility and the ingratitude with which the seekers for truth and justice are met by the prejudices of the world.[68]

Colenso knew only too well.

Three months after Colenso's death Bishopstowe caught fire and was totally destroyed. Frances Colenso moved into one of the farm cottages. In 1886 her daughter Frances Ellen, (whose lover Colonel Durnford had been killed at Isandlwana), sailed for England to work on an autobiography of the Bishop, but she died the following year. Frances Colenso died at Bishopstowe on 23rd December 1893 and was buried at Pietermaritzburg. Her other two daughters Agnes and Harriet died within a few weeks of each other in 1932 and were buried with their mother. A.L. Rowse has commented:

Colenso left a legacy in South Africa, not only in his ideals but in good works...[69]

The same could also apply to the Colenso women.

One other prominent Cornish family to arrive in Natal under the Byrne scheme was that of Baragwanath which today is a household name throughout the length and breadth of South Africa by virtue of the fact that the country's largest hospital serving the black population bears the name Baragwanath. Many people quite wrongly have thought the name to be of Indian origin but translated into English it means wheaten bread the Cornish equivalent of the surname Whitbread.

Baragwanath Hospital, Johannesburg takes its name from the farm on which it was established, and which was named after the owner John Albert Baragwanath. John's father – also John – was a Cornish sea captain (on the Cape route) who had obviously seen enough of South Africa to join the Byrne scheme. He sailed on the *Lady Bruce* in 1850 accompanied by his wife Wilmot and their four children, Elizabeth Grace, John Albert, Orlando and Emily. A fifth child Charles was born at sea en route but died aged eight weeks, his death being recorded in the *Natal Witness* 31st May 1850. The family settled on a farm called Isipingo just south of Durban. Little is known about John and Wilmot other than that John returned to England for medical treatment; where he died probably in 1873.

John Albert Baragwanath was apprenticed to a saddle maker but later opened his own trading store near Lady Frere in today's Eastern Province. Obviously deciding that only a Cornish wife would do, he married Adelaide Trennery, a daughter of Joseph and Hannah Trennery, at Queenstown. John and Adelaide had six daughters and four sons, of whom Orlando was destined to become the best known Baragwanath.[70]

To those already mentioned can be added Joseph Rapson, a tailor from Falmouth who arrived with his family to join his brother Josiah, a Cornish carpenter who had sailed on the *Dreadnought* in 1849, and John Rowe who arrived in 1856 on the *Portia*. The latter turned out to be a thief of merchandise and then horses.[71]

Dickason has shown the significance to Natal of the Pascoe family from Penzance and how E.J. Pascoe, having found coal deposits on his farm, became the forerunner to the development of a huge coalfield in the region.[72] Bishop Colenso himself had noted the existence of coal during his first visit, and how it was used in the sugar crushing mills.[73] However, large scale coal mining in Natal did not really begin until the late 1880's, with the arrival of the railway. Other members of the Pascoe family became engineers, blacksmiths, storekeepers and farmers, and all contributed to the building up of Natal into a viable Colony. A number of Cornish miners were employed in the coal mines.

Two Cornishmen who did not arrive in Natal until 1872 – but one of whom was to establish a notable legal family – were the Brokensha brothers from St. Just. Thomas Henry Brokensha left his home in Cornwall for Durban aged eighteen and at first hunted and traded throughout Zululand, travelling through the Orange Free State and Transvaal before returning to Natal to marry Sarah Brillianso, in 1881. He worked first as a Postmaster at Umsinga in 1883, then as Deputy Sheriff for the Dundee district, finally acting as Magistrate and Attorney of Natal's Supreme Court, practising as a law agent at Dundee where he was Deputy Mayor on two occasions. His brother Francis Carne, (six years older), having had commercial training in Penzance – he received the Freedom of the Town in 1901 – settled in Durban joining the Cornish firm of Harvey, Greenacre & Co., of which he eventually became Manager and finally Director. Francis was also very active on the Durban Methodist circuit. He died in 1923, a year before Thomas and was described as one of the oldest and most esteemed residents.[74] Both brothers had very large families. Francis who had married Ellen Baines in 1875, had thirteen children, whilst Thomas and Sarah had ten.

Commenting on the range of his family's contribution to South Africa Don Henwood wrote:

the field is as wide as the country and as varied as its topography, and the contribution continues.[75]

This is rather an apt comment that could apply to the many other Cornish Pioneers who each, in their own way, made a major contribution to the colony which had become their home.

Port Nolloth brass and reed band 1906. Top row from left to right: M. Harris, H. Rogers, S. Cornish, W. Chudleigh, H. Woodland, H. Leairy, G.R. Palmer.

Middle row: A. Harris, Band Master, W. Grose, B. Opie, J. Opie, J. Goodfellow, G. Woodland, G. Leairy, J. Reynolds.

Lower row: Band Masters' son, K. Woodland, F. Tucker, E. Cooper, B. Leairy, M. Doble, B. Cooper.

Notes – Chapter One

1. C.P.M.N., 8th SEPTEMBER 1910

2. Richard Lander, *RECORDS OF CAPTAIN CLAPPERTON'S LAST EXPEDITION TO AFRICA, 2 VOLS.,* (LONDON 1830) p.8 Lander was famous for discovering the source of the River Niger and his statue stands at the top of Lemon St. in Truro. His great-granddaughter Mrs. Joan Rowland (née Bentley) was a prominent member of the Rhodesian Cornish Association and now lives in Durban.

3. See Robert Hughes, *THE FATAL SHORE* (LONDON 1987) and Payton, *THE CORNISH MINER IN AUSTRALIA*

4. *THE ROYAL CORNWALL GAZETTE, 7th AUGUST 1819*

5. The members of Osler's party were as follows

   Benjamin Osler (44) w. Jane(45) d. Susannah(20) Stephen (15) d. Mary(12) Amelia(10) d. Elizabeth(6) James Ball(44) w. Ann(45) s. James(6) Richard Blee (22) w. not named John Bridgeman(19) John Dale(22) w. Mary(17) Richard Eva (24) w. Elizabeth (23) Henry Goodman(23) w. Elizabeth (20) William Mallet (45) w. Elizabeth (46) Charles Pearce(35) Joseph Richards (22) w. Sarah (21) d. Sarah (3) d, Phyllis(1) James Weeks (29) w. Grace (25) d. Elizabeth (2)

   Compiled from Dickason, *CORNWALL IMMIGRANTS* AND E. Morse Jones, *ROLE OF THE BRITISH SETTLERS IN SOUTH AFRICA* (CAPE TOWN 1969).

6. Dickason, *CORNISH IMMIGRANTS* p 20-21

7. Donald Woods, *ASKING FOR TROUBLE* (LONDON 1980) p 23

8. H.E. Hockley, *THE STORY OF THE BRITISH SETTLERS OF 1820 in SOUTH AFRICA* (CAPE TOWN 1957) p 115

9. See Eric W. Turpin, *BASKETWORK HARBOUR,* (CAPE TOWN 1964) p.129-13

10. *IBID.,* p129

11. Letitia Elizabeth Harriet Cock (1852-1951) was the daughter of Cornelius and Letitia Cock and thus Williams' granddaughter. She died in Kimberley aged 99 years 3 months.

12. *GRAHAMSTOWN JOURNAL,* 20th OCTOBER 1849

13. W.A. Maxwell & R.T. McGough Ed., *THE REMINISCENCES OF THOMAS STUBBS* (CAPE TOWN 1978) p.210

14. Turpin, *BASKETWORK HARBOUR* p.2

15. Ed. F.G. Van Der Reit, Rev. Henry Hare Dugmore and Rev. L.A. Hewson *REMINISCENCES OF AN ALBANY SETTLER (GRAHAMSTOWN 1958*

16. *GRAHAMSTOWN JOURNAL,* 14th FEBRUARY 1876

17. *IBID.,* 18th FEBRUARY 1876

18. *WEST BRITON,* 15th FEBRUARY 1877 Coode had been knighted for his services in 1872 which included giving advice on the building of the Thames Embankment. Coode died at Brighton 2nd March 1892. See *THE TIMES,* 3rd March 1892 and *NATAL WITNESS,* 4th March 1892 for obituary.

19. *WEST BRITON,* 3rd MARCH 1820

20. *CAPE TIMES,* 3rd FEBRUARY 1904

21. *WEST BRITON,* 13th JULY 1950

22. *THE JOURNAL OF THE TREVITHICK SOCIETY,* No:11 1984 p.43

23. D.D. Hall, *THE STORY OF A SOUTH AFRICAN PIONEER AND HIS FAMILY, RICHARD THOMAS HALL (1823-1889)* privately published.

24. *IBID.,* p.68.

25. *IBID.,* p.76

26. Lawrence G. Green, *SECRET AFRICA* (LONDON 1936) p.56

27. Dickason, *CORNISH IMMIGRANTS* p.37

28. *IBID.*, p.38

29. Lawrence G. Green, *SO FEW ARE FREE* (CAPE TOWN 1946) p.145

30 Dickason, p.38

31. Green, p.148

32. *CORNISHMAN,* 4th DECEMBER 1918

33. *C.P.M.N.,* 10th SEPTEMBER 1914

34. *MINING JOURNAL,* 16th FEBRUARY 1907 p.219

35 Tutworkers were paid for the amount of rock broken. Tribute work paid a varying proportion of the value of the ore raised and thus tribute workers had a chance to make more money than other miners.

36. Kenneth Brown, *THE INCREDIBLE O'OKIEP COPPER MINE :ITS RICHES, ITS RAILWAY AND ITS CORNISH ENGINES. JOURNAL OF THE TREVITHICK SOCIETY* (No.11) p.41-59

37. Green, *SECRET AFRICA* p.55

38. Green, *SO FEW ARE FREE.* p.133

39. *IBID.,* p.126

40. Hall, *REAPED MY MEALIES* p. 29-30

41. Oliver Ransford, *THE GREAT TREK* (LONDON 1974) p.127

42. In 1841, 23, 950 emigrants left England for Canada, 14, 552 for Australia and New Zealand but only 130 went to the Cape. See Sir G E Cory, *THE RISE OF SOUTH AFRICA 6 VOLS. 1910-30* (VOL. IV p.391)

43. Alan F. Hattersley, *THE BRITISH SETTLEMENT OF NATAL : A STUDY IN IMPERIAL MIGRATION* (C.U.P. 1950) p.171

44. *THE HISTORY OF THE HENWOODS 1856-1956* (privately published) p.9I Oom is a term of respect meaning Uncle.

45. Information supplied by Don Henwood.

46. *NATAL WITNESS,* 14th DECEMBER 1907. Paul Henwood is buried at New Barnet, North London England

47. Most of the information re: John Henwood comes from *THE HENWOOD FAMILY PAPERS* and has been supplied by the Killie Campbell Africana Library.

48. Much of the information concerning the Acutt family was supplied by Lambert Truran who made notes from Yvonne Miller, *ACUTTS IN AFRICA*, (privately published in the early 70's and limited to 500 copies) and from Shelagh O'Byrne Spencer, *BRITISH SETTLERS IN NATAL 1824-1857 A BIOGRAPHICAL REGISTER* (VOL. 1) (PIETERMARITZBURG 1981) p.4-6. A descendent of the Acutts was Peter Burns, who in 1939 founded Treverton School at Mooi River, Natal. The name Treverton apparently comes from the village of Treverton in Cornwall from which the Acutts emigrated. Sidney Hudson Read, *HOPE BEYOND. A MEMOIR OF TREVERTONS FIRST TWENTY ONE YEARS 1964-85* p.3

49. *CORNISHMAN,* 10th SEPTEMBER 1896.

50. Shelagh O'Byrne Spencer, *BRITISH SETTLERS IN NATAL 1824-57 A BIOGRAPHICAL REGISTER* (VOL. 2) (PIETERMARITZBURG 1983). p.104-106

51. *NATAL WITNESS,* 28th SEPTEMBER 1901.

52. Information re: the Harvey family and the Hitchen brothers supplied by Lambert Truan and P.M. Hitchens

53. W. Rees, *COLENSO LETTERS FROM NATAL* (PIETERMARITZBURG 1958) p.319

54. *PERSONALITY,* 24th NOVEMBER 1966, Michael Allwright, *THE WAYWARD ONE* p.101

55 J.W. Colenso, *TEN WEEKS IN NATAL A JOURNAL OF A FIRST TOUR OF VISITATION AMONG THE COLONISTS AND ZULU KAFFIRS OF NATAL* (CAMBRIDGE 1855)

56   *PERSONALITY,* 24th NOVEMBER 1966 Allwright p.105

57.   Rees, *COLENSO LETTERS FROM NATAL* p.113 Theophilus Shepstone was one of the original 1820 Settlers. He came from Gloucestershire with his parents when only 3 years old.

58.   Colenso, *TEN WEEKS IN NATAL,* p.269

59.   Daphne Childs, Ed., *A MERCHANT FAMILY IN EARLY NATAL,* Diaries and letters of Joseph & Marianne Churchill 1850-1880 (CAPE TOWN 1979) p.64

60.   *IBID.,* p.64

61.   Sol Plaatje dedicated his book *NATURE LIFE IN SOUTH AFRICA* to Miss Harriette Colenso in recognition of her unswerving loyalty to the policy of her late distinguished father. See Jeff Guy, *THE HERETIC* (LONDON 1983) p.353

62.   Rees, *COLENSO LETTERS* p.283

63   T.V. Bulpin, *TO THE SHORES OF NATAL* (CAPE TOWN 1953). p.180

64.   C.T. Binns, *THE LAST ZULU KING* (LONDON 1963) p.214

65.   Henry Rider Haggard, *DAYS OF MY LIFE* (LONDON 1926) p.56

66.   *IBID.,* p.63

67.   *IBID.,* p.66

68.   Rees, *COLENSO LETTERS* p.330

69.   A.L. Rowse, *THE CONTROVERSIAL COLENSOS'* (LONDON 1989)p.30 The *controversial Colenso*s were John and his cousin William. William went to New Zealand where his work among and for the Maori people was to his credit, although his relationship with a Maori girl, resulting in the birth of a son, brought a public scandal, with William being cast out from the Mission

For a full account of the Langalibalele Rebellion and the relationship between Colenso and Shepstone see Donald R Morris, *THE WASHING OF THE SPEARS: THE RISE AND FALL OF THE ZULU NATION* (LONDON 1965)

70.   Orlando Baragwanath (1872-1973) was without a doubt one of Rhodesia's (now Zimbabwe) great pioneers.

71.   See also Spencer, *BRITISH SETTLERS IN NATAL 1824-57 A BIOGRAPHICAL INDEX VOL. 1 & VOL. 2*

72.   Dickason, *CORNISH IMMIGRANTS* p.25 Edward Jasper Howe Pascoe died of fever 29th JULY 1875. See also *NATALIA,* DECEMBER 1982 No. 12. Sheila Henderson, *'COLONIAL COALOPOLIS' THE ESTABLISHMENT AND GROWTH OF DUNDEE.*

73.   Colenso, *TEN WEEKS IN NATAL* p.170-171

74.   *CORNISHMAN,* 21st FEBRUARY 1923

75.   Letter to author 3rd SEPTEMBER 1988

CHAPTER TWO

THE ZULU WAR AND
FIRST BOER WAR 1860-86

The Zulus have no wish whatever to fight if we leave them alone.[1]

Bishop Colenso

*If I were a younger man he shouted in a strong crescendo I would go
and fight for the Boers – fight for the Boers, fight for the Boers.*[2]

Edward John Trelawny aged 89

Following the agreements known as the Sand River and Bloemfontein Conventions (1842 and 1854) the British made no further attempts to extend their rule or encroach upon what was then officially recognised as Boer territory – namely the Orange Free State and Transvaal. That did not stop them, however, from taking territory elsewhere – such as Basutoland in 1869, or their even more dubious annexation of Griqualand West in 1871 (and with it a fortune in diamonds, see chapter 3). The British were also wary of hostility between the Boers and their African neighbours, especially the Pedi led by Chief Sekhukhune and the Zulus led by Chief Cetewayo. Ironically the hostilities that followed involving the Pedi, Zulu and Boer were all to be at British expense.

The town of Pretoria in Transvaal had been founded in 1855 and Marthinus Wessel Pretorius had, since 1857, been President of the South African Republic. He had tried, though unsuccessfully, to bring about union with the Orange Free State actually being its President as well from 1860-65. In 1872 he was succeeded by the Rev. Thomas F. Burgers, who had the idea that the Republic would be better federated with Cape Colony, an idea which lost him much support. Burgers' main problem however, was to prevent the Republic from becoming bankrupt, for the country was in a state of economic collapse. It was for this reason he set out for Europe in 1875 in an attempt to find financial backing. With the idea of building a railway between the Republic and Delagoa Bay whilst in Cape Town, he sought the service of a Cornishman who had already proved his engineering ability by the building of the railway line from O'okiep to Port Nolloth, and having surveyed the line from Cape Town to Kimberley. Richard Thomas Hall was appointed Railway Engineer to the South African Republic in March, 1875, and he and his son Harry were soon surveying the best possible route of a railway line from Pretoria to Delagoa Bay. In a letter to his wife, written in camp about eighty miles from Delagoa Bay and dated December, 1875, he claimed a railway could easily be made, but pointed out the dangers of the tsetse fly – his own horse having died 5 days after leaving Delagoa Bay. The countryside was all grassy hills without a bush or a rock to vary the scene. Whether or not Burgers succeeded in getting the money to build a railway, Hall had already decided not to quit the Transvaal yet and urged his wife to join him at Pretoria so they could all eat Christmas dinner there.3 It was duly reported in one of the Republic's newspapers that:

> *Mr. Hall, the Railway Engineer for the line between Delagoa Bay and Pretoria is settling permanently in the Transvaal. His wife and family in company with other English families (future Transvaalers) passed the Tugela last week, en route for the Transvaal.*4

Mrs Hall, with six of her children, sailed to Durban and then went by coach to Maritzburg. The rest of the journey to Pretoria was made by ox-wagon beginning in heavy rain on 6th November which was a new experience, for Mrs Hall wrote that the children were very restless. Then a wagon they were travelling in caught fire, a number of oxen fell sick – some died or had to be shot – and still more rain, thunderstorms and dense fog. On 18th November she wrote:
*Still floods of rain, no moving from the wagon – this is the third day of rain, wet, everything wet – roads are very bad.*5

R.T. Hall, Railway engineer. Photographed c. 1875

Hugh Lanion Hall in his autobiography seemed unperturbed by the rain – it was not even mentioned – for having bought a gun and ammunition in Durban he was more interested in relating how he hunted game thus making sure the party had game to eat every day, adding it was some little compensation for the long slow, weary journey with its many hardships that must have been very trying to his mother.6 On reaching Pretoria they were reunited with Richard Thomas and Henry, the two men having completed the survey. Such was the state of the Republic's economy – it was practically bankrupt – that the Halls could not be paid in hard cash for their work but were offered land instead. Unfortunately for Richard Thomas Hall he turned down the offer of a farm in the Eastern Transvaal on which gold was later discovered. When President Burgers returned from Europe he was faced with a revolt by Sekhukhune and the Pedi in 1876. An army of Boers led by Burgers himself suffered a defeat mainly because the Boers had little confidence in him as leader. As Sekhukhune and his tribe began to raid more openly throughout the Transvaal Britain saw the opportunity for stepping in to annex the Republic. According to Hugh Lanion Hall:

> *A letter was written from Pretoria to the British Government in Maritzburg drawing their attention to the state the Republican Government was in, pointing out that further native risings in the neighbourhood of Sekukini's country were expected, that a raid from the Zulus was feared, that the country was bankrupt and that the Boers were dissatisfied with President Burgers. This document was signed by the British in and around Pretoria.*[7]

This was all Britain needed to annex the Transvaal officially and on the pretext of saving the Boers Sir Theophilus Shepstone, the Secretary for Native Affairs – whom Fisher has described as one of the most remarkable of Queen Victoria's Empire builders[8] – was assigned to the task. He was assisted by two Cornishmen. On 27th December 1876 Shepstone wrote:

> *I left Pietermaritzburg in a mule wagon for my mission to the Transvaal I was accompanied by Dr. Lyle as a permanent companion.*[9]

Photograph taken on the annexation of the Transvaal 1877. The central, seated figure is Shepstone. To the right seated is Lyle and behind him Morcom. The author Rider Haggard is lying in front of the group.

Dr. John Vacy Lyle had been born in Cornwall (Stratton 1826) and after a period spent in Edinburgh studying medicine had returned to Cornwall to reside at

Launceston where he had attended school as a boy. Unfortunately ill health in 1859 encouraged him to seek a drier climate in South Africa. Having attempted, like so many other settlers to grow sugar, Lyle became for a short time Editor of the *Natal Herald* at Durban. Like Colenso he became a close friend of Shepstone – he was also the family doctor – often accompanying him on his many travels into Zululand. Lyle's medical background also led him to discover a cure for Bilharzia (a blood fluke).

The other Cornishman to whom Shepstone turned for assistance with his task was William Boase Morcom from Redruth. Morcom had arrived in 1861 in Natal aged 15 years with his father. He first gained employment with the *Natal Witness* and the newspaper became his ticket into law which he studied in his spare time. Barry Ronan later wrote in 1923:

> *There are no Natal journalists of the old school – they are either dead or limbs of the law, having availed themselves of the old system whereby a newspaper reporter who had attended a specific number of sittings of the higher courts became qualified to practise as an attorney. The late W.B. Morcom was a type of this class.*[10]

When Shepstone sought Morcom out he was Clerk to the Attorney General of Natal but took the position of Shepstone's Private Secretary and Legal Advisor, although his main role was to be the draughtsman of the actual proclamation of annexation. Another secretary Shepstone took with him was Rider Haggard who remembered the journey to Pretoria taking thirty-five days to traverse the four hundred odd miles in an ox wagon.[11] Shepstone (recently knighted and therefore Sir Theophilus) and party arrived in Pretoria on the 22nd January 1877 being enthusiastically received – over a hundred Boers escorted him into town some outspanning (unharnessing) his horses and drawing the vehicle themselves.[12] He set upon a programme of winning over the Boers. Morcom kept a diary which Shepstone called *Family Notes*. It provides a valuable insight into the social side of the annexation episode. Morcom has been described as a hawk-eyed scribe and it is not surprising that Shepstone often wrote in the margins of the diary, *Not on any account be made public*.[13] Caustic remarks, criticisms and comments about Boer barbarism would certainly not have endeared Shepstone to the Boers or helped his cause. A combination of threats and cajolement hinting at the growing danger from the warlike Zulus was enough to get the Boers to accept annexation. During the eleven weeks leading up to the declaration Morcom noted no less than fifty-nine social functions such as dinners, dances, picnics, whist drives and moonlight parties – all in honour of or given by Shepstone, although Rider Haggard did wonder who was paying the bill. The proclamation of the annexation of the South African Republic by Britain was issued on 12th April 1877 with Rider Haggard himself raising the Union Jack. Shepstone became the Administrator of the new

Colony – an Act of Parliament the same year united the Orange Free State and the Transvaal to Natal and the Cape – under a newly appointed High Commissioner Sir Henry Bartle Frere. According to Hugh Lanion Hall:

*The 13th Regiment of Light Infantry arrived in Pretoria about the end of April with their band. The band played as they passed farm houses, and were very much appreciated by the Boer women and children, who often followed them for miles, dancing to the music, for they had never heard a band before. A common saying was that the band had captured the Transvaal.*14

With the annexation of the Transvaal Richard Thomas Hall was unemployed. He and his wife returned to Cape Town where he began working once more for the Cape Railway.

Shepstone appointed Lyle as his Superintendent of Education although his appointment apparently

*raised the prejudice of many and the jealousy of more but he performed his work with the same zealous care which had always distinguished him and disarmed exception to his appointment on the ground of his want of acquaintance with the Dutch language receiving high testimony to the value of his work from Sir Bartle Frere during his recent visit to the Transvaal.*15

Lyle was in charge of Education from 1877-79 and Lyle's success was measured by the increase of the number of schools from 15 to 20 and of pupils from 442 to 838 during that period. Lyle encouraged local communities to set up their own schools and provided state aid to help them do it. He even went so far as to write a report on Education in the Transvaal, in which (among many things) he recommended adequate training for teachers. His death on the 28th June 1879 after a three-month illness was received in Natal with universal regret.16

The same did not apply to Lyle's fellow Cornishman William Morcom. Shepstone had appointed him Attorney General of the Transvaal but he only held the post a short while from February 1880, to August 1881. He referred to the Boer menfolk as uncommonly rough looking but having exemplary conduct, although his remarks as regards the Boer women were disparaging to say the least, for he considered them a sorry looking lot but then Morcom never married.17 He returned to Natal where he entered into partnership with his brother R.F. Morcom, (in Maritzburg) until he was appointed Attorney General of Natal in 1890 (he had been Acting Attorney General on three previous occasions). In 1888 he had been appointed Queen's Consul – the only Advocate to receive such an honour – until Natal received responsible Government, in 1893. Morcom was then pensioned off from the service only to re-enter public life when he was elected as

Pietermaritzburg's Member for Parliament in 1897 – a post he held until his death. In 1903 he became Minister of Justice in the short-lived Hine Administration, being the first Natal Minister to hold such a title. Following his death on 23rd April 1910 his obituary appeared on the front page of the *Natal Witness* where he was described as a notable Natalian, a man held in the highest respect by all classes of the community and one of South Africa's ablest lawyers.[18]

The High Commissioner of South Africa decided that for peace to prevail and possible confederation in South Africa, the natives would have to be subdued. Unfortunately the defeat of the Boers by Sekhukhune, had led Cetewayo, the Zulu King to gain confidence in his own power. He who had been crowned King in 1872 – by Shepstone of all people and had come to power with British help, the British had even supported his claim over disputed territory with the Boers. Having built up his army with rigid discipline, re-introducing the Zulu custom of a ban on marriage for warriors until they had proved themselves in battle – the traditional *"washing of the spears"* – Cetewayo had looked set to do battle with the Boers when the British had entered the Transvaal. Frere's policy of attempting to subdue the natives now led to conflict with the Zulu as three columns of British troops under the command of Lord Chelmsford crossed the border into Zululand in December 1878. What followed was the Zulu War. There are many excellent accounts of the Zulu War[19] though not from a Cornish perspective. The annihilation of one of the columns at Isandlwana on the 22nd January 1879 was followed by British military honour being upheld the following day with the heroic defence of Rorke's Drift. The Zulus massacred part of the 80th Regiment at Ntombe River (12th March) before being themselves defeated at the Battles of Khambula (29th March) and Ulundi (4th July) with Cetewayo being finally captured on 28th August. The disaster at Isandlwana has been attributed to the incompetence of Lord Chelmsford in splitting his force – he himself being out of camp with his staff and thus lucky to escape – and not having constructed adequate defences.[20] One man who paid with his life for these fundamental mistakes was Cornishman Teignmouth Melvill from Lostwithiel who was to play an heroic part on that eventful January day. Melvill was a Lieutenant Adjutant who had already expressed his concern over Chelmsford's lack of defences at the camp saying:

> *These Zulus will charge home and with our small numbers we ought to be*
> *in laager or, at any rate be prepared to stand shoulder to shoulder.*[21]

When the Zulus did strike and all seemed lost Melvill was given instructions to save the Queen's Colour of the 1st Battalion 24th Regiment. With the road to Rorke's Drift already blocked by the enemy Melvill set out across country on horseback with a few others heading for the Buffalo River which, if crossed, would give them safety. It was not to be. Melvill was unhorsed crossing the river but held on to the Queen's colour when he was joined by Lieutenant Coghill, who had also been unhorsed. The two men were to die together.

Many days later on the 4th February a volunteer party led by a Major Black went in search of the two officers. They found Melvill's and Coghill's bodies lying on a path in a glen 300 yards from the water alongside several Zulu bodies.22 The colour, which was recovered further down river by Black, was handed over to Colonel Glynn at Rorke's Drift. A simple grave was dug and the two men were buried near where they had fallen – an official burial ceremony took place in April.

A memorial cross presented by Sir Bartle Frere was placed on a rock just above the graves with the inscription:

> *In memory of Lieut. Adjt. T. Melvill and Lieut. N.J. Coghill, 1st Battalion, 24th Regiment, who died on this spot, 22nd January, 1879, to save the Queen's Colour of their Regiment.*23

Memorial window at St.Winnow's church to Lieutenant Melvill V.C.

Had the two men survived they would have been awarded the Victoria Cross for their bravery and a note to that effect appeared in the *London Gazette* 2nd May 1879 but there were no posthumous awards then. This was rectified in February 1907 when regulations changed and King Edward VII awarded Melvill and Coghill the first two posthumous Victoria Crosses. The high number of 11 Victoria Crosses awarded to men at Rorke's Drift has tended to overshadow the bravery of Melvill and Coghill. In Cornwall Melvill's young widow received from Natal a bloodstained photograph of her late husband which had been picked up on the battlefield, having presumably slipped from his pocket during the flight.24 Meanwhile it was announced that a window was being dedicated to Coghill in Cork Cathedral from funds raised by public subscription which led the *West Briton* to ask

*Will there be a memorial erected also in Cornwall to commemorate the heroism of Lieut. Melvill of Ethy?*25 The answer was not long in coming. A stained glass window was dedicated to his memory at St. Winnow Church, which is beautifully situated beside the River Fowey, just south of Lostwithiel.

Also among those who died at Isandlwana were Cornishmen Lieutenant Porteous from Falmouth and Corporal Phillip Nicholls from Redruth but one who had a very lucky escape was Lieutenant Horace Smith-Dorrien from the Scilly Isles. He said later in his memoirs that he believed he owed his life to the fact that he had been wearing a blue jacket and commented that the only five other officers to escape that day were also wearing blue coats.26 How he escaped riding a "broken-kneed old crock" was related to his father in a letter27 Interestingly when Smith-Dorrien gave an account of his escape in his autobiography he mentioned being passed by first Coghill and then Melvill. Smith-Dorrien was also recommended for the Victoria Cross but,

> *these recommendations drew laudatory letters from the War Office with a regret that as the proper channels for correspondence had not been observed, the Statutes of the Victoria Cross did not admit my receiving that distinction and having no friends at Court the matter dropped.*28

At Helpmakaar Smith-Dorrien caught typhoid and it was touch and go for two months as to whether he would live, but he recovered to return to his regiment.

Another Cornishman lucky to escape with his life was W.S. Musgrove from Redruth who was serving with Colonel Wood's column and became involved in a skirmish whereupon he had to beat a hasty retreat down a hill pursued by a large body of Zulu. In a letter to his uncle at Port Elizabeth Musgrove wrote of his most miraculous escape, and how he had been as cool and collected as if he had been playing a game of football. At the Battle of Khambula the following day, which saw the first major British victory over the Zulus Musgrove related how he and his volunteers

> *rode after them for six or seven miles killing them as they went. We found on the bodies of the Zulus Martini Henri rifles, braces, belts and several other things that they took from our soldiers at Isandula. It was a ghastly sight to see all the dead lying about camp, some with their heads cloven.*29

Two young men from Hayle also saw action in the Zulu War. One, John Luke, was with Colonel Pearson's column which was besieged at Eshowe until relieved by Chelmsford. The other Cornishman – called King – served with Colonel Wood, who was promoted to Brigadier General following his success at Khambula. In Cornwall there was a particular interest shown towards Henry Evelyn Wood, for he had Cornish connections – his family had once resided at Truro where he still had relatives. His right hand man, Colonel Redvers Buller, was also partly of Cornish stock, and held a large estate near Redruth.

Meanwhile Lord Chelmsford had been joined by Prince Imperial Louis Napoleon, the heir to the throne of France. Unfortunately, when the Prince was on a routine patrol, he was ambushed and killed by a Zulu war party. Rider Haggard wrote of the horror and shame that this news sent through all the land.30 The blame for his death fell on the officer in charge of the patrol – a Lieutenant Cary. Buller apparently said to him "By God, Sir, you deserve to be shot, and I hope you will be, I could shoot you myself!"31 Although Cary was court martialled he was not shot. Serving with Buller was an ex-Redruth Rifle Corps. volunteer whose letters home, like Musgrove's, were published in the local Cornish newspaper. Writing to a sister the young Cornishman – unfortunately not named – told how the victory at Khambula was marred by the death of the Prince, whose body was found with 14 wounds and one of his eyes knocked out. At the funeral parade

> *Lord Chelmsford wept like a child all the time. He looks years older than when I first saw him and it is expected he will be recalled from the command of the troops here. What with the Isandula massacre and then the death of the Prince Imperial (after he was cautioned to take special care of him, poor fellow) I feel sorry for Lord Chelmsford. It seems that luck has left him altogether.32*

The Prince Imperial had been killed on 1st June but the final battle with the Zulus at Ulundi did not occur until 4th July. The Zulus were no match for the Gatling guns and cannon and were soon put to flight, the Zulu War ending on 28th August with the capture of Cetewayo. He was taken to Cape Town where he was imprisoned in the castle. Smith-Dorrien, who was himself passing through Cape Town on his way home, saw the Zulu King but described him as a pathetic figure, his "huge obese body bathed in perspiration".33 Later in 1882 Cetewayo visited England and even had lunch with Queen Victoria. He returned to South Africa and in 1883 was once more allowed to rule again in Zululand but over a much smaller area. Shepstone was again on hand to formerly *enthrone* him but credit goes to Bishop Colenso who had been mainly responsible for getting Cetewayo reinstated. Colenso said of Cetewayo he ruled his people well, according to his lights.34 Cetewayo died in 1884, a few months after Colenso. Shepstone considered the Bishop's death more important for he remarked that it should help to settle the political situation.35 How wrong he was!

Lord Chelmsford had resigned on 15th July 1879 being replaced by Sir Garnet Wolseley. Wood and Buller had both been knighted for their services and in addition Buller had received the Victoria Cross on Wood's recommendation. Wolseley considered that the two of them had been the bright spots of a miserable war,36 and offered them the chance to lead the campaign against Sekhukhune but both men declined. Buller returned to a hearty reception at his family home at Crediton, Devon, whereas Wood was given the honour of escorting the Empress Eugenie to the site where her son, the Prince Imperial, had been killed. A Cornish musician who played before the Empress while she was en route was William Coulsen Tregarthen of Penzance. Tregarthen had only just arrived in South Africa himself having been appointed Organist and Choirmaster of St. Mary's Collegiate Church, Port Elizabeth. When Wood himself returned home both he and Buller were invited by Disraeli, the Prime Minister, to his home at Hughendon Manor – no invitation was given to Lord Chelmsford. Wolseley, with the help of a large force of Swazi quickly dealt with Sekhukhune by burning down his stronghold at Tsate on 28th November 1879 and capturing him. With both Cetewayo and Sekhukhune in prison, all threat from the Zulu and Pedi tribes to the Transvaal was removed. This was to prove unfortunate for the British but favourable to the Boers. Despite the annexation of the Transvaal the political situation was still extremely volatile. Hugh Lanion Hall aptly summed up the situation:

> *The feeling between the Boers and the British Government had become very strained. Now that the Zulus and Sekukini were conquered, the Boers were relieved of those dangers and they wanted the Republic back. We all felt that rebellion might break out any day.*[37]

Shepstone's term as Administrator of the Transvaal had been brief for he had been replaced in March 1879 by Colonel Owen Lanyon. Lanyon according to Lehmann was the worse possible choice to govern the Transvaal.[38] It was a view shared by Lanyon's contemporaries. John Nixon blamed the autocratic rule of Lanyon as being the major cause of the war that followed,[39] whilst Hall commented that Lanyon was a soldier, and, like many British officers he despised the Boers as fighting men and the Kaffirs too.[40] In his previous post as Governor of Griqualand West Lanyon had gained a reputation as a tough administrator and before that he had served in the West Indies. Unfortunately due to his dark complexion many Boers believed, although quite wrongly, that he actually had black blood and were convinced that the British had appointed a Kaffir Governor over them. His origins were in fact Cornish, although his family had been living in Ireland for some generations. Lanyon did not help matters himself for he was openly rude to the Boers to the point of refusing to shake hands with them. However, he performed his duties – which mainly consisted of restoring the Transvaal economy by collecting taxes – so diligently that Wolseley recommended that he be knighted for his work, which he was. Wolseley left South Africa early in 1880 being replaced by Sir George Colley.

A valuable insight into how high feelings ran in the Transvaal between Boer and Briton can be found in a series of letters written by Cornishman Charles W. Deecker, a journalist from Liskeard. He arrived in South Africa at Port Elizabeth in

1876, initially to take up the post as sub-editor on the *Diamond Field News* (Kimberley). However, he first went to Grahamstown to work on the *Journal* for three months and when he eventually did get to Kimberley he found the *News* over staffed. He therefore trekked up by ox-wagon to Transvaal where he became Special Correspondent for the *London Standard*, the *Natal Witness* and the *Cape Times*:

> *One of the first acts of Sir Theophilus Shepstone's Administration was to arrange a fresh Govt. Printing Contract, which Mr. Deecker secured… the contract consisted of the printing of the Government Gazette and all other printing required in conjunction with which Mr. Deecker ran the first English newspaper the old Transvaal Argus which soon became a power in the land.*[41]

When the Zulu War broke out Deecker became a Captain in the Pretoria Volunteer Rifle Corps, and in a letter home to his father remarked that it was fortunate the Zulus did not know their own strength, or Pretoria would have been in ashes long ago. He also warned that the Boers were instigating trouble adding confidently that any attack by the Boers would see them getting "a flea in their ears".[42] His next letter said that the Boers seemed determined to have a row and the sooner they fought the better.[43] A third letter showed Deecker in better spirits for he had just received a cheque from the Government for his Corps. services. It amounted to £350 – Deecker's share being £30, at the rate of 15s a day. Deecker was looking optimistically to the future pointing out Transvaal's great mineral wealth, and how he had been instrumental in starting up a chamber of commerce and agriculture and hoped once the iron horse reached Transvaal, Pretoria would soon become a second Chicago.[44] Taking the opposite view Leonard Courtney, the Cornish M.P. for Liskeard said:

> *We annexed the Transvaal country and it has brought nothing but trouble with it. Instead of wishing to suppress the Transvaal because it was less perfectly organised than we were, we should have allowed it to act as a barrier between us and a country of savages. The Boers of the Transvaal are a civilised people.*[45]

To Sir Garnet Wolseley, Courtney had been "that pestilent M.P. doing much mischief",[46] but to the Boers he and other Liberals became their only hope. The chance of the Boers regaining their independence was greatly enhanced when the Liberals under Gladstone – who had strongly condemned the policy of annexation in his election campaign – won the British General Election in April 1880. In the Transvaal, with ex-President Burgers having been pensioned off to virtual exile in the Cape – he died there in December 1881 – the Boers looked for a leader of a different calibre. They in fact found three – ex-President M.W. Pretorius, Petrus

Jacobus (Piet) Joubert and Stephanus Johannes Paulus (Paul) Kruger. It was Kruger who eventually emerged as the most prominent of the three, being almost the opposite to the highly sophisticated Burgers. William Morcom, who had met Kruger, described him as:

> *an elderly man, decidedly ugly, with a countenance denoting extreme*
> *obstinacy, and also great cruelty. He was also seen to comb his hair*
> *during a public luncheon and to put his napkin to strange uses. Moreover*
> *his dirty wooden pipe was visible, for it stuck out of his breast pocket.*[47]

What Kruger lacked in etiquette he more than made up in his single-minded desire for Boer self-determination. Devoutly religious and overtly racist Kruger came to symbolise all that was Boer. A survivor of the original Great Trek – he was eleven at the time – Kruger had stood alongside the men inside the laager at Blood River. Between the ages of 21-42 he fought in no fewer than nine major campaigns. Kruger, having become the pivot on which the Boer desire for independence balanced, led deputations to London in 1877 and 1878 in which he presented such a well-prepared case for independence that it seemed obvious he had been helped by an English politician or at least a Cornish one:

> *the culprit was almost certainly Leonard Courtney, the member for East*
> *Cornwall... it could well have been Courtney who, as an English friend of*
> *the Boers, presented Kruger with a gold ring engraved with the words*
> *'Take courage, your cause is just and must triumph in the end'.*[48]

With the new Liberal Government in power, and Gladstone more concerned about affairs in Ireland than in the Transvaal, the Boers decided to make their move. The timing was perfect for not only had the Transvaal already been denuded of British troops under Wolseley and Lanyon but Colley had taken many veteran volunteers from the Transvaal to put down a revolt by the Basutos in the Cape in September 1880. Sir Owen Lanyon's total intransigence over tax collecting provided the spark that led to the first Anglo-Boer War which lasted for three months. This followed a Boer declaration of independence in the first weeks of December 1880. The South African Republic was to be led by a Triumvirate – with no actual President. Kruger was Vice President, Joubert was Commandant General and Pretorius was included because he had once been President. Their policy was certainly an indictment of British rule in South Africa that was echoed in the last issue of the *West Briton* for 1880, which claimed, "if Mr. Courtney's advice had been taken we should have been spared this miserable news from Transvaal". [49]

On 20th December 1880 British troops on their way to Pretoria from Lydenburg were fired upon by Boers at Bronkhorst Spruit. Over two-thirds of the British force were killed or wounded in a skirmish that lasted less than an hour. Lanyon sent for

Colley who marched from Newcastle in the New Year only to be met by a Boer force under Joubert at Laings Nek near the Natal-Transvaal border. On 28th January 1881 the British were defeated – British losses ran into hundreds – whereas the Boer dead hardly reached double figures The British disaster went into the military annals to be followed quickly by another for 8th February again saw defeat for Colley at Ingogo Hill. During both battles Hugh Lanion Hall used his ox-wagons to fetch and carry the wounded.

Meanwhile inside the Transvaal Pretoria was cut off when the Boers set up a blockade on 18th December. Lanyon imposed martial Law and business came to a standstill A Volunteer Corps. of about 800 men was raised plus a civil guard. Deecker said:

> *I assisted in the establishment of the forces but did not join in as I contemplated having something to do in connection with business at the camp.*[50]

What he did was to move the printing machinery of his newspaper, the *Argus*, into the military camp and in conjunction with Charles Du Val, a travelling entertainer, began publishing a small, four page, tri-weekly newspaper, price 6d, called the *News of the Camp – A Journal of Fancies, Notifications, Gossip and General Chit Chat Published in the Military Camp of Her Majesty's Forces*

News of the Camp headquarters during the first Boer War. The paper was produced by Charles Deecker who is the figure under the right hand word 'CAMP'.

Defending the Beleaguered Inhabitants of Pretoria. It has been described as probably one of the greatest journalistic curiosities.[51] Deecker and Du Val worked from a tent, Deecker providing the technical printing skill, while Du Val wrote many of the articles During the blockade, which lasted 100 days, Deecker printed some 40 issues, the first appearing on Christmas Day 1880 – the last on 9th April 1881. The paper contained a unique record of most events that took place in Pretoria during that period as well as running a lottery as to when relief would actually arrive. There were reports also of the many social occasions ranging from athletics, military band concerts and dances, to a cricket match between the Military and Civilians (in which Lanyon was run out for 1 run!). Deecker even organised a performance of *Hamlet.*[52] Several attempts were made by the besieged garrison to attack the Boers who were, according to Deecker:

> *like bandetti and fight according to the guerilla style. They are plucky*
> *enough as long as they are hidden safely behind a stone, but they are*
> *scarcely ever seen fighting in the open.*[53]

At Laings Nek Colley had desperately wanted the Boers in the open, especially as the news from Britain was not to his liking. Gladstone's Government, rather than run the risk of facing a possible wholesale insurrection of Boers throughout South Africa, had decided to give in. It was conveyed to Colley that if the Boers ceased their hostilities then favourable discussions on self government would follow. Colley, angry over what he saw as a virtual surrender to the enemy, wanted at least one military victory before the politicians ordered him to the negotiating table. He gave the Boers a mere 48 hours to comply, which was a practical impossibility, considering that the Triumvirate would need longer than that just to meet together. Colley then made his next move and – as it happened – his final blunder.

On 26th February he personally led 400 men to the top of Majuba Hill to overlook the Boer position. Having thus gained an advantage, like Chelmsford before him, he did not take the necessary precautions, such as digging trenches or erecting barricades for defence. The following day Joubert sent 150 Boers up Majuba where they achieved total surprise. Colley, although killed outright, was held responsible for the virtual massacre of his small force, which was seen as the third disaster (after Laings Nek and Ingogo).

Although reinforcements had arrived under Wood – now a Brigadier General – and with Colley's death, the Acting Governor of Natal and High Commissioner of the Transvaal – they were denied any form of retribution upon the Boers as Wood had been ordered by the Government to the negotiating table. He met with the Triumvirate on 14th March, Colonel Redvers Buller V.C. having joined him to take over military affairs – the Boers considering his presence in South Africa to be equivalent to a reinforcement of ten thousand men for the British.[54] Within three weeks Buller himself was promoted to Brigadier General. After some tough negotiating on the part of Wood and Kruger the Triumvirate signed with the British the peace treaty of 23rd March, and the Boers lifted their blockades of the British garrisons in the Transvaal.

Although Wood had acted on orders – if reluctantly – he gained the stigma of having actually signed the peace. For that Wolseley ensured that Wood never had a command in South Africa again but before he left Wood prophetically announced, "in a few years… we shall have to take over the country".55

If the *West Briton* considered Gladstone to have been magnanimous and merciful56 in making peace, this was hardly the view of Richard H. Scaddow. Originally from Redruth but living in the Cape, Scaddow thought it:

> *Peace without honour… is it possible that Great Britain can submit to such humiliation, after having been thrice defeated by a handful of insurgent Boers.*57

Deecker was in no doubt, saying he scarcely knew how to express the disgust he felt at the humiliating peace which had just been concluded with our enemies the Boers.58

Deecker's letter printed in the *West Briton* brought a swift reply from a Cornishwoman, unfortunately not named but which shows that not all agreed with his jingoistic point of view, accusing Deecker of being

> *another victim of those false ideas of so called honour, glory and courage… what an idea that further bloodshed in retaliation and revenge can 'wipe out' a supposed defeat.*59

Transvaal was formally handed over to the Boers after the Convention of Pretoria on 3rd August 1881. Sir Owen Lanyon, having been dismissed, had departed some months earlier and he died in 1887. Deecker also left the Transvaal – the last copy of his *Transvaal Argus* being printed 12th November 1881 – but he remained in South Africa. A large number of troops were stationed at Newcastle in Natal and Deecker, assuming it was to become a permanent base, started the *Newcastle Echo* but it collapsed when the troops were withdrawn soon afterwards. Deecker then went to Durban to work on the *Natal Mercury* before moving on, in 1883, to East London, Natal, where he acquired the *Farmers' Chronicle* which he later sold in order to acquire the *East London Advertiser.*

During the days following the Boer War and leading up to the granting of independence one more Cornishman had a part to play. The Standard Bank of South Africa had, in 1877, opened offices at Potchefstroom, Pretoria and Lyndenburg, so that when the war broke out and the whole question of independence arose, the bank was naturally concerned over £500,000 of its money that was tied up in the Transvaal. So concerned was the Bank that its loans in gold were paid back in gold and not by inflationary notes, that it sent in person the Assistant General Manager Lewis Michell to the Pretoria Conference in order to seek the Triumvirate's full guarantee that any loans would be repaid in full and that the money in the Transvaal banks would be protected.

Michell, was from a very old Cornish family of Penzance. He entered the Penzance branch of Bolitho's Cornish Bank, a position which had first been offered to Leonard Courtney but who went to Cambridge University instead. Within a few years Michell joined the London and South Africa Bank and was soon transferred to South Africa – he was still only 22 years old. On his arrival at Cape Town in 1864, the Bank immediately entrusted him with £10,000 which he had to deliver personally to a branch of the bank at Wellington. Thus within three days of his arrival Michell had traversed the entire railway system of South Africa as it then existed.[60] Michell was soon appointed Manager of the London and South Africa Bank at Port Elizabeth but resigned in 1873 to join a rival bank – the Standard Bank – becoming Manager of its Port Elizabeth branch. Within 5 years he presided over the liquidation of his former bank. He moved to Cape Town, where the Standard Bank had its headquarters, and became its Assistant Manager, in 1881. Michell travelled to the Transvaal via Natal and Newcastle where he met Dr. Jorrisen, whose son was in the Bank. Dr. Jorrisen was an attorney who had accompanied Kruger on his mission to London so was able to introduce Michell to the *Triumvirate*. The meeting took place in a tent which the three Boer leaders were using as temporary headquarters. Michell noted:

> *Oom Paul smoked a short pipe as he sat in the only chair with a decent back to it. He looks a shrewd, hardheaded obstinate old boy and they all paid him great deference. Pretorious also, I should say, is a man of ability, though he looks old-fashioned. Joubert on the other hand was well dressed and looked like a fine old English gentleman or a country magistrate.[61]*

Apparently Michell took Kruger completely by surprise by first thanking him on behalf of the Bank for having taken care of the Bank's branches in the Transvaal, upon which Kruger replied that Michell's were the first kind words he had heard from anyone holding a responsible position in the country[62] and promised Michell further protection for the branches. Michell had also met and become a close friend of President Brand of the Orange Free State. Although the Boers had agreed to honour their debts to the Bank – by paying them in sterling and not in depreciated Transvaal Currency – the Imperial Government seemed about to renege on its commitments by claiming that the money which the bank had originally lent to the Transvaal when it was annexed, was now the responsibility of the newly independent Transvaal. Michell took legal advice and found in law he was entitled to prevent anyone who owed a debt – in this case the Imperial Government – from leaving the country, so Michell sought an injunction to stop the Imperial Government's Representative – the Administrator Sir Evelyn Wood – from leaving the Transvaal until the debt was paid. Michell found himself summoned by one very angry Administrator but in the course of the conversation it transpired that the two Cornishmen were related – Sir Evelyn's mother being a Michell, and that they had mutual friends in Cornwall.63 Needless to say the Bank's money was secured. Not long after Michell's return to Cape Town he was promoted to Joint General Manager of the Standard Bank in 1883.

Although the Transvaal was once again independent not all the Cornish were prepared to leave. A number of Cornishmen in particular had already seized on the potential of the Transvaal, especially in terms of setting up a business. Paul Henwood had opened stores at Pilgrims Rest and Lydenburg in 1874 and Pretoria in 1877. General Manager for all the Henwood stores in the Transvaal for a time was Cornishman Thomas John Rodda. Having arrived at Durban from Penzance in 1872 he was sent by Henwood to open the Pretoria branch. In 1886 he opened another Henwood branch at Barberton. Married with six children, Rodda lived at Pretoria where he was a Trustee of the Pretoria Wesleyan Church. His brother – William – also lived in Pretoria having come to South Africa from the U.S.A. where he had been for nearly five years. William Rodda was first the Managing Foreman to the building contractors Thomas Drew (who were responsible for building Pretoria's Town Hall, Catholic Church and school) before he set up his own contracting business. Like his brother, William Rodda was also a Trustee of the Wesleyan Church as well as Treasurer of the Pretoria Master Builders' Association. Another Penzance man, Robert Hamilton, became a member of the first elected council of Pretoria and later Vice President of the Chamber of Commerce. Married in 1881 to Mary Evans Hamilton had nine children.

Without a railway in the Transvaal perhaps the most lucrative if not dangerous business was that of transport rider or carrying provisions by wagon. An insight into the work and life of the transport business can be found not only in Hugh Lanion Hall's autobiography but also in Percy Fitzpatrick's *Jock of the Bushveld.* Fitzpatrick, (later Sir Percy and Chairman of the Chamber of Mines as well as a member of the South African Parliament 1911-20) originally wrote the story of his dog Jock for children. Fitzpatrick learnt the business of transport rider from Hall who was considered at that time to be Eastern Transvaal's most successful rider and a crack shot to boot.64 The latter skill led Hall into a little trouble. He and Fitzpatrick were returning from Lourenco Marques to their base on one occasion when arriving at their camp they came across some natives attempting to steal their oxen. Hall actually fired his shotgun when the natives turned to run, killing one of them which according to Fitzpatrick was murder without extenuating circumstances.65

Both Hall and Fitzpatrick had to make a run for it to avoid capture by Portuguese troops. A watered down version of the episode is related in Jock of the Bushveld 66 with Hall escaping on his horse Tsetse Fly – so called because being a salted horse it was tsetse fly proof.67 Hall and Fitzpatrick then lay low for a while in Swaziland. When they emerged it was to head for the goldfields.

What was to link Cornwall to South Africa and make South Africa more important to Cornwall than any other part of the world where Cornish miners could be found was the discovery in South Africa of diamonds and then gold:

> *History offers no comparable phenomenon. For two hundred years southern Africa had been vegetating; it was barely known to the rest of the world and it seemed doomed to mediocrity. Then suddenly twice within twenty years, its earth revealed treasures; all eyes turned towards it, and the obstacles along the road to its future seemed to have vanished as if by magic.*68

1. *WEST BRITON*, 24th April 1879

2. William St. Claire, *TRELAWNY.* p.197
   Trelawny in his youth like Byron had
   fought in Greece for Greek independence.
   Trelawny died 13th August 1881 and was
   cremated, his ashes being buried alongside
   the grave of the poet P.B. Shelley in Rome.

3. D.D. Hall, STORY OF A SOUTH
   AFRICAN PIONEER. p.93

4. *THE TRANSVAAL ARGUS &
   POTCHEFSTROOM COMMERCIAL
   GAZETTE* 3rd DECEMBER 1875

5. Hall, *SOUTH AFRICAN PIONEER* . p.98

6. Hall, *REAPED MY MEALIES.* p.35

7. *IBID.*, p.43

8. John Fisher, *PAUL KRUGER, HIS LIFE
   AND TIMES* (LONDON 1974). p.43

9. C.J. Unys IN THE ERA OF SHEPSTONE
   (being a Study of British Expansion in
   South Africa 1842-77) (Cape Town 1933)
   p 245

10. Barry Rohan, *FORTY SOUTH AFRICAN
    YEARS* (LONDON 1923). p.224

11. Henry Rider Haggard, *DAYS OF MY LIFE*
    (LONDON 1926). p.76

12. *TRANSVAAL ARGUS*, 26th JANUARY
    1877

13. C.J. Unys, *ERA OF SHEPSTONE.* p.238

14. Hall, *REAPED MY MEALIES.* p.44

15. *NATAL WITNESS*, 28th June 1879

16. IBID., 28th JUNE 1879

17. Unys, *ERA OF SHEPSTONE.* p.268. One
    contemporary author claimed Morcom was
    the most unpopular member of the Lanyon
    Administration. See John Nixon, *THE
    COMPLETE STORY OF THE
    TRANSVAAL* (LONDON 1885) p 152

18. *NATAL WITNESS*, 25th APRIL 1910

19. See especially Donald R. Morris, *THE
    WASHING OF THE SPEARS: THE RISE
    AND FALL OF THE ZULU NATION*
    (LONDON 1966) Frank Emery *THE RED
    SOLDIER: THE ZULU WAR 1879*
    (LONDON 1977) Michael Barthrop, *THE
    ZULU WAR* (POOLE 1984) and Ian
    Knight and Ian Costello *ZULU WAR 1879
    – TWILIGHT OF A WARRIOR NATION*
    (LONDON 1992)

20. See Joseph Lehmann, *THE FIRST BOER
    WAR* (LONDON 1972). p.59-60

21. Barthrop, *THE ZULU WAR* . p.49

22. *REDRUTH TIMES & CAMBORNE
    ADVERTISER, 11th APRIL 1879*

23. *WEST BRITON, 12th JUNE 1879. See also
    Patrick Coghill, WHOM THE GODS
    LOVE* (LONDON 1968) p 110-123
    52 Officers (more than had been killed at
    the battle of Waterloo) and 806 men were
    killed at Isandlwana.

24. Melvill's widow was placed on the Civil
    List with a pension of £100. One of her
    two sons, Brigadier General C.W. Melvill,
    greatly distinguished himself in the
    1914-18 War. He also wrote a biography
    of General Redvers Buller.

25. *WEST BRITON*, 27th MAY 1879

26. Sir Horace Smith-Dorrien, *MEMORIES
    OF FORTY EIGHT YEARS' SERVICE*
    (LONDON 1925)

27. *REDRUTH TIMES & CAMBORNE
    ADVERTISER, 14th MARCH 1879*

28. Smith-Dorrien, *MEMORIES OF FORTY
    EIGHT YEARS SERVICE.* p. 16-18

29. *REDRUTH TIMES & CAMBORNE
    ADVERTISER, 23rd MAY 1879*

30. Rider Haggard, *DAYS OF MY LIFE.*
    p.145. Although Queen Victoria was very
    upset at the death of the Prince, the Prime
    Minister, Disraeli had little sympathy
    referring to the Prince as *that little
    abortion.* See Robert Blake, *DISRAELI*
    (LONDON 1966) p.670. The spear that

may have killed the Prince Imperial can be seen at *Cotehele House*, a National Trust property in Cornwall.

31. Leigh Maxwell, *THE ASHANTI RING* (LONDON 1985). p.120

32. *THE CORNUBIAN & REDRUTH TIMES*, 1st AUGUST 1879

33. Smith-Dorrien, *MEMORIES OF FORTY EIGHT YEARS SERVICE*. p.29

34. Binns, *THE LAST ZULU KING*. p.214

35. Peter Hinchliff, *JOHN WILLIAM COLENSO* (LONDON 1964). p.195

36. Maxwell, *THE ASHANTI RING*. p.123

37. Hall, *REAPED MY MEALIES*. p.79

38. Lehmann, *THE FIRST BOER WAR*. p.62

39. See John Nixon, *COMPLETE STORY OF THE TRANSVAAL*. p.121

40. Hall, *REAPED MY MEALIES*. p.49

41. *THE NORTH WESTERN PRESS*, 14th MAY 1912

42. *THE WEST BRITON*, 10th APRIL 1879

43. *IBID.*, 24th APRIL 1879

44. *IBID.*, 4th SEPTEMBER 1879

45. *IBID.*, 27th NOVEMBER 1879. Courtney was elected M.P for Liskeard in December 1876 and re-elected April 1880. He considered annexation as unjustifiable as well as calculated to be injurious to the interests of the United Kingdom and of its colonies in South Africa. See Nixon, *STORY OF THE TRANSVAAL*. p.48 & 96

46. Lehmann, *FIRST BOER WAR*. p.80

47. Fisher, *PAUL KRUGER*. p.64

48. *IBID.*, p.84

49. *WEST BRITON*, 30th DECEMBER 1880

50. *IBID.*, 19th MAY 1891

51. *THE NORTH WESTERN PRESS*, 14th MAY 1912

52. *NEWS OF THE CAMP*, – there is a bound volume in the Pretoria Museum. I used an almost complete volume that is held by the Commonwealth Library, London.

53. *WEST BRITON*, 19th MAY 1881

54. Maxwell, *THE ASHANTI RING*. p.171

55. Lehmann, *FIRST BOER WAR*. p.306

56. *WEST BRITON*, 19th MAY 1881

57. *CORNUBIAN*, 20th MAY 1881

58. *WEST BRITON*, 19th MAY 1881

59. *IBID.*, 2nd JUNE 1881

60. *THE CAPE TIMES*, 30th OCTOBER 1928

61. J.A. Henry, *THE FIRST HUNDRED YEARS OF THE STANDARD BANK* (LONDON 1963). p.56

62. *IBID.*, p.57

63. *IBID.*, p.58

64. A.P. Cartwright, *THE FIRST SOUTH AFRICAN. LIFE AND TIMES OF SIR PERCY FITZPATRICK* (CAPE TOWN 1971). p.21

65. *IBID.*, p.27

66. See also, Hall, *REAPED MY MEALIES*. p.98

67. *IBID.*, p.90 Salted meant having immunity to the horse disease by having survived an initial attack.

68. Robert Lacour-Gayet, *A HISTORY OF SOUTH AFRICA* (LONDON 1977) p.153

CHAPTER THREE

LAND OF DIAMONDS 1870-99

By 1870 bullock-carts were jolting the Cornish miner from Cape Town to the newly-discovered fields at Kimberley.[1]

A.K. Hamilton Jenkin.

The discovery of the first diamonds between 1866-70 in South Africa is well documented.[2] A vivid recollection of what life was like on the diamond fields during their formative years is presented by Cornishman John Angove in his book of reminiscences *In the Early Days*.[3] Angove arrived on the diamond fields in 1870 and told how the early digger was faced with dust, flies and fleas – these came free everything else cost. There was no poverty in the camps although provisions were exceedingly dear, a loaf of bread, weighing one and a quarter pounds, was a shilling. A shilling also bought a pound of sugar, but it cost three shillings for a pound of ground coffee. Vegetables were almost unobtainable and were at famine prices – carrots were three shillings for a bunch of twelve, whilst one cabbage, if we are to believe Angove, cost as much as ten shillings![4] When water was scarce during 1878 Angove remembers that well owners sold it for five shillings per hogshead. The price of firewood sold at the morning market ranged from £8 to as much as £45 per wagon-load. Life on the diamond fields during the early years was certainly tough and dangerous. Sanitary conditions were primitive and with the great amount of sickness it was not surprising that a hospital was soon built. Dry weather brought the inconvenience of dust storms whilst wet weather brought flash floods. The first snowstorm experienced on the fields in 1875 was followed by an even worse one the following year and Angove commented the snowy landscape that presented itself was a relief from having to view a dry and dreary waste. Ordinary storms brought their own dangers and after lightning struck a tent, killing a woman, it was considered advisable to put glass bottles over the iron tent pegs. Although Angove mentions little crime, stern justice was handed out and punishments included flogging, tar and feathers and the occasional lynching.

It was not all hard work. 1872 saw the first horse race meeting and Angove gives a delightful description of the event with the crowds, the three-card tricksters, the bookies, the fair sex and the obligatory fights. Diggers could drink in public houses with names such as the Australian Arms, The Diggers Rest and The Crystal Palace. Gradually the diamond fields became more civilised. The first church built in 1870, albeit a simple construction of reeds over upright wooden poles, no doubt pleased many Cornishmen for it was a Wesleyan Chapel. This was followed by St. Mary's Anglican Church, the first to be built out of bricks and mortar. A Roman Catholic church, a Dutch Reform church and a Jewish synagogue soon followed and Angove comments that services were well attended

There has been some confusion over whether the John Angove who wrote *In the Early Days* was the same person as the Josiah or Joseph Angove who became a well known newspaper editor and proprietor in South Africa. They were brothers. Their father, Josiah Angove senior, was born at Sithney near Helston in 1818 and was a prominent mining engineer at Camborne. He came to South Africa in 1862 with his wife Salome (née Reynolds). Described as a skilled miner and mineralogist, Josiah Angove Senior became a superintendent of the Maitland lead mine near Port Elizabeth. There his reputation was one of having had extensive experience overseas. Angove was engaged to survey a number of farms around the Transvaal when Pretoria consisted of little more than half a dozen houses. At a public meeting on 31st October 1867, in the old Transvaal capital of Potchefstroom, Angove gave an address during which he emphasised the great mineral possibilities of the Republic. Although he did not find gold – he was actually looking for lead – he did discover deposits of excellent coal and copper. A collection taken at the meeting to pay for his expenses raised a sum of £23-6s-0d. From there Angove travelled to Kimberley with his family in 1870. In his book John Angove mentions that it was Captain Josiah Angove who suggested the adoption of the Cornish whim for hauling broken ground out of the claims and personally superintended the erection of the first horse whim.[5]

Josiah Angove Sen., John Angove and Josiah Angove Jr. are all registered as voters for the district of Kimberley giving their place of residence as Old De Beers. *The Diamond News* deeply regretted the death on the 24th March 1880 at Bultfontein of Josiah Angove Sen. after a painful illness in his 62nd year.[6] In 1883 *The Diamond Fields Advertiser* announced the death of Mr. Rice Angove, the 24 year old brother of the proprietor of the *Dutoitspan Herald*. Rice Angove had served with the Natal Mounted Police and been in the Zulu War, during which he had gained a medal, being with Lord Chelmsford's column at Isandlwana. He had also been in the Basuto War and been present with the Diamond Fields Volunteers at the Relief of Leribe. Having been in Zululand, where he had contracted dysentery, he was on his way to Kimberley but only reached Griquatown. The fact that the *Advertiser* stated that one of his brothers proceeded by postcart to Griquatown but was too late to be of any assistance, or even to see deceased alive,[7] suggests that John and Josiah Jr. were brothers rather than one and the same. Any further doubt however, is finally removed by Barry Rohan, who says in his book *Forty South African Years* that when Josiah Angove went to Johannesburg to start up a newspaper he was later assisted by his brother John.[8]

Josiah Angove, who is easily the most prolific of all the Cornish newspaper proprietors in South Africa, was born in Camborne 2nd April 1854. He began his journalistic career in 1878 with the publication of the *Diamond Fields Daily* at Kimberly. According to another source, however, he had first trained as a printer on the *Grocotts Penny Mail* at Grahamstown between 1873-77 and established his first newspaper at Kimberley, *The Diamond Fields Herald* a tri-weekly newspaper which became an instant success.[9] This was followed by *The Diamond Field Times* which Angove acquired in 1882. The canvas city mining camps were soon replaced by the bricks and iron of the municipal towns. Dutoitspan and Bultfontein gave rise to Beaconsfield, named after the Prime Minister, whilst New Rush and De Beers became known as Kimberley, after the Secretary of State for the Colonies. Josiah Angove himself became the Chairman of the Beaconsfield Town Council in 1884 and it was said he was not afraid to speak his mind whether it was over council spending or pushing Beaconsfield's interests at the expense of Kimberley.[10]

Another insight into the early days of Kimberley comes from Norman Garstin. Although Irish born he was later to adopt Cornwall as his home becoming a member of the colony of artists that flourished at Newlyn and St. Ives during the turn of the century. Garstin described the diamond workings as dangerous as they were unique.[11] In an area about the size of Trafalgar Square roads were marked out by the Diggers Board, some 60 feet apart, whilst on either side of the road would be a perpendicular drop which grew deeper by the day. Garstin highlighted the two main difficulties facing the early diamond diggers. One was not surprisingly the collapse of the walls of the roads as the diggings deepened. This often occurred at night when the air cooled. In 1878 there was a collapse of a million tons of debris covering nearly a quarter of the Kimberley Mine. To remove the fallen rubble cost money – Garstin claimed that the Mining Board spent some £300,000 doing just that the following year. Water, the other difficulty, swamped the workings of Old De Beers and Du Toits Pan creating a virtual lake before being pumped out. The whole organisation of diamond mining was to undergo a radical change. Shaft sinking and amalgamation were inevitable. Individual digger claims were parceled and sold to partnerships of diggers and then eventually, as the shafts went deeper and steam engines began to replace the horse whims, foreign capital and expertise were required to buy and run the heavy machinery. (Harvey's of Hayle sent three beam engines to Kimberley in 1876).[12] Industrial Mining Companies were thus formed and by 1880 the majority of claims lay in the hands of about a dozen companies, and it was the amalgamation of these that became the next problem. Instrumental in this change were men such as Joseph Benjamin Robinson, Jules Wernher, Alfred Beit, Harry and Barney Barnato – all of whom became millionaires.[13] But all these were to lose out in the final amalgamation struggle to the one man whose name was to become synonymous with the diamond industry – Cecil John Rhodes.

Garstin knew Rhodes well, having camped with him during the early days. He described Rhodes as a long headed youth[14] but although Garstin visited Rhodes when he was at Oxford University, he was not to share in his great diamond enterprise. Garstin quickly tired of diamond digging and after a short spell in the Civil Service he became Assistant Editor to the *Cape Times* in Cape Town. He returned to Ireland in 1877 before finally moving, in 1879, to Newlyn in Cornwall to work as an artist, his work being regularly exhibited at the Royal Academy.

Another Cornish artist to be found on the Diamond Fields was Henry Charles Seppings-Wright from Stithians. Like Garstin he was one of the first artists to record the early scenes on canvas and his many paintings included portraits of Rhodes and Barnato. Although he later moved on to the goldfields in the Transvaal, (such as the one centred on Pilgrims Rest) an exhibition of his work celebrated the opening of the McGregor Alexander Memorial Museum, Kimberley, in September 1907. Seppings-Wright later became a war correspondent for the *Illustrated London News*. He died in 1937 aged eighty-eight.

It was two Cornishmen in particular who were to assist greatly in the career of Cecil Rhodes. One already mentioned – Lewis Michell – who had come to prominence in the Standard Bank, was to become his personal financial advisor and biographer. The other – Francis Oats – was (at first) a potential stumbling block to Rhodes' grand scheme of amalgamation by the De Beers Mining Company.

Directors and officials of De Beers in 1896. On the left of the front row is Francis Oats. In the centre of the front row is Cecil Rhodes.

Francis Oats (born Golant 1848) began work as a 13 year old boy in the Botallack Mine, near St Just. where he rose to the position of mine Captain. As a young miner he had been sent by the Cornish miners to represent them at the first Miners World Congress in Paris in 1867 during which his knowledge and expertise of mining was recognised. The Crown Colony Office of Griqualand West recommended him to the Kimberley Mining Board and in January 1875, less than a year after marrying Elizabeth Ann Olds of St. Just, he set out for South Africa as a mining engineer and Inspector for the Griqualand West Government on a salary of £600 per annum. Unfortunately he arrived in Kimberley just when the diamond industry was in crisis – the price of diamonds had dropped – and many men were out of work. Oats remained for twenty months and then returned home to Cornwall to take up his old position at Botallack. His obvious mining talent had been noted, for he was soon on his way back to Kimberley, this time to look after the interests of Messrs. Baring Gould Brothers and Atkins, diggers in Kimberley; he also secured a seat on the Kimberley Mining Board. In 1877 he became the Manager of the far from prosperous Victoria Diamond Mine and from a shaky start and low profits it was turned into a profitable concern through the perseverance of Oats, linked with the considerable mining skill he had obtained in Cornwall. To show their appreciation towards Oats the owners of the mine presented him with the most generous sum of £6,500, whilst the *Diamond Fields Advertiser* claimed there had been more mining ability deployed in opening up the Victoria Mine than in any other on the field.[15] In 1886 when Rhodes and his De Beers Company made their final bid to secure control of the whole of the Kimberley diamond field the hardest company to crack and the last to fall was the Victoria.[16] The take-over was only achieved by Rhodes getting his friend Alfred Beit to buy up Victoria shares secretly in the European market until De Beers had a majority holding. With the amalgamation Oats was retired as Manager, a presentation being made to him the following year when he was described as an engineer of eminent ability and unwearied diligence. In appreciation of his services he was handed an 18 carat gold lever watch with a massive gold 'Albert' and locket suitably inscribed,[17] while his wife was given a gold watch and chain. Oats did well out of the amalgamation and he was obviously held in high regard by Rhodes and Beit for in 1890 he was given a seat on the De Beers Board of Directors.

Oats was to make a number of visits home to Cornwall where his high position in South Africa meant he was held in even higher esteem amongst the Cornish mining community. His wealth enabled him to become a major shareholder in the Basset Mines at Camborne and the Levant Mine at St. Just; holding some 800 shares (from a total of 2,500) he was the largest shareholder. The *Mining Journal* reported that the Levant Committee consisted mainly of merchants but:

a new broom recently appeared on the scene in the person of Captain Oats... returning with a large fortune from the management of De Beers diamond mine to his native parish.[18]

Oats later had a mansion built for himself and family (he had three sons and one daughter) but although they paid visits to Cornwall the family base remained firmly in South Africa. Their Cornwall residence at St. Just, still stands high on the cliffs at Cape Cornwall, with a superb sea view. Oats had come a long way since working as a lad at nearby Botallack for he had risen from being a labouring miner to being a wealthy man amongst wealthy men:

There must have been an element of immense pleasure in being able to return and demonstrate his success to those who had previously been his social superiors.[19]

Headgear for a hoisting shaft at the De Beers diamond mine.

Oats must have also enjoyed recalling the early days in South Africa sharing with an audience at St. Just on a visit to Cornwall in 1895 memories of when:-

Kimberley mine was surrounded by windlasses and was in 200 different holdings at an average depth of 100 feet and all the workings were in the open... round the margin of the mine there were some 2,000 or more labourers who were watched and directed by a large number of overseers... Now all this has changed. most modern steam machine engines are able to draw 8,000 tons through one shaft... they in fact drew up as much stuff out of De Beers in one day as was drawn out of Levant in 16 weeks. Skilled miners now had to be employed to supervise the blacks and to do the more scientific part of the work.[20]

It is said a prophet is not without honour except in his own country but this was not the case with Oats, when on a visit to Cornwall in 1899 he received what must have been a most memorable welcome home by the St. Just Working Men's Club. A genuine recognition of their favourite son's ability and worth was illustrated in an official address of hearty welcome, which spoke of the intense gratification Oats had given to St Just by his successful career, added to which were many congratulations on his recent appointment to the Cape Parliament as the Member for Namaqualand. Oats who had come home on the same ship as Cecil Rhodes spoke of their friendship although Oats pointed out that he was not one of those who thought Rhodes a God. Although Mr. Rhodes was a friend of his, and he admired him Rhodes also made mistakes. Commenting on the voyage home Oats wished that it took less than the month it did because a month makes a big hole in the life of an elderly person[21] – he was only 51 years old and his crowning achievement in South Africa was yet to come.

Another successful Cornishman at Kimberley, also from St. Just, was William James. Like Oats he had spent his boyhood down a mine, in his case Levant, but then moved on to the U.S.A. to work in the copper and iron mines of Michigan and Idaho. From there he travelled to Kimberley and using his knowledge and experience in mining, worked as a contractor and acted as an arbitrator for the Government. Having made a fortune he returned to Cornwall to stay. He became Manager of Wheal Basset and worked the mine so successfully, despite difficulties with excess water, that when the mine amalgamated with South Francis he was put in overall control. In an interview with the Editor of the *Cornish Post & Mining News* he showed himself as a hard task master. James also made rather disparaging remarks concerning the differences between working in the mines in Cornwall and those on the diamond fields. For instance he claimed the men worked harder and longer in Kimberley; he considered the Cornish miner at home to be less industrious but explained this by saying that the best miners tended to emigrate while Cornwall was left with,

immature youths not seasoned to hard work, the elderly men who had eased off a little, the lazy louts who only make a pretence of working, those of feeble constitution who felt it too risky to emigrate and finally those who had little ambition.

To round off his condemnation of the Cornish miner as a worker he said:-
Mind you, the men themselves are not altogether to blame. Indolence is inherited in most cases. If the mother is dawdling about and gossiping

with neighbours over the hedge instead of looking after her housework the chances are her offspring will not be particularly energetic. The example of the parents is another force which may lead the miner to degenerate.[22]

James, like Oats, knew Rhodes and thought him the most impressive speaker he had ever heard. One piece of advice James took from Rhodes was that no one in charge of a group of men was fit to remain in charge if he could not discharge some of them.

Compound for native workers at the Kimberly Mine.

With the amalgamation of the dry diggings and the emergence of the big mining companies, control was established not only over the buying and selling of diamonds but also over the black labour force. The diggers had attempted to control their own affairs in 1875 when they had hoisted a Black Flag in staging a rebellion with the hope of setting up an independent state. It came to nothing but at least the episode had passed without bloodshed.[23] Behind this protest was the rather sinister desire of the diggers to remove their economic rival – the native. The digging for diamonds had created a huge demand for labour and at first thousands of natives – especially Pedi – travelled to and from the diamond fields exchanging their labour for money in order to buy guns. Natives were prevented from holding a claim or dealing in diamonds; as the buying and selling of diamonds was severely restricted and purchases could only be made in the offices of licensed bankers or diamond dealers. There was plenty of evidence that Illegal Diamond Buying (I.D.B.) or Kopje Walloping (the selling of diamonds that had been stolen) was being carried out. Much of the blame for this was put on the native. John Angove remarked that as Kaffir eating-houses were used for passing illegal diamonds a move to prohibit Kaffir canteens from being within a five mile radius of any mine was only prevented by the liquor interests.24 Instead the natives had their movements restricted by means of a pass and contract system – any native found on the Diamond fields without a pass and not under contract could be searched and flogged. In contrast when (in 1883) the mine owners proposed to search whites the men went on strike and the proposals were dropped. Eventually the native was to be confined to barracks or compounds. It was Thomas Collingwood Kitto, a Cornish Mining Inspector, commissioned by the new Administrator Sir Charles Warren in 1879 to write a report on the diamond industry, who suggested a similar system to that which he had witnessed in the diamond industry of Brazil. Kitto believed that for the South African diamond industry to be profitable the present production methods were anything but efficient and the key to greater profits lay with a cheap but highly organised labour force in plentiful supply. Company barracking and white overseeing Kitto argued, would permit employers to free themselves from dependence on uncivilised people and instead acquire a workforce regimented to the demands of mining.25 Closed compounds became as much a landmark of Kimberley and the Diamond Industry as the Big Hole itself. The native became a migrant labourer being confined to the rigid, degrading and barbaric system of the compound where,

> *the precautions which are taken a few days before the natives leave the compound make it an utter physical impossibility for them to retain any diamonds they may have swallowed.*26

As the diamond fields prospered communication and transport with Kimberley and the outside world improved rapidly. The diamond fields were some 640 miles from Cape Town, and whereas it had taken James Eddy of St. Just 22 days to reach Kimberley by ox wagon from Beaufort West in 1876,27 relays of coach and horses soon cut the travel time between the Cape and the diamond fields to no more than 10-12 days. James Truran, another Cornish miner and blacksmith by trade, also travelled up to Kimberley by ox wagon, although when his wife joined him in 1887 she was able to make a more comfortable journey by train, the railway line having been completed some two years earlier.28 The railway lowered transport costs so living on the diamond fields became relatively cheaper. One of the first stores to open in Kimberley was a shack type shop opposite the Big Hole belonging to a Cornishman – Samson Rickard Stuttaford:

> *Few know that the great commercial enterprise known as Stuttafords of Cape Town was made possible as a result of trading and diamond buying activities along the Vaal river and the mines around Kimberley.*29

Alfred Henwood was in Kimberley during 1882 in order that a Henwoods Store could open the following year and as well as the Cornish shops there were at least two Cornish builders, probably brothers. Thomas Bond Tredrea had arrived from

Estimates
given
for all
Classes
of
Work.

  &   &

Jobbing
in all
its
Branches
Executed
with
Despatch.

WM. J. TREDREA, *Builder & Contractor,*

42, Dunell Street, KIMBERLEY.

Tel. No. 48.

Wm. Tredrea Established 1889.

Thomas Tredrea Established 1888.

Penzance in 1888 aged 19 years. He built up a large and very successful business at Bean Street to occupy a prominent position among the many builders. His excellent workmanship was known near and far and evidence of his ability as a builder is to be seen in numerous constructions throughout Kimberley.[30] Tredrea operated from a large two-storey business employing some fifty workers, of whom no doubt some were fellow Cornishmen. William James Tredrea arrived in Kimberley from Cornwall in 1889 aged 25 years. Like his namesake he also built up a successful building and contracting business which was established in Dunell Street. In 1911 he was joined by his brother-in-law (Harry Oats) from Penzance. Oats was building St Augustine's Church, West End and was looking forward to the completion of the Cathedral chancel which had just been commenced when he died aged 38 years.[31]

Thomas Rogers arrived from Camborne in 1896 to lecture at the newly opened Kimberley School of Mines and later went to work at the Bultfontein Mines; his brother Tobias left the South Crofty Mine in Cornwall to join him. Within sight of South Crofty today stands the famous Camborne School of Mines. It was Professor James Gunson Lawn, the Principal of the Camborne School of Mines, who became the first Principal of the Kimberley School of Mines when it opened on 10th August 1896. After a brief spell at the school, Lawn became a Consulting Engineer for Barney Barnato's Consolidated Investment Company. Fellow Cornishman Owen Letcher wrote:

> It was in no small degree due to Lawn's organising ability as well as to his sterling character and technical knowledge that the House of Barnato became, and has continued to be such a powerful concern in the world of gold mining.[32]

The school, which had received financial assistance from De Beers, was transferred in 1903 to Johannesburg where it merged with the Transvaal Technical Institute becoming in 1922 the University of Witwatersrand.

With the amalgamation of mines at the dry diggings individual prospectors could still chance their luck and hope to gain wealth and fortune at the river diggings but it was a risky business. Describing it as nothing but a lottery, where one man makes a few pounds, there are twenty who lose more two Cornishmen from Camborne writing home in 1896 described anything but an easy life with its dangers and difficulties of heat, dust storms and the swarms of locust sometimes 3 to 6 miles long and as many miles wide and deep which darken the sun and devour everything green as they come.[33]

The river where they worked caused other problems and although it had not rained for four months, when it did there were instant floods, the two men having seen the river rise 10 feet in one night. At the time of writing they had just experienced a national holiday on account of the virulent cattle disease

Rinderpest[34] with special prayers being offered to the Almighty. Before the Cornishmen had even begun to work their sifting and washing machine on their 60 by 30 feet claim, it had cost them 5 shillings for a miners' certificate plus 10 shillings for a licence – which only lasted three months. To run a machine required water, which meant digging wells 60 to 80 feet deep. A barrel held 68 gallons and cost a shilling and on average it took 15 barrels a day to run a machine, whereas working by hand used only 4 barrels a week. It went without saying that profits were marginal.[35]

Life was not much better for many at the dry diggings and in some cases worse. James Thomas, a 28 year old married miner with two children who had only left Cornwall but 3 months ago for the Cape Diamond Fields was killed at Kimberley when turning a drill and was hit on the head by falling rock.[36] John William Farnham of Wadebridge, Samuel Brown of Perranzabuloe and William Tallack of Carnon Downs all died from accidents in 1882.[37] Charles Tregonning of Stithians was killed in a mud rush at De Beers. He had only been married a year, having left his wife 48 hours after the ceremony. His wife had not yet left Cornwall to join him, so his chief mourner was his brother – although many Stithians men attended the funeral, including Messrs. Dunston, Peters and Opie.[38] William Pearce of Redruth committed suicide at Kimberley by cutting his throat[39] whilst Joseph George of Wendron was found dead at the open mine at De Beers 200 feet below the surface.[40] Thomas Dick was just one of a number of Cornishmen to meet with a fatal accident at De Beers.[41] and John Rowe was fatally injured when, in July, 1889 he slipped and fell at the Kimberley Mine.[42] None of these deaths are recorded by Dickason but those that are show that many Cornish who are buried at Kimberley came from St. Just such as James Dennis (1897), Thomas Oats (1891), John Nankervis (1896) and Richard Thomas (1879), the last three having been accidentally killed in the diamond mines. The same fate befell Alfred and Edwin Penrose from Lanner in 1892 at the Kimberley Mine. The average age for all the deaths of miners recorded is in the middle twenties. It was not only miners. Francis Oats and his wife Elizabeth suffered a double tragedy – their infant boy Francis died in 1878 at three months, followed by the death of son Victor in 1882 at eight months.[43] Today two grave-stones can be found in St. Just churchyard Cornwall recording the death of William Roberts, who died at Kimberley 21st September 1884 age 47 years and William his son, who also died at Kimberley 10th January 1884 age 23 years. Presumably the bodies lie in South Africa.

There was always a large contingent of Cornish miners at Kimberley especially as the mines went deeper and the demand for the skills of the Cornish hard rock miner increased. A large number of miners in Kimberley came from St. Just, either because of Francis Oats, or simply due to the fact that so many of the mines in the St. Just district had closed down by 1880. The year before, *The Cornishman* reported that in St. Just:

Out of 1,440 houses, 350 or nearly one quarter are now standing empty...
Of fourteen mines in the district only Botallack, Wheal Owles, Levant, N.
*Levant, St. Just Amalgamated and a small mine are now open.*44

According to the *West Briton* the population of St. Just had been reduced by
more than a thousand.45 The previous year some 70 people had left St. Just district
for New Zealand.46 The prominence and contribution to the South African
diamond industry by the men of St. Just – to say nothing of their sacrifice
(including that made by their women) has never been more vividly shown than in
what has been called the worst mining disaster yet recorded in South Africa46
which took place on 11th July 1888 at De Beers.

The De Beers fire of 1888 showing dense smoke from underground workings. The cross (+ ringed) on the front
right hand side shows the shaft through which many miners escaped.

Accidents were the major hazard of mining and the accident feared most by
miners was that of fire underground. There had already been an accident
underground at De Beers which inadvertently became the cause of the fire. Two
skips for hauling broken rock had been derailed in No. 2 shaft causing serious
damage to some shaft timbers. Repair work had begun but during a change-over of
shifts early Wednesday evening fire broke out at the 500 feet level. The precise
cause was never determined53 although the De Beers General Manager Gardner
Williams later wrote that it was probable that one of the native miners had placed a

lighted candle so carelessly that the flame ignited the timbers.[47] One thing was certain; the fire spread rapidly and smoke quickly filled the two main shafts. Clarence S. Lindsay, the Underground Manager and six miners had only just gone down the shaft when the fire alarm rang. The real danger was that some 685 men were working on levels below the fire. Williams, who was about to leave for home, immediately took charge above ground sending two men down to warn Lindsay and his team. The two men were beaten back by the smoke. Williams could not understand why Lindsay did not give the signal to be hoisted back up the shaft. The reason was because Lindsay and his team were already dead – suffocated by the smoke which was now pouring out from both the main shafts. Although Williams was now getting a signal from the men below the fire he hesitated to give the order to hoist the skip which was at the 600 foot level, as the risk of hoisting a skip load of men through the stifling smoke was appalling.[48] He had no idea what the situation was below the fire as the telephone connection had broken. When he eventually decided to respond to the signal and gave the order to hoist up the skip disaster struck. The skip, with four men in it, was about 300 feet from the surface when the wire rope, virtually melted by the fire, broke and the skip crashed back down the shaft – the four men being killed instantly. Tension mounted as the men above ground could make no contact with those below. Fortunately a small ventilation shaft although partially blocked led out of the side of the mine into the old workings of the big hole. This was to provide the escape for some 42 white men and 441 native miners but 24 whites and 178 natives lost their lives in the levels and passageways charged with deadly smoke.[49]

The disaster or most terrible calamity as the *Diamond Fields Advertiser* called the fire became a story of heroism and acts of bravery many carried out by Cornishmen. It was also a tragedy for the Cornish town of St. Just as expressed in a telegram sent from Kimberley at 11.10am. Saturday and received at the St. Just Post Office at 1. 55pm. the same day

> *Postmaster, Saint Just, Cornwall, De Beers mine on fire. Maddern Leggo,*
> *Thomas Nankervis and Benjamin Thomas killed. All the rest of the men*
> *from St. Just safe and well. Make this known publicly. John Vingoe.*[50]

Warren, the Postmaster, communicated the news around the district reluctantly to some, eagerly enough to others. Francis Oats was at St. Just himself and as befits a De Beers Director he received his own personal telegram which listed the other deaths. Out of the total of 24 white miners who were killed – 7 were Cornishmen.[51] The three St. Just men who died had only left Cornwall the previous February. Maddern Leggo, aged 29 left a widow and child. Benjamin Thomas, aged 42, had farmed at Bosovern and only a month before he left St. Just had been driving the omnibus between St. Just and Penzance. He had also been a much respected teacher in the Wesleyan Sunday School. Thomas left a widow, seven daughters and a son. Thomas Nankervis, aged 23, was described as a quiet and better principled young man ever to have left St. Just and one of the principal members of Trewellard Cricket Club[52] whose match against Penzance was postponed as a mark of respect by his colleagues. The De Beers Company provided for all sixteen widows and thirty eight children the pension list remaining open for many years[53] which no doubt gave some comfort.

A number of Cornishmen escaped the fire including Henry Trevarrow, E. Angwin, James Kitto, E. Trevithick, W. Polglasse, T. Polglasse, John Leggo, H. Rowe, A. Angwin, W. Mitchell, Thos. Carter, John Kitto, Richard Leggo, and Henry Paull. The last three named all performed acts of extreme bravery. John Kitto was leading a number of men towards the ventilation shaft when they met with dense fumes. Many were for turning back immediately but Kitto however, pluckily kept on his way and was thus in no small measure instrumental in saving the large party he was with.[54] Richard Leggo also saved a number of lives simply

Coffins of Cornish victims after the fire at De Beers mine in 1888.

by his pluck and his knowledge of the underground workings of the mine. Many times the men who accompanied him had given up the struggle and sat down to die had Leggo not encouraged them to persevere.[55] The real hero of the fire was without a doubt Harry Paull from Scorrier. Having escaped the fire himself Paull then went back underground, leading a rescue party consisting of Cornishmen F. Clemo, W. Bawden, F. Hutchings, W.M. Coward, Stephen Oats and John Vingoe, (who sent the telegram). Paull gave a lengthy interview to the *Diamond Fields Advertiser* afterwards, in which he showed that he had the presence of mind to take the leadership when others seemed undecided as to what to do. He told how, at one stage, to keep up their spirits it was agreed to sing a hymn, and all the men joined in one of Moody & Sankey's hymns. It was also said that some of the sights experienced by survivors and rescue men were almost too harrowing to describe.[56]

A few days after the fire Gardner Williams went down the mine with the Assistant Inspector of Mines, Captain Hambley from Cornwall. They found that lower down part of the shaft had caved in from the heat. The removal of the bodies plus the clearing out of the shafts and pumping out the water, took time. It was to be nearly four months before the mine was back in full production, and it was estimated that the fire had cost De Beers £250,000. Such a disaster did not stop men from Cornwall leaving for South Africa; no less than 15 miners from St. Just district left Penzance by the 2.15 p.m. train[57] one Thursday late in November. Neither did it see an end to further tragedy for the people of St. Just and the next mining disaster struck closer to home. In 1893 the other feared accident – that of flooding – occurred at the St. Just mine Wheal Owles. Twenty men were drowned. Money for the victims' families was expected from South Africa where there were many St. Just men.[58] Two years later Wheal Owles was closed, bringing more hardship to the St. Just district.

Captain William Hambley, who had accompanied Williams down the mine after the fire, was just one of a number of Cornishmen who rose to a pre-eminent position in the mining industry as Inspector of Mines. Hambley had previously been Manager of the Wheal Uny Mine in Redruth, Cornwall, and during a visit home he told a meeting at East Pool that if the meeting were transplanted to Kimberley on a Saturday night they would think they were in another Camborne – so numerous were the Cornish miners.[59] When Hambley left Kimberley for another visit to Cornwall a year later the Kimberley *Daily Independent* said that while he had been on the Diamond Fields his services have been sought-after far and wide both by diamond and gold mining companies for inspecting and reporting on properties and his urbanity and geniality to all with whom he was brought into contact, made a host of friends.[60]

Such a send-off was perhaps to be expected by a Kimberley newspaper whose Editor (Moses Roberts) was a Cornishman. Roberts, a former Cornish journalist from Truro, was one of the prime movers in organising a Cornish Association at Kimberley and the Annual Cornish Dinner on New Year's Eve. He first proposed the idea in his own newspaper on 14th December 1889 and gave notice to 'One & All' that anyone interested was to attend a meeting at Spargo's Gladstone Hotel at

8.30 p.m. Monday 16th December[61] so that a committee could be set up. Optimistically Roberts hoped that large numbers would turn up, and they did. The first committee, with Roberts as Chairman, consisted of James Reynolds, Harry Blewett, S. Quick, F.H. Clemo, Paul Eva and A. Tregarthan. The main item on the agenda was the organisation of the New Year's Eve dinner which was held at the Gladstone Hotel run by William Spargo from Lanner. The meal consisted of a fine choice of soups, meats, vegetables and pastries; guests included newspaper editors and mining officials. With some twenty-five Cornishmen in attendance it was a modest beginning. Captain W. Erskine, the Government Inspector of Mines, was

PROPOSED
CORNISH DINNER.

NOTICE TO "ONE-AND-ALL."

AS it is proposed to hold a " Cornish " Dinner in Kimberley on or about New Year's Eve, all Cornishmen on the Diamond Fields are requested to attend a Meeting at SPARGO'S Gladstone Hotel at 8·30 on MONDAY Evening Next, 16th inst., for the purpose of electing a Committee for carrying out the necessary arrangements. It is hoped that men hailing from the "One-and-All" County will roll up in large numbers, in order that the gatering may be as representative as possible.

83x   MOSES ROBERTS.

The Daily Independent 14th December 1889.

the principal guest and he proposed a toast to the success of the Cornishmen on the Diamond Fields and to *One & All*, adding there was no doubt in his mind the success of the Diamond Fields was in great measure attributable to the steadiness and the reliability of the many Cornishmen employed in them. Roberts in reply expressed some disappointment at the low turnout but hoped it would be the forerunner of many a successful annual gathering.[62] He was not to be disappointed. The Annual Cornish Dinner on New Year's Eve was to become very much a Kimberley Institution. At the dinner the following year over 80 zealous and enthusiastic Cornishmen sat down to eat but disappointment this time was expressed over the menu which contained not one pasty, or a junket or clotted cream and it was felt mine host clearly wanted a little more gastronomic teaching. Paul Eva did sing *Trelawny*, however, and Captain Erskine, the principal guest again, took as his theme the Cornish motto *One & All*, for it meant unity and strength, loyalty and support. He believed the English nation would look to Cornishmen as one of the strong factors of prosperity at home and abroad.63

The majority of the subsequent dinners were chaired by Thomas Quentrall of Wendron. Quentrall, after Oats, was the next most influential Cornishman at Kimberley. He had been Manager of the East Lovell and New Trumpet Mine near

Directors and officials of De Beers in 1902. On the left hand side, seated, are Dr. L.S. Jameson (outer) and Francis Oats (inner) Fourth from the left seated is Alfred Beit and next right is Sir Lewis Michell then Chairman of De Beers. Thomas Quentrall is second from the right of the middle row.

his home at Wendron and was much esteemed in the whole neighbourhood.64 Leaving Cornwall in June 1889 he was eventually to become Inspector of Mines for Kimberley and Barkley West covering a wide area including the copper mines of Namaqualand. Quentrall often represented the Inspectorate at the funerals of those miners killed in accidents. He also on one occasion appeared in court to give evidence when fellow Cornishman Walter Whitburn killed a native. Whitburn, who worked at De Beers, had hit the native on the head and was charged with culpable homicide. He was committed to trial but the *Cornishman* did not record the outcome.65

Another Cornishman who found himself on a charge was Thomas Cornwall Holman, a foreman moulder at De Beers workshops. He was accused of rape but was acquitted.66 Holman was from St. Just but remained at Kimberley becoming one of De Beers' oldest employees. Although he was described as one of the band of Cornishmen who did such excellent Pioneer work in the diamond industry and being the owner of one of the finest palm gardens in Kimberley he still kept links with Cornwall, being a member of the Old Cornish Society as well as playing a prominent part in the Annual Dinner.[67] His funeral in June 1931 was well-attended. William Spargo was another Kimberley Pioneer as well as being one of the most ardent promoters of the Cornish Association at Kimberley.[68] Despite that, he returned to Cornwall with his wife Ellen (née Penrose), and died at Truro in 1930 aged 87 years. His son Sydney, however, remained in South Africa.

One sport the Cornish introduced to Kimberley and elsewhere in South Africa was that of Cornish wrestling. In February 1886 over a hundred miners watched the St. Just Pug fight Captain Tom to a draw over 3 rounds,[69] and the following year John Vingoe and James Quayle were in contest. A champion Cornish Wrestler in Kimberley before the Boer War was Richard Eddy from Pendeen who because of his short and square physique was known as Little Dick. Like so many other Cornishmen he often went back and forth between Cornwall and South Africa. He died from gallstones on 26th February 1896 at Pendeen and was therefore buried in Cornwall.[70]

Not all the Cornish at Kimberley were involved in mining. Thomas Pooley of Penzance spent some 30 years with the Old Cape Railways and when he retired in 1921 was presented with gold mounted pipes and a cigarette case while his wife was given a brooch with a Kimberley ruby.[71] Pooley remembered that when the Kimberley railway platform had been built, Rhodes had ordered it to be double the length, because it would be needed one day, this proved to be the case when the troops moved there during the Boer War.[72] Pooley died in Cornwall at Heamoor aged 75 years. William Thomas Hoal from Fowey was the Chief of the Postal and Telegraph Departments at Kimberley and enjoyed the confidence of the public being highly respected and esteemed by his assistants and subordinates.[73] He left Kimberley in 1889 for Port Elizabeth because of illness in his family and when he died in 1910 flags were flown at half mast on the various Telegraph and Post Office buildings throughout South Africa.[74]

Sooner or later most Cornish on the diamond fields made at least one visit back to Cornwall. Fred Bennetto, a wagon shop foreman at De Beers and a regular at the Cornish dinners, left it for some twenty-three years before returning to Newlyn East to visit his aged mother and other relatives in 1914. His colleagues presented him with a purse of sovereigns before he left Kimberley.[75] J.W. Pope who had been one of the first on the diamond fields in 1870, made his first visit home to Cornwall thirty-five years later in 1905 – he was not in any way atypical.[76] Some, of course, left it too late, such as John Berriman of Penzance who was a regular at the Annual Dinner. Having begun work at De Beers in 1879 he was described as an old and respected employee being 69 years old when he died in 1910 at the residence of Fred Bennetto. He left two married daughters at Pretoria. At his funeral the wreath sent by Kimberley Cornish simply said *One & All.*[77]

When Edward John Kitto of Kimberley returned home to Cornwall it was to stay. It was remarked how industrious and fortunate in the land of diamonds he had been for he had made enough money to build a ten-roomed house for himself near the top of Vogue Hill, St. Day.[78] There are no records of how many Cornish went to Kimberley or just how many were to come back to Cornwall – what is clear is that many like Bennetto paid a visit, many like Berriman stayed in Kimberley, for one reason or another, and many – like Kitto – returned home. There were of course others who went elsewhere. Captain Hambley moved on to Australia to manage a mine, whereas Moses Roberts moved only as far as Johannesburg. On leaving Kimberley Roberts was presented with a gift from his many friends by Captain Quentrall. Not everyone from Kimberley even made the short distance to the gold fields:

> *A Mr Montgomery on his way to Barberton in a wagon when near the road saw a pair of boots at the edge of a 60 foot precipice at the bottom of which was a river... one of the other travellers looked over the edge and saw a man lying on his face, his hat off and blood all around him for about the space of 4 ft. square. The man died the next day and Montgomery had him buried. Later discovered the man was Jim Shequin, late Captain of Namaqualand Mine, a Cornishman, a miner, who also worked some time in the Victoria Diamond Mine Company, De Beers. Kimberley.*[79]

Not everyone headed immediately for the gold fields either. To the north of Kimberley lay two short-lived Boer Republics. Vryburg was the capital of the Stellaland Republic, which had been founded in 1883 along with the other Republic, Goshen. Conflict between the Boers and neighbouring tribesmen resulted in an expeditionary force in 1885 being led by Sir Charles Warren to the area – of which the Kalahari Desert comprises a major portion. The outcome was the annexation of the republics and the establishment of another British Colony – Bechuanaland (now Botswana). Further north of Vryburg, Warren founded the town of Mafeking, both towns becoming the focal point for some very adventurous Cornish folk.

One Cornish Pioneer who followed in Warren's wake was Josiah Angove. He left Kimberley taking his printing plant with him in order to establish at Vryburg another newspaper, *The Vryburg Advocate and Government Gazette*. Again there is confusion as to whether it was Josiah who went or his brother John. Maybe both the brothers went to Vryburg, for the *Advocate* recorded on 25th March 1886 that Johannes de Meillon, the Market Master of Vryburg had brought a charge of criminal libel against John Angove, Proprietor of the Paper. Angove had attacked the way the market was conducted, especially over the bidding for wood – a sparse commodity in what was virtually a treeless area. Angove had practically accused

Meillon of theft. Although the court found Angove guilty and imposed on him a £10 fine or a month's imprisonment, Angove's fine was immediately paid for by public subscription, his health being toasted with great enthusiasm, which was followed by three loud cheers, at which

> *The late criminal expressed himself highly gratified at this public demonstration in his favour and hoped that wherever he might be, he should at all times thus merit the goodwill of the public.*[80]

Neither Angove remained at Vryburg for long, nor did they return to Kimberley because, with the discovery of gold on the Rand they were soon, along with their printing press, en route for Johannesburg.

The Land of Diamonds had attracted many young Cornishmen to travel to Kimberley but perhaps the most extraordinary was Llewellyn May. Born in Fowey in 1864 May reached Cape Town in 1880 and became a Supervisor at the Docks. Like many others he was lured to Kimberley with news of the diamond rush. However, it was not as a digger that he was to earn a living but rather as a security guard on the train carrying the diamonds from Kimberley to Wellington. The city fathers of Kimberley must have placed a very high premium on the young man's performance and abilities because they immediately offered him the position of Town Security Chief.[81]

At some time before 1886 May changed his name to Frederick de Witt Tossel in order to be accepted as a Dutchman. Both Harry Zeederberg and Maria Vorster who have written short biographies on May/Tossel claim he learnt to speak fluent Afrikaans by the ingenious method of comparing his own English Bible with a High Dutch Bible. He was obviously very gifted, for in addition to English and Afrikaans he could speak Portuguese and Spanish plus a few native languages. Whilst still in Kimberley May met his brother Phillip who, having been a member of the Salvation Army in Cornwall, had been posted to Kimberley where he had lost no time in forming a Corps.[82] There followed an emotional reunion between the two brothers. Zeederberg and Vorster then claim that May (or Tossel, as he was now calling himself) went direct from Kimberley to Johannesburg. This was not quite the case for as Tossel himself relates, having resigned from the Kimberley Police,

> *I left Kimberley on horseback on March 1st, 1886, and took with me a pack horse laden with belongings and provisions. Upon arrival at Vryburg, I put up at the Queens Hotel... After meeting old friends, I met Mr. P.J. Truter, Resident Magistrate formerly Crown Prosecutor of Kimberley, who told me that as civil government had just been inaugurated, he was looking for just such a man as myself whom he could appoint to the post of Chief Constable... He added that as pay was small he could make it decent enough by adding the posts of Sanitary Inspector,*

Field Cornet, Deputy Sheriff, Pound Master, Controller of Traffic, etc., etc., which altogether made up one way and another about £50 a month as salary![83]

Not surprisingly Tossel accepted the offer and remained at Vryburg for at least a year.

After short stays the Angoves and Tossel moved on but the Rouncivell family from Cornwall were to make Bechuanaland their home. John James Rouncivell with his young wife Harriet sailed to South Africa in 1882 on board the *Durban*, under the Agriculture Settlers' Scheme. Rouncivell came from St. Columb Major (where his parents had a farm) and had married Harriet Lane, a miner's daughter from Golant. On arrival in South Africa the Rouncivells first lived at East London, Natal. Although allocated land in Knysna John worked for a time at the East London Brick Works during which time three children, John James Jnr., Louisa Agnes and Mary, were born. In 1888 the family moved to Mafeking where John James became a shopkeeper. Although a fourth child, Harry, was born the same year, tragically Harriet died ten days after the birth. John James later remarried, his new wife being an old friend Kate Broad, a blacksmith's daughter from St. Neot in Cornwall. When she arrived in Cape Town she was met, not by her future husband, but by five of his most trusted servants. Kate, who had never met a black man before, then travelled with them by ox wagon taking five weeks to cover the journey of some 850 miles to Mafeking. Once married to John James the couple added four more children to the Rouncivell family. Marie Broad Rouncivell (born 23rd March 1893) was the first white woman to be born at Macloutsi, Bechuanaland where her father now traded. The family then moved to Francistown, on the border of Bechuanaland and Rhodesia, where the other three children were born. Reginald (born April 1896) became a sampler on the gold mines at Brakpan, Transvaal; Beatrice unfortunately died aged 2 years in 1898 and Charles (born 1901) went into the printing business.

In 1905 John James built the first double storey building in Francistown in which he had his store. He was now trading in cattle and sheep. As expected the store stocked everything, most goods being imported from Britain. According to his granddaughter, John James was also a watch-repairer and photographer having a wonderful sense of humour, very generous to the poor but not to anyone imbibing too freely in alcohol! Apparently he had a lot of money owing to him when he eventually gave up the shop. The children were all taught at a small school in Francistown – the Bishop of Francistown teaching mathematics and Latin – which Harry considered a waste of time. Kate Rouncivell acted as a local midwife.

One of the visitors to the Rouncivell store was the Great Chief Khama of the Bamangwato tribe travelling from his headquarters at Serowe. For his comfort his retinue would lay Karosses (wild animal skins sewn together for mats) on the verandah of the store. (It was Chief Khama's grandson who became Sir Seretse Khama and who married an English girl in the 1950s causing outrage in many circles, both in South Africa and Britain.) John James Rouncivell left Francistown in 1921 for Cape Town where he had another business. He died in 1923; his wife Kate died in 1937, in Rhodesia. John James had 8 children, 16 grandchildren 28 great-grandchildren and 35 great-great grandchildren.[84]

John James Rouncivell and his wife Kate (Broad), store owner and mid-wife c.1915.

1. A.K. Hamilton Jenkin, *THE CORNISH MINER* 3rd Ed (Newton Abbot 1972) p.329

2. See especially Brian Roberts, *KIMBERLEY TURBULENT CITY* (CAPE TOWN 1976) William H. Worger, *SOUTH AFRICAN CITY OF DIAMONDS MINE WORKERS AND MONOPOLY CAPITALISM IN KIMBERLEY 1867-1895* (YALE UNIVERSITY 1987) which is described by John S. Galbraith as the definitive work on the diamond fields.

3. J. Angove *IN THE EARLY DAYS* (KIMBERLEY & JOHANNESBURG 1910)

4. George Lacy (1844-1904) an early Pioneer, trader and explorer of South Africa claimed he once gave twenty-six shillings for a cabbage on the diamond fields and boiled it in water that cost 2s 6d a bucket. See *CORNISHMAN* 28th OCTOBER 1886 p.4

5. Angove, *EARLY DAYS*. p.150 Whim is a Cornish word for a winding device to haul men and ore up from a mine shaft. Whims could be worked by horses, water wheels or steam power.

6. *DIAMOND FIELD NEWS, 30th MARCH 1880*

7. *DIAMOND FIELDS ADVERTISER*, 19th JANUARY 1883. See also *WEST BRITON* 15th MARCH 1883.

8. Rohan, FORTY SOUTH AFRICAN YEARS p.221

9. Additional information re the Angoves was supplied by Mrs. L. Brits, African Librarian Kimberly. She wrote even our historian Eric Rosenthal failed on that point and considered John and Josiah to be one and the same. I think they were brothers. THE SOUTHERN AFRICAN DICTIONARY OF NATIONAL BIOGRAPHY (LONDON 1966) as compiled by Eric Rosenthal states Joseph Angove as being born in Penzance 1853. This could lead to the suggestion that there were in fact four brothers – John, Joseph, Josiah and Rice. However, I firmly believe there were but three Angove brothers – John (the eldest) who wrote the book, Josiah – sometimes called Joseph being the newspaper proprietor and Rice the youngest who died from dysentery. In his newspapers Josiah Angove is sometimes called Joseph but never John.

10. *DIAMOND FIELDS HERALD,* 23rd APRIL 1885

11. *C.P.M.N.,* 1st OCTOBER 1896

12. See D.B. Barton, *THE CORNISH BEAM ENGINE* (LONDON 1969). p.150

13. *C.P.M.N.,* 24th DECEMBER 1895. The paper stated that Beit was worth £10 million, Wernher £7 million, Robinson £6 million, Rhodes £5 million and Barnato £4 million.

14. *IBID.,* 1st OCTOBER 1896

15. *DIAMOND FIELD ADVERTISER,* 26th JUNE 1886

16. Brian Robert, *CECIL RHODES: FLAWED COLOSSUS* (LONDON 1987). p.77

17. *DIAMOND FIELDS ADVERTISER*, 28th MAY 1887

18. *MINING JOURNAL,* 22nd SEPTEMBER 1888. p.1077

19. G. Burke, *THE CORNISH MINER AND CORNISH MINING INDUSTRY 1870-1921* (Unpublished Ph.D. Thesis London University 1981). p.119-120

20. *CORNISHMAN*, 3rd JANUARY 1895

21. *IBID.,* 16th FEBRUARY 1899 – See also *IBID.,* 9th FEBRUARY 1899

22. *C.P.M.N.,* 27th FEBRUARY 1896. See also H. Thomas Cornish Mining Interviews (Camborne 1896)

23. See Robert Turrell, *THE 1875 BLACK FLAG REVOLT ON THE KIMBERLEY DIAMOND FIELDS* (O.U.P. 1981)

24. Angove, *EARLY DAYS* p.67

25. Warger, *SOUTH AFRICA'S CITY OF DIAMONDS* p. 43.See also Marks, Shula & Rathbone Richard, Editors. *INDUSTRIALISATION AND SOCIAL CHANGE IN SOUTH AFRICA, AFRICAN CLASS FORMATION, CULTURE AND CONSCIOUSNESS 1870-1930* (LONDON 1982) See especially introduction and Chapter 1 *KIMBERLEY: LABOUR AND COMPOUNDS 1871-88* by Rob Turrell.

26. *C.P.M.N.*, 9th MAY 1895

27. *CORNISHMAN*, 15th MARCH 1906

28. *KIMBERLEY ADVERTISER*, 10th FEBRUARY 1931

29. J.T. McNish, *GRAVES AND GUINEAS KIMBERLEY 1871 – 73* (CAPE TOWN 1969)

30. *KIMBERLEY ILLUSTRATED*. p.82. No date – photocopy supplied by Kimberley Public Library.

31. *CORNISHMAN*, 21st OCTOBER 1925

32. Owen Letcher, *THE GOLD MINES OF SOUTHERN AFRICA* (LONDON 1936) p.468

33. *C.P.M.N.*, 14th NOVEMBER 1896

34. *Rinderpest,* a most destructive disease amongst cattle hit South Africa in 1896. The fact that 15th October 1896 was appointed a day of prayer indicates not only the devastation the disease caused among the herds of cattle but also showed how helpless the authorities were in preventing its spread. Cattle died within hours of catching the disease – over 30 percent of the cattle on the high veldt died – a whole breed, the Matabele cattle being virtually wiped out. See S.P. Hyatt, *THE OLD TRANSPORT ROAD* (LONDON 1914) p.293

35. *C.P.M.N.*, 14th NOVEMBER 1896

36. *CORNISHMAN*, 2nd APRIL 1885

37. *WEST BRITON*, 17th AUGUST, 9th NOVEMBER & 8th JUNE 1882

38. *DIAMOND FIELDS ADVERTISER*, 12th MARCH 1894

39. *CORNUBIAN*, 6th DECEMBER 1895

40. *IBID.*, 21st MAY 1897. George had left Cornwall 13 years previously for Australia, where he worked for 10 years prior to going to Kimberley.

41. *DIAMOND FIELDS TIMES*, 19th NOVEMBER 1886

42. *STANDARD AND TRANSVAAL MINING CHRONICLE* 27th JULY 1889

43. Dickason, *CORNISH IMMIGRANTS*. p.87-117

44. *CORNISHMAN*, 23rd JANUARY 1879

45. *WEST BRITON*, 23rd JANUARY 1879. A Census of St. Just in 1871 was 9, 011, dropping to 6, 109 in 1881 and further declining to 5, 646 by 1901.

46. *CORNISHMAN*, 26 SEPTEMBER 1878

47. H.A. Chilvers, *THE STORY OF DE BEERS* (LONDON 1939) p.75

48. Gardner Williams, *THE DIAMOND MINES OF SOUTH AFRICA SOME ACCOUNT OF THEIR RISE OF DEVELOPMENT* (LONDON 1902) p.29

49. *IBID.*, p.30-32

50. *CORNISHMAN*, 19th JULY 1888

51. From the list given by Chilvers, John Faull was from Truro and William Timmins was also Cornish. The other two Cornishmen I have been unable to identify. See Chilvers, *STORY OF DE BEERS*, p.79

52. *CORNISHMAN*, 19th JULY 1888. Nankervis's father died in Cornwall from mine injuries, one brother died of fever in Johannesburg, another died in the Kimberley mine – such were the dangers. *C.P.M.N.*, 26th MARCH 1896

53. Chilvers, *STORY OF DE BEERS*, p.79.

54. *DIAMOND FIELDS ADVERTISER*, 16 July 1888

55. *IBID.*, 16th JULY 1888

56. *MINING JOURNAL*, 18th AUGUST 1888 p.928

57. *CORNISHMAN*, 29th NOVEMBER 1888

58. *CORNISHMAN*, 20th JANUARY 1893. In the same year disaster struck at two other Cornish mines. At Wheal Agar, between Redruth and Camborne 12 men were killed when a piece of machinery fell into a shaft and 8 men were entombed at Dolcoath mine – there was only one survivor. For details of these and other mine disasters see Cyril Noall, *CORNISH MINE DISASTERS*, (REDRUTH 1989)

59. *MINING JOURNAL*, 21st APRIL 1888 p.451

60. *IBID.*, 27th JULY 1889 p.853

61. *DAILY INDEPENDENT*, 14th DECEMBER 1889. See also *DIAMOND FIELDS ADVERTISER*, 21st DECEMBER 1889

62. *IBID.*, 3rd JANUARY 1890

63. *CORNISHMAN*, 29th JANUARY 1891

64. *MINING JOURNAL*, 22nd JUNE 1889 p.712

65. *CORNISHMAN*, 7th JANUARY 1898

66. *IBID.*, 3rd JUNE 1898

67. *IBID.*, 25th JUNE 1931

68. *IBID.*, 17th APRIL 1930

69. *DIAMOND FIELDS ADVERTISER*, 16th FEBRUARY 1886

70. Information supplied by Olive Bennetts, Richard Eddy's granddaughter who lives in South Africa.

71. *CORNISHMAN*, 22nd JUNE 1921

72. *IBID.*, 15th AUGUST 1935

73. *DIAMOND FIELDS ADVERTISER*, 17th AUGUST 1889

74. *C.P.M.N.*, 24th NOVEMBER 1910

75. *CORNISHMAN*, 9th JULY 1914

76. *C.P.M.N.*, 18th MAY 1905

77. *IBID.*, 10th MARCH 1910

78. *IBID.*, 9th JULY 1896

79. *DIAMOND FIELDS TIMES*, 9th OCTOBER 1886 Shequin was probably the wrong spelling for the Cornish name *Chegwin.*

80. *VRYBURG ADVOCATE & GOVERNMENT GAZETTE FOR BRITISH BECHUANALAND*, 25th MARCH 1886

81. *SERVAMUS*, NOVEMBER 1986 article *FREDERICK de WITT TOSSEL = KRUGERSDORP SE'INGEVOERDE' POLISIEHOOF* by Maria Vorster.

82. *PERSONALITY*, FEBRUARY 1970 article *PRESIDENT KRUGER'S FOREIGN POLICE CHIEF*, by Harry Zeederberg.

83. *THE KRUGERSDORP STANDARD*, 25th MAY 1928

84. Information re: the Rouncivell family supplied by Vera Kirby.

CHAPTER FOUR

LAND OF GOLD 1870-99

Gold! Gold! Gold! Gold!
Bright and yellow, hard and cold
Molten, proven, hammered and rolled,
Heavy to get and light to hold.
Hoarded, bartered, bought and sold,
Stolen, borrowed, squandered, doled:
Spurned by the young but hugged by the old
To the very verge of the churchyard mould,
Price of many a crime untold
Gold! Gold! Gold! Gold!

Standard & Transvaal Mining Chronicle.[1]

We rode across vast plains, quite flat, never arriving at the horizon,
most wearying to the eye, but at the time relieved by countless herds of
big game, blesbok, gnu and zebra. I never saw the like before or since,
incredible even when seen. As the springbok came to the wagon road
they would bound gracefully into the air and clear it. When some
hundreds were thus in the air at the same time the appearance was
that of a bridge spanning the track

Bishop Wilkinson.[2]

Bishop Wilkinson was just one of the many Cornish to be found travelling around the Transvaal in the 1870's although whereas the Bishop went in search of lost souls, most Cornish went in search of gold. Wilkinson had originally led a mission party of eight from Falmouth in July 1870 and had spent some six years in Zululand where he had been Bishop. According to Chilvers, Wilkinson was the real founder of the Pretoria Diocese despite not being appointed when it was constituted in 1878. Wilkinson has left clear evidence that Cornish miners were working in the Transvaal well before the discovery of the Rand gold field in 1886. In 1879, two hundred miles north of Pretoria at a place called Eersteling, the Bishop found a number of Cornish from Hayle working one of Harvey's steam engines. On leaving their mining settlement Wilkinson received presents of salt beef and cheese from "these hospitable Cornish people".[3] Gold was first discovered in South Africa in the Eastern Transvaal from about 1871 onward in a number of places – the most notable being at Pilgrim's Rest, Lyndenburg and Barberton. When Francis Oats visited the only gold mine at Pilgrim's Rest in 1874 he found two St. Just men working there.[4] One of the first gold Pioneers from Cornwall was Mark Reed Pascoe of Crowan who was prospecting in the Transvaal as early as 1870. Together with his brother and William Hosken of Hayle he walked the 170 miles from Pilgrim's Rest to Lourenco Marques in order to catch a boat to Durban. There Pascoe established his own drapery business and later floated a number of mining companies on the Rand, such as the Blue Sky and Agnes Munro.

Twenty-three year old William Hosken, who was to become perhaps the most influential of all Cornishmen in the Transvaal, recalled many years later how he had made a tour of the Transvaal, inspecting its mining resources. He came to the conclusion that the Transvaal was going to be one of the greatest mining centres in the world. It was not a case of having the benefit of hindsight either, for at the time he had sent letters to the Cornish newspapers pointing out the favourable conditions, in particular for Cornish miners, in the Transvaal.[5] Another Cornishman, Thomas Collingwood Kitto, as Official Assayer during the short-lived Shepstone Administration 1877-81 found in the Transvaal that every person who held a farm believed himself to be the possessor of great mineral wealth.[6] Ironically the very farm that Richard Thomas Hall had turned down as payment for his railway survey became the site for the Sheba mine. This mine,

> *of which the brother of Lewis Michell was in charge, had the honourable*
> *distinction of being really rich, its capital had been subscribed, partly in*
> *groceries, mining stores and even liquor, by thirty men, and when it paid*
> *a first dividend of 170 per cent the £1 shares rose from par to £105 each.*[7]

T.R. Parkyn, a son of Capt. Parkyn of Roche, returned to Cornwall in 1885 and also reported favourably on some gold fields he had inspected in the Transvaal.[8] Two of the Acutt family from Cornwall who arrived at Barberton to seek their fortune were William Acutt, who ran a successful transport business at Barberton until his death there in 1896, and Leonard Acutt, who gave up sugar farming, being driven presumably by his Cornish blood to try his hand at mining. He eventually became Manager of a gold mine at Barberton. Lewis Michell arrived at Barberton from Cape Town in April 1886 to open up a branch of the Standard Bank:

> *While there, he attended a sitting of the Circuit Court on which the jury,*
> *in comic opera style, acquitted every prisoner as a protest against the*
> *condition of the jail, which, by nightfall, had only one occupant – the*
> *Public Prosecutor himself, who in a fit of bibulous temper had insulted*
> *the Judge and been committed for contempt.*[9]

There were fortunes to be made at Barberton. Frank Stevens, a Cornishman from Gulval, was worth his thousands and set himself up as a merchant in Durban where in 1887 he married Kate Green from Maritzburg – they had six children. Another Gulval pair quickly got together above £70,000.[10] Just outside Barberton could be found Thomas's Reef:

> *The proprietors are brothers and Cousin Jackys (in fact we are all over the country). They have a nice hole of gold and discovered quite accidentally. They have followed it down about 60 feet and the further they go the richer it gets... and I hear they get out 150 ounces in one week... they have made a pile.*[11]

Johannesburg in 1886

According to Hugh Lanion Hall the strike by the Thomas brothers had occurred when one of the brothers had pitched his tent on a spot just vacated by a gold digger called Sievwright:

> *Sitting next morning on the same rock on which Sievwright had so often sat and watched his kettle boil, he casually struck the rock, chipping off a piece with a prospecting hammer he happened to have in his hand. Picking up the rock he saw it was rich in visible gold. He pegged off the ground, which became Thomas Reef. He and his brother, both Cornish miners, put up a small stamp battery and recovered gold to the value of £1000 or more out of it.*[12]

The Thomas brothers had formerly been railway contractors in Natal although they had some mining experience in a copper mine near Maritzburg. They were described as hard working Cornishmen until then poor men toiling with their own horny hands with pick and shovel.[13] They were now very rich and still very lucky, for they decided to sell their mine to a company for £10,000 cash and 10,000 fully paid-up shares. Thomas sold these at £2 per share and went back to Cornwall with the proceeds.[14] The Thomas brothers had recovered 1000 ounces of gold from thirty-two tons of ore but the company which bought the mine and was floated with tremendous excitement only had a poor return.[15] Unfortunately Richard Thomas Hall having retired from the Cape Railways arrived in the Transvaal to take over as Manager of the Thomas mine. His son Hugh Lanion, however, had already some doubt as to the continual good fortune of the mine. This was confirmed when he was given the contract to cart the ore:

City & Suburban Gold mining Company – Surface scene.

Ferreira Gold Mining Company 350ft underground.

I had my suspicions that something was wrong, and before beginning to cart it, I took my own samples and panned them off. I found that it was only worth a few pennyweights to the ton. I told my father so, but he would not believe me. The director insisted it was to be taken to the mill, so I carted it all down. The result was very disappointing: it only went to five dwts to the ton, which did not pay for the transport, let alone the crushing of it.[16]

Hugh Lanion Hall found fortune of a different kind for it was at Barberton he married Grace Donaldson, a sister of one of Barberton's many storekeepers. Hall's father Richard was less fortunate; on his way to Bloemfontein to take up the position as Chief Engineer of the Orange Free State Railways he caught a chill and died at Johannesburg on 21st August 1889. The Thomas mine was managed for a time by Hugh's brother – George – but it soon collapsed, the fate of many companies at Barberton, which once had over 100 companies – including the Cornish Gold Mining Company[17] – listed on the local Stock Exchange. Then came the news in 1886 that gold had been discovered on the Witwatersrand centred on what was to become Johannesburg.

There have been many contenders to the discovery of what was to become the most significant goldfield in South Africa. Pieter Jacob Marias, a young Boer, had found traces of gold whilst prospecting in the Transvaal in 1854. Later main candidates for the honour were the Struben brothers – Fred and Harry – George Harrison, George Walker and George Honeyball. Walker's gravestone at Krugersdorp claims him to be The Man who discovered the Main Reef Series of the Witwatersrand of Langlaagte in February 1886.[18] Harrison is also said to have made the first claim.[19] However, according to Hedley Chilvers it was F.P.T. Struben and to him alone that the honour of having discovered the Witwatersrand belongs.[20] According to Chilvers, Walker had a companion who was a Cornish carpenter named Honeyball who spoke with a drawl,[21] but Honeyball was half Boer and half English.[22] However, Harry Struben openly admitted that he and his brother were assisted by a Cornishman. Having purchased Geldenhuis Farm, Wilge Spruit in 1884 Struben said:

I engaged a Cornish miner named Arnold and started him working on Wilgespruit under Fred's supervision. The man was afterwards quoted as 'a discoverer', whereas he was merely a labourer in my employ.[23]

It has been suggested that with the discovery of the Witwatersrand goldfield, or Rand as it became more commonly called, Cornishmen began to pour like a flood into South Africa.[24] This could hardly have been the case, for a major problem with the new goldfield was its inaccessibility. With no railway, at first, travel to the Rand was by ox wagon, which was slow and difficult. There could hardly be a

Miners at Ferreira gold mine.

rush. One route to the Rand meant travelling due west from Delagoa Bay – a distance of 150-250 miles, depending on the actual track taken. Another route from Durban involved travelling 300-400 miles, much on foot. George Lacy, ex-elephant hunter, gold prospector and experienced traveller in the Transvaal, wrote to the Editor of the *Cornishman* warning the Cornish miners that if they valued their lives they were to avoid the shorter route between the months of October and June, claiming the route was a graveyard to Europeans. Lacy then set out a complete guide for would-be gold diggers going to the Rand, including advice to take three blankets due to changes in temperature when the sun went down and to take no notice of snakes which would take no notice of them. He described the Boers as lazy rogues and warned that life on the goldfield would be decidedly dear.

Manager of the Simmer & Jack mine for six years, the Glencairn for two years, the East Rand Proprietary mine for three years and the Sheba gold mine for five years. William Whitburn from St. Day was Manager of the Henry Nourse mine for two years and then left for Europe to become Manager of the Forbes Reef mine in Switzerland. His brother James, who had begun work at the Tresavean mine, St. Day, had been Manager of the City & Suburban mine for two years, then the Jumpers mine before replacing his brother as Manager of the Henry Nourse mine. He remained Manager for nearly 15 years before he returned to Cornwall to retire in 1905.

William Morris Prout of Redruth, like so many of the Cornish managers was a product of the Camborne School of Mines. He was a student there from 1892-95 before going to South Africa as Surveyor Draughtsman at the Ferreira mine. He gained rapid promotion, for in 1899 – still only 29 years old – he was appointed Manager of the Jumpers mine. In 1903 he became Manager of the larger Witwatersrand mine. Sidney Penlerick of Falmouth arrived in South Africa in 1893, and after six years as Mining Engineer & Surveyor at the Roodepoort mine became Assistant Manager at the East Randfontein mine. Charles Pearce of St. Austell worked at the Sheba mine before becoming Foreman at the George Goch mine. He was eventually appointed Manager of the Van Ryn Apex & Kleinfontein group of mines in 1905.

Not all the Cornish managers came direct from Cornwall. Rowe, like so many Cornish miners, had gained valuable experience working in the U.S.A. as had Williams, who had also worked in Australia. James Whitburn came to South Africa direct from the mines of Chile whereas James Donald of Perranuthnoe had been working for twenty years in the gold mines of California before he arrived in South Africa to become Manager of the Nourse Deep mine. The most respected of all the Cornish managers in South Africa had previously worked in India. John Henry Johns, or J. Harry Johns, as he is best known, was born 5th December 1857 at St. Hilary overlooking Mount Bay but was brought up in the heart of mining Cornwall at Camborne, where his father was a competent Mine Agent at Dolcoath. In 1881 Johns went to India[38] where he was Manager of the Nine Reefs gold mine until 1888, when he was appointed Manager of the Ferreira & Wemmer mines. Johns as Manager contributed to no small degree to the success of the Rand being noted for his technique and administrative abilities.[39] It was Johns who turned the Ferreira mine in one of the most profitable of all the gold mines on the Rand, being able to announce to its shareholders a 100% dividend by the time he left. Such was his standing amongst the other mine managers that in 1893, when the Mine Managers' Association for the Witwatersrand was formed, Johns was elected its first President. The Association was second only to the Chamber of Mines as the most influential group in South Africa's gold mining industry. The Chamber, set up in 1887, was concerned totally with the interests of the mine owners.

Another successful Cornish mine manager was John Whitford. Born in 1858 at Newlyn East, he grew up at Mithian, near St. Agnes, where from the age of 10 years he walked the 5 miles from his home to West Chiverton mine (a rich lead mine until its closure in 1886). Later, having worked at Blue Hills and then Wheal Coates – two of the richest tin mines at St. Agnes – Whitford left for Brazil in 1881. Although he returned to Cornwall in 1889 he left the same year for South Africa to start work at the Salisbury mine. His stay there was short as he explained, "I got sacked the first time in my life because I did not touch my hat to the boss". It proved to be a blessing in disguise for he soon found work at the Robinson Mine, where he worked for seven years from Shaft Man to Shift Boss and eventually became Foreman at the Moderfontein. From there Whitford was eventually appointed Manager of the Robinson Central Deep mine where under his skilful management the mine made handsome profits. In July 1908 he was appointed Manager of the City Deep, a mine then still in its infancy but with a promising future. When asked as to what he attributed his success he replied "Work, work, work". John Whitford was married to Anne Searle Hooper and they had four sons – one, Ernest Howard worked at the Robinson and Crown mines – and two daughters. The Whitfords, like so many others eventually returned to Cornwall where they purchased a house called Rose in Vale at Mithian (now a hotel).[40]

A Cornish manager who held the record for the longest spell, twenty-two years of uninterrupted management of one particular mine property, was Charles Gluyas of the Jubilee gold mine. Gluyas was born in 1865 at Wendron near Helston where his father had been Manager of a number of mines, including Wendron Consolidated. As his father then moved to the United Phoenix mine in East Cornwall so Charles and his brother Richard gained their mining experience here, in the Caradon copper district. In 1887 both brothers travelled to South Africa to become Managers – Richard at the Nigel mine and Charles at the Moss Rose mine. Within a few months Charles was appointed Manager of the Jubilee mine at only 23 years of age. Like Johns he was an active member of the Mine Managers' Association. When Gluyas died in 1908 the Jubilee mine itself was coming to an end as a gold producer so that Gluyas had been Manager from start to finish. For that reason he was considered to be the Father of the Rand. His long service and successful work had been greatly valued by his Board of Directors, and to mark its appreciation of his sterling qualities and faithful management the Board not only gave Gluyas a £500 bonus but granted him six months' holiday on full pay. Unfortunately he caught scarlet fever, followed by pneumonia and died on the very day he was to have left South Africa. His funeral was held on Whit Monday. The obituary in the *Cornish Post and Mining News* under the heading *A Pioneer Randite and a Worthy Cornishman* praised him not only for having had a genial and hearty manner but above all for being popular. Evidence for this was apparent at his funeral attended by over 400 native employees of the mine along with numerous mine officials and other mine managers making up some thirty carriages in the cortege. Gluyas was buried in Braamfontein Cemetery, Johannesburg, alongside his wife who had died in 1897. The Chairman of Directors remarked "We feel we have lost a personal friend."[41]

Another long serving manager on the Rand was James Johns, Manager of the Ginsberg, Randfontein and Witwatersrand Deep mines. On the death of his wife in 1921 he returned home to Cornwall with his two children. He was a cousin of J. Harry Johns as was Samuel Johns, Manager of the Consolidated Langlaagte mine. Other Cornishmen who managed gold mines during the industry's formative years were Jacob Laity at the York Mine, Sidney P. Jennings at the Crown Reef mine and H.S. Vyvian of St. Germans at the Robinson Deep mine. When Vyvian died at Cape Town in 1897 aged 47 years his death was considered a great loss by the men at the mine.[42]

A Manager's pay was very lucrative. The Jumpers mine offered a manager's salary of £1,200 p.a. in 1890 and when Gluyas died in 1908 his salary was £2,500 p.a. A successful manager was often presented with a bonus – J. Harry Johns had £500 in 1896[43] – and they often received gifts in appreciation of their services to a particular mine,or when leaving for home. The employees of the Nourse Deep mine gave James Donald a diamond ring[44] while at the Glendenhuis mine a gold watch was presented to John Pope.[45] There were also disadvantages, for the position of manager was not only a position of responsibility but carried with it an element of risk. Joseph Jeffrey of Linkinhorne had been mining in Cornwall and the U.S.A. before arriving in South Africa in 1892. While Manager of the Randfontein mine he appeared before the Landdrost on a charge of falsifying two mine boys' passes. Although Jeffrey pleaded not guilty, adding that the compound manager could have altered them, as manager he was held responsible and ordered to pay a £7-10s fine or undergo five days' imprisonment. He chose to pay the fine.[46] Jeffrey was later Manager of the Ginsberg mine and then the South Randfontein mine. Peter Quentrall Treloar of Crowan, Manager of the Princess Mine was charged for not taking sufficient caution when one of his men, J.H. Glasson, was seriously hurt.[47] Treloar had only been in the job a few months having previously been Underground Manager at the Lancaster mine where W.H. Rodda of St. Just was Manager. William Thomas Reed of Sithney who had been Manager of the Heriot mine had only just been appointed Manager of Glencairn mine when he tragically met his death. He dropped 180 feet when the rope to the cage in which he was being brought to the surface broke – when extricated from the cage he was found to be still alive but expired upon being brought to the surface.[48]

Harry Teague, an Underground Manager at Tincroft mine, Redruth went to South Africa, having secured the position of Manager of the French Western Nigel and Nigel mines on the recommendation of J. Harry Johns. Unfortunately Teague committed suicide within a month by shooting himself. Apparently he had made a fortune by speculation but then lost it all. His funeral was well attended by a great number of Cornish. By 1908 another Cornishman called Curnow was Manager of the Nigel group of mines.

One criticism levelled at the Cornish Managers in South Africa was that they tended to favour Cornishmen. J. Harry Johns certainly secured Teague his position and for James H. Andrews of Penzance, the post of Manager of the East Orion mine[50] but Johns always maintained, like Oats at Kimberley, that men were employed on their ability and merit rather than the fact they were Cornish. Similar criticism was aimed at Treloar who took a number of his own men with him to the Princess mine. It was considered normal practice amongst the Mining Companies.[51] Neither was it unusual for Cornish Mine Managers to replace each other. When J. Harry Johns left the Ferreira mine in 1902 his post as Manager was filled by Joseph Richards of Pool who had been Manager of the Ferreira Deep mine for nearly fourteen years.[52] Richards was in turn replaced at the Ferreira Deep mine by another Cornishman, called Mitchell.

Gold mining was a much younger industry when compared to either the Cornish tin or copper industries but the more modern approach led many Cornish mine managers to make the trip to South Africa not to work but see for themselves the new techniques. Captain Josiah Thomas returned to Camborne having derived great benefit from his trip to South Africa.[53] Thomas was the Manager of Dolcoath, Cornwall's premier copper and tin mine. Both of his sons gained mining experience on the gold fields. Ernest was Manager of the Worcester mine before he left in 1896 to become a Consulting Engineer for a group of mines in Western Australia. R. Arthur had been a Pioneer of the Barberton gold mines before becoming Manager of the City & Suburban mine. When his father retired R. Arthur returned to Cornwall to take his place as Manager of Dolcoath. Later he became a Director of Dolcoath and Chairman of the Cornish Chamber of Mines, being awarded an O.B.E. for his services to the mining industry. His death in 1949, aged 82 years, removed from Cornish public life one of its last remaining figures of a famous generation.[54] Josiah Paull managed the Ferreira Deep mine before returning to Cornwall to become Manager, first at Clitters mine, Gunnislake and then South Crofty mine, Camborne.[55] Another Manager of South Crofty, James Thomas of Redruth, had also been in South Africa as Superintendent of the New Heart Gold Mining Company. Cornwall's mining industry certainly benefited from the experience gained overseas and men who returned to run Cornish mines were seen as the first returns on the huge investment of men and machines that was flowing out of Cornwall to the 'Land of Gold' in South Africa.[56] In reality, though, with the rapidly falling number of Cornish mines – 302 in 1873 to 81 in 1880 [57] –

it was South Africa rather than Cornwall that gained the most from the Cornish managers.

Johannesburg was officially founded on 20th September 1886 and from a couple of tin-shacks and half a dozen tents[58] known as Ferreira's Camp it soon began to resemble an American city.[59] The Cousin Jack Corner where Cornishmen used to assemble on Saturday nights to exchange gossip became lost under bricks and mortar[60] with well built houses and wide streets and tram cars running through them. The population of 3000 in 1886 rapidly increased to 30,000 in 1890, 80,000 in 1894 to reach an official census figure of 102,078 in 1896.[61] The mines on the Rand goldfield spread from East to West some thirty odd miles from the town centre. Hugh Lanion Hall in August 1889 called Johannesburg a dusty mining village.[62] When William James of Pendeen, arrived in 1892 Johannesburg was small; the Nourse Mines were worked with a whim or derrick instead of a head gear. The City & Suburban was bare veldt and a few houses in Fordsburg and Jeppestown.[63] Charles Downing from Camborne came to Johannesburg in 1889 when the town was an infant. He stayed eighteen months before moving on to California. When he returned in 1897 he was amazed at its growth remembering only three small stamp batteries – one on the Jubilee, one on the City & Suburban and one on the Robinson. The Wemmer had a windlass hoisting gear. His brother William had "got out" the first foundation on the Ferreira.[64]

Travel to the land of gold became easier as railway links connected Cape Town and Johannesburg in September 1892, Delgoa Bay and Johannesburg in October 1894 and Durban and Johannesburg in December 1895. William Jas. Hancock from Penzance was just one of the many Cornishmen who helped with the railway construction. He later worked as a foreman carpenter at the Robinson Deep mine.[65] The longest railway embankment near Krugersdorp was built by the son of Capt. J. Prisk of Redruth.[66] Mining skills could easily be adapted to railway construction and many Cornish miners had worked on the building of the North Cornwall Railway 1886-95 between Launceston and Wadebridge.

Despite the initial uncertainty of Johannesburg's future at least two Cornishmen had the vision to see that it was not going to be merely a boom town and suffer the fate of Barberton. In the very year Johannesburg was founded Paul Henwood the Cornish Pioneer from Tideford opened a small wood and iron store[67] facing Market Square. Such was his belief that Johannesburg had a future that in 1888 his two-year old store was pulled down and a new double-storied building – the first of its kind – was built in its place. Those who thought Johannesburg had but a short future called the palatial edifice, Henwood's Folly,[68] but Henwood was proved right. By 1891 the building itself was too small for Henwood's rapidly expanding business and Paul Henwood came himself to Johannesburg taking the decision to rebuild yet again. A three storey building on a site 50 feet by 200 feet

Henwood's store in Johannesburg 1888.

Henwood's rebuilt store of 1892.

arose in its place along with Henwood's Arcade, where a small band or orchestra played in the afternoons or evenings.[69]

The other Cornishman with vision was Samson Rickard Stuttaford. He purchased the corner of Pritchard and Russik Streets for £40,000 and by 1898 his company had expanded into storing, packing and shipping.[70] Many people had considered him mad[71] at the time, but the business flourished and his store became a permanent landmark. Just opposite Stuttafords was the Grand National Hotel which many Cornish patronised:

> *At the corner of Pritchard and Van Brandis was Heath's Hotel, a corner that was to become known as Cousin Jack Corner. It was here on Saturday night that Cornishmen and their womenfolk would gather to promenade down the length of the street and back, exchange news of friends and family, at home in Cornwall or scattered all over the developing mining communities strung along the line of the reef. The men would recognise each other as Cornish by the Cornishman's handshake, the palm outwards, followed usually by 'where be'ee workin'' or 'ows everybody'ome?'*[72]

Another Cornish landmark in Johannesburg was Mounts Bay House – a draper's store at the intersection of Pritchards Street with Eloff Street. The owner – Charles Chudleigh – had arrived in South Africa from his home in the Scilly Isles in 1875. Born in 1854, Chudleigh on leaving school, had become an apprentice to a Penzance outfitters. In South Africa he began work for a general merchant at Queenstown in the Eastern Cape, but when gold was discovered at Pilgrim's Rest, like so many young Cornishmen he went in search of fortune. He was unlucky and left early in 1879 to work at Pretoria, Potchefstroom and Kimberley before returning to Queenstown. There he married and, having made enough money to start his own business was joined by his brother Sam. In 1890 the Chudleighs came to Johannesburg and established a firm of drapers; their advertisements even appeared regularly in the Cornish newspapers. In 1893 when the first municipal town council of Johannesburg was created, Chudleigh was elected Vice Chairman of the Health Committee. In the same year Chudleigh embarked on the first phase of a rebuilding programme for his premises.

An early Cornish Pioneer of the Transvaal gold rush, John Albert Baragwanath, turned his hand to running a hotel. Built just outside Johannesburg, the Concordia Hotel was the ideal stop for travellers en route for Johannesburg from Kimberley. Once in Johannesburg itself Cornish miners could head for Frederick Street where:

> *Mrs Doney from Penzance ran a most popular boarding house. It was a lively place and on Sundays, the miners would invite their compatriots. Very often 200 Cornish miners would sit down to a Sunday dinner of*

Stuttaford's store with the Grand National Hotel opposite.

Chudleigh's drapers shop next to Heath's Hotel.

*Cornish pasty, heartily relished and washed down with beer, the beer being provided by themselves, not Mrs. Doney.*73

The Cornish out shopping in addition to visiting Stuttafords and Chudleighs, could call in at Kneebones the Outfitters and Penrose the Jewellers in Commissioner Street. In 1910 a letter from South Africa boasted that there was scarcely a business in the city of Johannesburg in which a Cornishman was not to the fore. There was Bailey for beef, Chudleigh for clothes, Pearce for pop (ginger), Penrose for pipes, and Wallace for whiskies, to name but a few. The Cornish must have felt very much at home, for Johannesburg was indeed a suburb of Cornwall.74

Two of the most wealthy and generous Cornishmen in Johannesburg were Albert Charles Collins from Stithians and William Mountstephens from Falmouth. They had much in common, for not only were they born in the same year – 1859 – they were also Methodists, non-smokers, and teetotallers. They arrived in South Africa in 1880, originally having planned to emigrate to the States but when at Plymouth, rather than wait for a ship to New York, they boarded one immediately for Cape Town. From there they moved on to Port Elizabeth, then to Grahamstown and finally Kimberley where they made their fortune, not as diamond diggers but as builders. In 1886 they arrived in Johannesburg and set up in partnership their own building business, becoming,

> *wealthy as a result of their hard work as builders, their shrewdness, their sound business investments and their sobriety of life. Mountstephens married and lived simply in a pleasant house in Parktown. Collins remained a bachelor and lived extremely frugally in a room in Pritchard Street.*75

Both Mountstephens and Collins were staunch supporters of the Methodist Church in Johannesburg. One of the first couples to be married in the church on 29th August 1888 were John Henry Marshall from Penzance (who ran a quarry business in the Orange Free State) and Sophia Lucy née Lehmon. Sophia was one of the first Sunday School teachers at the church and her two sisters also married Penzance men. The three sisters must have made some kind of a record as they all, along with their husbands, celebrated their golden weddings. Sophia died in 1942.76

Another Cornish builder in the mould of Mountstephens and Collins, in that he was also a teetotaller and non-smoker, came from St. Ives to South Africa in 1876 – the journey on the *Asiatic* taking forty-four days. William Berriman

> *was amongst the first on the Rand. Not long after his arrival in Johannesburg, which was then only a scattering of tin shanties, Mr. Berriman was asked by the officials of the Standard Bank if he would take*

*a quantity of bullion through to the coast. The feat Mr. Berriman
accomplished without any escort and the money was delivered safely.*

Berriman was not to stay in Johannesburg for he returned to Natal to set up in
partnership with F. Stevens as a builder and contractor. He married a Miss
Jennings and they had five children (one – W. Berriman – becoming a dental
surgeon). On his death in December 1912 the paper described William Berriman as
the St. Ives man who built Maritzburg, for he had laid the first water mains in
Pietermaritzburg, built the Town Hall, Legislative Buildings, Colonial Offices,
Post Office, Government House, the Asylum and many other major buildings. It
was said the splendid workmanship exemplified in the buildings stand as a lasting
testimony to the deceased's thoroughness. Although often asked he had always
refused to stand on the council.[77]

The administration of Johannesburg was first carried out by a Diggers'
Committee and then a Sanitary Board of which two of its seven nominated
members were Cornishmen – Charles Arthur Claud Tremeer and Charles William
Deecker. Tremeer on coming to South Africa in 1875 had seen action in the Gauka
and Galeka Wars as a member of the Cape Frontier Armed and Mounted Police.
He had also served under Wood but with the discovery of gold was soon on the
Rand where he set up the business of Tremeer and Cummings. Charles Deecker
arrived on the Rand with his wife early in January 1887 after a long but pleasant
trip of a month by ox-wagon through the Free State[78] from Natal. The Deeckers
began publication of the *Transvaal Mining Argus*, the first daily paper on the Rand,
the first issue being published on 25th February 1887. They operated from an
office of canvas over a wooden frame and carried out their journalistic duties
under exceptionally onerous conditions.[79] The paper itself was first printed in
Pretoria but then Deecker bought and moved the machinery of his last newspaper –
the *East London Advertiser* – to Johannesburg. The Deeckers ran the *Argus* for
seven years, Charles being assisted by his wife Mary and his brother Sam plus
another Cornishman by the name of Holman. Mary Deecker was in fact one of the
first women to live in Johannesburg as were two other Cornish women – a Mrs.
Courtney Acutt and Sophia Lucy Marshall.

The next paper to be published on the Johannesburg streets was the *Standard
and Transvaal Mining Chronicle* on 12th March 1887. It obviously had Cornish
connections – or at least was aimed at a Cornish audience – for early issues
contained an occasional series known as *Cornish Yarns*. Titles included *Old
Nancy's Cow* and *Cornish Ferrits!* Its great rival was the *Diggers News* which in
one edition included the following poem poking fun at President Kruger's rule
over the influx of foreigners or *Uitlanders* of which so many were obviously
Cornish:

My name is Oom Paul
And I'm boss of the Transvaal
*And Lord of one and all.*80

When the two papers combined in 1890 to become *The Standard & Diggers News* there was still a Cornish flavour about the paper which ran for a time a column called *Cornishman's Corner*. This was not surprising, as its Editor for a while was Cornishman Moses Roberts, previously Editor of the Kimberley *Daily Independent*. Two other Kimberley newspaper men reached Johannesburg although Cornish brothers Josiah and John Angove had a much more eventful journey than the Deeckers. Angove

> *shifted his plant from Potchefstroom, swept away by the gold rush and lost much of his type by a wagon turning turtle in the Vaal River, so that his journal for a time presented a very 'Pi-bald' appearance.*81

The Angoves published the first evening paper – *The Evening News* – in Johannesburg. Never able to stay in a place for very long Josiah Angove, by 1894, had moved to Port Elizabeth where he established yet another newspaper – *The Looker On*. Joseph Dunn, a former journalist for the *Cornishman* had been Editor of the *Natal Advertiser* at Durban for some five years before being appointed to the Editorial staff of the Johannesburg *Star* in 1896. With the *News* supporting Kruger and the *Star* Rhodes, Cornish newspaper men found themselves in opposite camps.

The Deeckers were influential and prominent figures in Johannesburg's early history. Mary helped to raise money – £5,000 in one morning82 – which helped fund the building of Johannesburg's first hospital, whilst Charles was Chairman of the Hospital Board for a time. He was also instrumental in organising the first horse race in Johannesburg on the 1st January 1887; the one and a half mile course ran between the Ferreira and Wemmer mines. Later the Deeckers moved to Krugersdorp where they published *The Krugersdorp Times & Roodepoort Mail*. It must have been tragic for the Deeckers to have to record the death of their own child in December 1895. Their son was balancing on a pole over the York Dam when he fell in and drowned.83

Early law enforcement on the Rand owed much to one of the most intriguing of all the Cornishmen (already mentioned in Chapter 3) to be found in South Africa. Llewyllen May (or Frederick de Witt Tossel, as he now called himself) was to have his name engraved in the annals of the history of the town forever and ensure him a particular place in the history of the Z.A.R.P. (Zauid Afrikaansche Politie or the Old South Africa Republics police force).84 Arriving on the Rand from Vryburg he recalled much later:

I became so broke that I went to Pretoria, presented my letters of introduction to his Honour President Kruger and Judge Esseeln, and as consequence, I became Sergeant in the first Police Force for the Witwatersrand. From there I was appointed to Krugersdorp in February 1888.[85]

Tossel was obviously a remarkable character, being described as a man of great physical strength but with his knowledge of languages he was considered by his superiors as one of the outstanding men in the force.[86] Within two years of joining the force, Tossel was appointed Police Chief of Krugersdorp, the appointment itself being unusual in that it was the one and only occasion that the President – who regarded Krugersdorp as his Kindergarten – chose a person from outside the so-called 'Pretoria Establishment' to fill any government position in the town which had been named in his honour.[87] Tossel's jurisdiction lay between Magaliesburg and Gatsrand:

Llewellyn May alias Frederick de Witt Tossel.

When I took over the police organisation of the new district... Plenty of prospecting was going on practically everywhere, scenes and happenings were frequently in evidence on pay days, which called for both brute force and tact to deal with... Womenfolk were scarce and there were men in plenty so for distraction the bars and canteens were popular resorts. One individual named Perkins, a Cousin Jack, like myself never used to miss a big binge on his pay day.[88]

In saying that Perkins was a Cousin Jack like myself Tossel comes the closest to revealing his true identity – that of a Cornishman, although President Kruger *was* apparently aware of his origins.[89] Tossel makes no mention, however, of two other episodes that have become part of the legend of this Cornish lawman.

One incident tells how on his arrival in Krugersdorp, which was more like the sort of lawless town to be found in the American Wild West, Tossel had first to tame the town's nuisance, a big burly miner called Adriaan Vys. The first meeting between the two men erupted into a saloon brawl with Vys ending up in a pathetic heap on the floor his face "a bloody mess".[90]

The other episode is even more like a scene from the Wild West and involved a bank raid by two outlaws. Having knocked the Bank Manager senseless the two robbers made off with £1,935 in notes, £1,500 in gold and some hard silver. Tossel immediately gave chase and, when his own horse began to fade, he commandeered a race-horse called Atlas. A ten-mile chase followed with a shoot-out – during which Tossel shot one of the outlaws in the arm. With the arrival of reinforcements both robbers were arrested and later sentenced to 25 years hard labour. Although the money was recovered, the gold and silver had been lost during the chase, but the Bank still presented Tossel with a gold watch bearing the inscription 'Awarded by the Standard Bank to Sergeant Tossel for his brave action in Krugersdorp on the 29th of August 1889'.[91]

The incident earned Tossel further promotion for within a couple of months President Kruger elevated him to the rank of Lieutenant. In December 1895 at Varley's Hotel, Krugersdorp, a public banquet was held in honour of Tossel on his further promotion and transfer as Chief Detective to the newly created Johannesburg Investigation Service.[92]

It was not clear until the middle of the 1890's that Johannesburg was to be a permanent establishment on the Rand. Lewis Mitchell, who visited Johannesburg in May 1887, despite finding that building was going ahead at a pace considered it hardly justified.[93] It says much about early Johannesburg that in 1888, long before main sewers were even thought of, the first telephone had been installed.[94] One Cornishman who lived in Johannesburg described it as a health hazard claiming it was an unpaved, undrained and jerry built city of death.[96] For all too many leaving Cornwall fate lay not with fortune but with an early grave. In March 1890 one Cornishman wrote home that:

> *Camp fever is all the go – over 500 sick – some days over 20 have been covered up in the cemetery.*[95]

One writer has estimated that in the early days of Johannesburg between one third and one half of all deaths were caused by contagious diseases like typhoid and fever.[97] Many of the deaths were of Cornishmen such as William Bottrell and Gabriel Cosley from St. Just who had only been in Johannesburg a few months before they both died from typhoid.[98] The same occurred to William Jeffry and William Hunkin, both from Pendeen.[99] Justinian Hosking – a 25 year old miner from St. Just – had been in Johannesburg but five months when he contracted typhoid. Attempting to return to Cornwall he died at sea.[100] Scores of Cornishmen who died from either typhoid or fever in South Africa are listed amongst the pages of the Cornish newspapers. Cornwall itself was not unaware of typhoid, there being outbreaks in Redruth in 1896, in Camborne and St. Agnes in 1898 and Flushing in February 1899.

In 1889 the state of Johnnesburg's sanitation had been called a standing disgrace and the situation had hardly improved when at a Sanitary Board meeting on the 10th September 1896 the medical officer remarked that the Johannesburg death rate was the highest of any civilised town in the world.[101] The ill-health of W. Tresize of Camborne was reported in the *Cornishman* as being attributed to President Kruger's insanitation.[102]

It was a serious matter for as the *Post* had stated earlier that year:

Every mail seems to bring news of death from accident or disease. This week we hear of three deaths of Gwennap men and other cases of men in hospital while St. Agnes, Camborne, Redruth and St. Just are startled almost every week by the news of deaths of even young and stalwart men at Johannesburg... those who emigrate... ought to be tough, temperate and cautious men who will remember the conditions under which they are working.[103]

Commenting again on the many deaths a few months later the *Post* compared Johannesburg's death rate of 50 per 1,000 to that of Truro's which was only 14 per 1,000. It also suggested that, as the large percentage of Cornishmen who succumb to the ravages of fever were young men, then perhaps only those over 30 years of age should go as they seemed to have a better chance of standing extremes of heat and cold, privation and driving work.[104]

William Hosken on being questioned about the high mortality rate of Cornish miners in South Africa put it down largely to the men's own ignorance of elementary principles of sanitation and their careless manner of living.[105]

With the vast extreme of heat and cold, especially working in the mines, it was not surprising that many Cornish miners died from pneumonia, such as Benjamin Wallis, who had been six years in South Africa and was described as one of the best draught players in St. Just, and Thomas Hattam, also from St. Just.[106]

When Arnold Whitburn, an Assayer on the Rand for twelve years, died from a combination of typhoid and pneumonia, his death was the fourth recorded within two months of St. Day miners in South Africa.[107] As late as 1897 a number of Cornishmen from Tuckingmill were content to be employed at Cape Town at about £15 a month which taking into account the better sanitary arrangements was considered equal to 20 shillings a day at Johannesburg.[108] Jack Clemo from Tuckingmill, who did reside in Johannesburg, died there from an illness the same year.[109] There was a smallpox epidemic at Johannesburg in 1893-95 although according to the Cornish press it seemed endemic, the *Cornishman* noting in 1896 that cases of smallpox there and other parts of the Rand were increasing.[110] Less than two years later more letters to Camborne from Johannesburg told of an outbreak of smallpox.[111] It was not just at Johannesburg either, for James Trembath died from smallpox in 1898 at Kimberley. The following year at Johannesburg Richard Henry Rowe, a Cornish blacksmith at Germiston succumbed to smallpox[112] along with Joseph James, a prominent Wesleyan and Shift Boss at the Durban Deep mine.[113]

Another frequent cause of death was dysentery. John Stephens of Redruth who was employed at the York mine died from it at Krugersdorp; so did John T. Rule – a former jeweller of Camborne. When John Permewan the youngest son of Dr. J. Permewan of Redruth and a former student of the Redruth School of Mines died from heart disease, he was only 27 years old. Permewan's funeral at the Johannesburg cemetery was attended by a large number of fellow Cornish miners from the Nourse Deep mine, where he had worked for seven years.[114] Some unfortunate Cornish met with death after less than a year in the land of gold. Matthew Peak from St. Just was one and another, who died in the same year – 1896-, was John Michell of Camborne, who had not been there for more than a few weeks.[115] Both men left behind in Cornwall widows and children; in neither case was the cause of death recorded by the newspaper. A study of the Cornish newspapers shows this was the rule rather than the exception. The deaths of Richard Gerrans, B.V. Rowse, Joseph Phillips, Samuel Stephens, John Terril (the last three from Redruth), Joseph Keverne, Simon Hocking, Walter Peters (St. Agnes), Frederick C. Bennetto, Charles Bennett, William Henry Roberts are others whose cause of death is unrecorded. This lack of information makes it difficult to draw any valid conclusion as to how many Cornish died from disease – or from which disease – during the formative years of South Africa's gold industry. What is clear, however, is that the number of deaths amongst the Cornish – in particular the miners – was extremely high. In April 1896 the *Post* commented that the mortality among St. Just men in South Africa had been very high of late, every mail bringing news of one or more deaths.[116]

Later that year the *Post* commenting on the high number of Cornish deaths in South Africa remarked that with such a great population of Cornish at Johannesburg it would be strange indeed if there were no deaths.[117] This could hardly be a consolation to those in Cornwall left to suffer the loss of their relatives and friends.

Cornishmen of all ages – and from all parts of Cornwall – died from accidents in the gold mines. Henry Carveth of St. Agnes fell 750 feet in the Glen Deep mine[118] William James Rodda, one time landlord of the Basset Arms, Pool, was repairing a shaft in the Woolhunter mine with his brother Frederick when the ground suddenly gave way and killed him. It was a tragic coincidence that on the very day he was buried in South Africa his mother, back in Cornwall, attended the funeral of his father and nephew. Rodda left a wife and three brothers in Africa, a mother and brother in Penzance.[119] When 21 year old Bertie Cowling from Camborne fell to his death down a 180 foot shaft he earned the sad distinction of being the first white man ever killed at Ferreira Deep mine.[120] Walter Harris, Shift Boss from St. Just, was found at the bottom of a shaft in a terrible condition after falling 600 feet at the Ferreira mine[121] and within three months a similar fate befell Richard Hocking – also from St. Just.[122] Nicholas Davey, who was described as a young Cornish miner and an active member of the Devoran Cricket Club had just married before leaving for South Africa. Having worked but two weeks at the Robinson mine he fell down a shaft and was killed.[123] Richard Ivey, a Cornish carpenter was also killed when he fell down a 220 foot shaft.[124] Despite having survived a snow slide which had nearly killed him whilst mining in Arizona – he was pulled out by his brother – Edmund Harvey from Redruth died in a mining accident at Ferreira mine one week before he was to be married. Although another of his brothers went to his assistance, this time his luck had run out. The paper commented that Johannesburg could do with more miners like Harvey and his brothers describing them as quiet, unassuming, hardworking, highly respected young Cornishmen.[125]

Charles Harvey of Chacewater died at the Robinson mine under a fall of rocks, and a similar accident occurred to Samuel John Peters of Gwennap who was crushed to death at the Simmer & Jack mine. James Henry Wallis also met with an accident at the Simmer & Jack and died two weeks after his leg had been amputated. Both Justus Angwin and George Eddy died from injuries received in mining accidents whereas Fred John Bray was a victim of gas at the Henry Nourse mine where his father, Charles, was Captain. At the same mine Joseph Blewett of Camborne was killed when a kibble hit him on the head.

Fatal accidents involving skips were quite frequent. W. Taylor of St. Just was killed when a skip overturned at the Balmoral Reef mine (his brother had been drowned three years earlier in 1893 when the Cornish mine Wheal Owles had flooded). A skip which struck Fred James at the Treasury mine resulted in his death, while a month earlier at the Langlaagte Deep mine three Cornish miners – Fred Oliver, Alfred Greenwood and Harry Crouch – were killed when they were all tipped out of a skip and plummeted down a 1,280 foot shaft.[126] Another Cornish miner, Charles Trudgeon, although badly injured escaped death by clinging to some timbers. William Francis and Frederick Bowden, who were both from St. Day were with a Camborne miner in a skip descending a shaft at the Simmer & Jack mine when it was hit by a piece of falling timber. All three miners were mangled to death[127] and John Luke, a timber man at the Glencairn mine, was just one more Cornish miner to be killed in a descending skip that broke free.

Accidents involving explosions, although less frequent, often resulted in a far greater loss of life. A dynamite explosion killed four Europeans and fifteen natives at the New Kleinfontein mine – the Europeans were all Cornishmen – J. Ball (Truro), John Nicholls (St. Day), J. Martin (Redruth) and John Oats (St. Just).[128] The following year – 1897 – a mysterious explosion on the 13th April at the

Langlaagte mine claimed 34 lives including 8 white men – of which 7 were Cornishmen. All the men had died from the inhalation of fumes. Three of the dead Cornishmen – John Barnes, Henry Caddy and William Brown – were married. The other four – Richard Brown, Richard Mitchell, Arthur Paull and Ronald G. Thomas – were single. Brothers Richard and William Brown were found lying dead together, one having in his possession a ticket showing he had been due to leave for Cornwall the following day. The "melancholy and gruesome" job of recovering the bodies fell to John Treloar – another Cornishman – who with two others was the first to descend the mine following the accident.[129] Thomas Henry Hocking, a 38 year old miner from Tuckingmill, blasted himself to death at the Crown Deep mine. His funeral was well attended by fellow Cornishmen John Craze (Mine Foreman), John Knucky (Shift Boss), J.H. Hocking, G.W. Hocking, Joseph W. Hocking (three nephews), Thomas Pearce (Shift Boss) plus some seventy others. In Cornwall Hocking left a widow and six children.[130] When Solomon J. Edyvean was killed at the North Randfontein mine this popular employee on the property had only just returned from Cornwall and his home town of Helston. His funeral was attended by his brothers R.J. Edyvean and Fred Edyvean, his brothers-in-law H. Thomas, A. Thomas and F. Thomas plus W. Morcom (engineer) and many more.[131] So often the funerals of those who died in the mines were on a large scale as the attendance would include virtually all those employed at the mine. Thus when F.E. Parkes of St. Columb, who was described as one of the most prominent and generally popular Cornishmen who have emigrated in recent years, died at the Ferreira mine, his funeral was so well attended that the great mine stopped in respect.[132]

In 1895, a Cornishman who returned to Cornwall from South Africa claimed:
the papers do not report the deaths that occur in the hospitals. I found around Johannesburg in the hospitals that about 10 people were dying every week – mostly white men under 30 years of age. One week the number of deaths... was 25.[133]

Some mining accidents happened above ground although they could be no less as horrific, as when John Retallack of Camborne fell into a cyanide tank – he was buried at Krugersdorp Cemetery.[134] Tom Bickle – a representative of the Cornish engineering firm of Harvey & Co. Hayle – had visited mining camps in Mexico, Canada and the U.S.A. but met his death at Johannesburg when he was trying to remedy defects of some machinery just erected.[135]

Thankfully not all the mining accidents on the Rand ended in death; James Rule of Camborne was lucky to escape after having a serious fall whilst erecting some mining machinery. He ended up in hospital with a double fracture of the leg below the knee, and a broken nose and arm.[136] Joshua Rowe escaped serious injury when he was hit on the back by falling rock at the Crown Reef mine and on the same day the three St. Day men were mangled by a skip, John Harper of Redruth suffered a broken thigh.[137] John White Ellis of St. Just lost an arm and an eye in an accident on the very day his wife reached Cape Town to join him from Cornwall.[138] Thomas Eastlake, a Cornish miner working at the Ferreira mine, had a miraculous escape when he fell fifty feet down the ladder way of the new shaft. His only injuries were two broken ribs and a cut head.[139] Capt. Rodda was thrown out of his trap and sustained some injuries to his side, although fortunately they were not serious,[140] and the *Cornubian* was sorry to hear that Mr. Kitto of St. Day, now in South Africa, had met with a slight accident to his thumb.[141]

There were of course deaths unconnected with mining. Harry Rodda, a Cornish grocer at Johannesburg died in 1896. John Roseveare (Paul Henwood's nephew) was killed in Johannesburg the same year when he was knocked down by a tram.[142] Roseveare had retired from Henwoods; he had also been a Director of the Natal Bank. In 1881 he had been Mayor of Maritzburg. Another Cornish Mayor was S.J. Sowden from St. Cleer. He had built up a successful business which was one of the most prosperous in Bloemfontein. He was elected Mayor of Bloemfontein in 1896 but died two years later, aged only 42 years.[143] Thomas Nicholl an auctioneer from Redruth died at Port Elizabeth and J.W. Hoskins a printer from Truro died at Cape Town. Henry Boase from St. Ives, one of the oldest and most respected inhabitants of Somerset West died aged 88 years.[144]

At least one Cornishman was murdered in Johannesburg. Thomas James was found on Tuesday 15th March 1892 with his skull smashed in, having been robbed of his gold watch and chain.[145] He left a widow and six children home in Cornwall at St. Just. John Craze on the other hand narrowly escaped a violent death when he was mugged on the Rand by three whites.[146]

Samuel Rogers of Gwinear died while duck shooting. Apparently a native boy fell into a dam and Rogers in trying to save him was pulled under and drowned.[147] Death by drowning was also the fate of six people from Redruth in what the *Cornubian* described as a *Terrible Boating Disaster* in Johannesburg. The tragic incident occurred on the 17th April 1895 at the Wemmer Dam when John Bawden – an engineer driver at the Wemmer pumping station – and four ladies – Mrs James Hammil, her sister Mary Mitchell Tremberth, Mrs. William Hammil (née Launder) and Mrs. Eustace – with three infant children went for an afternoon's sail. One of the Mrs. Hammils had declined to join the party but despite that, the boat was still overloaded, and it capsized. The Mrs. Hammil on the bank jumped into the water in an attempt to save her child but alas she had got in among the reeds, and entangled in their cruel clutches sank with her child. Bawden also became entangled in the reeds whilst attempting to save the other Mrs. Hammil and they – along with Miss Mitchell and another child – drowned. Only Mrs. Eustace, who could swim a little, managed to grab the third child and cling to the upturned boat holding on until rescue finally came. The six bodies were recovered the next day and at the funeral later the four hearses were followed by over 50 carriages containing relatives and friends.[148]

As there were comparatively few Cornish women in the mining areas it is hardly surprising that accounts of their deaths rarely figured in the newspapers. The greatest danger they faced was often childbirth. Mrs. Treloar of Tuckingmill, who ran the California Boarding House in Johannesburg and who died within four weeks of giving birth to a son is but one example.[149] In some cases it was the infant children who died. Cornish couple Charles and Annie Pyatt lost their 3 month & 22 day old daughter at Johannesburg[150] and another Cornishwoman (not named) lost her child through lack of medical treatment.[151]

At least one Cornish woman – Lillian Ball from Camborne – committed suicide in Johannesburg.[152] Women would hardly have been encouraged to leave Cornwall in 1888, upon reading one Cornishman's opinion of Johannesburg where he claimed:

> *every man has a woman but they have no marriage certificates and the biggest men have their 'Tart' as they call them. All the bar girls are what they are and do a large business;but drink and disease puts them out of court in time. Sodom was destroyed on account of wickedness...*[153]

On the other hand they were probably more encouraged in 1895 to learn that in South Africa women were paid higher wages and there was employment for them in schools and many other occupations. The average wage for a domestic female servant was £22 – £27 a year although on the Rand 'she could receive as much as £40 – £50 or even £60 a year.[154] However, as late as 1897 the *Cornubian* claimed that women were probably put off going to South Africa by stories such as that of the wife of a Cornish miner:

> *sometimes after taking her walks abroad, she has been obliged to strip to the skin to rid her clothing of fleas, which live in the dry grass and multiply enormously. She has suffered severely from fever and has been almost frightened out of her life by snakes – one in her kitchen.*[155]

However, many Cornish women did go to live in South Africa. Lily Bawden left Redruth to marry Harry Williams – also Redruth – at Maritzburg Wesleyan Church and Minnie Rickard left Camborne to marry Richard Trezona, who worked at the Princess Roodepoort mine. Ellen Thomas from St. Just married William Nankervis of Botallack on the Rand. When Henrietta Spargo married William Nankervis both bride and groom were from Illogan. There were even first generation Cornish women in South Africa such as Mary Jane Brokensha, niece to Thomas Brokensha solicitor of Dundee, who married Alfred James Marshall. They received many presents from the bride's relatives in St. Just, Cornwall and spent their honeymoon in the Orange Free State.156 In order to get married in the Transvaal the law stated that the banns of marriage had to be published back in Cornwall as well.

When Edith Rodda left Redruth in 1895 a big gap was left in the ranks of Cornish vocalists. Arriving at Cape Town on the *S.S. Arundel Castle* on Monday July 1st she reached Johannesburg by rail on Thursday July 4th, where she was met by friends. She then married Ernest Davey, Manager of the Meyer & Charlton mine (son of T. Davey, Redruth) at St. Mary's Church on Saturday 6th July. Her father having remained in Redruth, she was given away by R.H. Heath.157 Robert Hainsworth Heath was in his day one of the best known musicians in Cornwall. He had been the organist of the Redruth Weslyan Chapel and not only had he composed the popular song *Kitty Cornish* but had produced his second volume of Cornish carols in September 1891. Heath was appointed organist of St. Mary's Church, Johannesburg at a handsome stipend158 in 1894. At a farewell concert held in his honour at Druids Hall, Redruth, the Redruth Freemasons voted their fellow Brother-Mason a purse of money; he was also sent money from the Johannesburg boys.159 He left his home and was in South Africa by the end of the year being joined by his wife and family within a few months. Heath was certainly a driving force behind Cornish musicians on the Rand, and was responsible for the organisation of many music events at which Edith Davey (née Rodda) often performed.

Cornish music was much in evidence on the Rand especially since many of the mines had their own bands and choirs. The Nigel mine had a brass band which included Cornishmen John White and James Waters, (both from Redruth).160 One feature at Johannesburg which almost became an annual event was the contribution made by the Cornish at Christmas which is best described in the following report under the heading *Christmas in Darkest Africa:*

> *Christmas Eve – down Pritchard Street at 10.30 p.m. comes a waggon full of Cornishmen & Cornish lasses.Suddenly we heard the chords of the fine old carol "Sound sound your instrument of joy"*
>
> *Everyone without exception stopped and enjoyed the really good music. ' Earlier in the evening Tom Andrews (Illogan) had led the Ferreira Band on a march playing Cornish carols starting at 8p.m. under Chudleigh's verandah and ending up at the Goldfields Hotel which was owned by Messrs Hocking & Patterson. Hocking was from Penzance, his hotel being well frequented by Cornish*

The report ended with the comment:

> *My son, 'tes better than Doctors Medicine!*161

The Cornish miners who arrived in the land of gold from 1886 onwards certainly lived up to the description of roving miner and also gave confirmation that where ever a hole had been dug in the world a Cornishman would be found. For some it was no distance whatsoever to the Rand as they were already in the Transvaal working on the gold fields at Pilgrim's Rest and Barberton. S.J. Ferkin (Lanner) had been 18 years at Barberton and then, in 1892, rode four days on horseback to start work at the Glencairn mine. Another Cornishman – James Pellow – had also been in the Transvaal since 1874 and worked at the Sterling mine which had the first ever Reef Battery. James Eddy (St. Just) was just one of the scores of miners who made the short trip from Kimberley and the diamond fields to the Rand. Others in South Africa had slightly further to travel. John Trenwith (Penzance) was at the Cape in 1882 and arrived in Johannesburg in 1887 when there were no houses – only tin shanties. Richard Trevethan (Truro) had come to the Cape in 1877, having worked some three years in Moonta & Wallaroo in South Australia, although he did not make his way to the Rand until 1897. J.F. Hoskin came to Johannesburg in a mail coach whereas Edward Doble (Penzance) in 1889 had to journey all the way from Ladysmith, Natal by ox-wagon. Many Cornish miners came direct from Cornwall – such as James Oats (Chacewater), Charles Trenwith, J.G. Thomas (both Penzance), George Habe (Marazion), James Skewes (Goldsithney), Jack James (Breage), John Merrit (Gwennap), Josiah Wills, Edwin & James Jennings, Joseph Mitchell (all Redruth), John Angwin and John Lutey (both St. Just) the latter being a survivor of the Wheal Owles' flooding disaster. When James Bawden (Camborne) arrived on the Rand in 1893 there were only two or three levels working at that time. Bawden worked in the blacksmith's shop at Driefontein, East Rand. Some Cornishmen came from other parts of Britain, such as Vivian Rosewarne, who had worked at the East London Waterworks before moving to the Rand as an engineer on the Champ D'Or mine. John James (St. Just) had worked in Cumberland most of his life before going to the Rand in 1894. F. Peak (St. Just) was in Ireland working in 1895 but was on the Rand a year later. For many Cornishmen the trip to the land of gold was made from much further afield. William Spargo (Illogan) became Shift Boss at the Wemmer mine after some 8 years spent working at the Real del Monte silver mines, Mexico. C. Newton Lander (Redruth) – whose sister had drowned in the Wemmer Boating Disaster – was mining in Pachuca, Mexico in 1885 but was on the Rand by 1888. He then moved on in 1898 to Rhodesia. By 1907 he was back in Johannesburg as Manager of the Rose Deep Mine. Richard Penberthy (Carbis Bay) came to the Transvaal direct from Michigan U.S.A., whereas James Thomas and William Hosking left Butte City, U.S.A., in 1896 travelling to Johannesburg via Cornwall. W.J.T. Lanyon (Perranporth) had spent two years in the States and R. Hawkey (Truro) eight years there before going to the Rand. In 1895 John Arthur (Gwinear) had left Cornwall for the States where he worked as far north as Alaska and as far south as Texas before going to South Africa to work on the Rand at the Robinson Deep mine. William Henry Thomas, who had put down one of the first shafts on the Rand on the Old Nigel mine had previously worked in Norway, Michigan, Colorado and Utah between 1879-87. John Paul Northey spent some seven years in Utah at Salt Lake City before going to the Rand in 1896 to work at Knights Deep. James Harvey (St. Just) came to the Rand having worked fourteen years, mining near Lake Superior and J. Menhennet (Camborne) had been three years at Red Jacket, Lake Superior and Bingham Canyon, Utah, before coming to the Rand in 1898. Walter Pearce had spent fourteen years in the States and two years in Brazil before going to South Africa in 1897. James Stephens (Camborne) had worked for the John Taylor Company in India, California and Venezuela before coming to the Rand and William May had spent three years at the Mysore gold mine, India, coming to Johannesburg in 1899. J. Hodge had spent twenty-seven years in the copper mines of Chile before going to the Rand as Foreman Smith at the Wemmer mine. His son, who had been with him in Chile, accompanied him. John Harris (Lanner) had also worked in Chile, as well as Bolivia and Peru, before he went to the Rand. John Williams (Penzance) arrived on the Rand from Australia in 1891. Finally Ben Trembath (Churchtown) had worked in New Jersey (U.S.A.), Cape Town, Kimberley, Barberton and finally Johannesburg, but mostly on railway construction.[162]

These men show the extraordinary mobility of the Cornish miner and help to explain why the actual extent of the Cornish diaspora is extremely difficult to quantify.[163] Of seven men who left their homes in St. Just in March 1899, by November James Olds and Richard Hocking were the only two still in South Africa. William Thomas and William Mason had returned home, Amos Mason had died from fever, William Woodcock had been killed in a blasting explosion, whereas Henry Eddy had been buried alive.[164] Then there was the added complication that some of the Cornish on the Rand, though not even born in Cornwall, still saw themselves as Cornish. John Eastwick (Mexico) and W.C. Bray (Australia) both had fathers who came from Redruth.

From a number of letters and articles written to the Cornish press it is possible to build up a picture of what life must have been like for the Cornish miner in the land of gold although some of the points of view are conflicting. F.J. Tiddy, correspondent to the *Cornishman* and himself from the Scilly Isles wrote a number of articles showing what sort of life the Cornish miner actually led in South Africa and especially the Transvaal. Frederick Tiddy was not a man to mince his words – he was an outright imperialist and at times what he wrote appears – especially today – biased, racist, and offensive. Nevertheless he gives a flavour of the times, as well as providing interesting information;and occasionally some amusing anecdotes.

Describing the Cornish miner in Johannesburg he wrote:

A Cousin Jack sheds a lot of his clothes and perhaps more of his accent, in the land where his wages multiply by ten. At home his clothes and his *tongue stunk of the Bal. Here he is not a miner after he leaves work. He lives well, dresses well, enjoys himself well and invests in shares.*165

The Cornish miners apparently lived in comfortable rooms, built of galvanised iron and lined with wood or brick. They had their meals at a boarding house on the mine, and pay ranged from £5-10s to £6-10s a month. The miner ate well – meat three times a day, and many different dishes at each meal. The quantity was unlimited, and the variety great. Having probably risen at 5 a.m. the miner worked his 10-12 hour shift, ate his excellent meals and then his time was his own. The mining companies provided reading rooms, libraries with books and magazines of all kinds including copies of Cornish newspapers. At the Simmer & Jack mine the library was a fine building with billiard room and theatre attached. Most Saturday evenings, or on the pay day of each month miners generally travelled into Johannesburg, travelling first class on the train at a cost of 3d a mile.166

Tiddy also claimed the Cornish miners were a sober and well behaved lot and very very seldom did they figure in the law courts167 which is borne out by the papers of the day. Two who did, however, were William Henry Rule, who received four months' hard labour for theft from the Jumpers Mine,168 and Edwin Williams, who was caught illegally gold dealing.169 In 1894 there were apparently no postmen – you either had to send or fetch your own letter', but there must have been by 1896 for Cornishman Francis Long was fined £3-8-6 for hitting one!170

Sunday for many miners, if not working, was spent in Church or Chapel – the Cornish Methodists being particularly active and doing all in their power to ameliorate the conditions of the native labourers171 commented Tiddy. It was perhaps to appease the Methodists at home that Tiddy pointed out that,

*it was not considered irreligious to gamble here. Hundreds of church members enter the lotteries and deal in the share market. Religious men even swear a bit without getting off the Church roll.*172

A miner could thus try his luck with a ticket from the Phillips and Moss Sweep stake or lottery. Charles Bunney of Camborne did, and won himself £900.173 Jonathan Luke (Illogan) and William Gould (Redruth) were the lucky winners of £1,000 each in the Johannesburg Summer Horse races, better known as the Phillip Sweep Stake.174 However, it was the share market which, according to Tiddy, was the very heart and pulse of Johannesburg life.175 There was definitely money to be made and lost.

Movements in the Johannesburg share market were followed closely in Cornwall for many Cornish had invested their capital in the land of gold. When miners were doing well, their women folk in Cornwall wore ostrich feathers in their hats and handcrafted gold brooches often in the design of a crossed pick and shovel which were known as 'Cousin Jacks'. Miners on leave would gather daily in the Pendeen

Miners' Institute to study the newspapers, especially the South African ones sent home, with a view to deciding in which mine or mines to invest their capital and to which they should return to work. Such sessions were apparently well-attended when a miner had just arrived home with "hot tips".[176]

The Cornish miner could indulge in many forms of entertainment which included wrestling, boxing, horse racing, rock drilling contests and rugby. On 17th July 1897 at the Crown Reef mine the Redruth Johannesburgers gathered in a room where hung a placard claiming it to be the Red Lion Hotel, Redruth. Jas Davey & Rd. Coad Proprietors. Five casks of ale – labelled *Redruth Brewery Company* – were available and despite it being July the men ended up singing carols, *Auld Lang Syne* and *Trelawny*. Funds were raised for the Redruth Rugby Club back in Cornwall.[177] In April 1899 another report on a rugby match held at Roodepoort said how the biggest part of both teams were Redruth boys but also mentioned were A. Merrit (Truro), Olivey (St. Day) and Hosking (Camborne).[178] Later in the year it was announced that three Redruthians had been honoured with places in the Transvaal team in an inter-colonial game – they were H. Williams (back), Sam Hosking (three quarter) and C. Pearce (forward).[179] Another form of entertainment enjoyed by Cornish miners was a social gathering where singing would often take place, a typical example being on Midsummer's Day 1898 at the George Goch mine in the room of James Teague, W. Moyle and Tom Fowler. Also in attendance were some thirty Cornishmen from the Chacewater district.[180] The room must have been very large or the men were very cramped but occasions such as these would no doubt help prevent the men from being lonely or homesick. For all too many Cornishmen on the Rand, however:

> the greatest hardship and injury in every way from which they suffered was the absence of the other sex. It was rather a melancholy thing to see hundreds of men moping in front of their doors, who if in dear old Cornwall would be at these evening hours with their happy wives or their still happier sweethearts. They looked prosperous but not happy.[181]

On some mines Christmas was celebrated in style, as for instance in 1890 at the Simmer & Jack mine, where each man received £40 as a gift from the Company, and despite the intense heat the men participated in an athletics match. The day finished with a concert in the stamp battery house, the natives being treated to a few carols rendered with true Cornish gusto.[182]

Another group of Cornishmen the same year – to celebrate New Year's Eve – held a Cornish banquet in Pretoria. The Secretary, H.J. Tonking (Penzance) who had been in the land of gold and diamonds for the past eight years – charged each guest two guineas. At the head of the room the Cornish Arms and Motto were draped by the Union Jack and the Dutch Flag. Among the 44 men present were men from St. Ives, Buryan, Redruth, Camborne, Falmouth, Marazion, Newquay,

Gulval, St. Austell etc. Flowers also decorated the room and the diners managed to get one Cornish delicacy on the bill of fare, this being fried pilchards. Music and singing were much in evidence with T. Lanxon singing *Trelawny*, C. Hollow, *One & All* and H.K. Tucker *Good Company*. The Cornish toast *Fish, Tin & Copper* was made.[183] The Cornish miners certainly seemed to club together, and as one Cornishman pointed out

> *it is a good sight especially on a Sunday morning to see a meeting of Cornishmen, who perhaps have not seen each other for years with the inevitable 'Halloo Jan wart thee doing out ere?' followed by a hearty shake of the hand, and of course the usual*
> *'Let's gone an ave a wet!* [184]

With an estimated 5,000 Cornish miners in the land of gold a Cornish Association for the Rand became a possibility following a meeting held at the Goldfields Hotel in Johannesburg on Saturday 17th August 1895. That afternoon William Hosken was elected Chairman and George Olver Secretary. Special mention was made of N.T.Williams who had been a prime mover in forming the Association and the genial host (Mr.Hocking) of the Goldfields Hotel who was on holiday in Cornwall but had tried in the early days, to bring about a union of Cornishmen.[185] The plan was for the Association to supply mutual aid for its members, arrange hospital visits, hold an annual meeting and provide a club house. The actual Cornish Association was formed within a couple of months with William Hosken as its first President and Vice Presidents comprising R.J.Gluyas, F.W.Bawden. J.H.Johns, J.Whitburn and W.Stephens. A committee was also appointed although Hosken expressed regret at the meagre attendance by Cornishmen in general.[186] The first Annual General Meeting of the Cornish Association was held a year later when J.G.Oliver,the Secretary was able to inform the 50 members present that the Association had 313 paying members and he himself had made 40 visits to hospital, taking papers,stamps and confectionery to sick Cornishmen. Messrs.W.Pope,W.Hosken and J.Hosking were nominated for President and Pope was elected by a large majority.[187]

Without a doubt the social highlight for the Cornish Association in Johannesburg was the five month tour made by the *Cornish Nightingale* - Fanny Moody - in 1896.[188] When she was only eighteen this beautiful young singer,at a concert given in 1884 at her home town in Redruth,had caused business at the Mining Exchange to practically come to a standstill and such was her popularity scores of people were unable to get in.[189] In 1890 she married Charles Manners - another opera singer - and, forming their own Company, they toured America in 1893 and Australia in 1895 - where she sang in front of some 2,000 Cornish/Australians. Her triumph came with her visit to South Africa, for as she wrote later:

I shall never forget the scene when I arrived at Johannesburg. A red carpet had been put down from the carriage door all the way along the platform which was crammed with Cornish people, all pressing forward to shake me by the hand. I was escorted by a prominent member of the large Cornish community in the city, and the whole-hearted enthusiasm of the good, kind Cornish bodies made me feel like a queen. My hotel was near the famous Town Clock in Johannesburg where on Saturday nights all our dear 'Cousin Jackies' were wont to congregate to talk over the home news. Very soon the piano was pulled out on to the balcony and I was singing 'Home Sweet Home' to my fellow exiles far from home but still true Cornish people.[190]

At her farewell concert,during which she sang from a wide repertoire with *Trelawny* as an encore,she was presented with a tiara on behalf of the Cornish Association.The tiara was valued at £500 and consisted of Transvaal gold and Kimberley diamonds - its design consisting of a pyramid of 15 big diamonds surmounted by a tiny pick and shovel.On the left side was the coat of arms of the Transvaal and on the right that of Cornwall - the whole is encircled with diamond letters spelling 'One & All'.Fanny said "I need not say that I treasure this gift, coming from my own dear people above all other presentations".[191] A diamond ring was given to her husband and when she sang in Kimberley the Cornishmen there presented her with an uncut diamond.[192] After her visit R.Arthur Thomas - who was then at Barberton - not only sent her some gold nuggets but expressed the feelings of all Cornish when he said:

Your triumphant tour through South Africa has aroused all of us from our lethargy and it has done more to unite the Cornish people of this community than any other event in its history.[193]

Traction engine on a Rand mine c.1900.

1. *THE STANDARD & TRANSVAAL MINING CHRONICLE* 16th JUNE 1888

2 Hedley A. Chilvers, *OUT OF THE CRUCIBLE* (LONDON 1929) p.53

3 *WEST BRITON*, 15th MAY 1879 Bishop Wilkinson (his other names are illegible in the Register for 1879-80) is not the same man as George Howard Wilkinson, who became the second Bishop of Truro. I thank the Rev. Canon H. Miles Brown for his assistance on this point. Wilkinson returned to Cornwall where he became Rector of St. Michael's, Caerhays

4 *CORNISHMAN*, 3rd JANUARY 1895

5 *C.P.M.N.*, 8th SEPTEMBER 1910. On another occasion Hosken claimed the first gold mine in the Transvaal was opened with an entire workforce of Cornishmen in the year 1874. See CORNISHMAN, 8th FEBRUARY 1912.

6 A.P. Cartwright, *THE GOLD MINERS* (CAPE TOWN 1962) p.36

7 J.A. Henry, *THE FIRST HUNDRED YEARS OF THE STANDARD BANK*, p.60

8 *WEST BRITON*, 19th FEBRUARY 1885

9 Henry, *THE FIRST HUNDRED YEARS*, p.60

10 *CORNISHMAN*, 28th OCTOBER 1886

11 *IBID.*, 4th November 1896

12 Hall, *REAPED MY MEALIES*, p.117

13 *CORNISHMAN*, 6th JANUARY 1887

14. Hall, *REAPED MY MEALIES*, p.117

15 T.V. Bulpin, *THE GOLDEN REPUBLIC* (CAPE TOWN 1953) p.325

16. Hall, *REAPED MY MEALIES*, p.118

17. Dickason, *CORNISH IMMIGRANTS*, p.54

18. Cartwright, *GOLD MINERS*, p.52

19. Chilvers, *OUT OF THE CRUCIBLE*, 2nd Edition. p.20 – footnote.

20. *IBID.*, p.20 Fred Struben died 8th SEPTEMBER 1931, Newton Abbott, Devon England aged 81.

21. *IBID.*, p.15

22. Eric Rosenthal, *GOLD! GOLD! GOLD!* (London 1970) p.129

23. Owen Letcher, *THE GOLD MINES OF SOUTHERN AFRICA*, (LONDON 1936). p.70

24. Jenkin, *THE CORNISH MINER*,. p.330-331

25. *CORNISHMAN*, 28th OCTOBER 1886 p.4

26. Wheatcroft, *RANDLORDS*, p.112

27. The term Randlords was used by the English press in the 1890's. See especially Wheatcroft, *RANDLORDS*

28. *CORNISHMAN*, 12th NOVEMBER 1936

29. I thank Joseph Jeffrey's granddaughter Maureen Prout for this information. Joseph Jeffrey died in Wales. Rose Jeffrey died 1953 in Launceston, Cornwall.

30. Marks & Rathbone, *INDUSTRIALISATION AND SOCIAL CHANGE IN SOUTH AFRICA* – article entitled *LABOUR IN THE SOUTH AFRICAN GOLD MINING INDUSTRY, 1886-1914* by Peter Richardson and Jean Jaques Van-Helten. p.79

31. Eric Rosenthal, *GOLD!GOLD!GOLD!* See especially Chapter 24 *The Cyanide Case* p.213-219. The author Elizabeth Longford credits the rise of Johannesburg to Cyanide James who she says discovered that cyanide would make deep level mining possible on the Rand. This somewhat overstates the case! See Elizabeth Longford, *JAMESON'S RAID. THE PRELUDE TO THE BOER WAR* (LONDON 1982) p.13

32. *CORNISHMAN*, 21st DECEMBER 1893

33. *C.P.M.N.*, 12th DECEMBER 1895

34. *CORNISHMAN*, 28th OCTOBER 1886. By 1899 Cornishmen on the Rand were earning £20 per month, compared with £5 per month in Cornwall. See *C.P.M.N.*, 25th MAY 1899

35. *CORNISHMAN*, 3rd AUGUST 1899

36. *IBID.*, 4th FEBRUARY 1897

37. *C.P.M.N.*, 12th AUGUST 1933

38. *IBID* 1st October 1896. The story of the small number of Cornish miners who worked on India's Mysore goldfield has yet to be told but besides Johns other Cornish mine managers in India included Joseph Pryor (Redruth), Arthur Llewellyn (Redruth) James Rowe (Camborne) Capt. Hambly (Hayle) John Gilbert (Camborne) Capt. Martin (St. Day)

39. Letcher *GOLD MINES* p.129

40. *C.P.M.N.*, 16th JUNE 1910 Additional information re: her grandfather, John Whitford supplied by Phyllis Ferguson.

41. *C.P.M.N.*, 16th JULY 1908

42. *MINING JOURNAL*, 23rd JANUARY 1897

43. *C.P.M.N.*, 2nd APRIL 1896

44. *CORNISHMAN*, 13th JUNE 1895

45. *IBID.*, 22nd AUGUST 1895

46. *KRUGERSDORP STANDARD*, 17th DECEMBER 1898

47. *IBID.*, 13th SEPTEMBER 1899

48. *STANDARD & DIGGERS NEWS*, 11th APRIL 1891

49. *CORNISHMAN*, 26th MARCH 1896

50. *C.P.M.N.*, 23rd JANUARY 1896

51. *KRUGERSDORP STANDARD*, 1st JULY 1899

52. *C.P.M.N.*, 2nd JANUARY 1902

53. *MINING JOURNAL*, 20th JULY 1895 p.871

54. *CORNISHMAN*, 2nd June 1949. Dolcoath was managed by three generations of the Thomas family – Charles, Josiah and R. Arthur.

55. *IBID.*, 13th FEBRUARY 1947. Josiah Paull died at Camborne aged 77 years.

56. Burke, *THE CORNISH MINER*, . p.124

57. *IBID.*, p.82

58. Jenkin, *CORNISH MINER*, p.329

59. *CORNISHMAN*, 7th NOVEMBER 1899

60. Jenkin, *CORNISH MINER*, p.329

61. *GOLD FIELDS NEWS & BARBERTON HERALD*, 27th OCTOBER 1896

62. Hall, *REAPED MY MEALIES*, p.125

63. *CORNISHMAN*, 14th MARCH 1907

64. *IBID.*, 3rd JANUARY 1907

65. *IBID.*, 14th MARCH 1907

66. *CAMBORNIAN*, 7th JUNE 1890

67. *THE HISTORY OF THE HENWOODS 1856-1956* . p.19

68. W.H. Somerset Bell, *BYGONE DAYS* (LONDON 1933) p 134

69. G.A. Leyds, *A HISTORY OF JOHANNESBURG* (LONDON 1964)

70. *SUNDAY TIMES* (JOHANNESBURG) 20th MAY 1973. Colour Magazine *RULE OF THE FOUR RICHARDS* by George Aschman.

71. Leyds, *HISTORY OF JOHANNESBURG*

72. Dickason, *CORNISH IMMIGRANTS* p. 62

73. *IBID.*, p 62

74. CORNISHMAN 14th APRIL 1910

75. W.G.A. Mears, *THE EARLY HISTORY OF ST. STITHIAN COLLEGE* (RANDBERG 1972) p.3 I would like to thank Carol Botha, Librarian of St. Stithians College for the above book and other information.

76. *CORNISHMAN*, 24th SEPTEMBER 1942

77. *IBID.*, 30th JANUARY 1913

78. *NORTH WESTERN PRESS*, 24th MAY 1912

79. Chilvers, *OUT OF THE CRUCIBLE*, p.249

80. *THE DIGGER NEWS*, 20th NOVEMBER 1888

81. Barry Ronan, *FORTY SOUTH AFRICAN YEARS* . p.159

82. Chilvers, *OUT OF THE CRUCIBLE*, p.62

83. *KRUGERSDORP TIMES*, 28th DECEMBER 1895

84. *SERVAMUS*, NOVEMBER 1986

85. *THE STANDARD*, 25th MAY 1928

86. *PERSONALITY*, FEBRUARY 1970

87. *IBID.*, p.67

88. *THE STANDARD*, 25th MAY 1928

89 Zeederburg – *PERSONALITY*

90. Vorster – *SERVAMUS*

91. *IBID.*, *SERVAMUS*

92 Extract from *STANDARD* DECEMBER 1895. I thank the Krugersdorp Library for all their help and in providing the articles, letters and extracts on Tossel.

93. Henry, *FIRST HUNDRED YEARS OF THE STANDARD BANK* p.94

94. Wheatcroft, *RANDLORDS* p.114

95 *CORNUBIAN*, 14th MARCH 1890

96. *C.P.M.N.*, 12th MARCH 1892

97. Brian Kennedy, *A TALE OF TWO MINING CITIES, JOHANNESBURG AND BROKEN HILL 1885-1925* (MELBOURNE 1984) . p.51

98. *CORNISHMAN*, 2nd JANUARY 1896

99. *IBID.*, 2nd APRIL 1896

100. *C.P.M.N.*, 10th DECEMBER 1896

101. *IBID.*, 10th SEPTEMBER 1896

102. *IBID.*, 24th SEPTEMBER 1896

103. *C.P.M.N.*, 23rd APRIL 1896

104. *IBID.*, 17th DECEMBER 1896. A report a month later put Johnnesburg's death rate at 59 per 1000. See *CORNISHMAN*, 21st JANUARY 1897

105. *C.P.M.N.*, 19th SEPTEMBER 1896

106. *CORNISHMAN*, 13th APRIL 1899

107. *C.P.M.N.*, 21st MAY 1896

108. *CORNISHMAN*, 27th May 1897

109. *CORNUBIAN*, 24th APRIL 1897

110. *CORNISHMAN*, 17th SEPTEMBER 1896 – Cornishmen also died from smallpox elsewhere such as Pachuca,Mexico. *CORNUBIAN*, 24th MARCH 1893

111. *IBID.*, 18th AUGUST 1898

112. *IBID.*, 13th JULY 1899

113. *THE STANDARD*, 7th JANUARY 1899

114. *THE CORNUBIAN*, 24th MARCH 1899

115. *C.P.M.N.*, 3rd DECEMBER 1896

116. *IBID.*, 9th APRIL 1896

117. *IBID.*, 17th DECEMBER 1896

118. *CORNISHMAN*, 13th MAY 1897

119. *IBID.*, 12th JANUARY 1899

120. *CORNUBIAN*, 5th MAY 1899

121. *C.P.M.N.*, 10th SEPTEMBER 1896

122. *IBID.*, 10th DECEMBER 1896

123. *CORNUBIAN*, 8th JANUARY 1892

124. *IBID.*, 23rd SEPTEMBER 1898

125. *STANDARD & DIGGERS NEWS*, 28th MARCH 1890

126. *C.P.M.N.*, 15th OCTOBER 1896

127. *IBID.*, 29th DECEMBER 1898

128. *IBID.*, 22nd OCTOBER 1896

129 *CORNUBIAN*, 23rd April 1897, 14th MAY 1897

130. *IBID.*, 27th JANUARY 1899

131. *THE STANDARD*, 22nd APRIL 1899

132. *C.P.M.N.*, 28th MAY 1896

133. *IBID.*, 19th DECEMBER 1895

134. *CORNUBIAN*, 2nd JUNE 1899

135. *C.P.M.N.*, 17th FEBRUARY 1898

136. *CORNISHMAN*, 24th DECEMBER 1896

137. *IBID.*, 18th JULY 1895

138. *IBID.*, 2nd SEPTEMBER 1897

139. *CORNUBIAN*, 28th APRIL 1893

140. *KRUGERSDORP TIMES*, 8th AUGUST 1896

141. *CORNUBIAN*, 24th MARCH 1899

142. *CORNISHMAN*, 23rd JULY 1896

143. *C.P.M.N.*, 27th JANUARY 1898

144. *CORNISHMAN*, 7th DECEMBER 1893

145. *CORNUBIAN*, 15th APRIL 1892 and *MINING JOURNAL* 16th APRIL 1892. p.431

146. *C.P.M.N.*, 13th APRIL 1899

147. *CORNISHMAN*, 28th NOVEMBER 1895

148. *CORNUBIAN*, 17th MAY 1895

149. *CORNISHMAN*, 30th JULY 1896

150. *IBID.*, 16th FEBRUARY 1899

151. *IBID.*, 24th SEPTEMBER 1896

152. *C.P.M.N.*, 2nd MARCH 1899

153. *CAMBORNIAN*, 8th MARCH 1888

154. *CORNISHMAN*, 21st NOVEMBER 1895

155. *CORNUBIAN*, 7th MAY 1897

156. *IBID.*, 4th MAY 1894

157. *CORNISHMAN*, 8th AUGUST 1895

158. *CORNUBIAN*, 5th OCTOBER 1894

159. *IBID.*, 19th OCTOBER 1894

160. *IBID.*, 26th AUGUST 1892

161. *IBID.*, 25th JANUARY 1895

162. See a series of reports by Tiddy – especially *CORNISHMAN*, 15th MARCH, 5th JULY, 13th SEPTEMBER 1906, 3rd JANUARY, 14th MARCH 1907 and *C.P.M.N.*, 2nd NOVEMBER 1905, 22nd FEBRUARY, 1906, 5th APRIL 1906, 2nd AUGUST 1906, 24th JANUARY 1907, 14th NOVEMBER 1907

163. Burke, *CORNISH DIASPORA* . p.64 For an example of one family's mobility see *CORNISHMAN*, 9th FEBRUARY 1905

164. *CORNISHMAN*, 21st NOVEMBER 1899

165. *IBID.*, 9th JUNE 1899 *Bal* was a Cornish word meaning *Mine*.

166. *IBID.*, 15th MARCH 1900

167. *CORNISHMAN*, 15th MARCH 1900

168. *C.P.M.N.*, 19th SEPTEMBER 1896

169. *CORNISHMAN*, 19th JANUARY 1899

170. *IBID.*, 2nd APRIL 1896

171. *C.P.M.N.*, 3rd SEPTEMBER 1896

172. *CORNISHMAN*, 5th OCTOBER 1899

173. *IBID.*, 2nd FEBRUARY 1899

174. *CORNUBIAN*, 27th JANUARY 1899

175. *IBID.*, 5th OCTOBER 1899

176. For more information re. the brooches see CORNISH WORLD Jun/Jul/Aug. 1996 Issue 9 p.18-19.

177. *CORNUBIAN*, 20th AUGUST 1897

178. *IBID.*, 14th APRIL 1899

179. *IBID.*, 23rd JUNE 1899

180. *IBID.*, 5th AUGUST 1898

181. *CORNISHMAN*, 15th MARCH 1900

182. *C.P.M.N.*, 31st JANUARY 1891

183. *CORNUBIAN*, 20th JANUARY 1891

184. *IBID.*, 20th APRIL 1894

185. *CORNISHMAN*, 19th SEPTEMBER 1895

186. *C.P.M.N.*, 21st NOVEMBER 1895

187. *IBID.*, 31st DECEMBER 1896

188. The Moody/Manners Company was paid £1,500 with all expenses covered. *IBID.*, 15th OCTOBER 1896

189. *CORNUBIAN*, 7th NOVEMBER 1884

190. *CORNISHMAN*, 7th NOVEMBER 1923. See also *IBID.*, 18th MARCH 1897

191. Fanny Moody retired in 1903 at the peak of her fame. During the Second World War in 1940 she gave the diamond tiara to the British Red Cross *to help the maimed and wounded*. C. Berry, *PORTRAIT OF CORNWALL*. p.74-75

192. *CORNISHMAN*, 9th MARCH 1950

193. *CORNUBIAN*, 2nd April 1897

CHAPTER FIVE

SOUTH AFRICA OR STARVATION
1870-99

We ask no charity... on the one side we are offered South Africa or starvation, on the other side we are sure of a most determined effort to support our local industry and to better the condition of our people.

The Cornishman.[1]

The mining industry of South Africa is far and away more important to Cornwall than mining in its district.

Mining Journal.[2]

In 1861 the official census figure for the population of Cornwall was 369,390 – it had in fact reached its peak for the century. At the peak production of the Cornish copper and tin industries in 1863 there were 377 mines (157 copper and 220 tin). By 1870 a combination of a drop in the price of copper and the competition of cheap copper from abroad saw the number of copper mines in Cornwall fall to 80, although only two – Caradon and Marke Valley in East Cornwall – were of any major economic significance. Also a complete overhaul of the mining work force led to the number employed in the Cornish mining industry being reduced drastically from 26,500 in 1873 to 13,730 by 1878:

> *The decline in the number of working mines in Cornwall and Devon in the period 1874-76 was dramatic. In 1873 there had been 230 mines in existence and out of these 47 closed down in 1874, 48 in 1875 and a further 37 in 1876. Thus 132 mines were abandoned out of 230 in this three year collapse, leaving 98 working in 1877. The effect upon Cornwall of this rapid decline in the scale of mining can well be imagined, producing a depression as severe as had occurred in the late 1860's with the decline in copper. Then there had been the existing tin mines to which some working miners could turn, whereas now there was nought but emigration to fall back upon.[3]*

As the Cornish copper and tin mines continued to close down rapidly during the late nineteenth century Cornwall saw a migration of its work force unequalled to that in any other county in England as thousands of men were thrown out of work and hundreds of families were on the verge of starvation.[4] The Cornish china-clay industry was able to provide employment for some but for others the choice lay between South Africa or starvation.

The year 1879 was a year of distress and disaster for both Cornwall and South Africa. The chief topics of conversation in the New Year were the closure of the Cornish Bank at Falmouth and the Union Bank at Helston plus the hardship being faced in the country's mining districts due to another drop in the price of tin – to below £80 per ton. A Cornwall County Distress Fund and a County & Wesleyan Relief Fund were soon set up, and as the Cornish began to read in their newspapers the first accounts of the annihilation of British soldiers at Isandlwana and their bravery at Rorke's Drift the first soup kitchens began dispensing quarts of soup to the starving of Cornwall. At Truro two hundred quarts of soup a day[5] began to be distributed, and in the months that followed appeals for help went out from Helston, Hayle, Redruth and Bodmin. At Hayle the distress was not of individuals but of the whole population for all the mines in the district had closed and formerly one mine employed 1,800 persons.[6] In the St. Agnes and Breage districts the situation was as serious and emigration became the word on most miners' lips. Thirty miners were reported to have left Redruth for the Cape[7] at the end of March, their destination being Kimberley and the diamond fields. This was not surprising for in the same month the number of people attending the Redruth soup kitchen was 1,535 which was 260 more than the previous last month.[8] At Hayle, Harvey & Co, one of the biggest engineering firms in the county reduced the men's wage by ten per cent. In the Breage district 70-80 quarts of soup were being delivered twice a week at the price to the poor of 1d a quart.[9] In Gwennap Parish at Carharrack, Scorrier and St. Day where the richest copper mines in Cornwall had once been worked it was remarked that where twenty-five years ago £33,000 a month had been paid in miners' wages alone, now the figure was less than a £100[10] and,

> *once busy and relatively prosperous mining settlements such as St. Day,*
> *Carharrack, Lanner and Chacewater grew silent and depopulated, with*
> *houses and shops half derelict and deserted. Grass grew over the*
> *neglected metals of the railways that had served the mines and on the*
> *once busy wharves and quays at Portreath and Devoran and Hayle.[11]*

Some relief did arrive from South Africa but only in small amounts such as a donation of £55 to the Relief Fund in April.[12] Many families would have received individual help but of course this would not have appeared in the press. The papers continued to tabulate those Cornish who emigrated to South Africa as well as California and Australia – Cornwall's Distress Committee received some £1,150 for the relief of suffering in Cornwall from the Cornish/Australians.[13] Depression remained acute in St. Just where there were only four mines in operation, but near the end of the year in October relief appeared as the tin price began to rise once more. Soup kitchens were in evidence, however, at Falmouth, Truro, Lostwithiel, Helston and the Gwennap district throughout the 1879-80 winter.

Despite a slight recovery in the Cornish tin industry between 1880-82 the Relief Committees remained and during the 1880-81 winter, soup kitchens helped to prevent starvation in Truro, Penryn, Bodmin, Falmouth and Camborne. An added disaster in Cornwall was a storm which sank some fishing boats in Mounts Bay, Mr. Rogers a kind-hearted Cornishman in South Africa collected over £70 for the Mounts Bay Relief Fund.[14]

The mass exodus of the Cornish miners in the 1870's to the diamond fields of South Africa was evident in the 1881 Census for Cornwall which showed that in the mining districts the population had plummeted. The St. Agnes district was down 2,346, St. Ives 1,156 and even the heart of mining Cornwall – Redruth and Camborne – had seen a drop of 1,350 and 432 respectively.[15] Emigration continued. There were no new diamond mines being discovered at Kimberley and the diamond field alone could not have sustained the collapse of the Cornish mining industry nor could it have soaked up the vast numbers of Cornish miners who found themselves out of work. It was the discovery of gold in the Transvaal and the establishment of Johannesburg on the Rand goldfield in particular that saved many a Cornish family from starvation from the 1880's onwards. However, it could be even tougher for a miner out of work on the Rand for as one Cornishman warned:

> they will find that however, good a new country may be to work in, it is about the worse place to starve in, there are no guardians or philanthropists there to lend a helping hand.[16]

The effect of migration on Cornwall, especially the migration of the so-called roving miner caused many problems especially to the county's Board of Guardians.[17] The Penzance Guardians had to take in 6 children named Williams[18] when their mother died and their father was in South Africa. Married miners in South Africa who failed to send home remittances to wives and families caused further problems for the Boards of Guardians. A woman who applied to Redruth Guardians was typical of many; her husband had been in South Africa over three years but had only sent her £17 in nine months. The Board Chairman said the number of these deserted cases was almost unlimited.[19] Caroline Gay and her five children were given relief by the Redruth Board of Guardians, amounting to 5 shillings and 5 loaves when her husband failed to send money,[20] and the wife of James Moon of Barripper was given 4 shillings and 4 loaves when she applied for herself and four children. The Guardians were quick to point out that a miner could often afford the £20 or £30 to go away while leaving them to care for their families, but Moon could hardly be blamed for not sending money, for a couple of months later the news of his death arrived from South Africa.[21] When Ben

Hocking, who was working at the Simmer & Jack mine, had only sent his wife Minnie and their two children at Camborne, £22 in the last two years and Minnie's brother had also written to say that Hocking had left the mine and gone on a drinking spree, the Chairman of the Redruth Guardians said he would make enquiries as he knew some parties connected with the Simmer & Jack Mine.[22] This method was to be used to good effect, as many of the mines were run by Cornishmen who were well aware of the importance to a family home in Cornwall of the remittance sent by the husband.

A story is told of a certain Cornish miner who had failed to send a remittance home and his wife wrote a letter of complaint to the mine Manager The Manager sent for the miner and said he had received a letter from the miner's wife who had stated that if he didn't send money soon she would have to go into the workhouse, and what did he propose doing about it? To which the miner replied, "Tell her to wait a bit, and I'll come home and go in with her".[23]

Nevertheless the failure by some Cornish miners to send remittances led many women to the workhouse. Pauperism was very much in evidence.

The Redruth Board of Guardians in January 1897 noted a large increase in the number of paupers – 225 against 209 the same time the previous year and the number of out-paupers being 1653 against 1518 the previous year. The comment was made that the destitution of the neighbourhood had increased very considerably.[24] Within five months the conditions had obviously worsened for the number of paupers had risen to 240 compared to 204 the same time the previous year.[25]

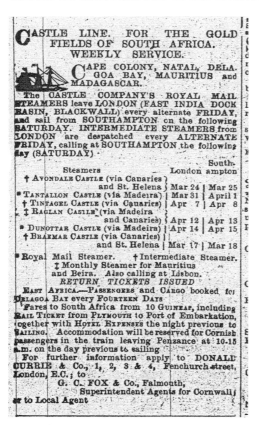

Castle Line advertisement of 1890's

Along with the now regular reports that appeared in the newspapers of deaths of Cornish miners from disease or accidents in the mines, the women of Cornwall were not only having to make a sacrifice but were paying a high price. When the appalling loss of life in South Africa is catalogued alongside those deaths in the U.S.A., Mexico, Australia, India and elsewhere, to say nothing of those who perished in the mines at home then it is without a doubt that the success of the mining industry worldwide owes a considerable debt to Cornwall, its miners and above all to the Cornish women.

Every Friday morning (from 1890 to 1900) the up train from West Cornwall, included special cars labelled Southampton, the embarkation port for South Africa.[26] During those years the number of people emigrating to the land of gold and diamonds fluctuated and not just with the price of tin or the closure of another mine in Cornwall. The abandoned mines in the St. Austell, Gwennap, Breage, St. Agnes, Marazion, St. Ives, Lelant and other districts have caused these places which used to blossom as the rose, to become to a large extent as deserts claimed the *Cornubian* in 1891.[27] In the same year the official census figure for Cornwall was 322,589 a further drop of 8,097 from ten years before.[28] In 1892 with the price of tin reaching £100 per ton in price the *Mining Journal* optimistically announced Cornwall breathes again,[29] and there was an actual demand at some Cornish mines for men which was hoped would relieve Camborne, Redruth, Goldsithney and St. Just of the unemployed caused by the shut down of mines such as Penandrea and West Seton.[30] The following year saw just how over-optimistic the *Mining Journal* had been, for 1893 saw the flooding at Wheal Owles leaving 20 miners drowned and partial closure of the mine, the last of the Redruth mines – Wheal Uny, and East Uny – close and a further disaster near the end of the year, when eight miners were entombed by a fall of rock at Dolcoath. There was only one survivor. Added to this came news of the closure of 318 silver mines in Colorado which saw the neighbourhood of Camborne "getting full of the billy cock hats and watch chains which denotes the distress in American camps".[31] As the Rand goldfield therefore offered the best means of employment in no time the labour market at Johannesburg became completely glutted and worse – the mine owners reduced the wages.[32] Despite the many warnings from the Cornish and Cornish/Americans – many of whom had travelled direct from Butte City – to their fellow Cornishmen not to leave Cornwall, in 1895 with the tin price at an all time low of £57-17-6 a ton, emigration from the county hit an all time high. Twenty miners left Redruth one Friday in February, the same month that Wheal Owles began to be wound up. In April the stoppage of Botallack threw a number of men out of employment at St. Just, some of whom had already left for South Africa and others were expected to follow.[33] In May with flood waters rising at Wheal Agar the men refused to go down the mine. Instead seven hundred went on a march:

The crowd of miners from E. Pool, S. Crofty, Carn Brea & Tincroft
marched into Redruth in free and easy order. Some were chewing pasties,
others carrying large sticks or wearing azaleas from Mr. Bawden's

> *garden. Some sprang into a passing cart and had a ride into town, while*
> *others hung on to the rear of a bus.*[34]

This rather-light hearted demonstration resulted in the men returning to work after some meetings with the mine owners.

Friday 13th June 1895 was proclaimed a record day as far as Cornish emigration was concerned. It was said 80 people left Penzance, Camborne, Redruth and other West Cornwall stations for South Africa and the station platforms were thronged with friends who came to wish them goodbye.[35] Throughout 1895 the *Cornishman* kept track of those emigrating to South Africa and elsewhere. In June scarcely a man was to be seen at Barripper and Penponds, Camborne, so strong had been the tide of emigration. In July the paper told of how the exodus to South Africa continued. In September the paper again spoke of "Starvation or South Africa" as another contingent of Cornish Miners left West Cornwall for South Africa In November at St. Just there was "Wholesale Emigration with 120 booked for South Africa".[36]

As Christmas approached the numbers leaving began to dwindle but Cornish emigration to South Africa from Jan. 4th to the end of 1895 had seen no less than 2,086 leave Cornwall – the highest number in one week being 127, for the week ending November 8th. In that month 226 left Cornwall for the Transvaal.[37] It was believed that out of the total number 1000 miners were from the districts of Camborne and Redruth alone.[38]

Although at the end of 1895 there were still, according to the *Mining Journal*, 56 mines producing tin, some of these were but mere scratchings where the working staff did not amount to more than the proverbial 'two men and a boy'.[39] Only Dolcoath, East Pool and Levant were mines producing tin in any quantity and at a profit. At the Basset mines even the intervention of Francis Oats, who was mainly responsible for the amalgamation of Wheal Basset with South Francis, could not stop some 500 hands (including 232 miners) being discharged.[40] A fall in the price of silver had increased the threat from the Malay Straits with its vast alluvial tin deposits and cheap coolie labour, for now the Straits companies could

> *get gold for their tin and purchase two depreciated silver dollars, with*
> *which to pay the men for about the same amount that would formerly only*
> *purchase one silver dollar.*[41]

The state of Cornwall's tin industry was put into perspective by J. Harry Johns at a banquet held in his honour by the Mining Association and Institution of Cornwall at Tabbs Hotel, Redruth Tuesday 8th October 1895, when he said:

> *Cornish people have got to regard South Africa as Greater Cornwall...*
> *the amount of money which at the present moment is finding its way to the*

old county from the Transvaal for the support of the families of the miners is astounding.[42]

A Cornish miner home a month later confirmed this by describing times in Johannesburg as brisk with miners getting about £5 a week and although most miners were working a 6-day week it was possible after expenses to save £15 a month.[43] Cornwall was certainly by now dependent on South Africa for as the *Post* commented Camborne had got a double bottom – its own tin industry and gold mining in South Africa, and in fact all over the world.[44] Such had been the decline of the home industry that the Cornish miners on the Rand almost outnumbered those still employed in Cornwall. The number of Cornish Miners in July 1896 were 3,772 underground and 3,793 above ground giving a total of 7,365 (1,336 less than in 1894). For the Rand the number of Cornish miners was close to 7,000.[45] Such had been the large number leaving in 1895 that for a while the Levant mine had been actually in want of hands.[46]

Although there was a temporary set-back in emigration to South Africa due to the Jameson Raid in 1895 (see next chapter) it was soon under way once more. On one Friday in July 1896 between 60-70 left West Cornwall[47] with equally large numbers in following weeks. In October emigrations were so numerous special trains were run from Penzance to Southampton as scores of miners left for South Africa.[48] The Cornish tin mining industry continued to decline as 200 men were about to be discharged at Carn Brea mine. It was thought that if Carn Brea was amalgamated with Tincroft then calamity to the Camborne neighbourhood could be averted.[49] Despite the two mines being joined with a third – Cooks Kitchen – in July a reduction of wages at the mines led to a demonstration but,

as the Cornish miners are without means and organisation which are necessary to the successful engineering of a strike the Carn Brea & Tincroft employees very sensibly contented themselves with a protest and returned to work.[50]

This was not a mistake the Cornish miners were to make in South Africa. For the men out of work in Cornwall there could only be help from the Miners Distress Fund and the Poor Law Guardians.

There may have been special trains to carry the large numbers of Cornish miners' to Southampton but although the numbers were large they only represented a portion of those who wished to go for many had to wait on account of the Cape boats being full.[51] When the weekly lists of emigrants given by the *Cornishman* appeared very meagre an explanation given was that the shipping agents had not provided the newspaper with their lists nor had the railway officials. It appeared there was rivalry between the agents and the unsuccessful ones had complained of adverse publicity.[52] This of course makes it virtually impossible to calculate with any accuracy the total number of Cornish who went to South Africa or to compile their names, but suffice it to say that throughout 1897-98 hundreds more left Cornwall to seek work in the South African El Dorado.

Harvey's Johannesburg office in 1893

As the Cornish mining industry went into decline many of the foundries and small firms connected with the industry went out of business. Dingeys Iron Foundry at Truro collapsed in 1890 along with others at Devoran, Perran, St Austell and St. Just. The larger firms managed to survive by taking the opportunity to develop new markets for their products overseas. So as South Africa began to draw the highly skilled, hard rock miner from Cornwall, in return the mines began to send back orders for much needed mining machinery and equipment. One advantage to the Cornish firms was that many of the South African gold mines had Cornishmen as Managers. As long as Francis Oats had influence at De Beers at Kimberley regular orders flowing into Cornwall were almost a certainty. As orders in the home industry shrank dramatically they were off-set by orders from the expanding gold mining industry. Therefore most of the major Cornish mining firms soon had their own agents in South Africa – especially on the Rand.

In Cornwall, at Hayle, there was Harvey & Co., the last major foundry in the county, with a high reputation for manufacturing mine machinery. In South Africa Harveys' contractors had already sunk shafts for De Beers at Kimberley with two 14 (inch) whims for Kimberley being shipped from Hayle in November 1876,[53] but it was the discovery of gold in the Transvaal that saw the orders increase. An advertisement in the *Transvaal Mining Argus* for October 1887 shows that Harveys had supplied stamp batteries for the Forbes Reef Mining Co., Jubilee Gold Mining Co., Pilgrim's Rest Mining Co., Salisbury Mining Co., and the May Gold Mining Co. For Harveys:

> *South Africa was now engaging the attention and aspirations of the Company and, among the new extensions to the works was a moulding shop devoted to the production of pipes for the Rand mines.*[54]

Tom Bickle, a foreman at Harveys, (he later met his death on the Rand in 1898) was sent out to South Africa in 1889 on what was really a fact-finding mission. On his return later in the year he recommended to the Company that Harveys needed a resident engineer in Johannesburg. G.N. Burden was appointed and sent out. The Company's agent in South Africa became the Hosken brothers (William, Samuel and James, were all from Hayle and brothers to Richard Hosken) who were trading as The Cornish Trading Company. Unfortunately the Hoskens ran heavily into debt with their suppliers in 1890 which resulted in a law suit with Harveys and they lost the agency. The new agent became William Francis Trevithick Harvey as Manager of Harveys' Johannesburg branch with G.N. Burden as his assistant. W.F.T. Harvey was the son of Harveys' Chairman – Frank Harvey – but was too young and had little experience of business. Harveys were now losing money both at home and abroad and the future of the foundry at Hayle was by no means secure. In October 1895 over 100 hands were discharged of whom 37 left the hammer mill department.[55] At every meeting of Harveys' Board of Directors one subject was brought up for 'full discussion' with monotonous frequency under 'Affairs in South Africa' and that was the economic viability of the Johannesburg Branch.[56] The news was not good. On a number of occasions both W.F.T. Harvey and Burden had returned to Cornwall to give reports on the South African situation. Now it was decided that one of the Board should go to South Africa. Major John Mead was the director chosen and he left Cornwall in 1897, although the *Cornubian* gave no sign that Harveys was in any sort of difficulty when it reported that Mead had left Cornwall for Johannesburg no doubt with a view to further the company's business. On arrival in Johannesburg Mead was faced with complaints from Harvey and Burden that the fault lay with mismanagement back in Hayle which had resulted in losses in money and custom[58] in South Africa. One surprising discovery made by Mead was that whereas Harveys specialised in pumping engines, unlike their Cornish tin mines there was little or no water in the mines on the Rand therefore Harveys' speciality was seldom required.[59] Mead returned to Cornwall but whatever plans he had made for the future of the Johannesburg branch were overtaken by the events of the Boer War (see next chapter).

The most successful Cornish engineering firm – and one still in existence under different ownership – was Holman Brothers Ltd., established at Camborne in 1801. During the period 1861-1901 when most towns in Cornwall connected to mining saw a decrease in their population, Camborne was one of the very few that actually increased its numbers (1,273 between 1861-1901) – the reason being that the decline of Camborne's mining activity was neutralised by the expansion of its engineering, and in particular by the rapid growth of the Holman enterprise.[60] Holmans began their trade with South Africa in 1889, their reputation being secured with the manufacture of their Cornish Rock Drill which was very successful, for by 1896 there were more than a thousand in use on the Rand and three years later the number had risen to two thousand. There was other equipment as well, for on one occasion the *Mining Journal* stated that two Cornish compressors, several pumping and drawing lifts & a good consignment of rock drills[61] were on their way to South Africa from Holmans. The agent for Holmans in South Africa was Howard, Farrar & Co. In the manufacturing of rock drills, competition for Holmans not only came from the American firm – Ingersoll Rand

– but also the fellow Cornish firms of R. Stephens & Son at Carn Brea, Redruth and between Camborne and Redruth the Tuckingmill Foundry Co. Numerous rock drill competitions were to be held over the years that followed as each firm tried to corner the market. Also based at Tuckingmill was Bickford Smith & Co. a firm which made safety fuse for the mining industry. In competition with Bickford Smith & Co. was the Roskear Fuse Works of Bennett & Sons at Camborne where another mining firm – W.J. & C. Tyack Ltd., was situated. Further afield in Birmingham the Cornish firm of Tangyes also manufactured mining equipment for South Africa and had an agent at Johannesburg.

Some Cornishmen even built up their own firms in South Africa itself. James Oliver Bartle of Tuckingmill had spent ten years visiting practically every great mining camp of the United States before moving to South Africa in 1886 to establish the engineering and mechanical firm of Bartle & Co. which represented numerous British manufacturing companies.[62] Ironically his firm produced the Chersen Rock Drill in South Africa which was in competition with Holmans and Stephens its two main Cornish rivals. Henry J. Rich of St Ives was the Secretary of the Transvaal Plumbers Society and gave another insight into the different working conditions found in South Africa. He warned other Cornish plumbers that in South Africa the materials used for plumbing were mainly galvanised iron or zinc, so that men accustomed to lead working were quite unable to find work at their trade.[63]

Henry Trembath of Penzance – brother-in-law to J. Harry Johns – was made President of the South African Pharmaceutical Society whilst James Stuthridge of Redruth was one of the largest brass manufacturers in Natal. From Camborne to the Cape in 1895 went S.A. Eddy where at Cape Town he built up a successful building business, being joined by his brother – G.A. Eddy – in 1905. The two men were not only active members of the Cape Town Master Builders' Association but were to hold high office. S.A. Eddy was President of the Cape Colony Builders' Federation and G.A. Eddy was President of the Cape Town Master Builders' Association. Both men represented Cape Town as delegates to South Africa's National Federation Congress of Builders.[64]

John Wevell, a Cornish blacksmith from Lostwithiel had first emigrated to Australia in 1884 but when the news of the gold strike reached him he was soon on the Rand. Joined by two younger brothers from Cornwall he established in the centre of Johannesburg the Blacksmiths, Farriers & Wagon Builders Firm of Wevell Brothers. By 1905 the firm claimed to be the finest farriers and carriage shop in South Africa – well stocked from horse-shoe nails to the best equipped motor car, and enjoying the patronage of the élite of the Rand.[65] Finally, despite having problems with Harveys, William Hosken built up a successful mining and commercial firm known as William Hosken & Co. Hosken was assisted by his brothers Samuel and James and later Richard, who came to South Africa in 1897. William Hosken was very much a commercial Pioneer. He became a director of a

Premises of Wm. Hosken & Co. in Johannesburg c.1900. The three brothers are standing in front.

number of gold mines including the City & Suburban, Nigel and Heriot which had offices in Natal. By 1896 Hosken was back in Johannesburg becoming the founder of the Johannesburg Chamber of Commerce of which he became President, a post to which he was elected six years running. William Hosken became a spokesman for the Cornish in South Africa and it is not surprising that in his role as President of the newly formed Cornish Association on the Rand his views were listened to with respect and given prominence in the newspapers. There is no doubt that many Cornish on the strength of what they heard and read were prepared to leave Cornwall to make South Africa, if not their home, then at least their place of work

Once in South Africa the Cornish were always ready to support those left behind in Cornwall. Whether it was in terms of collective donations to the various distress and relief funds or separate gifts from individual miners depended on the circumstances. Several young men from Stithians sent over £20 from Johannesburg to William Burley who had lost the use of his hand in a mining accident. It was hoped the money would help him set up business in Stithians.[66] Henry Kemp a young Cornish miner who was prospering in South Africa sent home five pounds to the Vicar[67] and the Vicar of St. Day received £17 towards the cost of a new pulpit for the church collected by Fred Bawden, an old parishioner in South Africa.[68] Francis Opie in South Africa who sent £1 to the Primitive Methodist Sunday School at Illogan[69] was just one example of a number of Cornishmen who sent small donations to their home church, chapel, band, or to a number of sports clubs and associations. The Cornish Salvationists at Johannesburg, who had links with Camborne, sent £13 from the gold region to the tin country.[70] Just how much was sent from South Africa would be impossible to calculate for there is no way of knowing just how many gifts went unrecorded by the newspapers or were sent privately. What is certain is that it was virtually a one way traffic – the help came from South Africa to Cornwall. Some of course brought their money back with them for John Bowden was at least one miner rewarded for his toil in South Africa.[71] He bought five cottages in Penrose Terrace, Helston.

Even before the Jameson Raid and Boer War South Africa had at least one political ramification for Cornwall. In the 1885 General election the Mining Division of Cornwall had rejected A. Pendarves Vivian, the official Liberal candidate and their M.P. for 15 years and replaced him with Charles Augustus Vansittart Conybeare, a radical Independent Liberal. He was re-elected with an increased majority the following year. Conybeare visited South Africa sometime in 1888 and Samuel Hosken recalled many years later how he and Conybeare along with R. Arthur Thomas and others enjoyed what must have been one of the first Cornish dinners in Johannesburg.[72]

In the Transvaal the Oceana Gold Mining Company had been set up in February 1889 and the Silati River Gold Mining Company in October the same year. Conybeare was the Chairman of the Oceana and a Director of the Silati. He had a large number of shares in both companies and had encouraged investment – an action criticised and resented by many Cornish who felt that any such investment should have gone into the ailing Cornish tin industry. Conybeare – who was not himself a Cornishman – was hardly supporting the home industry. The Manager of the Silati Company, James Williams of Redruth, a mine Captain of considerable mining experience in Cornwall, the U.S.A. and India, was according to the *Mining World* set the impossible task of bringing ounces of gold from quartz that only yielded pennyweights. In other words the Silati mine was virtually worthless.

Williams had sent home reports to Conybeare and his fellow Directors which hinted at such. Another mining expert was sent to check but when he corroborated Williams' figures the Directors replaced Williams with a Mr. Pedersen who sent back highly satisfactory accounts. Meanwhile Williams had been described as incompetent. Having had his professional ability called into question, especially by Conybeare, the position of Williams was left in no doubt for, as the *Post* asked the question, who in future would invest money in a mine managed by Capt. Williams if they believed Mr. Conybeare's word?[73]

In July 1891 Conybeare went out to South Africa again to visit the Silati Company himself. Later he told the *Mining Journal* how having reached Johannesburg it had taken,

> two days' journey by coach to Pietersburg and then there is a branch
> coach to Haenertsburg. From Haenertsburg I did the trip by means of a
> days ride on horse back which brings one to the Silate Camp.[74]

Conybeare had been accompanied by a number of Cornishmen whom he thanked for their advice and kindness.[75] Unfortunately a new scandal, entitled Mr. Conybeare and the Dying man, hit the pages of the *Post*. Charles Cadwell from Tuckingmill had died in the Johannesburg Hospital but had assisted Conybeare in his early days. Apparently whilst at Johannesburg, Conybeare had agreed to pay Cadwell's hospital fees but later refused for which he was called a mean man. This was seen as an insult to all Cornishmen on the Rand and would seem to suggest that they were incapable of keeping a promise.[76] Perhaps it was no surprise in the 1892 General Election that Conybeare, although he won the Mining Division, did so with a reduced majority.

Meanwhile Williams had gone to court to save his reputation. Messrs. Bewick, Moreing & Alford, mining engineers acting on Williams' behalf showed that the Silati mine was indeed worthless. Alford had inspected the Silati Company and condemned it and Conybeare attacked Alford with such a degree of acrimony – many were shocked when charges of so discreditable a character were brought forward in public against him.[77] Alford emerged from the Silati litigation with honour but not so Conybeare. By 1893 Conybeare was attempting to float yet another gold mining company – the Sheba Lode – in South Africa whereupon the *Post* once again took him to task for taking every opportunity in his power to speak against Cornish mining but using his position as an M.P. to encourage London and other capitalists to send their money to South Africa.[78] A few weeks later the *Post* condemned Conybeare as a man of no political principle claiming his one and only principle was South African Mining.[79] Just over a year later the *Post* resumed its attack when it claimed Conybeare's whole policy since he had first arrived in Cornwall, had been to ruin Cornish mining and to raise up that of South Africa.[80] Conybeare's days were numbered and in July 1895 at the General

Election he was defeated by Arthur Strauss, who in fact held the bulk of the shares in the *Post*. Conybeare was the first Cornish M.P. to be brought down by events in South Africa but he was not the last.

There is only one example of an attempt made by a Cornishman to bring a new business to Cornwall with the aim of exporting its product back to South Africa and that was by Francis Oats who in 1891 established the British & Colonial Explosives Company at Perranporth. As well as being in competition with the two main Cornish explosive companies – Curtis & Harvey Ltd., Kennal Vale and the Cornish Explosives Works, Hayle – it was felt that the new company could take a profitable share of the market. Its only rival in the Transvaal where a monopoly existed, was the all powerful Nobel Explosives Company. In 1893 the *Mining Journal* reported:

> *Information has reached Cornwall that the Nobels Trust people are in anything but a pleasant humour from the fact that the Cornish Company of dynamite manufacturers have been of late importing considerable quantities of their goods into South Africa. It is satisfactory, at least to Cornwall, that the Cornish Company is making such good headway. In the face of the prevailing mining depression, it is well to know that some industries are working their way successfully.*[81]

Sadly this was not to last.Within three months of this report, Nobels,by a combination of a price war and having inside information about the Cornish Company, staged a successful take-over of the British & Colonial Explosives Company:

> *Thus apart from the British and Colonial experience throughout the 1880's and 1890's the relationship between Cornwall and South Africa was, in effect a one-way one.The outflow of men, machinery and skills was not matched to the same degree by returning management or flamboyant prodigal sons.*[82]

1. CORNISHMAN, 18th July 1895

2. MINING JOURNAL, 14th April 1900

3. Barton, A HISTORY OF TIN MINING & SMELTING IN CORNWALL p.169. Competition saw the price of copper fall steadily from £115 a ton in 1860,to £80 a ton in 1870,to £60 a ton in 1885 and as little as £38 a ton in the 1890's.

4. Halliday, A HISTORY OF CORNWALL, p.298

5. WEST BRITON, 6th FEBRUARY 1879

6. IBID., 6th MARCH 1875

7. CORNUBIAN, 28th MARCH 1879

8. WEST BRITON, 6th MARCH 1879

9. IBID., 20th MARCH 1879

10. IBID., 3rd APRIL 1879

11. Barton, A HISTORY OF COPPER MINING IN CORNWALL AND DEVON p.90

12. WEST BRITON,10th APRIL 1879

13. IBID., 24th JULY 1979. Money also came from the Cornish community in Pachua,Mexico.

14. IBID., 10th FEBRUARY 1881

15. CORNUBIAN, 29th April 1861.
Population for Cornwall.
1841 - 341,269
1851 - 355,558
1861 - 369,390
1871 - 362,093
1881 - 356,266

16. CORNISHMAN, 12th SEPTEMBER

17. There were 13 Unions representing 221 Parishes in Cornwall.

18. CORNISHMAN, 10th OCTOBER 1892

19. IBID., 26th SEPTEMBER 1895

20. IBID., 12th JANUARY 1899. Ten other women were mentioned in the same case,their husbands being in America.

21. IBID., 6th MAY 1897

22. IBID., 26th JANUARY 1899. Bigamy was one reason why some men in the States didn't send money home according to the CALUMET WEEKLY NEWS, IBID., 12th OCTOBER 1899. See also IBID., 10th July 1902

23. Information supplied by Ken Sara who was from Scorrier and arrived in South Africa in 1929.He was the District Grand Master of the Transvaal and Orange Free State (Scottish Constitution) of Freemasons from 1956-60 being the only Cousin Jack to reach that position. In carrying out his masonic duties he travelled a great deal and met many Cornish people such as, Garfield Blight manager of Rooiberg Tin Mine who hailed from Tuckingmill near Redruth,he was followed by Oxley Oxland,a relative of the well known 'Parson Oxland' of Illogan,both ex-Camborne School of Mines, Pengelly, Manager of an Asbestos Mine in Swaziland,also ex. C.S.M. Fred Hosken,Underground Manager,West Rand Consolidated and others.

24. CORNISHMAN, 14th JANUARY 1897 Paupers lived in the workhouse whilst out-paupers lived in their own homes but still depended on relief.Many were old or sick.

25. IBID., 20th MAY 1897

26. Jenkin, CORNISH MINER, p.329

27. CORNUBIAN, 2nd OCTOBER 1891

28. IBID., 7th AUGUST 1891

29. MINING JOURNAL, 11th JUNE 1892 p.653

30. CORNISHMAN 13th AUGUST 1892. There was also employment required on the Delabole section of the North Cornwall Railway.

31. IBID., 14th SEPTEMBER 1893

32. C.P.M.N., 31st AUGUST 1894.It was claimed 1,000 were out of work.

33. MINING JOURNAL, 20th APRIL 1895 p.456

34. CORNISHMAN, 23rd MAY 1895

35. IBID., 13th JUNE 1895

36. C.P.M.N., 9th JANUARY 1896

37. IBID., 29th OCTOBER 1896

38. MINING JOURNAL, 28th SEPTEMBER 1896

39. C.P.M.N., 6th FEBRUARY 1896

40. CORNISHMAN, 26th SEPTEMBER 1896

41. MINING JOURNAL, 12th OCTOBER 1896 p.1242

42. CORNISHMAN, 21st NOVEMBER 1895.The latest reports were that about one thousand persons were every week passing through Cape Town on their way to Johannesburg,many of whom hail from Cornwall. CORNUBIAN, 15th NOVEMBER 1895

43. C.P.M.N., 12th DECEMBER 1895

44. IBID., 16th JULY 1896

45. The number was estimated between 6000 – 7000 but it was pointed out that there was three times that number in the U.S.A. (Butte City – 10,000, Cripple Creek – 5000 and Grass Valley – 3000) IBID., 12th MARCH 1896

46. CORNISHMAN, 11th JULY 1896

47. C.P.M.N., 30th JULY 1896

48. IBID., 1st OCTOBER 1896

49. IBID., 27th FEBRUARY 1896

50. MINING JOURNAL, 25th JULY 1896 p.967

51. CORNISHMAN, 15th OCTOBER 1896

52. IBID., 2nd MARCH 1896

53. Barton, THE CORNISH BEAM ENGINE p.150

54. E. Vale, THE HARVEYS OF HAYLE (TRURO 1966) p.305

55. CORNISHMAN, 3rd OCTOBER 1895

56. Vale, HARVEYS OF HAYLE

57. CORNUBIAN, 12th AUGUST 1897

58. Vale, HARVEYS OF HAYLE p.309

59. IBID., p.310

60. Bernard C.Hollowood, CORNISH ENGINEERS (HOLMANS 1951, 1st Edition – privately published) p.92

61. MINING JOURNAL, 30th NOVEMBER 1896 p.1470

62. C.P.M.N., 5th NOVEMBER 1908

63. CORNISHMAN, 30th JANUARY 1896

64. C.P.M.N., 16th FEBRUARY 1911. They left two other brothers in Camborne, T.Eddy who worked at Holmans and F.C. Eddy who worked at Roskear.

65. IBID., 28th SEPTEMBER 1905. See also Dickason, CORNISH IMMIGRANTS TO SOUTH AFRICA. p.60-61

66. CORNUBIAN, 13th DECEMBER 1895

67. CORNISHMAN, 6th AUGUST 1896

68. CORNUBIAN, 14th MAY 1897

69. IBID., 20th AUGUST 1897. The Methodists had split into the Primitive Methodists who, as their name suggests,went back to the early church methods of organisation and the Wesleyan Methodists who continued to follow Wesley's ideas.In 1932 all became united once more as Methodists although pockets of Primitive Methodists and Wesleyans can still be found around the country.

70. CORNISHMAN, 18th MARCH 1897

71. IBID., 2nd SEPTEMBER 1897

72. C.P.M.N., 24th NOVEMBER 1910

73. IBID., 9th MAY 1891

74. MINING JOURNAL, 6th FEBRUARY 1892. p.139

75. CORNUBIAN, 21st AUGUST 1891

76. C.P.M.N., 14th MAY 1892

77. MINING JOURNAL, 21st MAY 1892

78. C.P.M.N., 8th DECEMBER 1893

79. IBID., 15th DECEMBER 1893

80. IBID., 11th JANUARY 1894

81. MINING JOURNAL, 14th OCTOBER 1893 p.1145

82. Burke, THE CORNISH MINER p.134-13

CHAPTER SIX

BLOOD AND GOLD

THE JAMESON RAID AND
SECOND BOER WAR

It will be terrible when this topic is worn threadbare
Winston Churchill.[1]

All wars are avoidable. But this war was for the equality of the white race, humanitarian dealing with the blacks, honest and good government for all

William Hosken.[2]

The great upheaval to the Cornish in South Africa caused by the Boer War 1899-1902 was preceded by the Jameson Raid four years earlier. The story of the ill-fated Jameson Raid has been well documented and discussed[3] but it is one of those curious episodes of history where it seems the more that is written about the subject in order to clarify what actually happened, the more mysterious and complicated it becomes. As for the Boer War, Thomas Pakenham's book of that title[4] is considered by many as the definitive book on the subject. Admirable as it is, surprisingly, considering out of the many sources used, Pakenham completely ignores the Cornish newspapers, which all followed closely the events of the war – often with a greater insight, due to the Cornish-South African connection.

The Jameson Raid – a somewhat foolhardy attempt to overthrow President Kruger's regime in the Transvaal – had been planned in the main by Cecil Rhodes, the Prime Minister of Cape Colony. The gold rush had seen a large number of immigrants, mainly British, arrive in the Transvaal who were called Uitlanders by the Boers. Using the genuine grievances of the Uitlanders as a catalyst (such as being denied the rights of citizenship yet bearing the brunt of taxation) the idea was for the Uitlanders, led by a Reform Committee in Johannesburg, to rebel.[5] Then from across the border in support would gallop an armed force led by Dr. Leander Starr Jameson. In short the initial rebellion never happened and the raid that did, failed. The Uitlanders had already made an attempt to settle their grievances with Kruger by means of a National Union set up in 1892. The Kruger regime, which was considered corrupt, destructive and reactionary, remained intransigent. Kruger, despite being sixty-eight years old, was re-elected as President in 1893. The Union gave way to a Reform Committee which decided

The Reform Committee. William Hosken is standing second from left, back row.

that force was now the only way to topple Kruger. A new, independent Republic could then be set up in which the Uitlanders would be enfranchised and the mining industry would profit as a dynamite monopoly, restrictive railway tariffs, liquor monopoly and favouritism to the Dutch and Germans would all be swept away. At least two Cornishmen were Committee members. William Hosken was an ideal link between mine management – he was managing director of several leading Natal mining companies and a founder member of the executive committee of the Chamber of Mines – and the ordinary miners, of whom many were Cornish. The second Cornishman was C.A.C. Tremeer, an ex-Major in the Cape Frontier Police and considered as the ablest of the volunteer officers.[6] The Committee ringleaders were Frank Rhodes (Cecil's brother), George Farrar, Lionel Phillips and John Hays Hammond. Although it was up to the Reform Committee, when ready, to give the signal for rebellion, Jameson, over-confident and impatient, could not wait, and crossed the border on the evening of 29th December 1895. As the New Year arrived, Jameson's force, getting no further than Krugersdorp, was surrounded and captured all too easily by a strong force of Boers. Hosken and Tremeer, along with all the other members of the Reform Committee, were arrested and thrown in jail. Hosken, who claimed the Reform Committee had not been ready despite having amassed 2,200 rifles, 3 Maxim guns and spending £400,000 in laying up provisions against a possible siege, called Jameson an erratic individual who had claimed to be on the border with 1,500 men – but had only 480.[7] Jameson, on the other hand, was equally disgusted with the Johannesburg Uitlanders, who barked but did not bite.[8]

Although the abortive raid took place in the last week of December 1895 the news did not reach Cornwall until New Year, along with the Christmas letters and papers which did not carry any hints of the impending raid. Such was the anguish of relatives fearing the worst had happened in Johannesburg, that at Camborne the Town Crier was sent around the town with the good news that all was quiet [9] and a telegram was put up in the window of the Printing & Stationery Company telling of the capture of Jameson and his loss of about 70 men killed and 30 wounded.[10] The mood soon changed to anger when it was discovered that a number of Cornishmen were accused of cowardice for their apparent lack of support, and it was reported that on the eve of the raid 200 Cornishmen left Johannesburg for Cape Town and were presented at the railway station with white feathers.[11] Another newspaper claimed that Cornishmen were hooted in the streets as cowards.[12] There was strong anti-Cornish feeling in Natal and at Durban, police had to escort Cornish miners from the train, to avoid a hostile reception.[13] From the jumble of delayed and contradictory telegrams[14] it was not at first clear what exactly had happened. More credence was given to the statements of the actual miners, who soon arrived back in Cornwall.

The first boat to arrive at Plymouth from South Africa, carrying some seventeen Cornish miners on board, was the *S.S. Tartar,* on Sunday 19th January. Knowing that a revolt was imminent these Cornishmen had actually left Johannesburg before the raid but admitted the reason for this was because they had anticipated fearful consequences. They had been in no doubt that many of the miners had been armed with the guns smuggled in during the previous months by Rhodes, the purpose for which was breaking up the Transvaal Government.

One miner claimed he was not prepared to risk his life for the sake of a few capitalists who 'wanted to make wars for their own particular ends'. Another said that organisation of the rebellion had been conducted so secretly that it was not until the very last moment they knew of the probability of an early fight. None seemed surprised when told the news of the raid, having expected something serious to have taken place before their reaching Plymouth. As for the civil rights claimed by the Uitlanders this apparently had not greatly troubled the miners, whereas some others said that a large number of Cornishmen left the mines, on the grounds that bloodshed was not necessary in order to obtain desirable constitutional reforms. Other miners had been told that not to carry a rifle would lead to a forfeit of their wage and a few had actually come away from the Rand with money owed them.[15] The next boatload of Cornish miners to arrive home were even more united in their condemnation of the mine owners, claiming:

> *There was scarcely a Cornishman agitating against the Boers – unless perhaps a shift boss or capitalist. We did not know Jameson was coming but were told we should soon have to fight for our lives. We were given guns, enrolled in companies and stationed in forts - there was no proper organisation and if Jameson had reached Johannesburg things would be worse than they are now for there would have been bloody war.[16]*

Other miners in the group spoke of wanting wages more than votes and could not see why they should face bullets in order to get the ballot box. With the mines being closed and the threat of war scaring away native workers many of the Cornish miners who had come out to work thought it time to leave. The following week over 150 miners from St. Day, Redruth, Camborne, St. Agnes, Penzance and Liskeard landed at Plymouth. They also told of concealed arms on the mines but had not solicited Jameson's aid.[17] When about three dozen Cornish miners returned to St. Just the following week a few were lucky to find work at the Levant Mine.[18] The majority of the Cornish who arrived home saw the whole affair as an attempt to 'burst Oom Paul' and his colleagues from the responsible position which they held in the conduct of the affairs of their own country.[19] As another Cornishman pointed out, it was a well known fact that in Mexico and other foreign countries where Cornish miners were located, they had kept aloof from politics – their one object being to make money and return home to enjoy it.[20] Letters from Cornishmen in Johannesburg showed that at least on one mine Cornish miners were actually prevented from taking up arms, a notice being read out that Mr. Barnato had decided to give his men no arms but they were to lie neutral and work on the mine as if nothing was going on. Then later that day the men were paid off but as the roads into Johannesburg were blocked by armed Boers one Cornishman said "we did what we thought best, and made our way to the nearest railway station and took tickets for the Colony".[21]

The Cornish left the Transvaal for a number of reasons. Jameson had failed to take the miners into his confidence,[23] or the men refused to take up arms, or the men not having arms to take up, or the failure of the Reform Committee to win over the men's support. The over-riding question was *Were the Cornishmen Cowards?*[23] Many articles and even poems appeared in the Cornish press in an attempt to exonerate those who left, whilst numerous letters were written expressing opposing points of view in an attempt to answer the question. Guy Pollard of Egloshayle writing from Johannesburg said bluntly that the Cornish who had left had disgraced the name of Cornishmen although those who had remained to a certain extent had wiped out the stigma but Cornishmen 'will ever be a by-word here'.[24] Despite Cape Town correspondents telling of the Cornish miners being execrated as cowards and poltroons[25] the Cornish attitude at home was of tolerance and impartiality.

The view of the majority of the Cornish was that as the actual number who left the Transvaal was small compared to that which remained, then the principle embodied in the saying 'one scabbed sheep spoils a flock' should not apply.[26] William Thomas, the Secretary of the Cornish Mining Association, estimated that by not counting those Cornish who left Cape Town before the stampede from Johannesburg the rest who returned totalled no more than 175 men. He also pointed out that some of these would have been coming home in the ordinary course of events, while a number of the rest were young and inexperienced miners who had been unsure as to what to do when trouble unexpectedly broke out.[27] J. Harry Johns later claimed that out of 260 men, only 2 left for home from the Ferreira Mine.[28]

Much was made of the Cornish Brigade, formed in Johannesburg and numbering some 400 men, which easily outnumbered those who had returned to Cornwall. Under the command of officers such as Colonel James Hosken (Roskear), Captain Adjutant, Arthur Hodge (Redruth), Captains Davey, Pollard, Rundle and Eddy plus Lieutenants Simons and Williams the men were paraded in front of the Cornish Association Office before being marched back to the Wemmer mine. Then after two hours' drill the men paraded through the principal streets of Johannesburg proceeded by the One & All Band playing *Trelawny*. The men, who were frequently cheered as they marched, were distinguished by a white ribbon with the fifteen balls on it, worn on the left arm. It was said they were well supplied with food from the Commissariat Department under the direction of Mr Charles Rowe, Manager of the Llangaate United Mines. It was reported that Edward Doble of Penzance also took up arms as did Bernard Lyle from Marazion, who was drilling the people for defence.[29]

One Cornishman wrote to say the Jameson raid was the most exciting and curious week he had ever spent, telling of the trains to the Cape and Natal being overcrowded with women and children, and how the police or ZARPS were withdrawn so it had been necessary to equip a force although it had been a great surprise to them all and the Government when the Reform Committee were able to serve out many thousands of rifles. Jameson's arrest had come as a shock, and the

tide of opinion went against the Reform Committee – although the majority were
still eager to strike a blow at the Boers and march to Pretoria.[30] A St. Just man
writing home said the softest job he ever struck in his life was when the trouble
began. for he had £1 a day for walking around with a rifle in his hand.[31] Hugh
Lanion Hall was contacted by his old friend, Percy Fitzpatrick, who was now
working for Eckstein Brothers[32] but more importantly was Secretary of the
Reform Committee. Fitzpatrick requested Hall to supply the Committee with a
large number of cattle, sheep and horses – money being no object. Hall at first
assumed the cattle and sheep were to supply the natives on the mines with food.
With his brother George, Hall bought all the fat cattle he could get in the Eastern
Transvaal and soon had one thousand five hundred head of cattle, three hundred
sheep and twelve horses. Hall was aware by now that some trouble was brewing[33]
and had his own family safely removed to Bloemfontein. Hall and his brother then
took the livestock to Johannesburg, luckily by a back route for a group of ZARPS
had been waiting on the main road to arrest them and confiscate the livestock.
Once in town the cattle were guarded near the Bonanza mine. Some of the guards
were Cornishmen, who Hall noted were, not a bad lot and when they found out
that he was Cornish too, were quite happy. So they might have been, for they were
getting £1 per shift. Hall made many trips to the Reform Committee Headquarters
to pay in money from the sale of cattle to the town butchers. At night he had to
have a password:

> Cornish miners on guard at the mines would challenge me with 'Halt, be
> ye friend, or be ye foe ?'When satisfied that 'I be friend' they would ask
> for the password and wish me good night as I rode on. I soon saw that
> these chaps all untrained, and knowing nothing about a gun, would make
> no stand against the Boers[34]

With the arrest of Jameson, Hall and his brother quickly left Johannesburg to
join their family at Bloemfontein. A Marazion miner who was also on guard in
Johannesburg wrote that, with the arrest of Jameson:

> We received orders to lay down our arms that evening or Dr. Jameson
> and his men would be shot. This was done and we returned to our
> respective diggings (lodgings). I slept 18 hours and never budged as I do
> not think I had more than eight hours' sleep for the nine days and I felt
> done up. I fully expected to be shot... I am still on the mine and have
> started to work again. During the affair a cup of tea and a bit of bread &
> butter cost 1/6d and I gave as much as 5s for an apology of a meal.[35]

Even with news of the Cornish Brigade and letters such as these the charge of
cowardice was to rankle with Cornishmen for many months afterwards. The
Cornish motto was not exactly upheld either in a letter written by a woman in
defence of stalwart Penzance men:

*Will you kindly note that among so many 'White Feathered Men' who have returned to Cornwall from the Transvaal we (women) are pleased to say... that there is not one Penzance man returned out of so many hundreds we have here.*36

At home few would have disagreed with the eminent Cornishman Arthur Quiller-Couch who said at a Cornish Dinner in Birmingham that he had

*not lost faith in Cornishmen and saw no reason why our miners in the Transvaal should rise against armed Government forces when a stock jobber waved a Union Jack in their faces. At home Cornishmen play a fascinating game of hazard – their lives against £3.10s a month – and have again and again displayed pluck, heroism and fortitude. To cast a slur on Cornish miners as a class is the act of fools at large, who in most cases would shun the dangers of Cornish mining as they would the devil.*37

A few months later at the London-Cornish Association Dinner the M.P. for the Cornish Mining Division -Arthur Strauss- commenting on the charge of cowardice said, "It is libel and I know it".38

Of much more interest to Cornish people, was the discovery that some Cornishmen had actually been part of Jameson's force, including John Menheniot of Helston, John Miners of Wendron and E.W. Wenn, the son of Rev. T. Wenn, a Wesleyan Minister at Launceston.39 At least one Cornishman – a miner from Hayle – had witnessed Jameson's last stand and writing to his wife told of the horrors as the Englishmen fell one after another under the fire of the Boers.40 With the Battle of Doornkop at Krugersdorp over, the injured had to be taken care of and a makeshift hospital had been set up in the new stores of Messrs. Harvey & Greenacre & Co. in Ockerse Street. Mrs. Deecker volunteered her services and was appointed Matron. There were 50 patients at first – 13 Boers and 37 men of Jameson's force.41 Later an enquiry was held into the hospital after it was claimed Jameson's men received better treatment than the Boers – who were often left on the floor. Mrs. Deecker had the full support of Dr. Viljoen who described her as a lady of ability and whose work was admirable. Her powers of organisation and the excellent results attained by the patients were also to her credit. Mrs. Deecker testified herself that the work had been very hard, especially for the first few days, when the majority of the operations took place. With no professional nurses available the amateurs had taken over but the surgeons were perfectly satisfied. Then a testimonial letter to Mrs. Deecker and the other nurses was read out from the patients of the hospital in appreciation and it was signed by Jameson's men.42

On the 15th February Frederick Tiddy visited the battlefield himself and made the prophetic utterance:

If Mr Chamberlain should in any way repeat the mistake of Mr. Gladstone
– if he listens to stories of the so called magnanimity of the Boer and in
any way strengthens Boer Government - the day will come soon when the
business must be worked over again with a thousand times more bloody
results.[43]

Jameson and his men were eventually released, being shipped back to England for trial. Kruger had already proclaimed a general amnesty for all Uitlanders except the Reform Committee – the four leaders of which were sentenced to death. The others were given a 2 year jail sentence and were fined £2,000 each. Kruger then relented and reprieved the death sentences, and when one of the Committee members – Fred Grey – went insane and cut his throat (his funeral was attended by 3,000 people) Kruger bowed to public pressure and petitions and released all the remaining prisoners.[44] All the fines were paid by Rhodes and Alfred Beit.

Only Jameson and his officers were put on trial so his troopers were allowed their freedom. Back to Cornwall came Louis Anthony and a Mr. Cazalet – both former students at the Camborne School of Mines – H. Young from Penzance and Mr. Reynolds – a former member of the Camborne Police. All except Anthony were preparing to go back to the Transvaal, which is perhaps why Anthony seemed less reluctant to give the *Post* an interview.[45] Although originally a miner, Anthony had joined the Bechuanaland Mounted Police and on 6th December 1895 G and K troops were handed over to Rhodes' Chartered Company and the men had their old Henri Martini rifles replaced with new Lee-Metford ones. Anthony knew trouble was coming when he was handed 110 rounds of ammunition instead of the usual 10 rounds, but assumed the pending trouble was against some natives led by a chief called Linchway. On crossing the Transvaal border Anthony was told they were going to relieve the women and children of Johannesburg. On reaching Krugersdorp they expected to be met by reinforcements from Johannesburg but instead were met by a large force of Boers. Hopelessly outnumbered they surrendered to Cronje, the Boer Commander. After a short imprisonment Anthony was sent to Durban, put on board the *Harlech Castle* and sailed home. Anthony accused the Boers of having no sense of honour by using explosive bullets and claiming that they had only lost twelve men killed in battle when he saw more dead than that lying around the laager in the early morning; in his opinion Kruger was artful.[46]

Hugh Lanion Hall verifies this as he makes it quite clear that Kruger knew all about the smuggled guns, had deciphered the telegrams sent to Jameson and Rhodes and was fully prepared, knowing the exact moment Jameson crossed the border. As Hall put it the Reform Movement was an utter failure. The Government had the Reformers beaten from the start for their intelligence was too great for them.[47]

There is a definite mystery surrounding the part played by one Cornishman during the time of the Jameson Raid.

Maria Vorster claims Frederick de Witt Tossel (formerly Llewellyn May) played a very important role in the events leading up to the Jameson Raid but gives no precise details except to say, the Jameson Raid took its toll and in February Tossel asked to be transferred back to the uniform section![48] Harry Zeederburg is even briefer, by saying that Tossel resigned shortly after the Jameson trial and it was rumoured that he had left the Transvaal.[49] From Tossel there is no clue at all. However, if the papers are to be believed, Tossel severed his connections with the Johannesburg Detective Department but the announcement in the *Krugersdorp Times* that Tossel was being freed from his duties had caused surprise as well as no small amount of surmise.[50] Krugersdorp was very much Tossel's adopted home for in his own words it was there he had been married, his children born and some of them buried; they would know that if he ever talked of home he meant Krugersdorp. Dr. Viljoen had considered Tossel's appointment to Johannesburg a good and wise one,[51] so what had happened that resulted in Tossel being removed from his post? Whatever the reason it was not made public despite the *Krugersdorp Times* demanding it. Within a few weeks however, the same paper was able to announce:

> Under the heading 'A Good Appointment' the 'Potchefstroom Budget' says 'The appointment of Lieut. Tossel as the Chief of Police in the goldfields area of the Potchefstroom and Krugersdorp district is a step in the right direction. Our police matters want touching up badly. The Lieutenant will find that he has a wide area to keep his eye upon and a lot of curious police material to knock into shape.[52]

Tossel was not to remain in the Orange Free State for long, for within two weeks following this announcement the *Krugersdorp Times* reported that Jameson's Trial had been postponed to allow the appearance of some witnesses from South Africa. Lieut. Tossel and Lieut. Eloff were among the number of those about to take a trip across the herring pond.[53] The trial of Jameson, which began 20th July, ended nine days later with Jameson having been sentenced to 15 months. Ill health and a Queen's Pardon saw him released within four months. At the trial there is no mention of Tossel. On returning to South Africa Tossel must have resumed his duties with the Johannesburg Detective Department for in 1897 another Rand newspaper reported:

> Lieutenant Tossel is in retirement for a while having been temporarily removed from his position as Chief Officer for the working of the Immorality Law in Johannesburg. Pending an investigation the duties have been taken over by Sergeant Murphy of Jeppestown. The charge

*against the late Chief of Police for the West Rand is an ugly one whether
there be any foundation for it or not.*[54]

The Immorality Law was aimed at eradicating prostitution in Johannesburg
which had become a serious embarrassment to the town. A Morality Squad had
been set up by the police but unfortunately some of its members were bribed, and
whether Tossel was one of these is not clear.[55] In the meantime Tossel remained, as
the paper put it, rusticating at the Capital of the West Rand on the look out for
more worlds to conquer.[56]

The only other Cornishman who perhaps could have given a real insight into the
Jameson Raid from the Reform Committee's point of view, was William Hosken.
He returned to Hayle to stay with his cousin Samuel the head of Messrs. Hosken,
Trevithick, Polkinhorn & Co. and one of the greatest breeders of shorthorns in the
country, expertise he was later to take to South Africa. One of the terms of William
Hosken's release, as it had been for all the others, was that he was no longer to
interfere with the politics of the Transvaal; therefore when interviewed by the *Post*
he could make little reference to the Raid. Instead he concentrated on persuading
Cornish miners to go to South Africa. In an outline of the gold mining industry on
the Rand, where he estimated there were 7,000 Cornishmen employed, Hosken
claimed there was still a demand for the rock drill man who was sure of at least 20
per cent more wages and constant employment. It was the drill sharpener who
made the most money, however, but he was expected to sharpen 400 drills in an
eight hour shift for which he was paid £1 a day. In Cornwall the average was 200
drills a day for £1 a week.[57] After a short stay, Hosken returned to the Transvaal
and Johannesburg.

The Cornish miner needed no persuasion from Hosken to go to the Rand.
Although the Jameson Raid brought some miners home, such was the depressed
state of the Cornish mining industry that even as they arrived others were leaving
and those who had returned because of the Jameson Raid were soon on their way
back. One of these, William Hurley, who had come home with his brother to
Illogan, returned to the Rand and by May was back working in the same mine he
had left until he was killed underground.[58] Near the end of 1896 special trains
from Cornwall were once more in operation, and emigration to South Africa was
as high as ever. Since January over 1,000 miners from the districts of Camborne
and Redruth alone had left for the land of gold and diamonds.[59]

The political explosion caused by the Jameson Raid in January 1896 was
followed in February by an "almighty" dynamite explosion in the Johannesburg
suburb of Vriedendorp. The blast, which made a hole 40 fathoms long, six feet
wide and nine deep, 'created a Gwennap Pit in an instant'.[60] This Cornish idiom
was quite apt, for indirectly the explosion was linked to a Cornishman. It was
believed the dynamite which had been left exposed to the sun for some days in

Chapter Six

Blood and Gold. The Jameson Raid and Second Boer War

trucks at a railway siding, exploded due to a combination of the heat and the impact made when an engine began to shunt the trucks. According to Chilvers the explosion was a result of peculiar circumstances arising over the storage of dynamite after the Jameson Raid.[61] The dynamite should have been safely stored in a warehouse belonging to William Hosken. The explosion, which killed 80 people, occurred on Wednesday 19th February in the afternoon; as one witness later recalled:

> *About 3-15 p.m. I was walking along Henwoods Arcade Market Square*
> *when suddenly a shock lifted me from the ground and down came a*
> *shower of glass from Henwood & Souters building from the second storey*
> *which struck me on my hat which fortunately saved my head.*[62]

The Cornish Association Secretary, G.T. Oliver, was on his way to hospital to visit some sick Cornish, when the shock wave of the blast hit the hospital, smashing most of the windows. As £33,000 was raised almost immediately to form a relief fund – most of the contributors being Reform Committee members – Oliver considered this was enough to show the Government that the Uitlander is deserving of more consideration.[63]

1896 was certainly an eventful year for the Cornish in South Africa. If the excitement of the Raid, the explosion or the tour by Fanny Moody were not enough, then at least for the Cornish Methodists there was the visit made by Mark Guy Pearse. If strong emotional preaching was a keystone of Cornish Methodism then the Methodist Minister from Camborne was not to disappoint those in Johannesburg. Travelling with his wife and daughter his evangelistic tour lasted about five months. On reaching Johannesburg, which he thought was like another Cornwall, Pearse said:

> *I wished with all my heart that I could have sent home some of the*
> *prosperity of this new land for the dear old county. I had come with*
> *dreams of gold, gold, gold but I was blinded and choked and buried with*
> *dust, dust, dust.*[64]

Although Pearse was given an enthusiastic welcome from the Cornish, it was not so good from the Boers, mainly because he was outspoken about native drunkenness – which he believed was being fostered by the Dutch Government.[65] Pearse found Cornishmen by the hundreds – Tre Pol and Pen were everywhere,[66] and when he preached at the Wesleyan chapel in Johannesburg it was so crowded that the service commenced 40 minutes before time. He gave a whole week of lectures such as *'How I came to sign the pledge'*, and services which it was claimed would live long in the memory and hearts of all Cornishmen in Johannesburg.[67] Pearse was in Pretoria when a number of the Reform Committee, including Hosken were released, and he also visited George Farrar, (Holman's

Representative) in prison, noting that when Farrar was later released, he saw him arrive in Johannesburg with Lionel Phillips where they were lifted shoulder high and surrounded by thousands of friends borne in triumph to his office.[68] Pearse whilst in Pretoria, met and talked with Kruger's wife, whom he described as "a grand old mother in Israel".[69] Despite their delightful talk which lasted half an hour, Pearse continued to denounce the Boers:

> *I have heard of the outrageous conduct of the police and their dealings with the natives. I saw enough myself to stir my blood to a fever of indignation that I felt it difficult to control.*[70]

If the planning of the Jameson Raid had occurred in relative secrecy then the same could not be said for the eventual Boer War. As early as 1897 extra troops were being sent to the Cape and Cornishmen were arriving home talking about how another Majuba Hill would give them the chance to cast off the yoke of the Boer,[71] whilst the *Cornishman* reported on the *Uncertainty & Perplexity at the Rand* and speculated as to what would happen next? A number of mines had closed, wages had been reduced by as much as 25 per cent with shipping agents putting berths up for auction to the highest bidders to have the first chance to leave the city of gold, disease and dissatisfaction.[72] However, the situation seemed to improve and a rise in share prices at Johannesburg raised hope for the Rand's future. It was shattered at the end of 1898. Cornish miner Joseph Tucker explained the situation and the impending conflict in a letter to his son written 31st December:

> *Well things is in a very disturbed state again. One of the Dutch police broke open a man's door last week and shot the man dead and had no warrant nor summons to serve so the feeling in Johannesburg is very hostile to the Dutch...'* [73]

The failure of the Jameson Raid led to Cecil Rhodes' resignation as Prime Minister of Cape Colony. It had also humiliated the British Colonial Secretary, Joseph Chamberlain. Despite having denied any involvement in the Raid,[74] Chamberlain had given his encouragement and was now out for revenge on Kruger. He not only wrote to Kruger insisting that the Uitlander grievances be resolved but early in 1897 appointed Sir Alfred Milner as High Commissioner for South Africa and Governor of the Cape, and encouraged him to pursue a more aggressive policy towards Kruger. If the role of Rhodes had been taken over by Milner then that of Jameson had been taken over by Percy Fitzpatrick, the leading political mind among the Uitlanders.[75] Fitzpatrick also represented Ecksteins, the subsidiary company of Wernher-Beit, and Beit himself was also involved. The man shot in Johannesburg by the police was Tom Edgar, a miner and Uitlander, and his death was used as an excuse for mass meetings of the Uitlanders all along the

Rand. The all-important meeting came at Bloemfontein from 31st May – 6th June, when Milner met Kruger. The stumbling block was the Uitlander franchise qualification which required fourteen years' residence in the Transvaal before the vote was given. Milner wanted the qualification reduced to five years. Kruger, who had been elected for a fourth term as President the previous year, had no desire to see a situation develop where a majority of Uitlanders (who far outnumbered the Boers) received the vote and brought about an end to Transvaal independence by putting his country once more under British control. The meeting thus ended and war seemed unavoidable.

Following the shooting of Edgar an action of libel was brought against Cornishman Joseph Dunn (now Editor of the *Transvaal Critic*) for having shown racial favouritism in the paper.[76] The Cornish newspapers now began to carry headlines such as *Transvaal Powder Keg – Who will Strike the Match?*[77] and *Cornish Eyes Watch the Transvaal*,[78] telling of British subjects being shadowed and busy spies. Then came the curious episode of the arrest of eight men for high treason, on the 16th May. Amid much speculation as to whether a second Jameson Raid had been nipped in the bud concern was shown over the identity of a certain Colonel Richard Floyd Nicholls and a Lieutenant Edward John Tremlett. Although both were Cornish neither were British Officers. It turned out at their trial, in July, that Nicholls, a miner from Perranuthnoe, had been duped by Tremlett, who was paid by Boer detectives. The case was quickly dropped and it was not clear what the significance was of this Boer trickery and tyranny.[79] There was no mistaking the reasons behind a Uitlander demonstration organised by William Hosken and to avoid arrest Hosken had to escape to Natal, his leaving the Transvaal being considered a bad omen for peace.[80] The exodus from Johannesburg in 1899 had begun as early as June but by September the numbers leaving totalled 1,750 a day. For the Cornish miner it was almost a repeat performance of 1896 as once again he was shown the white feather and pelted with rotten eggs.[81] Why the Cornish miner should be singled out was obvious to one correspondent:

> *it is clear to me that the cleverness and industry of Cousin Jacks have rendered them the objects of very envious and malicious feeling from the unprincipled part of the community there who evidently require the fighting as well as the work done for them.*[82]

A much larger number of miners came back to Cornwall than during the Jameson Raid and trains which arrived in Redruth after an African liner reached Southampton were spoken of as "Afrikanders trains".[83] Most miners were returning because the mines had nearly all closed down, and once again many spoke of having no complaints against the Boers, and considered the present trouble as being brought about by the capitalists for sinister purposes. On the question of the franchise, many thought it would not affect the Cornish miners who were only birds of passage.[84] In the *Post* it was felt the granting of the franchise could lead to wages being lowered and many agreed that the franchise was not greatly wanted.[85] However, the miners were not happy paying the 18/6d per year Poll Tax especially when, if they lost their receipt, they had to pay again. It was obvious that most Cornish miners only went to the Transvaal in order to earn a high wage and return home to their wives and families as soon as possible.

If the Rand was the key to the paradox of prosperity presented by most of the villages and smaller Cornish towns then the prospect of war was viewed with considerable trepidation, for the stopping of remittances home meant hard times ahead.[86] At Camborne, businessmen had already noted a fall in money from Africa.[87] Whole communities in Cornwall such as St. Just were supported entirely by remittances. The advent of war was therefore seen as momentous to the Cornish people and especially around Camborne and Redruth where it was thought hundreds would be driven into the workhouse in an area where the percentage of pauperism was already the largest in England.[88] It was believed Cornwall would suffer more than any other county in England. As one newspaper pointed out:

> *Although tin mining has been practically dead for twenty years Redruth*
> *and Camborne are more prosperous today than ever. The shops are*
> *larger, better and constantly being rebuilt, the result of those bad laws we*
> *hear about in the Transvaal. One today sees dejected groups of men*
> *gathered at the corners of streets discussing the future of their source of*
> *income. Practically only one reply is made to the question. If the English*
> *take the country, what's going to become of we? (The Cornish miner still*
> *speaks of English as another people living East of the Tamar).*[89]

With so many Cornish miners returning home the *Mining Journal* thought they probably ran the risk that once the war was over the capitalist, having become disgusted at the action of the 'Cousin Jacks' would not be inclined to give them employment again.[90] It also raised the question of the collateral effect the returning miners would have upon the Cornish mining industry itself for the mining towns – particularly Redruth, Camborne and St. Just – 'were wearing an aspect singularly suggestive of the good old times when the mines were in full swing.'[91] Fortunately – unlike the time of the Jameson Raid – tin was a splendid price at £127 a ton and therefore the one bright lining to the cloud.[92]

Arriving home the Cornish Afrikander[93] found his county torn between the Imperialists and the Pro-Boers. When a Pro-Boer threw down the challenge that it would be impossible to go to Redruth or Camborne and try to get a meeting to pass a resolution in favour of war,[94] the Imperialists duly obliged. Within a month Chamberlain himself wrote:

> *It has given me much pleasure to receive the resolution passed at the*
> *public meeting held at Redruth... in which the electors of the Camborne*

*Division of Cornwall expressed their confidence in the efforts of Her
Majesty's Government, to secure for British residents in the Transvaal,
the same political rights and privileges as are enjoyed by the Dutch in
Cape Colony and their wish that a final and lasting settlement of the
South Africa problem may now be achieved.*[95]

Some of the men arriving home claimed they had been robbed by Boers while
several Camborne men who came home on the *Arundel Castle* had to leave a good
deal of clothing behind. Alfred Kempthorne and William James (both Illogan)
were "Sjamboked" and according to the *West Briton* an unnamed Cornishman was
so badly cut by a sjambok that he died on the *Arundel Castle*.[96] Henry Trembath
on the other hand reached Penzance after being befriended by a Boer burgher's
wife. Trembath, a chemist in Johannesburg, had already sent his wife and family to
safety back in May. He and his brother-in-law – J. Harry Johns – took a train to
Pretoria and Delagoa Bay, sitting in the cattle trucks. On crossing the Transvaal
border a wave of enthusiasm passed over the occupants and they spontaneously
burst forth into *Rule Britannia*. On their arrival at Lourenco Marques they could
not find a bed but the manager of the hotel happened to be a Truro man, and with
Cornish clannishness allowed them to sleep in the drawing room. They were
unable to board the *Arundel Castle* which was full – although her complement of
passengers was 400 or 500 she had 1,100 on board – so the two men had to wait a
few days before boarding another ship which was equally overcrowded. On
reaching the Cape they boarded the *Scott* and arrived safely at Plymouth. Trembath
believed he would be able to return in January, though he knew some people who
thought the war would not be over for five or six months. He had left his property
in Johannesburg in the safe hands of two Germans.[97]

Another Cornishman in Johannesburg who was given a warning to get out was
Frederick Tiddy, who had been running an anti-Government paper *The Skeptic*.
Tiddy had been afraid to leave earlier for fear of being called coward but then a
lady friend with burgher acquaintances told him his life was in danger if he stayed.
By bribing a policeman with ten shillings he was able to jump the queue at the
railway station and boarded a train to travel, like Trembath and Johns, in an open
truck. On reaching East London he found many Cornishmen living in tents above
the beach and amusing themselves by sea bathing, cooking, sitting in the sun and
drinking lemonade.[98]

Cornishman Tom Godfrey sent a letter home telling of how miners were offered
a £25 bonus to stay but how he, like so many others, caught a train out from
Johannesburg and travelled the 300 mile journey to Lorenco Marques which took
30 hours. After a one-night stay in a hotel, which cost him £1, he boarded the
Raglan Castle which was fearfully overcrowded but reached Durban where he
stayed in one of the best hotels at 12s 6d per day.[99] George Mitchel (Marazion)

rode a train from Johannesburg to Cape Town, the normal 50 hour journey taking 90 hours, for it was stopped and searched before leaving the Transvaal.[100] T. Edwards arriving home at Perranwell, told how a man he was with had £600 in gold taken from him.[101] Some were luckier – Joseph Tucker came home with £160 on him – but home for Tucker was not Cornwall. He had to travel north to join his family at Barrow-in-Furness, where there was a small Cornish community;[102] whereas Richard Angove made his way home to his family in the States, at the much larger Cornish community of Grass Valley, California.[103] Some even returned to homes in Australia.

The exodus from the Transvaal by the Cornish and others increased as war became imminent. With British troops gathering on the border and preparation being made to send out General Redvers Buller with a very large force numbering some 47,000 men, the numerical advantage lay with the Boers only if they struck first before Buller arrived. Facing them in Natal was the Cornish Major-General Sir William Penn-Symons with what amounted to only a token force of about 15,000 men, against which the Boers could muster some 40,000. The Boers therefore issued an ultimatum on 9th October 1899 which demanded the withdrawal of the British troops from the Transvaal's border. When this was rejected by the British the Boers declared war on 11th October 1899.

One returning Cornishman – W.J. Stephens (Camborne) – was able to give a valuable insight into Boer thinking at a high level. He carried out large plumbing contracts for the Pretoria Government, thus knowing many members of the government intimately, even working in Kruger's house where he had enjoyed having coffee with President Kruger and his wife and considered the Boers as his best friends. Despite being in what was obviously a privileged position, Stephens gave two reasons for leaving; firstly he was not prepared to fight against his own countrymen but neither was he prepared to fight the Boers against whom he bore no ill will. Secondly he had the safety of his wife and two children to consider. When asked what had induced the Boers to issue the ultimatum Stephens replied "I don't believe they thought England would go to war. I believe it was a move to drive England into acceptance of the seven years' franchise". The *Post* considered Stephens had been treated fairly by the Boer and added:

> If the same could be said of all Uitlanders we should have had no war...
> But we know that there was corrupt administration, injustice to
> Uitlanders and awful oppression of the native races, and the Boers will
> learn by bitter experience that the citizens of a world-power like Great
> Britain cannot be bled and defrauded of their rights, and that for their
> brutality to the black races they will have to pay with their blood.[104]

Much blood was to be shed by both sides before the signing of peace at Vereeniging on 31st May 1902. The Boers invaded Natal and Cape Colony and the

British troops went on the defensive until the reinforcements arrived from Britain. The Boers threw away their advantage with the futile sieges of Mafeking, Kimberley and Ladysmith. From 1900 a period of guerrilla warfare developed with the British trying to prevent Boer commanders from raiding isolated British units by erecting blockhouses[105] to protect railways and roads, and by moving Boer sympathisers into concentration camps:

> *Great Britain was humiliated, first by the incompetence of her Generals, and then by report of her inhumanity. In the end, she gave away at the conference table much of what she had gained on the battlefield – including control of the fate of black South Africans.*[106]

The first battle of the war came on 20th October when the Boer Commandant General Piet Joubert, having invaded Natal, clashed with a British force under the command of Penn-Symons at Talana Hill just outside the small coal mining town of Dundee. Lieutenant-General Sir George White, the Natal Commander-in-Chief, held his G.O.C. Major-General Sir William Penn-Symons in high regard, considering the Cornishman to be the most competent man to command an infantry division.[107] Penn-Symons who as a young subaltern, had been one of the lucky few to escape death from the Zulus at Isandlwana, had also seen action in India. There Winston Churchill remembered Penn-Symons, not only for his energy, his jokes and enthusiasm, but also for being intensely popular with his men.[108] Penn-Symons, although confident, had great respect for the Boer's love of independence his power of mobility and for his marksmanship.[109] Ironically it was Boer marksmanship which cost Penn-Symons his life. It appears that during a lull in the battle, Penn-Symons, in order to boost the morale of his men, deliberately showed himself to the enemy and was shot in the stomach. Despite having won a victory due to the leadership and somewhat foolhardy courage by Penn-Symons, his force had to make a tactical retreat to Ladysmith to join up with General White's troops. Dying, Penn-Symons, was left behind in a hospital tent, thus becoming a Boer prisoner. Seventeen-year-old Deneys Reitz (the son of F.W. Reitz, President of the Orange Free State 1889-95), came across the field hospital, flying the Red Cross:

> *One of the tents was a large marquee for wounded officers and here I saw General Penn-Symons, the Commander of the English troops. He was mortally wounded and the nurses told me that he could not last out the night. Next morning, as I was again on my way up to the camp, I met a bearer party carrying his body, wrapped in a blanket, and I accompanied them to where they buried him behind the little English chapel.*[110]

The Boer Commandant-General, Piet Joubert personally sent a letter of sympathy to General White in which he also expressed his sympathy to Lady Penn-Symons and hoped the war which had been brought about by unscrupulous

speculators and capit-
alists would soon stop.[111]

Winston Churchill,
while still at sea on his
way to report the war for
the *Morning Post* at £250
a month – all expenses
paid – read the news of
Penn-Symons' death at
sea when a passing tramp
steamer displayed the
news on a blackboard.
Churchill commented
that no-one would have
laid down his life more
gladly in such a cause
and hoped there would be
others like him.[112] There
were further Cornish
casualties, for many of
those who had remained
in South Africa had
joined the irregular
troops[113] such as the

General Penn-Symons from Hatt near Saltash.

Kimberley Horse, Thorneycroft's Horse and in
particular the Imperial Light Horse, which had
been formed at Pietermaritzburg being financed
and equipped mostly by Alfred Beit. The day
after the Battle of Talana Hill, a British force,
including the Imperial Light Horse, met the
Boers at Elandslaate, near Ladysmith. It was a
fierce and bloody skirmish which ended with
British lancers taking few prisoners. After the
battle Cornishman Rundle Oats, serving with the
Imperial Light Horse, said how the men slept just
where they fought and their food was dry bread
and water with a little bully beef. Oats thought

Memorial obelisk to General Penn-Symons at Saltash.

the courage of the Boers had been rated too highly for when the Lancers charged the Boers, they tied white handkerchiefs to the ends of their guns and cried for mercy.[114] The performance of the Imperial Light Horse went some way to remove the stigma that the Johannesburg Cornish were all white-feathered and Winston Churchill remarked "After this who will dare call Outlanders cowards".[115]

Buller and his army arrived in Cape Town on 31st October, by which time the Boers had laid siege to Ladysmith, Mafeking and Kimberley. Buller immediately split his force in order to relieve Kimberley and Ladysmith – Mafeking would have to wait. Lieutenant-General Lord Methuen was given the order to advance on Kimberley but it was not to be an easy task, for ahead he was to be met by two of the most experienced Boer Commanders, Koos de la Ray and Piet Cronje, the latter being a veteran of the first Boer War, as well as being responsible for Jameson's capture. Part of Methuen's force consisted of the 9th Brigade, which was led by the 50-year-old Major-General Reginald Pole Carew, a descendant of a very old Cornish family of Antony House near Torpoint in East Cornwall. Sir Arthur Conan Doyle thought Pole Carew was one of those finds which help to compensate us for war. *'Handsome, dashing, debonair, he approaches a field of battle as a light-headed schoolboy approaches a football field.'* [116] Also with Methuen and under the command of Colonel Aldworth was the 2nd Battalion of the Duke of Cornwall's Light Infantry (D.C.L.I.), itself part of the 19th Brigade under the command of Major-General Horace Smith-Dorrien, another Cornish survivor of Isandhlwana. Smith-Dorrien's A.D.C., was his own nephew, Lieutenant Edward Pendarves Dorrien-Smith. Methuen's force was quickly involved in three minor battles at Belmont, Graspan and Modder River, from where Private Albert Davey (Porthleven) serving with the 2nd Coldstream Guards sent a letter to his mother, claiming:

> the Boers are the biggest lot of cowards of men I have ever seen for when they see us get a bit close they put up the flag of truce to say they are our prisoners and then shoot at us… they did that yesterday but instead of taking prisoners we finished them off with our bayonets.[117]

Davey was wounded during the Battle of Modder River, but he was able to write to his mother, again describing the battle as hell on earth saying "You don't know the horror of war, I wish I had never seen it".[118]

As a wounded man Davey was sent home. In contrast, Gunner William P. Comerford (Penzance), serving with the 18th Battery of the Royal Horse Artillery, was of the opinion that the Boers were a fine lot of men.[119] This was perhaps more than could be said for the leadership of the British forces. In what became known as Black Week the Boers inflicted three defeats upon the British, who now completely outnumbered them. Starting in the Eastern Cape on 10th December General Gatacre tried to remove a Boer force from a strategic position at

Stromberg and lost a third of his men in the attempt. Later Sapper A.E. Trenoweth (Redruth) of the Royal Engineers wrote that although the Boers were very much afraid of Lyddite shells and the bayonet, "we cannot get them out in the open at all."[120] Then 11th December saw Lord Methuen's force beaten at Magersfontein and having to return to its base on the Modder River. The third defeat came in Natal where Buller made his first attempt to relieve Ladysmith. The Boers, under the command of Louis Botha (who had replaced Joubert) were dug-in at Colenso; following the battle Buller was forced to retreat, being given the nickname Reverse Buller by the British press. During the Battle of Colenso, in which many Cornishmen took part, the son of Lord Roberts was killed. Harry J. Tonkin (Penzance) complained of intense heat but obtained the autograph of Prince Christian Victor, Queen Victoria's favourite grandson, who later died at Pretoria from typhoid fever. Charles Hodge, also from Penzance, was with the Volunteer Natal Field Force but the squad he was in was lucky, as there were only three wounded.[121] Following Black Week Buller was relieved of his command which was given to Field Marshall Lord Roberts, sent out to South Africa with Major-General Lord Kitchener as his Chief of Staff. Gunner Comerford remarked that they should soon settle it.[122] Meanwhile Christmas 1899 was remembered in different ways by the Cornish soldiers serving at the front. Trooper Charles H. Osborne (St. Ives) who was serving with the Royal Hussars (Prince of Wales Own) was expecting a big battle on Christmas day, although he was looking forward to the Queen's Christmas pudding.[123] Sapper A.E. Trenoweth was to have no Christmas, being surrounded by bullets on that day.[124] Christmas dinner for Sergeant W.E. Perrin (Penzance) serving with the 2nd Battalion. D.C.L.I. was boiled beef, hard duff and one pint of beer.[125] Osborne's big battle was the Battle of Colesburg which he described as worse than murder adding,

> *my helmet was shot clean off my head and went spinning and humming like a telegraph wire... our Major was killed, four of my dear comrades killed and seventeen others wounded... my officer's horse was shot under him. I gave him mine and walked back to camp, thankful to get out of range... can you send me a few pairs of cheap socks... I have not changed for ten weeks.*[126]

Other Cornishmen were not so fortunate in battle. Bombardier J.G. Cowling, also from St. Ives, was killed in the following battle at Rensburg[127] as was Major G. Eddy, who was serving with the Victorian Rifles from Australia. Although listed as Australian, Eddy was of Cornish parentage; his father coming from St. Just, had visited Cornwall in 1898 and stayed with an aunt.[128] The New Year saw the arrival at Cape Town (10th January) of Lord Roberts and Kitchener, but the situation for the British – if anything – was to get worse. They suffered another defeat, this time at Spion Kop, a small hill overlooking the Tugela River. The

battle which took place on the 23rd and 24th of January was almost a re-run of
Majuba Hill. Led by Major-General Sir Edward Woodgate, the British reached the
top of Spion Kop only to be cut to pieces and Woodgate, like Colley at Majuba,
was shot and killed. Sam Thomas (Redruth) told of having marched 17 miles in
one day, 10 miles the next before crossing the Tulega River for the night attack on
the Boers at Spion Kop. Two of his comrades sent to the top were killed
instantly.[129] Bertie Heath (Redruth) was wounded in the arm and Edgar Watson
(Sennen) one of Thorneycroft's Scouts was also injured in the battle. Willie Corin
(Penzance) was at Spion Kop alongside two of the *Dorsets* at about 2pm when a
shell exploded and killed them both. Corin was himself struck in the back by part
of the shell and although he was knocked out for a time he carried on fighting until
being hospitalised.[130] There were three other Penzance men in his company. A
Cornishman named Jack wrote to his parents that it was at Spion Kop during the
battle that he thought of home. Having climbed the 3,000 foot hill by night, his
company (most likely Thorneycroft's) reached the top,

> *at 4am in the morning, cold, wet and hungry. We had just time to get a*
> *cup of coffee made when the Dutch opened fire on us. Well there we were*
> *with nothing but rifles and no trenches made. We sent for reinforcements*
> *but it took them 5 hours to come by that time we had nearly all the men*
> *killed. Well it was here that I felt it worse to see men lying, some with*
> *heads gone and some with both legs blown off... if a man has got a nerve*
> *it is a place like this where he is wanted. I managed to get down off that*
> *hill but how God knows ! We lost heavily and then had to withdraw from*
> *that position.*[131]

More direct in his condemnation of Spion Kop was Thomas Ham of St. Day
with the Imperial Light Infantry who said "What I saw I never wish to see again.
We were led into a death trap".[132]

Two Cornishmen, whose duty it was to go up Spion Kop and remove the
wounded, were S. Nicholls and Tommy Clifton of the Ambulance Corps. Their
search was in the dark and only by feeling could they tell if a man was living or
dead. They found one poor fellow propped up against a rock, bleeding badly from
a bullet wound which had entered his chest and passed out at the side. It took the
two Cornishmen hours to get him to hospital. Both men had been through the
Battle of Colenso where they had buried three lots of soldiers – seventeen in each
of three graves.[133] Nicholls was well known in Redruth and Camborne as a piano
tuner, whereas Clifton was a hairdresser, banjoist and cyclist from Camborne.
Although Nicholls made it safely home to Cornwall, Clifton died at
Pietermaritzburg shortly after Spion Kop and was buried with full military
honours. Much publicity was also given to the death at Spion Kop of Sergeant
Edgar Litkie, who had been a Camborne mining student. Litkie was leading a

platoon of Thorneycroft's men when he was killed by an exploding shell, and subsequently was buried in a grave on Spion Kop.[134]

Despite Buller having to undergo another reverse in his attempt to lift the siege of Ladysmith, the tide began to turn in Britain's favour. On the 15th of February 1900, after a siege lasting 124 days, Kimberley was finally relieved, the honour

Freathy Oats and his father Francis Oats in uniform for the defence of Kimberley

going to Major-General Sir John French leading a cavalry division. Even before the war had broken out Francis Oats was not only determined to remain in Kimberley but had sent for his elder son – Freathy – to join him. Francis Olds, who like Oats was from St. Just, said that among the defenders of Kimberley were Messrs. Tippett, Hocking, Barnes, Angwin, Holman and Batten, who were all from St. Just, and showed that Cornishmen were not 'White feathered'.[135]

Unlike Johannesburg, where there had been a mass exodus of Cornishmen, very few of the Kimberley men returned home during the war. One Cornishman from St. Just who arrived in Kimberley from the Orange Free State on the 30th of September 1899 kept a diary throughout the siege.[136] It shows some of the trials and tribulations as well as the horror – and sometimes humour – that the siege brought to the inhabitants of Kimberley. The siege lasted from the 15th of October until the 15th of February during which time food was rationed and Christmas was virtually ignored. De Beers built a 28 pounder gun christened 'Long Cecil' in retaliation for the Boers 'Long Tom'[137] and women and children took refuge in the mines. Lieutenant-Colonel Scott Turner, a son-in-law of Cornishman Lewis Michell was shot during the siege. The diary ends with a tribute to Cecil Rhodes who the diarist believed, by his presence, assistance, kind words and actions, did more than anyone to bring the people of Kimberley through the siege.

The De Beers Company had supplied the town with water and fuel and provided shelter and safety for the women and children down the mines but perhaps its most valuable role in the siege was to allow its workshops to be used for the manufacture of shells and the provision of armour plating for the train. Although nearly all the credit for making the gun known as 'Long Cecil' has gone to George Labrum, the man who actually rolled up his sleeves and got on with the job was Cornishman William Berry of Illogan. Having learned his engineering skills along with his father and brother at Tangyes' Cornwall Works in Birmingham, William Berry had travelled to South Africa and Kimberley to take up employment with De Beers. The idea of the gun was probably put to Berry as he was in day to day control of the workshops, but he had no direct experience of gun making. Following Labram's plans, Berry nonetheless built the gun and provided the shells to go with it being greatly assisted by another Cornishman, Thomas C. Holman. The gun when finished was toasted by Rhodes, Labrum and Berry with a single glass of soda water which the three men had to share there being only one glass available. Berry was to carry on working at De Beers being awarded his siege medal by the Mayor of Kimberley. Berry never married, and when he retired in the late nineteen-twenties he went back to Cornwall to live out his days at Looe where he died in 1941, aged 78.[138]

Along with Francis Oats, one of the first to volunteer for the Kimberley Town Guard had been Thomas Quentrall, but with a curfew at 9pm it was perhaps not surprising that the two men were unable to organise the Kimberley Cornish New Year's Dinner for 1899. H.H. Olds (St. Just) wrote to his parents to say that Christmas that year was not a merry one for he was on half rations, and down to a quarter near the end of the siege which he thought had been a terrible time.[139] Thomas Ennor, a Sergeant of the Kimberley Town Guard caught a chill and spent a fortnight in bed. He considered the Boers the dirtiest low people on the face of God's earth for "they surrounded us, stole our cattle, cut off our water supply and the shelling of the town was the worst of the lot".[140] Ennor played cribbage with Harry Carvolth and J. Harris of Redruth, two Cornish miners from Johannesburg who had got shut in there. Ennor's wife and children, plus servant, went down the mine and Robert Dennis (St. Just) also commented in his letter about the women and children going down the mine and how every comfort was made for them for sheets, mattresses and food were sent down to them – there were no fewer than 1,400 on the 800ft level he wrote.[141] James Wills wrote to his wife at Newlyn, sparing her nothing of the horrendous effect of being under fire at Kimberley from the Boers' 'Long Tom' gun.[142] Edward John Kitto, a contractor with De Beers, eventually became a Sergeant in the Kimberley Town Guard. When he arrived home in Cornwall at St. Day he talked to the *Post* of how he had eaten horse flesh and refereed a Cornish wrestling match during which a Penzance man, W. Freeman, came second-best to a colonial.[143] Another Cornishman in the Kimberley Town Guard was Arthur Kendall, and when he arrived home in Cornwall at Camborne he told the *Post* how the oil, in which the bread and mealie pap was fried, came from the stores of De Beers, being originally purchased for greasing machinery and that he had longed for a good old pasty many times. He also said that the Boers had shot the wounded who had been left on the battlefield. On returning to fetch them back to camp they were all found cold and dead having been shot through the head at close quarters by the Boers.[144]

Even before the euphoria of the relief of Kimberley had died down in Cornwall the news arrived of a major action involving the 2nd Battalion D.C.L.I. at the Battle of Paardeburg. An army of Boers led by Piet Cronje and numbering some 5,000 men was completely surrounded by the army of Lord Roberts, on the 18th of February. Unfortunately Cronje was in a good position and any attack on him would lead to heavy losses. Lord Kitchener as Commander-in-charge that day grew impatient and gave orders that half of the 2nd Battalion D.C.L.I. (they had been guarding the baggage), along with the Canadian Battalion were to cross the river and charge the enemy. Smith-Dorrien as Commander of the 19th Brigade, to which the Cornwalls and Canadians were attached, knew nothing of Kitchener's orders so was quite astonished to see his own men suddenly cross the river and make "a gallant charge, gallantly led, but the fact that not one of them got within 300 yards of the enemy is sufficient proof of its futility".[145] Lieutenant Colonel W. Aldworth who led the Cornwalls saying "We will make the name of the Cornwalls ring in the ears of the world, boys"[146] was shot in the head and killed outright. Twenty-five men of 2nd Battalion D.C.L.I. were killed with as many again wounded. Sir Arthur Conan Doyle later wrote:

> *If the miners of Johannesburg had given the impression that the Cornishman is not a fighter, the record of the county regiment in the war has for ever exploded the calumny. Men who were not fighters could have found no place in Smith-Dorrien's Brigade or in the charge of Paardeburg.*[147]

The battle itself was in the end a success, as on the 27th of February, Cronje, with just over 4,000 Boers, surrendered and was taken prisoner. Later Private J. Cronin wrote home to say he had seen Cronje last Thursday in a special military train as he happened to be on sentry duty at that time.[148]

Charles Osborne who had been at Paardeburg was soon writing home telling how he was in one of the first regiments to enter Bloemfontein, 'adding We are now in full pursuit of the Boers.'[149] He gave the names of other Penzance boys at the front including Sergeant Charles Tonkin, Privates Matthews, Dick Mann (who was fat), Clemo, Henwood, Ede and others. Mann was obviously thinking of his stomach when he wrote home, for having stopped at Elandsfontein for three days he noted the price of a half pound loaf was 2s, a tin of jam 2s, sugar 2s a lb, tin of Swiss milk 3s and a pound tin of butter 4s, commenting "very nice for a 'Tommy' who gets 1/3d per day".[150] Walter Matthews, a private in 2nd Battalion D.C.L.I. who had been an apprentice journeyman at the Cornishman offices, told of getting fresh beef and lamb taken from the Boers and gave an account of how he saved a man from drowning in the Orange River, the

IN MEMORY OF THE UNDERMENTIONED OFFICERS,
N.C.OFFICERS, AND MEN OF THE 2ND BATTALION
DUKE OF CORNWALL'S LIGHT INFANTRY,
WHO WERE KILLED IN ACTION AT THE BATTLE OF
PAARDEBERG ON THE 18TH FEBRUARY 1900.

OFFICERS:-LT-COL.W.ALDWORTH,D.S.O.
CAPT. B.A.NEWBURY,
CAPT.AND ADJT. E.P.WARDLAW.
SERGT. R.JORDAN,CORPL.W.OSTLER,
L-CORPLS:-W. ATKINS, W. MURRIN.
PRIVATES:- W.BANNISTER, A.BENTON,
A.DOWNES, B.EVANS, C.EWERS,J.HORAN,
C.HAYTHORPE, J. HOWKETT, E. JONES,
A.KING, W. KINNERSLEY, W. LOVALL,
I. LOVE, S. MAY, T. RUMBALL, W. TAYLOR,
W. VINEY, W. WASHBROOK, E.WEBBER.
ERECTED BY THE OFFICERS, NON-COMMISSIONED
OFFICERS, AND MEN OF THE REGIMENT.

D.C.L.I. memorial at Paardeburg.

man giving him 1/6d despite Matthews not wanting it.[151] Nearly all the men mentioned by Osborne were members of the Volunteer Service Company of the D.C.L.I. or the Cornish Volunteers. This Company under the command of Captain E.A.

Jackson (Truro) had left Cornwall in March for South Africa and was attached to the 2nd Battalion D.C.L.I.

The relief of Ladysmith occurred on the 28th of February, General Buller at last succeeding, with his fourth attempt. The Cornish newspapers had made little reference to the siege of Ladysmith as compared to the siege of Kimberley most likely because far fewer Cornish people had been trapped there. At least one Cornishwoman was, for Mrs W.H. Kinsman – sister to Captain John Penberthy and a cousin of Sir Henry Irving – brought back to Redruth a shell casing fired by the naval gunners of the *Terrible*[152] during the relief of Ladysmith; this she kept not only as a memento but to use as a dinner gong. Her brother, Capt. Penberthy, had as his souvenir a fine pistol taken from the body of a British Officer who fell at Spion Kop.[153] Private Edgar Perry (Penzance), serving with the 1st Battalion Gloucester Regiment, was just outside Ladysmith when he was shot in the hip and the arm, being picked up eventually and taken to the field hospital. He later gave an account of his journey back to the regimental barracks at Bristol.[154]

Lord Roberts captured Bloemfontein on the 13th of March but it was the news of the relief of Mafeking four days later that led to celebrations throughout Britain. At Mafeking a small unit comprising mainly some two hundred Bechuanaland and Rhodesian police and a large number of volunteers under the command of Colonel R.S.S. Baden-Powell had held out for over seven months. George Green (Penzance), a former smith and fitter for Holman Brothers, was in Mafeking during the siege and was unfortunate enough to have his foot blown off whilst another Cornishman was trying to extract a detonator from an unexploded shell. Arriving back in Cornwall later he told a reporter:

> *Whilst I was engaged in my work Mr. Gerrans, my employer - a native of Truro – was endeavouring to extract the contents of a Boer shell which had just been brought in. It was during his effort to remove the explosive that the projectile burst killing one man instantly. Mr. Gerrans had a miraculous escape, his only injury being a slight wounding of the fingers of his left hand. A portion of the shell struck my left foot to such an extent that its amputation was the only alternative.... while in hospital I was visited by that brilliant soldier Colonel Baden-Powell.*[155]

Joseph Gerrans had arrived in South Africa sometime in the early 1880's working for three years at Cape Town before moving to Kimberley to work for De Beers. He moved to Mafeking, setting up a wagon building and engineering business in 1891. Gerrans, who was a Baptist and member of the Wesleyan Church in Mafeking had great sympathy for the African Native who through long experience regarded him as their staunch friend. All the principal Bechuana chiefs knew and respected him.[156]

Also at Mafeking and serving under Baden-Powell during the 217 day siege was Courtney Vyvyan who had already seen action in the Zulu War 1879 and the Matabele War 1896. Vyvyan was a member of the old Cornish family -Vyvyans of Trelowarren – and had been a Brevet-Colonel during the 2nd Boer War.[157]

Other high-ranking Cornish Officers during the Boer War included Brigadier-General C. Porter (Trematon) with the 1st Cavalry Brigade, who replaced Kekewich as garrison commander at Kimberley. Lieutenant-Colonel William Lueg Harvey, a member of the engineering family – Harveys of Hayle – had a distinguished career in the D.C.L.I., being mentioned in dispatches twice during the Boer War and awarded the D.S.O. Another member of an old Cornish family who served throughout the Boer War, being awarded the Queens Medal with five clasps, was Colonel Edward Treffry of Fowey.

Major W.E.T. Bolitho (Penzance) was in command of the Devon Company of Imperial Yeomanry;with him was Lieutenant J.C.B. Lethbridge (Launceston). Major F.S. Garrat (Merefield) was with the 6th Dragon Guards as was Major C.H. Paynter (St. Buryan). Captain J.H. Tremayne (Cardew) was with the 13th Hussars, Captain H.B. Protheroe-Smith (Truro) with the 21st Lancers and Captain C.R. Jervis Edwards (St. Stephens, Saltash) was with the 2nd Battalion D.C.L.I. All these officers survived the war but many of the junior officers were not so lucky. Lieutenant Cowlard (Launceston) of the Cornish Volunteers died from disease and Lieutenant Percy Bickford-Smith (Trevano, Helston) serving with the 23rd Imperial Yeomanry was shot. Bickford-Smith had been at the front barely two months and his death came as a shock to the employees of the Bickford-Smith & Co. Fuse Works, Tuckingmill, of which he had been a Director.[158] He was only 28 years old. Captain Horace Mann, the son of Rev. Charles Mann, late Vicar of St. Issey, was with Thorneycroft's Mounted Infantry when he was shot through the heart. Trooper Smith (St. Austell) said he had helped to dig his grave and burnt an inscription on a cross.[159] Reports of death and injury were not confined to officers. Richard Rodda (Redruth) serving with Kitchener's Horse was severely wounded at Burgespruit, the bullet striking his wrist and passing out at his elbow. His horse having been shot out from under him Rodda, in trying to clear himself of the animal, became lacerated by barbed wire. He was eventually taken to the base hospital at Pretoria, the town having been taken by the British on 5th June.[160] Trooper Phil Hoar of the Natal Mounted Rifles told of a Cornishman named Vyvyan who was shot three times through the chest and as he fell shouted "One & All for ever! Give 'em Camborne!"[161] Another Cornish soldier from Penzance serving with Kitchener's Horse, told another grim story:

> *Two of our Corps. went out about 4 miles from the camp and was never in the firing line. One was found with 6 holes around his eye and the other with 6 holes around his heart, showing that they had been put up by the Boers as targets. Knowing full well that they were without arms. Then*

they took off their boots and took what money they had on them that is the
*sort of warfare that is going on.*162

A number of Cornishmen who were not in the armed forces were captured during the war and became prisoners. One of the first of these was John F. Christophers, a miner from Camborne, who was imprisoned right at the start of the war. He had been working at the Wemmer mine when it was taken over by the Boers on 1st November 1899. Refusing to work, Christophers – with a number of other Cornishmen – went to Government House to get the necessary papers in order to leave for Delagoa Bay. They were arrested and thrown in Johannesburg jail. The next day, having only been fed bread and water, they were put on a train to Pretoria with an armed guard. On reaching Pretoria they were put in jail – each in a cell 6 feet by 6 feet. On 4th November they were moved to the race course to join the rest of the British prisoners of war, which Christophers said numbered 1,275 British soldiers and Volunteers – who had been captured near Mafeking. The prisoners had a meagre diet, being allowed corned beef once a week and being fed bread and rice the rest of the week. The prisoner camp was divided into four – the Soldiers Camp, Mafeking Camp, Dundee Camp and Johannesburg Camp, which Christophers was in; he said they

> *held a kind of concert, each camp taking turns to sing songs and choruses*
> *etc. In fact we enjoyed ourselves immensely considering the*
> *circumstances we were under. It was amusing to see our Boer Guards*
> *marching up and down our respective camps with their rifles on their*
> *shoulders when we were holding our concert. I don't know whether they*
> *enjoyed it or not, but I must say they did not interfere at all.*163

Christophers noted in his diary, which he kept throughout his imprisonment, that their greatest danger came not from the Boers but the deadly tarantula which they sometimes found in their tents, and from snakes, which seemed to infest the place. On the 16th of November Christophers and the other Cornish miners were released, being marched to the station and put on board a train in a corn van without any food, water or daylight. Making holes in the sides with their penknives, for ventilation and daylight, they underwent a twelve-hour journey before being allowed off to stretch their legs. The next day at 3pm they reached the Transvaal border and were finally set free reaching Delagoa Bay at 7pm where they quickly found a restaurant and got food, which they needed after going two days without any. They had to wait ten days before they were able to get a passage to Cape Town and home.With Christophers were T. Pengelly (Zennor), W. Truscott, H. Roberts, J. Eathorne, W. Jones (all Camborne), A. Thomas (St. Just), J. Scoble (Redruth) and R. Davey (Chacewater).164 Charles Osborne wrote to say that Stephen Cara (also Penzance) had been nabbed and sent on to Pretoria free of charge and how he had only escaped the same fate by escaping on a mule and using his sling belt for a head collar.165 When Pretoria was taken, Cara and many others were set free, including Stanley R. James (Porthleven) who had been a Surveyor at the Glen Deep mine, Germiston before he joined the Cape Pioneer Railway Regiment.166 Lieutenant C.A. Percy Tarbut of the South African Light Horse (and a former student of the Camborne School of Mines) actually died in prison at Pretoria – he was only 24 years old. The cause of death was typhoid fever, a reminder that for many more during the war, death came not from bullets but from disease. Robert Tute, another Camborne mining student, died from enteric fever167 while on active service. In Cornwall at the Camborne Mining Students 5th Annual Dinner in May 1900, special mention was made of some twenty-five students who were in South Africa, mainly serving with the irregular troops.168 With the British in control of Johannesburg and Pretoria, and President Kruger having left the country for exile in Europe, on the 1st of September 1900 Transvaal became once more a British colony and Lord Roberts left South Africa to return to Britain and a hero's welcome. Lord Kitchener was left in command, and the war seemed as good as over. Joseph Thomas (St. Michael's Mount) became a Transvaal constable at Heidelburg; this made a welcome change, for he now had a roof over his head and what he considered "the greatest thing of the lot", he was now able to keep clean.169 His brother was at Lydenburg attached to General Buller's Staff as an orderly. Herbert Cara (Penzance) also joined the police. He had served with the 27th Company of Imperial Yeomanry and like his brother Stephen had been captured by the Boers, commenting, that when a man is facing death he thinks of his past life, but they had no time for that because the Boers were within 50 yards of them.170 Cornish Volunteer, J. Glasson (Hayle) wrote about guarding the Boers in Pretoria and how he went to the cell that Dr. Jameson had been in. The Boer prisoners were being kept in the same huts that had been built for Dr. Jims's men so Glasson thought the Boers were being 'paid back in their own coin'.171

At the end of 1900 the Annual Cornish Dinner was once again held at Kimberley, being presided over by Francis Oats, who paid tribute to those Cornishmen who had fought in the war – with special mention of Penn-Symons. Oats had actually visited the site of Penn-Symons' death. The *Post* named sixty-eight Cornishmen who attended the Eleventh Annual Dinner.172

The situation back in Cornwall had been grim, to say the least, and many families suffered acute hardship because of the war. The war had halted remittances; faced with unemployment in the home industry many miners and their families soon found themselves in dire financial straits. The Board of Guardians found the war made heavy demands on their relief funds, and had to grant relief – usually 3 shillings per week – to a number of families. One such case presented to the Penzance Board of Guardians concerned a young married woman who had appealed for relief for herself and three children because her husband, who had left two years ago, was ill in Cape Town. Before the war he had sent her £4 per month regularly. The Board believed the husband would have sent money to her if he could, so considered her a deserving case and granted the 3 shillings per week.[173] Another case which involved the Redruth Board of Guardians concerned a Cornish miner who had come home from South Africa because of the war but had been taken ill and been unable to work. With what money he had being soon used up he and his family were in a state of destitution – he was awarded the 3 shillings a week. Mrs Daddow unfortunately had her relief discontinued at Redruth when her husband, fighting with the Imperial Light Infantry, was killed at Spion Kop, for she was now entitled to a war pension.[174] Life was certainly not so pleasant at home, for despite a good tin price, more miners meant less money and wages were reduced to as little as £2 a month; the Redruth Board of Guardians noted that the return of miners was reflected in the increase in outdoor relief.[175] Perhaps that accounted for the news from a Cornishman in Michigan, U.S.A. that a large number of Cornish miners were coming to the state.[176] The Cornish M.P. Arthur Strauss estimated that 5,000 had returned[177] to Cornwall from South Africa although from the letters received in Cornwall the *Mining Journal* pointed out that many Cornishmen had actually stayed in South Africa or gone to Australia, in the hope of getting work there.[178]

The St. Just Urban District Council foresaw a future problem, as shown by the following dialogue between the Medical Officer and Nankervis the Chairman:

'Mr Nankervis:

'*The births have gone up and perhaps that will be better by next August or September*'
(laughter)

Chairman:

'*Do you attribute that to the influx from South Africa?*'
(laughter)

Mr Nankervis:

'*I shan't say any more.*'
(renewed laughter).[179]

Having come home some Cornish miners were soon to return to South Africa in order to fight – such as Alfred Nancarrow, William Penberthy, Edward Pearce, and Henry Penberthy – all from Illogan. Nancarrow had been home less than a month.[180]

For many other Cornish people, however, the idea of war and going to fight was anathema. Known collectively as Pro-Boers, they became influential through the

South African Conciliation Committee and the Stop the War Committee. Leonard Courtney, the M.P. for East Cornwall who had already been a champion of the Boers during the 1st Boer War has been described as:

> *one of the most well informed members of the House in South African affairs and subsequent events justify his being labelled the most disinterested, courageous and consistent of all the Pro-Boers.*[181]

Courtney was the President of the South African Conciliation Committee and was greatly assisted by his wife Kate, whose sister was Beatrice Webb. The Chairman of the Stop the War Committee was another Cornishman Silas K. Hocking who became the most outspoken of all the Cornish Pro-Boers. Hocking, born 1850 at St. Stephen in Brannel (near St. Austell), had been ordained as a Minister of the United Methodist Free Church in 1870. Better known as a prolific writer of novels and active in liberal politics, he had, in fact, been invited to become a Liberal candidate and to stand against the Liberal Unionist Arthur Strauss, M.P., in the Cornish Mining Division. When war broke out Hocking said:

> *I asserted my right to think and act for myself, I believed then, as I believe today, that the war was unjust and wicked and whatever the consequences might be I felt bound to protest.*[182]

Hocking called the war unholy and unchristian,[183] and in a typical letter to the newspapers he questioned whether, even if the quarrel with the Boers was a just one, how Christian people could think that the wholesale killing of people can be the best way of bringing it to a happy issue.[184] In another letter, this time to the Editor of the *Cornubian* Hocking, like many of the Pro-Boers believed that Britain had been jockeyed into war by 'unscrupulous' adventurers.[185] He soon became a target for the Jingoists and Imperialists, and was lucky to escape from a 'howling mob' after giving a speech at Maidstone. The same experience occurred at Birmingham where, again confronted by an angry crowd, Hocking had to leave by the back door. (A few weeks later another Pro-Boer – the young David Lloyd George – had to take the same evasive action in Liskeard). Hocking now found that bookstalls began to withdraw his books and one book – *Sword and Cross* – due to be published was not in print until 1914 because it was felt the book, which was based on Hocking's own experiences, might arouse ill-will.[186] In Cornwall Silas Hocking, who had been President of the Liberal Association, resigned over the war – as did John Vivian, Chairman of the Radical Association. In March 1900 there was an ugly incident at Redruth when Richard Glasson, a Pro-Boer and well known radical, was publicly tarred and feathered by a mob which also threw rotten oranges at him, burnt his effigy and pinned a placard, which stated '*The Death of Glasson*', to the town clock door. The police were unable to intervene other than to escort Glasson home after the incident, although even then a large crowd of a few hundred people followed and hustled and jeered him all the way. The *Cornubian* thought it a matter for regret but added:

> *we cannot help stating that the mob were not without some excuse for their conduct. So far as we can learn the only other towns in Cornwall where Boer sympathisers had any reasons for complaint were Penryn and Falmouth;but even they were not maltreated or held up to public ridicule like certain persons at Redruth.*
>
> *Seeing what has been done at Redruth the tarring of a Pro-Boer, it is said there are some at Camborne who are quaking and do not care to show out of doors.*[187]

The previous week an effigy of Kruger had been burnt at Redruth during a public demonstration for the war. There was much singing and banging of drums, and the *Cornubian* stated that the police – who were few in numbers – had wisely made no attempt to quell the popular demonstration.[188] A public meeting organised by the Pro-Boers at Liskeard and chaired by Arthur Quiller Couch, with Lloyd George and Courtney's niece, Emily Hobhouse, on the platform, was broken up.[189] A number of Stop the War Committee peace meetings had to be abandoned elsewhere, for fear of rioting and damage to property.[190] Leonard Courtney was called upon to resign as M.P. for Liskeard on account of his Pro-Boer sympathies, whilst on Mafeking Night a mob stoned Hocking's neighbour's house in the belief it was where Hocking lived.[191]

With the capture of Johannesburg and Pretoria the home government decided that as it had public support, it was the ideal time to call a General Election. Set for October it became known as the Khaki Election. In Cornwall, especially in the Mining Division, it was to be a rough contest between the Liberal Unionist, Arthur Strauss and the Pro-Boer W.S. Caine. Silas Hocking, who had been the original candidate for the Pro-Boers claimed he had won back the constituency to its old allegiance but had not been permitted to reap what he had sown.[192] Such were the feelings against Hocking in the Mining Division that he had been advised not to show his face in Cornwall again, if he valued his life. Therefore after a talk to Herbert Gladstone, the Liberal Chief Whip, although Hocking did not relish the idea of running away from a fight, he came away with the impression that in the interests of the party it would be better to stand aside for someone who had taken no active part in opposing the war and who was not a member of either of the committees.[193] Hocking resigned his candidature in favour of Caine, who was adopted in April. Neither Strauss nor Caine were Cornishmen but both had loyal support. Accusations were made by both sides in the run-up to the election, the underlying argument being whether or not after the war in South Africa the Cornish miner would be squeezed out by the mine companies on the Rand in favour of more natives or even Chinese labour (See Chapter 7 The Chinese

Chapter Six

Blood and Gold. The Jameson Raid and Second Boer War

Episode). The *Post* backed Strauss – perhaps not surprisingly as he had financed the newspaper for the past ten years. Strauss warned that the future for Cornish Afrikanders on the Rand would only be secure under British rule and asked them to think twice before they leant to a perilous policy and an unpatriotic politician and not to disgrace the country by returning a Pro-Boer to Parliament.[194] Strauss asked his opponents what possible benefits the capitalists could derive from the war, when the mines had closed down and the shares had

General Pole Carew of Antony House near Torpoint.

dropped in price. In the few weeks leading up to the election tension was high in the Mining Division. Rocks were thrown by a Pro-Boer at Strauss, when he was leaving a meeting at Mithian. One rock smashed the window of his carriage and another hit him, although causing no injury.[195] Caine, who was speaking at Hayle, saw his meeting end when fighting broke out between his own supporters and the Unionists with chairs and sticks being used as weapons. The police had to be called, although Rexford, a Cornishman just returned from Johannesburg, accused Caine's supporters of starting the trouble; the *Post* commented that their methods were so un-English that they were evidently borrowed from the Transvaal.[196] The Unionists used General Buller's support of Strauss at the last election to bolster his chances, adding that the General would vote for Strauss this time except he was busy fighting Boers – Buller actually left South Africa early in October just as the election was taking place. The Unionists also linked Caine to the last Liberal-radical M.P. for the Mining Division – the discredited Conybeare (now a Pro-Boer candidate at St. Helens in the North of England). Captain Joseph Thomas J.P., Manager of Dolcoath and probably the most respected of the Cornish Mine Managers was in full support of Strauss. Victory for the Unionists seemed certain but just as a final warning to the Cornish miner it was pointed out that on the Rand the miner could hardly accept employment from mine owners if they voted for Caine after he had called Johannesburg a nest of intriguing millionaires.[197] Despite that, the result of the vote in the Mining Division went against the national tide, for where Lord Salisbury's Conservative and Unionist Party won an outright victory at the polls, in the Cornish constituency Strauss lost to Caine by 108 votes. Caine claimed that out of 700 Cornish miners home from South Africa at least 650 had voted for him.[198] The Mining Journal stated that Strauss did not have the support of the St. Agnes men. Strauss, who was of German-Jew descent, may have been also the victim of anti-semitic feeling during the election although there is little evidence.[199]

Near the end of the year there was a great celebration in East Cornwall on the arrival home of General Pole Carew. He was quoted as saying he would like to go through the whole thing again – with the added experience gained during the past twelve months.[200] The General crossed the River Tamar in a specially decorated ferry and was received at Torpoint by the Earl of Mount Edgcumbe, who was Lord Lieutenant of Cornwall. Pole Carew thought although peace had its advantages he was not sure that war had not more when they thought how it brought all ranks and classes together.[201] The General was then escorted to his home, Antony House. A few months later when in London Pole Carew said:

> *There was little doubt that if the Boers had known their own strength at*
> *the beginning of the war and our state of unpreparedness they could*
> *easily have driven us to the sea ports and we should have found ourselves*
> *in a position of having to defend Durban, Cape Town and to reconquer*
> *South Africa from beginning to end.*[202]

At Truro, Pole Carew was honoured by becoming only the third person to be made a freeman.[203]

The Victorian Age may have come to an end with Queen Victoria's death on the 22nd of January 1901 but the Boer War was far from over. The war took on a more sinister aspect as Lord Kitchener became more and more frustrated by the guerilla tactics of the Boer Commandos – Louis Botha, Jan Smuts, Barry Hertzog, Koos de la Rey and especially Christiaan de Wet. Kitchener adopted less conventional warfare including the terror tactics of what amounted to a scorched earth policy – that of burning homesteads and slaughtering livestock. Blockhouses were built along the main transport routes, but worse was the internment of thousands of Boer women and children in concentration camps. There were other harsh measures, and Kitchener issued a proclamation saying that any Boers found with rifles on them would be shot. Cornish Volunteer Richard Mann was all in favour, adding that it ought to have been issued months before.[204] The new tactics were too much for at least one Cornishman from Camborne, who wrote home saying he was sick of war, tired of burning homesteads and killing young horses so they would not fall into the hands of the Boers.205 It was a Cornish commander Major General Charles Knox, who led the stern chase of the elusive De Wet.206 Archie Bennet, serving with French's Mounted Rifles, wrote to his brother in Redruth telling him how he had been chasing De Wet and burning houses, leaving not a house within 10 miles of the railway either side. They burnt them all down on their way to Krugersdorp and marched from there along the mines.207

Also involved in chasing De Wet was Norman Dungey (from Redruth) serving with the Border Horse Regiment. He believed the saddest sights of the war were when they gave order:

> to give notice to the Boer women that in ten minutes or so their homes
> (and sweet homesteads some of them were) would be burned to the
> ground. 'We often helped them to remove their personal effects and there
> the poor things were sitting on the veldt with their side of bacon or
> poloney in front of them, with their little children (four, five, six as the
> case may be) clinging to their skirts crying, their homes being burned
> before their eyes and knowing that the next house, three or more miles
> away was being treated in the same way so there was no shelter there for
> them. We hated and almost cursed ourselves for being the means of
> bringing about such desolation.208

Although Dungey was discharged from his regiment, having come through the war without a scratch, he had no intention of returning to Cornwall and went to stay with his brother at Beachgrove, Durban.

The Boers now invaded Cape Colony, and to prevent help being given to the Boers, martial law was declared. Cornishman Lewis Michell became President of the Martial Law Board which consisted of himself and two others. The Board had to consider all complaints regarding the administration of Martial Law in the Cape, and in ten months some 540 cases were dealt with. As sole manager of the Standard Bank since 1896 Michell's position on the Martial Law Board was only one of the contributions made by him during the war. When war had first broken out, Michell,

> Acting at his own discretion, but with a fine patriotism... undertook to
> meet all the requirements of the military authorities in the financing of the
> military operations and it was largely owing to the highly efficient
> measures that he took to this end that the whole of the war finances in
> South Africa were arranged without a single hitch.209

Meanwhile De Wet still had to be caught; the *Cornishman* said De Wet 'runs like one of our Penwith foxes'.210 With the Boers operating in Griqualand West, Private J. Cronin (Penzance) wrote to say that his company had been put on an allowance of one pint of beer a day.211 The next time he wrote he had been

Chapter Six

Blood and Gold. The Jameson Raid and Second Boer War

N.C.O's of the Second-Battalion Duke of Cornwall's Light Infantry at Bloemfontein in 1900.

promoted to Corporal, saying De Wet was even hated by his own men who would give in, except they were afraid of being shot by De Wet.212 Many Boers had given in, and some were now fighting on the British side. Known as 'hensoppers' or 'Hands-uppers' they were much despised by their own people. In contrast those who carried on the struggle against the British were called 'bittereinders' being prepared to fight to the bitter end.

At least for the Cornish Volunteers the war had come to an end. All Cornwall was overjoyed at the news, and towns were decorated and receptions planned throughout the County to welcome home the Cornish Volunteers. The Company, which in the main had been on outpost duty guarding communications and rebuilding bridges, had also formed a guard of honour to escort Sir Alfred Milner to Cape Town. It was at Bodmin that the Volunteers were first honoured in Cornwall. Having disembarked from the *Tagus* at Southampton they travelled down to Bodmin to be met by the Mayor of the Town. In his welcome speech he made special mention of Lieutenant Cowlard (Launceston), whom he believed was respected and loved by all, adding his name was revered in Cornwall. Cowlard was one of only three Volunteers to have died in South Africa from disease, the other two being Private T. Jones (Hayle) and Private Cox (Wadebridge). Out of the original ninety-three Volunteers sixty-eight had arrived home together (ten had been invalided home earlier), eight had been discharged, three had died from disease, three had come home early and one – Private Truscott (Wadebridge) – was too sick to travel. From Bodmin the Volunteers dispersed to their home towns and further Welcome Home celebrations. At Camborne drenching rain greeted the town's seven Volunteers, but the streets were decked with flowers, the crowds cheered and the band played *See the conquering hero comes*. The men were taken in procession through the town to Commercial Square for an official welcome address from the Town Council. At Redruth, Hayle and other towns throughout the county similar scenes were enacted.213

In Cornwall the loss of South African money was increasingly felt and was believed to have diminished the volume of trade and increased the difficulty of collecting cash, including the bulk of the rates.214 Camborne may have been cushioned somewhat by having Dolcoath mine, Holmans and other industries, but other parishes felt the loss. *The Mining Journal* commented that the number of Afrikanders to be seen in the Cornish towns had appreciably diminished but was unable to decide whether that was because the men had once more conformed to the customs and dress of the country of their birth or had gone to Australia, America or elsewhere.215 It was also noted on occasion in *The Mining Journal* that the mining industry of South Africa was far and away more important to Cornwall than tin mining in its own district216 and throughout the duration of the war it kept its readers informed as to the effect the war was having upon the people of Cornwall. An example of how seriously the South African War had affected the St.

Just neighbourhood was clearly indicated at a meeting at the Levant mine. According to Major White in six months he had taken on 100 miners who had previously worked in South Africa, men who seeing no prospect of return had been compelled to seek work in the district. For the first six months of the war the men had lived on their savings, but rather than entirely exhaust their resources they resumed their old occupations at wages much less than they could command abroad. *The Mining Journal* concluded:

> *There is no county in England, probably, which feels the continuance of hostilities so acutely because for every one Cornish miner at home there are 10 or more in the disturbed country, or still seeking refuge in Natal or Cape Colony, who are waiting eagerly for the time to come when they can resume their work and pay.*[217]

There were other problems to contend with, such as soldiers' pay not being sent home to the wives. W.S. Caine M.P. had to ask the Secretary of War if he was aware of this in relation to Edwin Paynter of Camborne, to which he was given the assurance that money would be advanced if the woman could produce reliable evidence that it was her husband's intention to remit.[218]

General Redvers Buller paid a visit to Cornwall, and at St. Michael's Mount was greeted by a cheering crowd. At the same time Caine gave a speech at the Town Liberal Club, in which he said:

> *This terrible war is weighing on us like a nightmare. It was preventing men going back to the mines in the Transvaal and was half ruining shop-keepers because money was no longer being sent home to the wives and families by the men who formerly worked in the mines. The prolongation of the war was due simply to the fact that the Government insisted on pursuing a policy of coercion instead of one of conciliation.*[219]

There were still Cornishmen at the front; Trooper Carne of Penzance, gave details of a tough and bloody encounter with De la Rey's Commandos during which his officer was hit in the hand and having dismounted along with a Sergeant to bandage it, the Boers got to him and shot him through the eye, then shot the Sergeant through the neck.[220] Carne eventually returned to Cornwall, although not before spending a fortnight in the Woolwich Hospital to get over the effect of fever. J.H. Brighton serving with the Duke of York's Light Infantry also saw his officer killed. The shot that hit Major Edwards struck him above the right eye and came out at the crown of his head.[221] Edwards was from Mount Edgecumbe and had been a great friend of another young Cornish officer – Guy St. Aubyn. Brighton's two Uncles – Alfred George Seccombe and James Edward Seccombe – were also in South Africa, the latter having fought in the Zulu War. Lieutenant Joseph Dunn, the Penzance journalist who had been on the Editorial Staff of the

Star, was serving with the Scottish Horse Regiment. In one letter home to his former newspaper the *Cornishman,* he spoke of how the climate of South Africa had changed him from the pale faced sickly lad he had once been.222 Twice captured by the Boers, Dunn had escaped each time but he died from an illness brought on by exposure, hard work and fatigue as a soldier.223 Corporal Charles Osborne made it safely home to Penzance, although Alfred Cara – having broken two of his teeth from eating biscuits – was unable to get a discharge, being sent from Kimberley back to garrison duty.224 Corporal T. Jenkins (Redruth) died from an attack of dysentery whilst in Eastern Pondoland, and was yet one more Cornishman to be laid to rest in far off South Africa whilst serving his King and country.225 Also from Redruth – and described as one of the coolest men in action – was Lieutenant H.E. Thompson, with 1st Brabant's Horse.226 Another Cornish hero was Staff-Sergeant John Carylon Hill from Helston, serving with Thorneycroft's Mounted Infantry. He died from wounds received during a fight with the Boers near Pietersdale on the 20th of January 1902. Hill, a chemist, had joined up at the outbreak of war and been promoted twice – first to Sergeant and then Staff-Sergeant. Two of his brothers had also seen fighting, Sam Hill – who had completed his service before going back into business at Johannesburg – and Cecil Hill, who was a member of the South African Constabulary. Staff-Sergeant Hill had been home on leave during the war and had received a welcome reception at Helston, during which he gave a speech but,

> *Half way through, the young Cornishman's voice was choked with tears*
> *'You must excuse me, 'said he, 'but I sometimes feel sad when I think of*
> *the brave men who laid down their lives, men we loved and followed, men*
> *who are now dead and buried – while we are here to receive the*
> *honours.*227

Hill also spoke in praise of General Buller and Colonel Thorneycroft and especially fellow Cornishman Captain Horace Mann. News of the deaths of Cornishmen was being reported almost on a weekly basis. Jim Bolitho of St. Just, with the Kimberley Light Horse, had been right through the war, only to be shot at the end of it.228 Ambrose Trembath, also of St. Just, died at Port Elizabeth from fever and Charles Richards of Tuckingmill, a storekeeper on the railway died from drowning.229 Equally disturbing to many Cornish was the news that some Cornishmen had actually fought on the side of the Boers. A Cornishman doing military duty at Ceylon where a number of Boer prisoners had been taken, came across a St. Ives man who tried to make out he wasn't who he was and also found a native of Redruth and one from Truro.230 The *Post* also told of a Cornishman who was one of the prisoners at the Boer camp at Umballa, in India, but commented, 'happily they are the very rare exceptions.'231 Although none of these are named, one Cornishman who did fight with the Boers was Frederick de Witt

Tossel. He served in the Pretoria Dorp Commando under General Smuts throughout the Boer War, and according to one writer was taken prisoner and sent to East London. After the war he was offered his old job back in the police force by the British Government but Tossel "could not see his way open to accepting it".232

Most of the Cornish-South Africans, those who had made South Africa their home, either took the side of the British or remained neutral. Hugh Lanion Hall wrote:

> *I had to be very careful when talking about the war. There were some foreign engine drivers who used to get papers from Natal and the Cape smuggled through to me, so I was kept posted, but it was a very anxious time.233*

With his family safe in East London, Hall remained on his farm near Nelspruit, although he often came under suspicion from the local Boers. President Kruger himself stayed at Nelspruit, and Hall watched him leave one morning with his shipment of gold:

> *I saw this gold loaded;... seventy-two boxes... When all was loaded, the train started off for Lourenco Marques. That was the last we saw of Krugers millions. No doubt they went with him to Europe and were used there to carry on the war. They have been much talked about, and many have thought they were buried. Futile searches, practically yearly, have taken place right up to the present time.234*

Cornish Post and mining News, August 1900

To all intents and purposes the war was over for the Cornish miner when Johannesburg was captured on the 31st of May 1900 and an early return to the mines was expected. They were not disappointed:

> *Several old hands at Camborne were telegraphed for last week to go to the Rand mines at once, presumably, we think, to pump the water out as*

*soon as possible, so that the main bulk of the refugees may soon be able to resume work. News has been sent to Camborne from South Africa that those Volunteers who left Cornwall to fight at the front, are to have their selection of situations on the Rand.*235

Such was the rush that some of the men reached Johannesburg only to be turned back. One Cornishman who received a wire to go to Cape Town en route for the Rand was just one of the many to get no further than the Cape; and told how many miners were stranded and in desperate straits. His Superintendent, having made a brief inspection of the mines at Johannesburg, had been ordered back to Cape Town and did not expect that there would be much mining done that year on the Rand, which turned out to be the case.236 In June a warning had been issued by the Colonial Office that miners would be delayed at the Cape and that it would be a couple of months at least before those already in Cape Colony and Natal would be able to return to work in the Transvaal.237 In October came better news that a batch of men had gone up to Johannesburg and were staying. The *Cornishman* reported:

*Many who left Johannesburg last summer to escape the dangers of the Boer War buried their tools and covered them with vaseline to prevent them from rusting. Some left their furniture behind and we are pleased to learn from recent letters that this has been recovered almost unhurt.*238

In the same newspaper, Corporal J.L. Roach (Penzance), serving with the Railway Pioneer Regiment reached his home in Johannesburg and was agreeably surprised to find it still in good order with the furniture virtually intact.239

Although the war was to continue for another eighteen months or more, in Cornwall all focus was now centred on the mining situation on the Rand. Lord Kitchener gave his consent for seven mines to resume work240 with fifty stamps each, but only on condition that no employee received more than 5 shillings a day with rations – all miners had to join the Rand Rifles as well.241 A Rand Mines Guard, consisting of some 1,000 men, was formed at the Cape and having first been inspected by Sir Alfred Milner at Cape Town, travelled to Johannesburg, which was completely surrounded by barbed wire, with only five entrances into the town, each closely guarded. The miners who refused to accept the 5 shillings a day wage – as some did – were sent back to the Cape or Natal.242

Most Cornish miners were only too willing to return to the Rand on Kitchener's terms, including many who had been staying at Durban and East London. There were others who opted for the United States of America, while Richard Thomas took with him a contingent of assistants and miners – chiefly from East Cornwall – to West Africa,243 despite a warning only a week earlier from William Petherick that the death rate of Cornishmen on the West Coast had been appallingly heavy.244

By October 1901 the Mines Guard at Johannesburg had been disbanded and the men had been provided with work in the mines although they still had to do service with the Rand Rifles without pay. The outlook for the gold industry seemed promising, as arrangements with the Portuguese authorities regarding the supply of native labour were being satisfactorily negotiated. Nine mines were now working – each mine requiring 1,000 – 1,500 natives – and Kitchener withdrew his proclamation which had limited wages to 5 shillings a day. In Cornwall:

> *welcome gifts in the shape of the old fashioned money orders were received by the South African mail at Camborne on Saturday... the good times of two and a half years ago begin to return sooner than most people thought they would.*[245]

However, at the end of the year it was considered a little unfortunate that the visit of the Royal Cornwall Show to Camborne should follow a long depression and stoppage of South African remittances.[246] In South Africa that Christmas a number of Cornishmen met on Christmas Eve at the house of James Trezona (Camborne), Shift Boss at the May Consolidated mine in order to celebrate the approach of Christmas in the old Cornish style of carol singing. Having paraded around the mine singing carols until early in the morning, they all adjourned to the residence of the underground manager Mr. John Rowe of Marazion for refreshments.[247]

At the beginning of 1902 came good news as the number of miners going up from Cape Town every week to Johannesburg was about 400.[248] The numbers increased with twenty miners leaving Camborne and ten women and children leaving Redruth with a large number of men during the last week of February.[249] The exodus of miners to South Africa from the Mining Division was so great that in April there was a scarcity of miners in the Camborne district, although part of the reason was also due to a number of miners having exchanged their jobs not for South Africa but for the more lucrative work on the surface with the Electric Tramway Company, which was building a three-mile tramway from Camborne to Redruth. On arrival in South Africa the Cornish miner still faced a problem, for a permit system was in operation. In May the Cornish M.P. for the Mining Division – W.S. Caine – asked the Secretary of War if he was

> *aware that a number of Cornish miners who left the country in January and February last under a War Office permit to take up their old employment in Johannesburg were detained at Cape Town and could not proceed further in consequence of the refusal of the permit office at Cape Town to grant facilities of travel.*[251]

Chamberlain replied, saying that the miners detained at Cape Town were either those who had not been employed on the Rand before the war or those whose mines had yet to begin working. Thirty mines had been working since March and in May another six – Glenn Deep, Ferreira, Crown Deep, Geldenhuis Deep, Geldenhuis Estate and Henry Nourse Deep – began work once more.252 At the end of the month came the news all Cornwall had been waiting for – the Peace of Vereeniging (31st May) had been signed – the war was finally over. For the Cornish, however, both at home and abroad, their problems were to continue.

Before leaving the subject of the Boer War, special mention needs to be made of one Cornish person – Emily Hobhouse – whom Gandhi called one of the noblest and bravest of women.253 The humanitarian contribution made by this extraordinary woman, was a credit to Cornwall even if not appreciated at the time.

Emily, youngest daughter of Reginald Hobhouse, Rector of St. Ive, near Liskeard, was 39 years old when the war started. Through her mother, she was descended from Sir Jonathan Trelawny of *Shall Trelawny Die?* fame whilst her uncle was Leonard Courtney. Working on behalf of the church, Emily Hobhouse was very much a social reformer who had already spent a number of years in the United States of America, where she worked amongst the Cornish miners. Returning from America in 1898, following a broken engagement – which would have involved her living in Mexico after marriage – she devoted her time and energy to working with the Women's Industrial Council in London, where she was particularly concerned about the exploitation of children working in industry. At the start of the Boer War, influenced by her uncle and aunt – the Courtneys – Emily Hobhouse became Secretary of the Women's Branch of the South African Conciliation Committee. For the first time in British history a broad spectrum of women became politically active.254 During 1900 when the attention of Emily Hobhouse was drawn to the plight of the Boer women and children in South Africa and despite initial difficulties her efforts led to the creation of a new charity – the South African Women and Children's Distress Fund. Described as purely benevolent, non-political, non-sectarian and national its main aim was to feed, clothe, shelter and rescue women and children whether Boer or British or others who had been made destitute and homeless by the destruction of property, deportation, or other incidents of the military operations.255

In order to visit South Africa Emily Hobhouse privately raised a sum of £300 to buy food and clothing for the inmates of the camp. She used her own money to pay for the trip to South Africa, and left Britain on 7th December 1900 to arrive at Cape Town two days after Christmas Day, having travelled second class and alone, using her time to learn Dutch. Armed only with the advice 'Be calm, be prudent', from her uncle and with a letter of introduction to Sir Alfred Milner, through her own personality and strength of character, she extended a 15 minute audience with Milner to well over an hour. During the interview Milner agreed she could visit the concentration camps, giving her a letter of authority. He also admitted in her presence that the order to burn the farms was a mistake. Then, perhaps to ease his conscience, he presented her with a truck – capable of holding 12 tons – which could be attached to any train. Before coming out to South Africa, Emily Hobhouse had heard only of the refugee or concentration camp at Port Elizabeth but she was soon made aware of other camps at Potchefstroom, Norvals Pont, Kroonstad, Johannesburg, Kimberley and Bloemfontein, which she decided to visit first.[256] On leaving Cape Town she said:

> *as the train moved off towards the strange hot war-stricken north with its accumulation of misery and bloodshed I must own up that my heart sank a little and I faced the unknown with great trepidation in spite of the feeling that the deep desire of months which had laid so urgent a call upon me, was indeed finding accomplishment.*[257]

It was a lonely journey that Emily Hobhouse made, and she recalled later the desolate outlook, passing as she did carcasses of horses, mules and cattle and a number of burnt out farms. Those still standing looked lifeless, with little evidence of any work being carried out in the fields.[258] On reaching Bloemfontein – a camp of some 2,000, including 900 children – Emily Hobhouse for the first time realised how great was the task that lay before her. She wrote:

> *The authorities are at their wits' end – and have no more idea how to cope with the one difficulty of providing clothes for the people than the man on the moon. Crass male ignorance, stupidity, helplessness and muddling. I rub as much salt into the sore places of their minds as I possibly can, because it's good for them; but I can't help melting a little when they are very humble and confess that the whole thing is a grievous and gigantic blunder and presents an almost insoluble problem, and they don't know how to face it.*[259]

Someone who agreed with her was Hugh Lanion Hall, who also considered the concentrating of the women and children as the biggest blunder made in the Boer War.[260] He believed that the rounding up of the women and children into camps enabled the Boers to carry on the fight much longer, for it removed their responsibility of having to feed the women and children. The rations in the camps were far from adequate, and worse was the lack of sanitation resulting in the rapid spread of typhoid, dysentery and diarrhoea. Whooping cough, measles, chicken pox and pneumonia also killed many of the young children, and the rate of mortality within the camps was extremely high. At Aliwal North camp Emily Hobhouse wrote:

> *It was a death rate such as had never been known except in the times of the Great Plagues. The whole talk was of death – who died yesterday, who lay dying today, and who would be dead tomorrow...* [261]

Emily Hobhouse.

Describing the emaciated children at Bloemfontein Camp as like faded flowers thrown away,262 Emily Hobhouse travelled north through a countryside where war was still raging. Her journey was slow due to the many checks made by the military of permits and passes. At Norval Pont she waited seven hours for a train, before making a melancholy journey to Kimberley, passing by the battlefields of Belmont, Modder River and Magesfontein and seeing the long trench from where the Boers shot down the Black Watch.263 At Kimberley she found a dirty and smelling camp with over-crowded tents, an army doctor who naturally knew little of children's ailments and three little corpses being photographed for the absent fathers to see some day.264 By now Emily Hobhouse had decided that she could do little more in South Africa:

> *Shocked at the misery I had seen and conscious that equal suffering prevailed in some thirty other camps, certain that with right administration much of it could be removed and strong in the faith that English humanity if made aware would not tolerate such conditions I formed my determination to return home and I left South Africa with poignant regret but with no delay.*265

Arriving back in Britain on the 24th of May 1901 she first appealed for help to Sir John Brodrick, the Secretary of War, but when that was ignored she began a strenuous campaign of letters to the press, pamphlet circulation and the organisation of public meetings. She said:

> *I spoke at forty public meetings in the course of the summer and with three exceptions (Bristol, New Southgate and Darlington) everyone was peaceful and orderly.*266

The Bristol meeting in particular caused offence to many Cornish, for she insinuated that when it came to the non-appreciation of sanitary conditions the Cornish were more blameworthy than the Dutch.267 Emily Hobhouse was labelled as a political agitator, a disseminator of inaccurate and blood-curdling stories and deficient as an investigator.268 At least one clergyman was so incensed by her speeches that he published his own pamphlet pointing out that war was not a Sunday School picnic and reminding his readers that the British had suffered too; he told of a Cornish couple who were turned out of the Transvaal, lost their savings and suffered illnesses because of the war, asking "Now where is Miss Hobhouse's womanly sympathy for them and where is her report of visits to them?".269

Emily Hobhouse returned to South Africa arriving at Cape Town on the 22nd of October 1901, but she was prevented from leaving the ship by a Royal Navy Lieutenant who said. "I have to inform you that you are not to be allowed to land in Cape Town, that you are to remain on the *Avondale Castle*, under strict supervision, that you are to hold no communication with anyone on shore either by word or letter and that it is proposed you should return by the *Carisbrooke Castle* leaving on Wednesday afternoon". The Captain of the *Avondale Castle* was then instructed that under martial law he was to be responsible for guarding Miss Hobhouse. When Emily asked on whose orders she was prevented from leaving she was told, "Of that I can say nothing". Although Emily pointed out that her work both in England and South Africa was purely and consistently philanthropic and not political it was to no avail. While remaining on board as a prisoner Emily wrote:

> *By a curious chance I hit upon a volume of McCaulay's history and found some stimulus in reading again how Bishop Trelawny (who happens to be an ancestor of mine) resisted with his colleagues the despotism of James II.*[270]

Although she was visited the next day by Colonel Cooper, the Acting-Commandant in Cape Town, Emily demanded to know the reason for her detention either from Sir Alfred Milner or Lord Kitchener. She also refused to make the return voyage, for she was now a sick woman suffering from the shock and strain of the ordeal. A Doctor was instructed to examine her and he arrived with two army nurses with orders to take Emily Hobhouse to the *Carisbrooke Castle* by force if necessary. Appealing to the two nurses that the laws of humanity and nature are or should be higher than military laws and not to mar their sacred office as nurses by molesting a sick woman the two nurses turned and silently left the room. The Doctor returned with two soldiers and asked her to co-operate, but she replied,

> *Sir, I cannot and will not give other reply than what I have said from the beginning. My refusal was based on principle and principles do not alter in a day, nor can they be frightened out of me by force. I am weak and ill, unfit to take this voyage. It is not a right thing in any case, and especially unreasonable to ask it without giving me previous rest. I will not go one step voluntarily towards the Roslin Castle. I beg you to leave me.*

> *'Madam' he said 'do you wish to be taken like a lunatic?'*

> *'Sir, 'I replied 'the lunacy is your side and with those whose commands you obey. If you have any manhood on you, you will go and leave me alone.*[271]

They did not. Her shawl was wrapped around her thus preventing her from using her arms and she was picked up by the soldiers and carried from one ship, along the dockside, and on to the other. After a 48-day voyage she arrived back in Britain weak, worn out and nerve-racked.[272] Despite the questionable legality of the incident, Emily Hobhouse was informed by a Government source that if she took any legal action against her arrest it would be defeated and any attempt to obtain an authoritative or useful decision on Martial Law would prove abortive.[273] At least one Cornish newspaper had little sympathy for Emily's deportation from

South Africa, suggesting that after wallowing so deep in pro-Boer mire – her vision has become distorted.274

To recover her health Emily Hobhouse went to Switzerland in April 1902, where she wrote *The Brunt of the War* and dedicated it to the women of South Africa. She showed that more adult Boers perished in the camps than fell in the field of battle with over four times the number of children – the book is a damning indictment of the war. Emily Hobhouse was one of the few people to welcome the arrival in Britain of the three Boer leaders, Botha, De la Rey and De Wet, who had come seeking compensation for the Boer people:

> *Botha a kindly person with very courtly manners and commanding air, De la Rey a patriarch, very gentle and quiet; and De Wet impressive. His face is enigmatical but stamped with the responsibility and the sorrow of the war... I felt they were not merely great soldiers, but great men.274*

She did return to South Africa in May 1903 and received a hearty welcome at Cape Town in Afrikander circles.275 After a short rest she

> *headed inland and passing so many bones of dead animals she was reminded of Tom Pearce's old mare 'ghostly white' in our West Country ballad 'Old Uncle Tom Cobbleigh & All'. She stayed at De Wet's farm and was shocked to find De Wet so thin but still with his dignity and a sense of humour.276*

Emily Hobhouse visited many towns, being welcomed especially by the Boer women and children. On one occasion, whilst travelling through the Transvaal, she wrote:

> *I got at last to Belfast, the highest town in the Transvaal. As we jogged along I dozed a little in the wagon, and when I opened my eyes I thought I saw our Cornish Kit Hill with the chimney on top, but it turned out to be the monument in memory of 1881, where Dingaans Day is kept in this district.277*

At Pretoria she stayed with General Smuts and his wife, but all around she could see the utter destitution and poverty facing many Boer families. A personal appeal made by Emily to the British Government resulted in an immediate grant of some £7,000 being sent. By the end of 1903 she was once more on her way back to England, unfortunately in ill health. After regaining her health, by resting at Lisbon, she travelled to the South of France and called on ex-President Kruger. She wrote:

> *Our talk was not long. I saw that already his mind was elsewhere and the world had ended for him... He wanted so much to know if I had seen his wife and when I told him that I had not been allowed to visit Pretoria*

*before her death, he seemed too disappointed to make further effort. The little modern French villa was a cheap and incongruous setting to that mediaeval and puritanical figure.*278

Kruger himself died just over a year later, in July 1904. His body was taken back to South Africa, where on December 16th it was finally laid to rest at Pretoria. The Post reported that Briton and Boer mingled in the crowd and there was no untoward incident.279

Instrumental in the reconstruction of post-war South Africa were a number of Cornishmen, including the two Hosken brothers. Richard Hosken, who had been an advisor to Lord Roberts, Lord Milner, and to the military police, had been one of the first civilians to enter Johannesburg after its capture by the British. He later earned distinction for his work among the refugees in Natal. It was his older brother – William – however, who was the more prominent. Like Richard, he had also served in an advisory capacity to Lord Roberts, and after the war Milner appointed him to Johannesburg's first Town Council in 1902. Re-elected as President of Johannesburg's Chamber of Commerce, William Hosken was to become very much its leading Cornishman. In April 1903, Hosken was selected as one of the Johannesburg members of the Transvaal Legislative Council.280

Equally important in aiding Milner with his reconstruction policy were two other Cornishmen; Charles Hitchens, took on a Chancellor of the Exchequer role,281 and the other, Lewis Michell, was overall financial advisor to Milner. Michell could easily have become finance minister of the Transvaal if it had not been for the death of Cecil Rhodes, for he felt bound by a promise to succeed Rhodes on the Board of De Beers and the Chartered Company.282 Michell had become very much Rhodes' financial wizard and Rhodes had the utmost confidence in the calm, confident, shrewd judgment of the Cornishman.283 Respect between the two men had been mutual. In 1890 when Rhodes become Prime Minister of Cape Colony, Michell had been put in charge of all his household and other expenditures. In return Michell had put the bank's resources at the disposal of Rhodes so that he could finance the expansionist policy which was to lead to the creation of Rhodesia (now Zimbabwe). It was perhaps not surprising that when in early 1902 Rhodes lay dying he sent for his closest financial advisor. "All right – then send for Michell", was his remark when Jameson told him that the end was near.284 During the evening of 26th March Michell spent the last few hours with Rhodes listening to the final instructions as executor to his will. Rhodes extracted from Michell a promise that he would continue his work. First Michell had to arrange Rhodes' funeral, and he was one of the chief mourners at the funeral held in Rhodesia.

In 1902 Lewis Michell reached the height of his career when he became a member of Parliament for Cape Town and Chairman of De Beers at Kimberley.

However, to carry out his duties as a trustee of the will – it was Michell who launched the Rhodes Scholarship – he resigned as General Manager of the Standard Bank. Before the year was out a further honour was bestowed upon Michell when he received a Knighthood for his war contribution.[285] Such had been his rise to prominence that many saw Sir Lewis Michell as a future Prime Minister but it was not to be. Michell supported Dr. Jameson for the leadership of the Progressive Party and served in Jameson's Ministry 1904-08 as Minister without Portfolio where he proved an ever-present help in trouble to other Ministers, and his great financial knowledge and experience were constantly at the disposal of the Government.[286]

Boer war memorial at Morrab Gardens,
Penzance (See also page 317)

1. Randolph Churchill, *WINSTON S. CHURCHILL,* YOUTH 1874-1900 (LONDON 1966) p.299

2. *C.P.M.N.,* 15th MARCH 1900

3. Elizabeth Longford, *JAMESON'S RAID. THE PRELUDE TO THE BOER WAR* (LONDON 1982)

4. Thomas Pakenham, *THE BOER WAR* (LONDON 1982)

5. Hosken claimed in a lecture he gave at Hayle that nine tenths of taxation was imposed on the Uitlanders (outlanders or foreigners). In other words 75,000 Boers paid one tenth, 175,000 Uitlanders paid nine tenths. See *C.P.M.N.,* 15th MARCH 1900

6. *CORNISHMAN* 19th SEPTEMBER 1896

7. *C.P.M.N.,* 15th MARCH 1900

8. *IBID.,* 9th JANUARY 1896

9. *IBID.,* 16th JANUARY 1896

10. *IBID.,* 9th JANUARY 1896

11. *CORNUBIAN,* 17th JANUARY 1896

12. *CORNISHMAN,* 16th JANUARY 1896

13. *IBID.,* 13th FEBRUARY 1896

14. *C.P.M.N.,* 9th JANUARY 1896

15. *CORNISHMAN,* 23rd JANUARY 1896

16. *C.P.M.N.,* 30th JANUARY 1896

17. *IBID.,* 6th FEBRUARY 1896

18. *IBID.,* 13th FEBRUARY 1896

19. *IBID.,* 6th FEBRUARY 1896

20. *CORNUBIAN,* 24th JANUARY 1896

21. *CORNISHMAN,* 26th MARCH 1896 Barney Barnato was one of the few Randlords to denounce the raid. He was not a member of the Reform Committee. He died in 1897 when he jumped overboard on his way back to England.

22. *CORNISHMAN,* 6th FEBRUARY 1896

23. *C.P.M.N.,* 23rd JANUARY 1896

24. *IBID.,* 30th JANUARY 1896

25. *C.P.M.N.,* 30th JANUARY 1896

26. *CORNISHMAN,* 13th FEBRUARY 1896

27. *IBID.,* 6th FEBRUARY 1896

28. *IBID.,* 30th JANUARY 1896

29. *C.P.M.N.,* 30th JANUARY 1896

30. *CORNISHMAN,* 30th JANUARY 1896

31. *C.P.M.N.,* 13th FEBRUARY 1896

32. The Eckstein brothers – Hermann and Frederick – had founded the Corner House, the name given to the company which was probably the most important financial group on the Rand. As one miner said it was simply an attempt of the Charter Company (by which he meant Rhodes) and Engstein (sic) Brothers, who own most of the mining properties in that district to get control of the Government and in this they were defeated. *CORNISHMAN,* 26th MARCH 1896. See also A. Cartwright, *THE CORNER HOUSE,* (CAPE TOWN 1958)

33. Hall, *REAPED MY MEALIES,* . p.155

34. *IBID.,* p.158

35. *CORNISHMAN,* 13th FEBRUARY 1896

36. *IBID.,* 6th FEBRUARY 1896

37. *C.P.M.N.,* 20th FEBRUARY 1896. Arthur Quiller Couch 1863-1944 'Q' of Bodmin of Fowey is considered to be one of Cornwall's greatest scholars. He became Chairman of the Cornwall Education Committee and was a great supporter in politics of the Liberal cause. Knighted in 1910, he became Professor of English Literature at Cambridge in 1912, a post he held until his death. During the 1914-18 war he equipped and trained a Pioneer battalion for the D.C.L.I. In 1928 he was made a Bard of the Cornish Gorsedd. He wrote over 21 novels.

38. *CORNISHMAN,* 14th MAY 1896

39. *IBID.*, 9th APRIL 1896 and *C.P.M.N.*, 23rd JANUARY 1896. The sons of eight Ministers of religion were riding with Jameson.

40. *C.P.M.N.*, 13th FEBRUARY 1896

41. *KRUGERSDORP TIMES*, 18th JANUARY 1896

42. *IBID.*, 1st FEBRUARY 189643. *CORNISHMAN*, 26th MARCH 1896. Winston Churchill was also aware that a war was coming, writing in 1896 or 1897 'Sooner or later, in a righteous cause or a picked quarrel, with the approval of Europe or in the teeth of Germany, for the sake of our Empire, for the sake of our honour, for the sake of our race, we must fight the Boers.' Randolph Churchill, WINSTON S. CHURCHILL, p.449-450

44. Two committee members actually refused to beg for mercy and were not released until 1898. See Longford, *JAMESON'S RAID* p.91

45. Louis Anthony had planned to go to Australia – However, he apparently changed his mind for the paper later reported he was returning to Transvaal. See *C.P.M.N.*, 28th MAY 1896

46. C.P.M.N., 26th MARCH 189647. Hall, *REAPED MY MEALIES* p.162

48. Vorster *SERVAMUS*, NOVEMBER 1896

49. Zeederburg, *PERSONALITY* FEBRUARY 1970

50. *KRUGERSDORP TIMES*, 28th MARCH 1896

51. *IBID.*, 7th NOVEMBER 1895

52. *IBID.*, 11th APRIL 1896

53. *IBID.*, 25th APRIL 1896

54. *ROODEPOORT MAIL, FLORIDA & MARAISBURG NEWS*, 24th NOVEMBER 1897

55. For more information on Immorality in Johannesburg see Onselen, *STUDIES IN THE SOC & ECON. HISTORY OF THE WITS, 1886-1914 NEW BABYLON*

CHAPTER 3 *PROSTITUTES AND PROLETARIANS 1886-1914*

56. *ROODEPOORT MAIL*, 2nd MARCH 1898

57. *C.P.M.N.*, 19th SEPTEMBER 1896

58. *IBID.*, 21st MAY 1896

59. *IBID.*, 29th OCTOBER 1896

60. *CORNISHMAN*, 27th FEBRUARY 1896. Chilvers claims the hole made by the explosion was 250 feet long, 60 feet wide and 50 feet deep see Chilvers, *OUT OF THE CRUCIBLE*. p.126. Gwennap Pit is a grass amphitheatre near St. Day, possibly the sunken roof of a mine. The pit is 300 yards around and seats thousands on grassy tiers. It has remarkable acoustic properties. See Arthur Mee *CORNWALL* (LONDON 1943) p.82

61. Chilvers, *OUT OF THE CRUCIBLE* p.125

62. *POTCHEFSTROOM BUDGET*, 29th FEBRUARY 1896

63. *CORNISHMAN*, 26th MARCH 1896. The actual relief total was £104 to £128.

64. *C.P.M.N.*, 30th JULY 1896

65. *CORNUBIAN*, 7th AUGUST 1896

66. *CORNISHMAN*, 13th AUGUST 1896

67. *CORNISHMAN*, 16th JULY 1896

68. *C.P.M.N.*, 30th JULY 1896

69. *CORNUBIAN*, 7th AUGUST 1896

70. *C.P.M.N.*, 30th JULY 1896 – Mark Guy Pearse died in 1930. His funeral was held at the West London Mission, St. James Hall, Piccadilly which he had begun some 42 years earlier.

71. *CORNISHMAN*, 13th MAY 1897

72. *IBID.*, 3rd JUNE 1897

73. Norman Hannan, *JOSEPH TUCKER LETTERS OF A SOUTH AFRICAN MINER*, 1898-1904 (Romford 1981) p.4

74. Rhodes said Chamberlain was in up to his neck, but neither man could bring the other down without destroying himself, so they both survived. See Wheatcroft, *RANDLORDS*, p.188

75. Pakenham, *BOER WAR* . p.48

76. *CORNUBIAN*, 20th JANUARY 1899

77. *C.P.M.N.*, 13th JUNE 1899

78. *IBID.*, 22nd JUNE 1899

79. *CORNISHMAN*, 31st AUGUST 1899. There is no mention of this episode in either Longford's *JAMESON'S RAID* or Pakenham's *BOER WAR*.

80. *C.P.M.N.*, 7th SEPTEMBER 1899. Pakeman, Editor of the *TRANSVAAL LEADER* was arrested on a charge of high treason whilst Monypenny, Editor of the Johannesburg *STAR* reached Natal safely with Hosken See also *STANDARD & DIGGERS NEWS* 9th SEPTEMBER 1899 for a description of Hosken's arrival in Natal.

81. *IBID.*, 14th SEPTEMBER 1899. This was denied by returning miners interviewed in the same paper.

82. IBID., 28th SEPTEMBER 1899. Rowe notes that during the American Civil War 1861-65 although a few Cousin Jacks may have fought in the Southern armies while quite a number enlisted on the Union side… it seems that the majority tended to look on the war as a purely American quarrel that was none of their concern. He added that if this reluctance to fight was misunderstood then so it was again in 1899 when rather than fight in a war they regarded as the result of the conflict of antediluvian Boer politicians, on the one side, and avaricious European and Semitic capitalists on the other, they left the Rand in hundreds to find other mining fields until the trouble was over. Rowe, *HARD ROCK MEN* p.149-150

83. *CORNUBIAN*, 29th SEPTEMBER 1899

84. *IBID.*, 13th OCTOBER 1899

85. *C.P.M.N.*, 5th OCTOBER 1899

86. *CORNISHMAN*, 19th OCTOBER 1899

87. *IBID.*, 12th OCTOBER 1899

88. *C.P.M.N.*, 24th AUGUST 1899, an extract from the '*Western Mercury*'.

89. *IBID.*, 12th OCTOBER 1899

90. *MINING JOURNAL,* 14th OCTOBER 1899

91. *IBID.*, 28th OCTOBER 1899

92. *C.P.M.N.*, 12th OCTOBER 1899

93. *CORNUBIAN*, 24th NOVEMBER 1899

94. *C.P.M.N.*, 12th OCTOBER 1899

95. *CORNISHMAN*, 2nd NOVEMBER 1899

96. *WEST BRITON*, 9th NOVEMBER 1899. A Sjambok was a whip made out of a single piece of rhinoceros hide.

97. *CORNISHMAN*, 9th NOVEMBER 1899

98. *IBID.*, 30th NOVEMBER 1899

99. *IBID.*, 16th NOVEMBER 1899

100. *C.P.M.N.*, 30th NOVEMBER 1899

101. *CORNUBIAN*, 24th NOVEMBER 1899

102. Norman Hannan, *TRAVELS AND HEARTACHES OF A MINING FAMILY,* (ROMFORD 1984) p.90. There were large numbers of Cornish miners working in the Iron Mines in the Dalton-in-Furness area.

103. *C.P.M.N.*, 21st DECEMBER 1899

104. *IBID.*, 11th JANUARY 1900

105. A blockhouse took 3 months to erect and cost between £800-£1,000 – it served a similar purpose to a Second World War 'Pillbox'. See: Emanuel Lee, *TO THE BITTER END*, (LONDON 1985).

106. G.H. Le May, *THE BOER WAR*. Article appeared in *HISTORY OF THE TWENTIETH CENTURY,* Chapter One p.13 (LONDON 1968).

107. Kenneth Griffith, *THANK GOD WE KEPT THE FLAG FLYING. THE SIEGE AND RELIEF OF LADYSMITH 1899-1900* (LONDON 1974) p.3

108. Winston S. Churchill, *THE BOER WAR LONDON TO LADYSMITH.* Ian Hamilton's March (LONDON 1989) p.6

109. Griffith, *THANK GOD WE KEPT THE FLAG FLYING* p.3

110. Deneys Ritz, *COMMANDO. A BOER JOURNAL OF THE BOER WAR* (LONDON 1983) p.33 Thomas Brokensha, leader of Dundee Ambulance

Corps during the war, was in conversation with Penn-Symons a few minutes before he was shot and after the war dined with the deceased General's brother and Lady Penn-Symons whose photograph she presented to him. The home of the Penn-Symons family was at Hatt House near the village of Botusfleming on the main Callington to Saltash road in east Cornwall. *CORNISHMAN*, 25th JUNE 1924.

111. Griffith, *KEPT THE FLAG FLYING* . p.65

112. Churchill, *THE BOER WAR* .p. 6

113. Over eighty irregular troops or units assisting the British took part in the Boer War. Cornishman C.R.C Tremeer assisted George Farrar in forming a number at the Cape. Tremeer later joined Lord Roberts' Staff as Field Officer for the Colonial Forces.

114. *CORNUBIAN*, 1st DECEMBER 1899

115. Churchill, *THE BOER WAR* p.21

116. A. Conan Doyle, *THE GREAT BOER WAR . A TWO YEARS' RECORD 1899-1901* (LONDON 1902) p.396

117. *CORNISHMAN*, 4th JANUARY 1900

118. *IBID.*, 25th JANUARY 1900

119. *IBID.*, 25th JANUARY 1900

120. *CORNUBIAN*, 19th JANUARY 1900

121. *CORNISHMAN*, 25th JANUARY 1900. A memorial obelisk to the Prince was later placed on Plymouth Hoe near the Citadel. Prince Christian Victor was the eldest son of Prince Christian of Schleswig-Holstein and Helena, fifth child of Queen Victoria.

122. *IBID.*, 25th JANUARY 1900

123. *IBID.*, 1st FEBRUARY 1900

124. *CORNUBIAN*, 19th JANUARY 1900

125. *CORNISHMAN*, 1st FEBRUARY 1900

126. *IBID.*, 15th FEBRUARY 1900

127. *CORNUBIAN*, 19th JANUARY 1900

128. *C.P.M.N.*, 15th FEBRUARY 1900

129. *IBID.*, 22nd MARCH 1900

130. *CORNISHMAN*, 23rd MARCH 1900

131. *IBID.*, 4th MAY 1900

132. *IBID.*, 1st JUNE 1900

133. *C.P.M.N.*, 7th JUNE 1900

134. *MINING JOURNAL*, 10th FEBRUARY p.170 and *C.P.M.N.*, 15th FEBRUARY and 1st MARCH 1900

135. *CORNISHMAN*, 5th APRIL 1900 – Tippet and Angwin both returned to Cornwall. Angwin went back to South Africa. *IBID.*, 2nd JANUARY 1902. Francis Olds was most likely Henry Francis Olds and therefore a nephew of Francis Oats.

136. The diary was reprinted in the *CORNISHMAN* between 27th APRIL – 3rd AUGUST 1933

137. The Boers had a great Creusot 5.9 inch gun known as 'Long Tom', so called because it had a range of 10,000 yards compared to the British field gun which only had a range of about 5,000 yards.

138. *WEST BRITON*, 27th DECEMBER 1973

139. *C.P.M.N.*, 5th APRIL 1900

140. *CORNUBIAN*, 27th APRIL 1900

141. *CORNISHMAN*, 29th MARCH 1900

142. *IBID.*, 22nd MARCH 1900

143. *C.P.M.N.*, 12th APRIL 1900

144. *IBID.*, 12th APRIL 1900

145. Smith-Dorrien, *MEMORIES* . p.154

146. *C.P.M.N.*, 8th MARCH 1900. According to a later edition of the *POST* Colonel Aldworth said This is to be a charge – a charge which shall live in all time to come, it is to be known as the Cornish charge. I have a £5 note to hand to the first man to get into the Boer trenches. The enemy are in a strong position; our firing line are tired; they only want a little spirit and dash infused into them by you; but the honour of the charge shall be yours alone. *IBID.*, 5th JULY 1900

147. Conan Doyle, *THE GREAT BOER WAR* p.331

148. *CORNISHMAN*, 5th APRIL 1900. Cronin seemed more concerned in his letter whether a box of chocolates he had sent

had reached home. It did and was displayed in a local shop window for a fortnight. The box was special, for each soldier had been sent one by Queen Victoria.

149. *IBID.,* 21st JUNE 1900

150. *IBID.,* 19th JULY 1900

151. *IBID.,* 24th MAY 1900

152. To match the range of the Boers' guns, naval guns were taken off ships such as the *Terrible*, and put on makeshift gun carriages. For more detail see Gerald Sharp, *THE SIEGE OF LADYSMITH* (LONDON 1976) Appendix III p.142-145

153. *CORNUBIAN,* 5th JULY 1901. Mrs Kinsman's husband Wm. Henry Kinsman was a well known resident of Natal, being the head of the West Country Association at Durban and one of the town's prominent citizens to welcome General Buller when he first arrived. He died in Durban in 1925 aged eighty-six. See *IBID.,* 9th MAY 1902 and *C.P.M.N.* 23rd May 1925

154. *CORNISHMAN,* 1st MARCH 1900

155. *IBID.,* 19th JULY 1900

156. *C.P.M.N.,* 15th JULY 1915

157. Vyvyan became Sir. Courtney Vyvyan and later served under Field Marshall Haig in World War 1. His brother Rev. Wilmot Lushington Vyvyan was Bishop of Zululand 1903-29 – he died at Grahamstown in 1937. Courtney Vyvyan died in 1941 aged 80

158. *IBID.,* 20th JUNE 1901

159. *CORNUBIAN,* 23rd AUGUST 1900

160. *IBID.,* 23rd NOVEMBER 1900

161. *C.P.M.N.,* 24th MAY 1900

162. *CORNISHMAN,* 13th DECEMBER 1900

163. *C.P.M.N.,* 8th MARCH 1900

164. *IBID.,* 8th MARCH 1900

165. *CORNUBIAN,* 24th JUNE 1900

166. *MINING JOURNAL,* 30th JUNE 1900 p.796

167. *IBID.,* 19th MAY 1900 p.611 Enteric fever is another name for typhoid.

168. *C.P.M.N.,* 31st MAY 1900

169. *CORNISHMAN,* 27th SEPTEMBER 1900

170. *IBID.,* 14th FEBRUARY 1901

171. *CORNISHMAN,* 27th SEPTEMBER 1900

172. *C.P.M.N.* 31st JAN 1901

173. *CORNISHMAN,* 9th August 1900

174. *C.P.M.N.,* 22nd MARCH 1900. Her husband is listed in Dickason, *CORNISH IMMIGRANTS.* p.91

175. *C.P.M.N.,* 30th NOVEMBER 1899

176. *CORNUBIAN,* 1st DECEMBER 1899

177. *MINING JOURNAL,* 11th NOVEMBER 1899 p.1346

178. *IBID.,* 9th DECEMBER 1899 p.1472

179. *CORNISHMAN,* 28th DECEMBER 1899. Nankervis was quite correct – 164 births were registered during the year, 82 males and 82 females – giving a birth rate of 26.80 per 1,000 against 24.35 per 1,000 for 1899 with 149 births. *IBID.,* 21st FEBRUARY 1901

180. *CORNUBIAN,* 22nd DECEMBER 1899

181. Arthur Davey, *THE BRITISH PRO-BOERS 1877-1902* (CAPE TOWN 1978) p.15

182. Silas K. Hocking, *MY BOOK OF MEMORY* (LONDON 1923) p.178

183. *CORNUBIAN,* 12th JANUARY 1900

184. *C.P.M.N.,* 11th JANUARY 1900

185. *CORNUBIAN,* 2nd FEBRUARY 1900

186. Hocking, *MY BOOK OF MEMORY* p.158. One of the books withdrawn was *Meadowsweet & Rue* which was based on the war and published in 1904

187. *CORNUBIAN* 16th MARCH 1900

188. *IBID.,* 9th MARCH 1900

189. Davey, *THE BRITISH PRO-BOERS* . p.158

190. *CORNUBIAN,* 23rd MARCH 1900

191. *CORNISHMAN,* 19th SEPTEMBER 1935. See also *CORNUBIAN* 8th JUNE 1900

192. Hocking, *MY BOOK OF MEMORY* . p.178

193. *IBID.*, p.184

194. *C.P.M.N.*, 27th SEPTEMBER 1900. Cornish Afrikander was a term used locally in Cornwall for the Cornish-South African miners.

195. *I.B.I.D.*, 4th OCTOBER 1900 Stones had also been thrown at Strauss the previous week, after he attended a meeting at Pool, but no injury was done. See *I.B.I.D.*, 27th SEPTEMBER 1900.

196. *I.B.I.D.*, 4th OCTOBER 1900

197. Caine had also apparently called the capitalists a gang of dirty, intriguing monopolists and Strauss a quack, humbug impostor and German Jew. *IBID.*, 4th OCTOBER 1900

198. *C.P.M.N.*, 27th SEPTEMBER 1900. Caine received 3, 100 votes – Strauss 2, 993 votes. Strauss later attributed defeat principally to the action of the 700 miners who had returned from South Africa. *CORNUBIAN*, 26th APRIL 1901

199. *MINING JOURNAL*, 25th OCTOBER 1900 p.4

200. *CORNUBIAN*, 14th DECEMBER 1900

201. *IBID.*, 21st DECEMBER 1900

202. *IBID.*, 17th MAY 1901

203. *CORNISHMAN*, 23rd MAY 1901 Sir. Reginald Pole Carew retired from the army in 1906. He was M.P. for Bodmin 1910-16 and died in 1924 aged 75

204. *IBID.*, 3rd JANUARY 1901

205. *IBID.*, 30th MAY 1901

206. *CORNUBIAN*, 21st DECEMBER 1901

207. *IBID.*, 15th FEBRUARY 1901

208. *IBID.*, 1st FEBRUARY 1901

209. *CAPE TIMES*, 30th OCTOBER 1928

210. *CORNISHMAN*, 10th JANUARY 1901

211. *IBID.*, 31st JANUARY 1901

212. *IBID.*, 9th MAY 1901

213. *C.P.M.N.*, 2nd MAY 1901

214. *IBID.*, 31st JANUARY 1901

215. *MINING JOURNAL* 3rd MARCH 1900

216. See also *IBID.*, 21st DECEMBER 1901

217. *IBID.*, 5th JANUARY 1901 . p.23

218. *CORNISHMAN*, 9th MAY 1901

219. *CORNUBIAN*, 19th APRIL 1901

220. *CORNISHMAN*, 11th JULY 1901

221. *IBID.*, 19th SEPTEMBER 1901

222. *IBID.*, 23rd MAY 1901

223. *IBID.*, 3rd JANUARY 1902

224. *IBID.*, 30th JANUARY 1902

225. *C.P.M.N.*, 23rd JANUARY 1902

226. *CORNISHMAN*, 30th JANUARY 1902

227. *C.P.M.N.*, 30th JANUARY 1902

228. *CORNISHMAN*, 30th JANUARY 1902

229. *C.P.M.N.*, 27th FEBRUARY 1902

230. *CORNISHMAN*, 10th APRIL 1902

231. *C.P.M.N.*, 30th JANUARY 1902

232. Vorster, *SERVAMUS* NOVEMBER 1986

233. Hall, *REAPED MY MEALIES* . p.172

234. *IBID.*, p.176

235 *CORNISHMAN*, 14th JUNE 1900

236. *C.P.M.N.*, 23rd AUGUST 1900

237. *CORNUBIAN*, 15th JUNE 1900

238. *CORNISHMAN*, 25th OCTOBER 1900

239. *IBID.*, 25th OCTOBER 1900

240. The Robinson and Treasury mines were started followed by the New Primrose, May Consolidated, Geldenhuis Estate and Geldenhuis Deep according to one source – the seventh mine is not named, it was probably Meyer & Charlton. See *MINING JOURNAL* 11th MAY 1901

241. Some Cornishmen died fighting for the Rand Rifles, including W. T. Jenkin (Gunnislake), A. Pengelly (Madron) and J. Thomas (Illogan). For Joseph Tucker's experience as a Rand Mine Guard see *HANNAN, JOSEPH TUCKER-LETTERS* p.6

242. *CORNUBIAN*, 6th SEPTEMBER 1900 See also CORNISHMAN 21 FEBRUARY 1902

243. *C.P.M.N.*, 24th OCTOBER 1901

244. *IBID.*, 17th OCTOBER 1901

245. *CORNISHMAN*, 5th DECEMBER 1901. The great copper mine of Devon Great Consols, just over the Cornish border in Devon, had begun to close down, which did not help employment in East Cornwall. See *MINING JOURNAL*, 21st DECEMBER 1901

246. *C.P.M.N.*, 5th DECEMBER 1901

247. *IBID.*, 20th FEBRUARY 1902

248. *CORNISHMAN*, 30th JANUARY 1902

249. *C.P.M.N.*, 3rd APRIL 1902

250. *CORNISHMAN*, 24th APRIL 1902

251. *CORNUBIAN*, 9th MAY 1902. According to *THE MINING JOURNAL* the two Geldenhuis mines were already at work. See Footnote 240.

252. *IBID.*, 16th MAY 1902

253. *THE COLLECTED WORKS OF MAHATMA GANDHI VOL. 31* p.132-133

254. Emanuol Lee, *TO THE BITTER END* (LONDON 1985)

255. Emily Hobhouse, *THE BRUNT OF WAR AND WHERE IT FELL* (LONDON 1902) p.94

256. In total there were 136,000 Boers in some 50 camps and 115,000 Africans in 66 camps.

257. Ruth A Fry, *EMILY HOBHOUSE (London. 1929)* p.88

258. Emily Hobhouse, *TO THE COMMITTEE OF THE DISTRESS FUND FOR SOUTH AFRICAN WOMEN AND CHILDREN. REPORT OF A VISIT TO THE CAMPS OF WOMEN AND CHILDREN IN THE CAPE AND ORANGE RIVER COLONIES* (LONDON 1981) p.38

259. Fry, *EMILY HOBHOUSE* . p.106

260. Hall, *I REAPED MY MEALIES* p.103 One of his sons – Harry – was given the task of bringing fresh spring water to the concentration camp at Middelburg.

261. David Harrison, *THE WHITE TRIBE OF AFRICA* (LONDON 1981) p.38

262. Hobhouse, *REPORT* p.5

263. *IBID.*, p.8

264. *IBID.*, p.10

265. Hobhouse, *THE BRUNT OF THE WAR* p.125

266. *IBID.*, p.143

267. *CORNUBIAN*, 19th JULY 1901

268. Hobhouse, *THE BRUNT OF THE WAR* p.144

269. Rev. J.C. Harris *REFUGEES AND RELIEF* (LONDON 1901)

270. Emily Hobhouse, *A LETTER TO THE COMMITTEE OF THE SOUTH AFRICAN WOMEN AND CHILDREN'S DISTRESS FUND*

271. Fry, *EMILY HOBHOUSE* p.175

272. *IBID.*, p.181

273. *CORNUBIAN*, 29th NOVEMBER 1901

274. Fry, *EMILY HOBHOUSE* p.183

275. *IBID.*, 25th JUNE 1903

276. Fry, *EMILY HOBHOUSE* , p.192

277. *IBID.*, p.207

278. Fisher, *KRUGER* , p.247

279. *C.P.M.N.*, 27th SEPTEMBER 1904

280. *IBID.*, 16th APRIL 1903

281. *C.P.M.N.*, 16th JANUARY 1908

282. Henry, *THE FIRST HUNDRED YEARS OF THE STANDARD BANK*, p.147

283. *CAPE TIMES* 30th OCTOBER 1928

284. Gordon Le Saur, *C.J. RHODES* (LONDON 1913) p.156 – 157

283. *CAPE TIMES* 30th OCTOBER 1928

284. Gordon Le Saur, *C.J. RHODES* (LONDON 1913) p.156 – 157

285. *C.P.M.N.*, 11th DECEMBER 1902

286. *CAPE TIMES* 30th OCTOBER 1928

Chapter Six

Blood and Gold. The Jameson Raid and Second Boer War

CHAPTER SEVEN

THE CHINESE EPISODE 1900-10

On the Rand the Cornish miner has resigned the pick and drill,
He sits upon the dump heaps and he sweareth with a will,
For up and down the shaft head come the gentlemen in blue,
The miners brought from China, by the men late of 'Peru',
In response to Israel's call, Come the Chinkies One and All,
Back to Cornwall go the Cornish
Bag and baggage One and All.[1]
Cornish Post and Mining News. 18th January 1906

Anyone wishing to read about *Chinese Mine Labour* in the Transvaal need look no further than the book of that title written by Peter Richardson.[2] However, the book has one major omission – there is no mention of the part played specifically by the Cornish miner – in fact there is no reference to Cornwall or to any Cornishman.[3] Any close examination of mining in the Transvaal between the years 1900-10 will clearly show that there was a definite link between the Cornish and the Chinese with each having an important effect on the other.

When it came to mining, the Cornish and Chinese had long been antagonists. The Cornish Tin Industry had suffered acutely from 1820 onwards, with the discovery of vast alluvial tin deposits in the Malay Peninsula where the majority of the work force consisted of Chinese coolie labour. The *Post* commented:

John Chinaman when well paid will work like a horse and anyone who has been down a tin mine 80 or 100 feet and ascended by one of the rough wooden ladders used therein for ascent and descent will testify.[4]

During the Boer War, with remittances halted and the prospect of large unemployment at home, as a glut of Cornish miners returned to Cornwall from South Africa, the spectre of the Chinese ousting the Cornish after the war was used by the radical supporters of W.S. Caine in the run up to the 1900 Election. In reply the *Post* – a Unionist backed paper – said,"the rubbish that Mr. Caine is circulating about Chinese labour is a miserable political dodge of the lowest order".[5] To the Cornish miner, Chinese labour in South Africa was a real threat. Only a few months previously the *Post* reported that Cecil Rhodes, faced with a labour shortage in Rhodesia, had advocated cheap Chinese labour.[6] The *Post* was quick to suggest, however, that the Cornish miners need not be alarmed for any decision by the Chartered Company to introduce Chinese labour into Rhodesian mines would have no effect on the employment of Cornish miners in the Transvaal.[7] This probably explains why such prominence was given in the election to a telegram sent by Rhodes to the *Post* expressing his strong opposition to the importation of Chinese labour into South Africa.[8] J.S.V. Bickford, a Cornish capitalist who had visited Johannesburg many times, was quick to remind Cornishman that the Colony of Natal had actually prohibited the importation of coolie labour, and that a newly elected government in the Transvaal following the war would probably do likewise.[9] If there were any doubts as to just what threat Chinese labour did present, then the Cornish miner could look to the warning given by Henry Copeland, Agent General for New South Wales, Australia:

> *We know the Chinese Question... we know its perils... he is content with a wage on which a Britisher would starve... we were compelled to pass restrictive legislation... we imposed a poll tax on every Chinaman who landed – £100 per head – this had effect. In 1891 – 14,156 Chinese in N.S.W.... in 1898 there were only 32 arrivals and 419 departures... wherever you want Englishmen to thrive and prosper don't import Chinese.[10]*

The Cornish miner needed no warning. He was fully aware of the effect of cheap Chinese labour, for he was working in competition with the Chinese coolie:'his wage was largely governed by the wages of those rice-eating Celestials thousands of miles away in the Malay Straits'.[11]

Opposition to the employment of the Chinese could also be found on the American continent. In British Columbia, in order to prevent Chinese from being employed, the authorities hit upon the curious but effective expedient of forbidding the employment on the mines of any man whose hair is more than 4 inches long.[12] The Cornish in the U.S.A. had actually worked with Chinese labourers for many years – especially in the rich gold mining areas of California and Nevada centered on Grass Valley and Nevada City. According to Rowe, although the Cornish and Irish had their antipathies they could unite in anti-Chinese agitation against cheap coolie labour, on the mere hint of an economic recession throughout the decades following the end of the Civil War.[13] In a more detailed study of society in Grass Valley and Nevada City during 1849-70, Ralph Mann has shown how the separateness of the Cornish and the Chinese, based on race, culture and occupation, remained constant, and the treatment of the Chinese remained a good gauge of whites' sense of security.[14] When a strike broke out in 1869 over the introduction of dynamite into the mines of Grass Valley – up until then black powder had been used, requiring two men to drill large holes – Cornish and Chinese clashed.[15] The use of dynamite meant smaller holes which could be drilled easily by one man, so the work force could be halved. The innovation also obviated Cornish Mine practices which used two-man teams, and Cornish expertise underground.[16] As an all-out strike developed and it looked as if the Cornish were about to be ousted by other ethnic groups willing to work the dynamite – one drill practice – the most dangerous potential ethnic conflict uncovered by the strike pitted the Cornish against the Chinese.[17] When the strike eventually ended and the Cornish miners went back to work there was little doubt that their jobs were under threat due to the presence of the Chinese. Anyone who supported the Chinese was seen as opposing the Cornish, and vice versa. The Cornish miner was therefore under no illusions, and the image of the Chinese as unfair labour competitors remained dominant.[18] When the Cornish radicals voted for W.S. Caine in 1900 they had partly done so in order to prevent the introduction of Chinese labour into South Africa but, whereas the Cornish Mining Division may have voted Radical, the majority of the country had voted Unionist. Not all Cornish perceived the Chinese as a threat. Captain William Teague, returning to Cornwall from Rhodesia at the end of 1900, passed a number of Cornish miners at Cape Town waiting to return to the Rand. He was sorry Strauss had been rejected and could not understand,

> *any Cornishman taking the part of the Boers and blaming those capitalists who had opened up South Africa as a great field of labour for miners, mechanics and traders. Another fairy story that helped to gammon the electors was Mr. Caine's invention of the Chinese labour bogey... Chinese labour has never been mentioned in connection with the Rand.*[19]

It was, however, to be no Chinese labour bogey; the introduction of Chinese labour into South Africa was to become a reality.

Johannesburg after the war belied the fact that the city was in dire straits. It was suffering acute overcrowding, large numbers of unemployed and a cost of living that was far too high.[20] Its economy had slumped because the mines were working at only a quarter of their capacity[21] due to a serious native labour shortage. The newly-created Viscount, Sir Alfred Milner, High Commissioner for South Africa, had based his entire reconstruction policy on the revenue which was to come from the taxation of mining profits, but unfortunately the mines were not working to anything like full production. Milner said, the scarcity of native labour constituted the greatest bar to further industrial progress.[22] The figures said it all; before the war, during August 1899, there were 96,000 natives employed on the Rand mines, but in November 1901 the number was as low as 16,000. Cornishman Frederick J. Tiddy blamed not the native labour shortage but the mine owners for creating it. Tiddy had just returned from a sea voyage to Argentina where he noted the Argentinian Government had given out 70 square miles of good land to the Boers for settlement of 200 or 300 families and commented that they could be spared.[23] Arriving back in South Africa in July, 1902, after nearly three years' absence he

was glad to be in dry sunny and dusty Johannesburg where no longer flies the
Dutch Vierkkur (fair colours) but the Union Jack floats proudly in the breeze.[24]
Tiddy also found lots of people but the shops with little stock and much
complaining. Rents had trebled and he added:

> *The millionaire has cut Kaffirs' pay down to 1s per day with the result*
> *that there are no boys coming in to speak of... Ferreira Mine has 600*
> *boys instead of over 2,000. I believe the boy question is only a dodge of*
> *the millionaire to keep the country back till Chamberlain makes a*
> *pronouncement as to our total war debt.*[25]

There may have been a shortage of native boys but the same could not be said of
Cornish miners who, since the ending of hostilities, had been returning to the land
of gold. In June 1902 the *Cornubian* assumed that within a few months the trade of
the town – meaning Redruth – would largely benefit from the remittances which
were soon expected home.[26] The *Cornishman*, equally optimistic, considered that
the exodus to South Africa was likely to be very great for a few weeks.[27] The
prediction of the exodus was proved correct, as large numbers left the mining
districts of Cornwall during the months that followed, with as many as 40-50
Cornish miners leaving each week. From America, where many Cornish miners
had congregated during the war, came the news that they were once more on their
way back to Johannesburg.[28] In Cornwall the Redruth Board of Guardians was
happy to announce that some women had actually taken themselves off the Poor
Rate, as the first money orders began to arrive back from husbands in South
Africa.[29] It all seemed reminiscent of the time before the war:

> *One of the sights of Camborne is to be witnessed at the P.O. after the*
> *receipt of an African mail... when women and even children in great*
> *numbers could be observed cashing their postal orders that had been sent*
> *them by husbands and their fathers abroad.*[30]

Sadly their optimism was misplaced, for by September the *Post* was warning
Don't Start for South Africa. Disillusionment had set in, as clearly expressed by a
Johannesburg hotel keeper who claimed two-thirds of Johannesburg discontent
was due to short native labour supply.[31] Tiddy was equally despondent, describing
Johannesburg then as a bad place to be in.[32]

Despite the warning, Cornish miners continued to leave in large numbers for the
Rand (9th October 41 miners left, 7th November 90 miners left and 4th December
52 miners left).[33] In November the Redruth Board of Guardians noted that the
number of paupers in the Union workhouse was rising whereas in the other Unions
in the South West it had been going down;the reason for this was said to be the
special circumstances Redruth Union was placed in regard to its population and
South Africa.[34] By the end of 1902 it was

regarded at Camborne that Christmas which will soon be on us will be one of the dullest seen for a great number of years. At the present time there are a great number out of employ… big firms have left for South Africa to solicit orders for the coming Spring. It is hoped that they may be successful…[35]

In South Africa, the hope for all Cornish miners on the Rand lay with a solution to the problem of how to entice the native boys back to work in sufficiently large numbers, so that all the mines could be re-opened. The setting up of a Miners' Association introduced a new factor to the industrial situation on the Rand. Such an organisation had been contemplated before the war, after a dispute at the Crown Deep mine,[36] but it was only in 1902 that it was actually formed. Prominent in the setting up of what was virtually a Trade Union in all but name was a Cornishman, Tom Mathews of Newlyn.[37] He was a miner at the age of sixteen, working in a Michigan copper mine for two years before moving first to Duluth, Minnesota and then Butte City and the silver mines of Montana. Having gained an engineer's certificate he worked his way up in the Miners' Union of Montana to become its President; he then turned to politics. In 1892 Mathews was elected, with a large majority, to the State House of Representatives as an independent, for he believed neither the Democrats or Republicans properly represented the labouring classes. At only 27 years of age he was the youngest speaker in any State legislature in America.[38] After a short visit home to Cornwall he arrived in South Africa just before the war and soon became involved in the labour struggle which itself was to take a new direction. In an attempt to solve the native labour shortage – and with such a large number of unemployed whites – the Village Main Reef Mine, under its Manager Frederic Creswell, experimented with cheap white labour and paid the penalty. Creswell argued that a few white artisans with machines could bring up the rock more economically than a much larger number of blacks without.[39] The Miners' Association denounced the so-called white labour policy in its own newspaper – *The Tribune* – claiming it was an attempt to virtually eliminate the services of the skilled miner.[40] The miners went on strike, and although the *Post* believed the miners had a perfect right to combine, it thought that to begin the re-opening of the Rand with a labour war to the death was calamitous in the extreme.[41] The mine owners seemed to agree, for the Chamber of Mines soon announced that the native labourers would in future be paid their old wages,[42] or about £2.10s per month. This was considered good news for all concerned and the *Post* rather prematurely claimed the end of the Transvaal Labour trouble was in sight.[43] Nothing could have been further from the truth as the problem was anything but solved.

Any initial euphoria at the ending of the Boer War had evaporated by 1903 for the Cornish miner. His only desire was to return to the mines, be given permanent employment and a chance to earn a high wage once more. He was now faced with little chance of employment, and ability to send remittances home. Worse than this were the frightening statistics of miners' phthisis (see Chapter 8 To Strike in the Land of Death). His future seemed to rest on the question of native labour, which, according to Tiddy was the one continued burden of life here now.[44] The whole question of native labour was treated on the one hand as genuine and indisputable and on the other as a bogus cry. The *Tribune* said:

> *Just think of it. People are making from 15 away up to 120 per cent whimpering because they have to pay a big strapping Kaffir 50 or 60 bob a month for doing work which would cost them in other countries £16 to £20 a month.*[45]

In desperation a Commission was set up to enquire into the actual amount of labour required and where the supply could be found. Members included William Hosken, Sir George Farrar (President of the Chamber of Mines), Messrs. Fusey and Perrow of the Mine Association, plus others. Its verdict at the end of 1903 was that there was a labour shortage in mining of 198,000 and a total labour shortage of 241,000 but worse, it could see nowhere in Africa which could supply the shortage.[46]

With British public money no longer being pumped into the Transvaal by 1903, its economy slumped. First-hand evidence of this can be gleaned from a series of letters written by Joseph Tucker, the Cornish miner from Barrow-in-Furness, who had returned to the Rand in 1901. Having served his time with the Rand Rifles, Tucker – who was 55 years old – was back working on the mines as an engine driver. A letter dated 17th January 1903 comments:

> *I see the chamber of mines has decided to give the natives the same pay they had before the war. If the boys will come back to work in sufficient numbers there ought to be a big boom and plenty of work shortly unless there is a terrible rush to South Africa.*[47]

As the politicians toyed with the idea of Indian,[48] then Italian labour,[49] before finally settling for Chinese, Chamberlain himself arrived on the Rand to reach some sort of settlement over the war contribution. Tucker was able to write that he saw Mr. & Mrs. Chamberlain last week as they passed through the Randfontein mine where he worked.[50] At the Chamber of Mines, after a visit to the Robinson mine, Chamberlain was introduced to an assembly of about a hundred mine managers by a Cornishman – J. Harry Johns, the President of the Mine Managers' Association.[51] Johns had, a few months earlier, resigned his post as Manager of the Ferreira mine accepting the more lucrative position of Consulting Engineer to the Consolidated Investment Company and Messrs. Barnato Brothers.[52]

the chief danger to wage earners does not arise from indentured Asiatics... but from the unchecked unregulated entrance of impecunious aliens of European extraction... who threaten at no distant date to oust our artisans from their hard won position, and permanently lower the standard of wages, which it is so important to maintain and improve.[88]

Michell and Oats were backed in their support of Chinese labour being introduced into the Transvaal by two other prominent Cornishmen, J. Harry Johns and William Hosken. All four men were Unionists, but as the *Post* claimed, they were four Cornish gentlemen of wealth, ability and experience, thoroughly conversant with the pros and cons of the questions affecting labour and capital in South Africa.[89] There had been some doubt as to whether Hosken would support the move for Chinese labour or not, and the *Guardian* asked:

Which way is Mr. W. Hosken M.L.C. going to vote?
The oracle of Nonconformity – is he going to vote for the yellow slave system, for the horrors of the compound and the iniquities that the Chinese hordes would bring? If so the Nonconformist conscience must be particularly elastic as exemplified in Mr. W. Hosken M.L.C.[90]

On this occasion Hosken went along with the economic argument, an argument the pro-Chinese lobby won. The anti-Chinese group secured the high moral ground; it was a stance Hosken himself was to take later, over another issue involving humanitarian rights.

The ordinary Cornish miner, however, probably took more notice of a man like Tom Mathews and the Miners' Association. Unfortunately the Association was experiencing difficulties of its own; only 40 per cent of the miners were members, so any idea of an all-out strike to keep the Chinese out seemed an unlikely proposition. There also seemed to be disagreement amongst the officers. William Mather resigned as Secretary of the Association in May 1903 due to ill-health but already he had accepted there was no alternative to Chinese labour. Tom Mathews had himself been ill with 'machine stomach' another name for miner's phthisis. The Butte City *Tribune Review*, whose Editor was Cornishman Sam Roberts of St Agnes reported that one of Mathew's lungs was totally destroyed and the other greatly ravaged by the dread disease.[91] This was reprinted in the *Cornishman* and is just one example of how news often reached Cornwall. The *Review* had also expressed doubt over the officers of the Miners' Association reporting that it was not yet perfect and that it did not pay to rely upon it as men do upon their Unions in America.[92] This seemed to be correct, and the Association became dissatisfied with the performance of W. Perrow (another Cornishman) on the Labour Commission and told him he was only sitting in a private capacity and not as President of the Association.[93] With a weak Association, Mathews, like Mather, also saw the introduction of Chinese labour as inevitable, but warned if Chinamen were made responsible for the firing of explosives it would be incredible and would create a tempest of trouble.[94] With the fear that replacement of Cornishmen by Chinese was being somewhat minimised by Mathews, the question of Chinese Slavery now became an issue, as expressed in a large demonstration – numbering some 70,000 – in London's Hyde Park. Banners were carried proclaiming "Slavery abolished in 1833 revived in 1904 after the sacrifice of 52,000 men, women and children and £250,000,000 spent to paint South Africa red. The Randlords now wish to paint it yellow".[95] W.T. Stead,[96] Editor of the *Review of Reviews*, looked at the Chinese slavery issue through a Chinaman's eyes and came to the conclusion:

> *the penniless and half-starved Chinese emigrant is likely to wonder at the meaning of the outcry against 'Chinese slavery' for 3 years contract with barrack life, a free passage home and a little fortune in his hands when he returns to the flowery land, did not strike him as slavery and he was willing to chance the risks just as have been the thousands of Cornishmen who during the last fifty years have swung their picks in Cuba & California, Alaska & the deadly coast of W. Africa, in Peru silver mines, in Afghanistan, Chile, Malaya & Russia & practically every land where the Pioneer might win a fortune or a grave. So far as John Chinaman is concerned the case would be quite as strong if instead of going to the Rand, he were to be indentured to work the disused tin mines of Cornwall.*[97]

The *Post* was quick to comment that there was little fear of that for many miners could only get a Chinaman's earnings in Cornwall. The same theme was taken up by Francis Oats, who said that there had been no more slavery than when he had gone to the Cape on a contract with the Government, on the diamond fields. The Chinamen were freely contracted and did not have to come. If they did, their wages were stipulated before-hand and at the end of their contract they were free to return to China.[98] However, Oats forgot to mention that he was not fingerprinted on arrival – the Chinese would be; he was able to move freely about Kimberley – the Chinese were to be kept in compounds their movement severely restricted, and he – Oats – was earning a very high wage, whereas the Chinese were to be paid at a fixed rate of a shilling per working day of ten hours.

On 18th June 1904 the first batch of Chinese labourers for the Rand arrived in Durban on board the *Tweedale* after a 25 day voyage from Hong Kong, which had seen three deaths from beri beri.[99] The batch, numbering around a thousand coolies, was put to work at the Comet and Cason mines. Before the Boer War the Comet Mine had employed 135 white skilled miners, but owing to the scarcity of native workers the number had dropped to 34. With the influx of a thousand Chinese by July the number of whites had increased to 96 and it was estimated that

143 white men would be employed when the mine was fully back to work. The pro-Chinese lobby seemed vindicated, and it was hoped that if the proportion of whites to Chinese was maintained then Cornwall would have no cause to grumble.[100] By November the Chamber of Mines was able to report that the number of Chinese on the Rand totalled 10,894 and there had even been a significant increase in the recruitment of native labour.

A Cornishman who saw the first of the Chinese miners to arrive was James Holman, a partner in the Cornish engineering firm of Holman Brothers and a Director of the Cornish mine – Dolcoath. He believed:

> *As far as Cornwall is concerned there can be no doubt that we stand to benefit materially from the introduction of Chinese labour. I spent two months on the Rand and I saw the first batch of Chinese coolies arrive and begin work. They are excellent miners and one on the first day bored a hole 3 feet deep – that was as good as a practised Kaffir would do.*[101]

Holman spoke also of the large number of unemployed Cornishmen he found on the Rand, and when he was reminded that the Cornishmen were not so doubtful of the Chinaman's knowledge of mining but were more suspicious that, despite the £500 penalty and the restriction of the Labour Ordinance, the capitalists would eventually substitute Chinese for White Labour, Holman replied:

> *That is not reasonable nor is it contemplated – I expect within the next twelve months 50 or 60 thousand Chinamen will be imported and this will necessitate the immediate engagement of skilled white miners as shift bosses, engineers and the like. I found this time that the very men who used to be most opposed to the idea of indentured labour are now in favour of it. Some people think a miner's leader like Mr. Mathews cannot be honest if he studies the facts and reverses his opinions... Our Cornishmen on the Rand will be wanted in considerable numbers and the stories of slavery and ousting white labour may be dismissed as unworthy of credence.*[102]

A Redruth miner who had described conditions as worse than during the long slump following the Jameson raid was eventually given a job at the Comet mine, where the Chinese were first employed. He had a gang of twenty coolies placed at his disposal and found them very tractable and on the whole they showed a strong desire to attain proficiency.[103] Cornish Mine Captain Joseph Richards of Pool was equally in favour of Chinese labour. With some 44 years of mining experience – 14 years as Manager of the Ferreira Deep – Richards was about to leave Cornwall, where he had been Manager of South Crofty, and take up the position of Manager in a mine in Bolivia. He was being replaced at South Crofty by Captain James Thomas of Redruth who, besides having considerable experience in Cornish mines, had also been in Central America and most recently in South Africa, where he had been Superintendent of the New Herriot gold mine. Whilst Richards had been Manager at the Ferreira Deep he had tried a white labour policy, but it had failed miserably and he remembered in one case:

> *I got 30 men to take a job in a stope and before setting them the task I*
> *took care to get all the Kaffirs out of their way knowing that the presence*
> *of the natives was objectionable. They had not been working many days,*
> *some not many hours – before all, save three, threw up the whole business*
> *and went on top... another trial was made on grass where I engaged a*
> *number of whites at the cyanide works. They worked one week and left.*104

At the Ferreira Deep mine Richards said that only 65 stamps out of a total of 120 were actually working, but he thought this would soon change with a regular supply of Chinese labour being provided. He also believed that if the Chinese were slaves for being engaged on a contract then hundreds of Cornishmen must be too. For Richards, Chinese labour meant:

> *more unskilled labour, more work for Cornishmen, more money for their*
> *wives and families at home, more money remitted to the home, more*
> *money spent amongst local tradesmen. This is what I think and I claim to*
> *know the needs of my fellow countrymen as well as anybody.*105

Probably few in Cornwall would have disagreed with him; neither would they have disagreed with Dr. L.S. Jameson (now, in 1904, Prime Minister of Cape Colony) who when asked by W.T. Stead whether there was a Chinese Difficulty replied there was no Chinese difficulty in South Africa but a Chinese success.106

However, there were some difficulties. Two Chinese were accidentally killed at the New Comet mine in an explosion, and the accident resulted in a revolt amongst the Chinese going on night shift, as they refused to work.107 Then sixteen Chinese deserted from the same mine but were eventually recaptured.108 Finally, a Chinaman who ran a laundry business in Johannesburg was arrested when he spoke to his compatriots in the New Comet mine, and convicted of trespassing, of refusing to move on, of speaking to a public meeting; he received a sentence of six months' hard labour.109 Perhaps not surprisingly all three adverse reports regarding the Chinese appeared in the *Cornubian*. The *Post,* on the other hand, was more favourable towards the Chinese, often showing how they were a benefit to the Cornish. The Editor of the *Post* – Herbert Thomas – interviewed three Cornishmen. The first, a miner who had worked in California, the West Coast of Africa and South Africa, having just heard the news that more than 1,500 white men had found work on the Rand, claimed the Chinese were doing a good service. The second Cornishman, described as a leading Natal townsman, having heard of the most recent fighting by the Chinese – again at the New Comet mine, where three overseers were killed and some 500 Chinese had a battle with 50 Kaffirs and had to be driven back with bayonets – dismissed it as nothing out of the ordinary. He could remember at St. Just:

> *When five or six thousand men were employed there, seeing after a payday teeth and pieces of clothing lying about the streets as relics of the punching matches. If this can be said even of Cornish miners, when money flows freely and the tide of feeling reaches high-water mark, how can we blame Chinese or Kaffirs if occasionally their human nature finds vent in fighting.'*

The third Cornishman, who apparently had been a Manager of Mines in South Africa, Australia, Wales and elsewhere said:

> *I do not know a case of any St. Just miner who is out of work on the Rand at the present moment... Men who were out of work more than a year have got work through the introduction of the Chinese but they are sending home less money... Some Cornishmen are working off arrears;others are prudently banking their money in Johannesburg which they can now do as easily as they could in any Cornish town.*[110]

Thomas himself was very much in favour of Chinese labour believing Cornwall suffered more than any other country by the war.[111] The home industry certainly had little to offer the Cornish miner. Francis Oats, who paid a visit to Cornwall during 1904, announced in September that the Levant Mine had made a loss of £627 during a period of sixteen weeks and said if Levant – the principal mine in the parish – was not able to make a profit with tin at £80 a ton, then he could see there was no hope of any other mine in the parish being restarted.[112] There were, however, other alternatives open to the Cornish miner, for by the end of 1904 there was a weekly exodus of miners leaving Cornwall, the majority going to the States.[113]

Throughout the year 1905 the life of the Chinese on the Rand was widely reported in the Cornish Press. Some Cornishmen were given work building the compounds for the Chinese. At first they received 12s a day but this was later reduced to 7s and they were coolly informed that if they declined to accept it, Chinamen would be substituted in their places.[114] A report of Chinese New Year celebrations ended in Chinese and Natives fighting with sticks.[115] There was a strike at North Randfontein mine when 2,000 Chinamen became dissatisfied with their wage,[116] and when 500 Chinese broke out of the Jumpers Deep compound they were rounded up by police with the help of Natives.[117] In addition to tales about Chinese gambling and opium-smoking in the compounds, it was the violence and crime that was seen by many to be the main disadvantage of having brought in the Chinese. In September it was reported that roving parties of Chinese

The Cornubian cartoon above of 1906 depicted the Chinaman based on reports of fighting but the postcard below of the same time is captioned 'hardworking men' by the Cornish sender.

continue to terrorise the occupants of lonely farm houses on the East Rand.[118] A small group of Chinese had apparently deserted and eluded attempts by the authorities to catch them; thirty-three Chinese who deserted from the Witwatersrand mine were caught and imprisoned,[119] while following a disturbance at the Langlaate Croesus mine the white miners asked for revolvers against the "chinkees".[120] A Chinese miner who murdered a fellow worker received one year's imprisonment, a punishment which was seen as lenient when compared to a Kaffir being found in possession of gold worth £14.4s.0d receiving eighteen months' imprisonment.[121]

In contrast to the Chinese outrages, there was also positive news on the benefit of Chinese labour. For a start, with the arrival of the Chinese, letters received from South Africa showed that no steady able miner need fear not having work there.[122] Some Chinese claimed they were living like mandarins[123] and in the same month – April – it was reported that 16,000 white miners were employed in the Transvaal mines, 4,000 more than before the Boer War. With total wages of £5 million per annum, an average miner could hope to earn about £300 per annum. Assuming therefore that 7,000 miners were Cornish it would mean they would earn over £2 million per annum altogether. If the cost of living on the Rand amounted to half their wages then there would be almost a million pounds either to be posted home to Cornwall or to be kept in hand by the Cornish on the Rand.[124] This was what Chinese labour meant to Cornwall. As more Chinese arrived – the number reaching 43,141 by July 1905, – there followed an increase of white labour, 560 more being employed during October, compared to September.[125] Some of these were Cornishmen like Arthur Eathorne from Penponds, who joined his brothers on the Rand[126] and J. Kellow, J. Kellow (father and son), R. Richards, J. May and W.H. Matthews, all from St. Day.[127] In one week some 30 persons left West Cornwall for South Africa,[128] and a few weeks later it was said that the majority who were leaving Cornwall had booked for South Africa.[129] In June Arthur Reynolds left Camborne as a representative of Holman Brothers. He came from a well-known St. Agnes family, his father being the Manager of Charlestown Foundry near St. Austell. Reynolds, it was claimed, had a thorough knowledge of rock drills,[130] and his trip to South Africa was obviously successful for in October it was announced that Holmans were busy with orders from South Africa.[131]

As well as being provided with work some Cornish had other reasons to be thankful for the presence of Chinese labour. W.T. Mitchell of Tuckingmill, upon leaving the Van Ryn mine to go to work elsewhere, was given some handsome and curious window blinds worked by the Chinese in the Van Ryn compound as a present from the Chinese.[132] When H.C. McDonald, the Manager of the Durban Deep mine, and his wife and family returned to South Africa following a six months' holiday in Cornwall, they were met by a reception committee at the Johannesburg station. Along with the Mine Captain, G. Gilbert (Illogan), were

Shift Bosses J.K. James, J. Wills and R. Angove (Redruth & Marazion) plus some thirty Cornish miners. As the McDonald family left in their carriage Chinese coolies employed on the property started firing crackers.[133] As to what else the Chinese thought about the Cornish there is little evidence other than two amusing anecdotes. One, reported in the *Post*, said:

> An English speaking Chinese who is a sort of headman at one of the West Rand mines was giving an exposition of his linguistic attainments. 'I know London-English' he said. 'I know Scotch-English and understand the compound Manager. I also learn German-English but the Cornishman-English down the shaft! I never learn that.'[134]

The other story tells how when the Chinese were imported to the Rand, they were disliked by the Natives, who had a saying:-

> Chinee man, no good – two years, no speak English, Cousin Jack, too clev (clever) two weeks – speak English.[135]

Without a doubt the Chinese miner was good at his job. A private drilling contest at the Lancaster West between a Chinaman and a Native resulted in:

> The Chinaman, drilling 153 inches in 6 hours, whereas the Kaffir champion collapsed when he had drilled 140 inches. The mines were content if the hammer boys drill 36 inches a shift. The Champion at Lancaster makes a £100 a year in addition to free food and house. There is a Chinese coolie on £14 at the Simmer Jack mine... [136]

Not everyone was in favour of what he read. John Carbis was just one Cornish miner who considered the Chinese as near useless,[137] while another said he saw letters in the papers in England of some poor fools writing home in praise of the Chinese only to keep in with the Manager and mine officials.[138] Not all Cornishmen were happy to work alongside or with the Chinese, either; Reuben James had started work as a miner at the age of fourteen at Blue Hills mine, at his home in St. Agnes. After eight years he left Cornwall for South Africa where, in 1895, he began work on the Robinson mine before moving after two years to the Ferreira, where he worked under the late Matt Mill, the Ferreira mine Captain. James established a reputation for being a first class miner and he was requisitioned by the Manager John Whitford to work with him at the New Modderfontein mine. When the Boer War broke out, James returned to Cornwall, but once it was over he took up his old position at the New Modderfontein, until the coming of the Chinese:

> John Ching Chinaman had never been a favourite of Mr. James and the little knowledge he had obtained of the 'Celestials' on the Van Ryn property was sufficient cause for him to leave.[139]

Whether Chinese labour had caused the increase in white labour depended on which newspaper was believed – if it were the *Post*, then there had been a significant increase; but if it were the *Cornubian* then there had been the opposite. By 1906, however, there was no escaping the fact that the mines on the Rand were back in full production and that the value of gold had risen. Hedley Chilvers wrote:

> *It can hardly be denied that the Chinese saved Johannesburg, the Rand and South Africa, and that, as the salvation of the country had been from the first the prime consideration, any less admirable features of the experiment must be regarded as of secondary importance.*[140]

It was these secondary features, however, that were considered to be of prime importance to the British Liberal Party believing strongly that the Chinese experiment, which it classified as slavery, must end. On 4th December 1905, this end suddenly seemed possible when Prime Minister, Arthur Balfour, resigned and a General Election was called. The main issue of the 1906 General Election was Tariff Reform but Chinese slavery came a close second. For one seat lost by Tariff Reform, said Chamberlain on 18th January, ten have been lost by libels and baseless stories about Chinese labour; Balfour, writing to Lord Stanley on 27th January, remarked that the constituency did not the least want to argue any question at all except Chinese labour.[141] One writer is doubtful whether Chinese slavery influenced the electorate to any significant extent[142] but it was certainly an important issue in Cornwall's Mining Division. With both Lawson and Strauss having decided not to stand again, the Liberal Radicals looked to A.E. Dunn and the Liberal Unionists to Sir Thomas Hewitt. Both sides were to use the question of Chinese labour to their advantage.

In Cornwall the *Cornubian* asked:

> *Will you vote for a Government that had ruined South Africa for the Cornish miner? Will you vote for Chinese labour? If it is not be a kind of slavery, what is it?'*[143]

The Unionists in the *Post* took the line that, if the Chinese were sent home, some 4,000 white miners would be thrown out of work and Cornwall would lose £2 million in wages. B.P.C. Gibbons, a former member of the Chamber of Mines who backed Hewitt and the Unionists, deeply resented the term slavery. Having resided on the West Coast of Africa, he knew only too well the horrors of real slavery.[144] The Unionists made political capital out of the fact that C.V. Thomas, a Radical and leading Wesleyan, was a large employer of Chinese labour in the Straits Settlement and they quoted Lord Mount Edgcumbe's comments on Chinese labour; he had reason to believe that eighty percent of the miners in the Camborne district were strongly opposed to the introduction of Chinese labour in the Transvaal but now had equally good reason to believe that they were quite satisfied

He also believed that the slavery cry was a purely bogus and dishonest argument in the mouth of those who approved the Indian coolie Ordinance in British Guiana.[145] Hewitt was also to use the last fact to his advantage for at one meeting, when tackled on the question of slavery, Hewitt read out the terms of the Radical Ordinance for Indentured Labour in British Guiana without mentioning what it was he was quoting:

Do you call that slavery he asked, to which the Radicals shouted 'Yes!'That, said Hewitt, is a Radical Ordinance passed by a Radical Government.[146]

In hoping to sway the Methodist vote the Unionists reprinted a letter from Bishop Hartzell (American Methodist Episcopal), who had made a study of the treatment of the Chinese in the Transvaal, coming to the conclusion that the cry of slavery was absolutely absurd.[147] Finally from South Africa came the support of Frederick Tiddy who had made his views on the forthcoming election known in his usual bombastic style saying:

I only hope Cornwall will regard the voice of her sons overseas who in every land, I am sure, detest the name and doings of the Liberal Party. I advocate the possession and use of the revolver by every white man on the mines as the real cure of the Chinese insubordination and disturbance. We are no longer afraid that the Chinese will take the white man's job – that fear has passed away.[148]

In Cornwall the election campaign proved violent. For the first time in the Mining Division a Labour candidate – John Jones – had been put forward. At Camborne Market House a meeting held by the Socialists, during which Jones and Will Thorne, the Labour M.P. for South-West Ham, were due to speak, ended abruptly when a crowd made a rush for the platform. Windows were smashed and missiles thrown as the speakers had to make a run for it. Jones left by a rear exit and although he was surrounded in a back lane by a crowd, during which he received several blows, and a heavy missile which was thrown struck him on the back of the neck, luckily for him Police Superintendent Banfield appeared and the crowd fell back. Jones was then escorted safely to Tyack's Hotel. Thorne was not so lucky. Being unable to follow Jones, he became surrounded in the hall by a hostile crowd and was badly mauled. However, luck then appeared in the guise of a number of Mining Students who came to his aid and half-carried, half-dragged him to the safety of Lawry's Hotel where he needed attention from Nurse Marshall, the Redruth District Nurse who happened to be nearby. Thorne's most serious injury had come from a kick to the ankle, and he was unable to walk for a few days. Other members of the platform had also been roughed up, and the *Post* thought the outrage to be the worst that had ever happened in the annals of even the Mining Division.[149] At the end of the day most Cornish believed that Chinese labour was ruining South Africa for the Cornish miner[150] and voted for the Liberal Radicals and A.E. Dunn. Hewitt claimed he had been defeated by a mixture of religion, politics, Chinese slavery and the big loaf, while the *Post* itself said:

> *We can pay Mr. Dunn M.P. the compliment that he is a past master in the art of electioneering. He thoroughly gauged the constituency, he started to work on an established foundation and he built it up, using big loaves, big pasties, Tory Gold and the Chinese slavery as cement and the structure has stuck together like concrete.*[151]

Dunn's maiden speech in Parliament was on Coolie Labour in the Transvaal; during this he pointed out that every Saturday night more money was spent in Camborne that had been earned in the Rand mines than had been earned in any other way, and thus unless the Chinese were repatriated they would eventually be used as skilled labour and so oust the white skilled labourers.[152] The *Post* argued:

> *Cornwall is getting more profit from Chinese labour in the form of employment and wages of white miners than any other county in England yet our mouthpiece in Parliament tells the country that we are opposed to the employment of Chinese.*[153]

Cornishman Albert Hicks, Head Carpenter at the Simmer & Jack gold mine, wrote that a change of Government would not help the white miners' position and that the Dutch were glad the Liberals were in, and he attacked the British Press for their anti-Chinese coverage. He complained that only crimes committed by Chinese received publicity, and accused the Liberals of being extremely biased. Not everything in the Press was true according to Hicks who noted:

> *The other day we noticed... about a riot in the Simmer Jack... we were surprised to see it because we did not know of this supposed riot. The Illustrated London News had a long article on the Chinese and they called Simmer Jack a Diamond Mine... this is the kind of thing you in the old country read... The Chinese are without doubt a great success and are absolutely necessary if the country is to go ahead and people kept in work.*[154]

Another letter, this from a Redruth miner, thought the people at home had been carried away by the hue and cry of Chinese slaves ousting the white workers[155] Perhaps not surprisingly, the most hostile condemnation of the Liberal victory came from the Agent of the Progressive Party, Frederick Tiddy who accused the Liberals of malicious interference, malignant lying and being religious sentimentalists.[156]

This somewhat overblown outburst from Tiddy was not the view shared by many of his party, who were disgusted by much of what he had written.[157] It did seem, however, that the conditions on the Rand once again were not in the Cornish miners' favour. There were reports of the decision of the Liberal Government to repatriate the Chinese as having a paralyzing effect on Rand enterprises of all kinds.[158] There was a general feeling of unrest and uncertainty and many miners returned home, the *Post* reporting in April that the homeward bound boats from Cape Town were said to be fully booked until June.[159] In May another report told of hundreds of Cornishmen back from the Rand and how Redruth railway station was crowded one Saturday evening on the occasion of the arrival of the South African train which contained numerous arrivals from South Africa.[160] One Cornish Mine Manager said, the married Cornish miner, getting £20 per month and having his family on the Rand is no better off than if he remained at home and earned £1 per week.[161] However, as one man put it although times were bad it was not the first time the Transvaal had been dull.[162]

Although a large number of miners headed for the States, and for Butte City in particular,[163] those returning to Cornwall found, for a change, conditions in their favour. Both the Cornish Tin and Copper Industries were enjoying a boom period. Tin selling at £161-15s-0d a ton in January 1906 quickly reached £200 a ton-and-over by May 1906, while copper rose from £79-10s-0d a ton in January 1906 to £107-10s-0d by the end of the year.[164] At Geevor Mine, near St. Just, a number of stamps slightly different in type from any in other Cornish mines were started by the South African Cornishmen who pluckily invested in this little venture.[165] By October it was announced that 110 men were taken on and it was thought the number would rise to 300.[166] In November it looked as if the Providence mine near St. Ives was about to restart, but more important was the news that Botallack, the mine where Francis Oats had first worked as a boy, was to reopen.[167] For once Cornwall was faced with a labour shortage,[168] despite a large number of Cornish miners back from the Rand. 'This is Cornwall's year'[169] claimed the *Post*, which later said Cornwall offered such return upon capital as left the golden dreams of South Africa far in the background.[170] It certainly did not seem South Africa's year and any idea that Cornish miners on the Rand were some kind of labour aristocracy was quickly dismissed:

> *Ye Gods! go up Market St. any day and see the aristocrats of labour hanging around the restaurant door begging for a meal. Go out any night twixt eleven and twelve and see the aristocrats of labour trying to make their bed on the hard veldt.[171]*

The whole subject of Cornish mining now developed a new dimension. The situation on the Rand between the Cornish and Chinese and the problem in Cornwall of getting enough Cornishmen home to work the reopened mines, albeit at lower wages than could be earned in South Africa or the U.S.A., were discussed in full. The Editor of the Butte City *Tribune Review*, Sam Roberts, entered into dialogue with the Editor of the *Post*, Herbert Thomas. Roberts criticised mining conditions in Cornwall, considering the men to be underpaid; he therefore could see no reason why Cornish Americans should want to return in a hurry to the land of pasties and cream.[172] As speculation continued as to when the Chinese would actually leave the Rand – Chinese recruitment having now been prohibited – it could not be soon enough for the *Cornishman*, which said:

> *The Liberal Government was returned to get rid of Chinese Labour but for six months it has engaged in postponing, delaying, adjourning and procrastinating. Their miserable shilly shally is ruining South Africa for white miners and capitalists alike... whole Rand is in a state of ferment and doubt... meanwhile the skilled white miner is being gradually forced out of the country.[173]*

The *Cornishman* and *Post* each presented the facts to show the advantage or disadvantage the Chinese had been to the Cornish miner. The *Cornubian* claimed:

> *the wages of the white miner had been cut by 8s 4d at the Comet mine – the first to take the Chinese. In 1899 there had been 18,000 skilled whites employed on the Rand – now there were only 13,000.[174]*

The *Post*, on the other hand, believed there were more than 18,000 whites employed on the mines whereas before the war only 12,000 were employed.[175] When the *Cornubian* noted that the number of men employed at the Glen Deep and Village Reef mines had been 750-800 before the introduction of the Chinese and only 500 white men after[176] the *Post* quoted a report from the Simmer & Jack mine. This not only showed the efficiency of Chinese labour but also the ratio of white to coloured labour, which maintained that with the Chinese 10.5 per cent more white labour was employed than with the Natives before the war.[177] The *Post* also printed in full an open letter to the British workman from the Johannesburg Chamber of Trade, showing the benefits brought to the Transvaal by the Chinese and what it might mean if they left, such as, a possible 5,000 miners being thrown out of work.[178] Both the *Cornubian* and the *Post* continued to make assumptions on a revival of the Cornish Mining Industry while contradicting each other as to the fate of the Cornish miner in South Africa, if and when the Chinese left.

Three events now took place in South Africa, each having an effect on the Cornish-Chinese situation. The first was the Transvaal election, which centred on the Chinese question but where instead of talking about repatriation, the word used was replacing. The Dutch orators admitted that the Chinese must stay until Natives could be found to take their place.[179]

The second event, was the introduction of a new smaller, rock drill. As early as 1878 Frederick Eckstein, at the annual general meeting of Rand Mines Ltd., had said that it would be a handy stope drill that would solve the labour problem. At the Robinson Mine the Gordon Hope Drill made by the American firm Ingersoll Sergeant, was about to bring about such an improvement in the method of obtaining gold ore from the underground working places known as stopes.[180] With the drill enabling a smaller number of natives to do the work previously done by a large number of Chinese, the question of the replacement of the Chinese was answered. However, the introduction of the new drill led to a feeling of distrust towards the Progressive Party, reflected later in their defeat at the election. The white miners feared that the Chinese and Kaffirs would ultimately be employed as skilled machine men. Thus to the question Will the Gordon Hope Drill solve the labour problem? the answer was quite prophetic:

> *the Gordon drill, if successful, unless worked exclusively by white labour,*
> *will be the cause of the greatest fight between labour and capital that has*
> *ever taken place in South Africa.*[181]

The third event, a direct response to the second, was a strike (see Chapter 8. To Strike in the Land of Death).

Meanwhile the Chinese were to be gradually repatriated and J.B. Robinson, so confident that an adequate supply of native labour was available once more, said, he was prepared to open eight new mines – if seventeen hundred Chinese at his mines left they could be supplanted immediately by Kaffirs.[182] The *Cornubian* therefore suggested that it may be with the return of the native, the Rand will be again to Cornwall what it was previous to the war.[183] In December 1907 came news from South Africa that large batches of Chinese were leaving the mines and considerable excitement prevailed at the Simmer & Jack Mine when over 1,000 of the coolies prepared to go.[184] As the Chinese continued to leave they seemed no longer important, as far as the newspapers were concerned. What little news there was of the Chinese was now of an adverse nature, such as reports of riots and murders. John Jacobs of Redruth was murdered by Chinese at the Glen Deep dump whilst on his way to the Witwatersrand Deep Mine, where he worked with his brother Daniel. He had already been attacked twice by Chinese, underground at the mine, each time being saved by other miners. On each occasion the Chinese miners responsible were arrested, and it was believed that the final and fatal attack had been an act of revenge on the part of the Chinese.[185] In 1909, a riot on the Rand resulted in some 800 Chinese at the Village Deep mine successfully driving back the police twice, before being brought to order – by which time six Chinese had been shot dead and fifteen wounded. It was said the riot had followed a misunderstanding of the interpreter in connection with the Chinese New Year Holiday.[186]

The Chinese decreased rapidly in numbers and by the beginning of 1909 there were not more than fourteen thousand remaining. A year later, when Dunn made an election speech in January 1910, there were only a thousand Chinese left on the

Rand.[187] By March the same year they had all gone, and the Chinese episode was over.

Camborne and the Colonial Office

Camborne to Winston Churchill; – When we voted Liberal, Winny, we meant business, not shilly-shally. When we said we didn't want Chinese labour we meant business too. Go back to your old ways, call a spade a spade, and slavery, slavery. We've got a motto for you, Winny: "Cut the cackle and get to work."

A Cornubian cartoon of 1908 expressing impatience with the liberal government and their Colonial Secretary Winston Churchill.

1. *C.P.M.N.*, 18th JANUARY 1906. These lines called *Song of the (White) Miner* appeared first in an issue of the *Tribune* and were repeated in the *Post*. The men late of Peru actually refers to the Peruvians, which was a euphemism for East European Jews. Many of the mine owners such as the Barnato brothers, Lewis Cohen, the Ecksteins and Samuel Marks all had Jewish backgrounds so response to Israel's call is a dig at them. 'One and All' was and still is the Cornish motto.

2. See Peter Richardson *CHINESE MINE LABOUR IN THE TRANSVAAL* (LONDON, 1982).

3. Some compensation for this omission is perhaps made by Richardson, with G. Burke, in their comparative study dealing with *Miners' Phthisis in Cornwall and the Transvaal* – see Chapter 8 *TO STRIKE IN THE LAND OF DEATH*

4. *C.P.M.N.*, 10th OCTOBER 1901

5. *IBID.*, 27th SEPTEMBER 1900

6. *IBID.*, 16th AUGUST 1900

7. *IBID.*, 23rd AUGUST 1900

8. *IBID.*, 11th OCTOBER 1900

9. *IBID.*, 4th OCTOBER 1900

10. *IBID.*, 16th AUGUST 1900

11. *IBID.*, 10th OCTOBER 1901

12. *IBID.*, 26th JULY 1900

13. Rowe *THE HARD ROCK MEN* p.118

14. Ralph Mann, *AFTER THE GOLD RUSH : SOCIETY IN GRASS VALLEY AND NEVADA CITY, CALIFORNIA 1849-70* (CALIFORNIA 1982) p.175-176. Rowse estimates that in 1852 Nevada County had 12,500 whites and nearly 4,000 Chinese. Rowse *THE CORNISH IN AMERICA* p.248

15. Todd claims the Chinese labourers at the Empire mine had been roughly handled by both Cornish and Irish alike. Todd *THE CORNISH MINER IN AMERICA* p.70

16. Mann, *AFTER THE GOLD RUSH* p.184

17. *IBID.*, p.188

18. *IBID.*, p.192

19. *C.P.M.N.*, 8th NOVEMBER 1900.

20. *IBID.*, 9th AUGUST 1900 *Cost of Living on the Rand*.

21 *IBID.*, 4th DECEMBER 1902

22. *IBID.*, 23rd JANUARY 1902

23. *CORNISHMAN* , 5th JUNE. Whilst in Argentina, Tiddy came across a number of tombstones erected for Cornishmen who had died there – most likely miners.

24. *IBID.*, 4th SEPTEMBER 1902

25. *IBID.*, 18th SEPTEMBER 1902

26. *CORNUBIAN* 6th JUNE 1902

27. *CORNISHMAN* 8th JUNE 1902

28. *IBID.*, 26th JUNE 1902

29. *IBID.*, 10th JULY 1902

30. *C.P.M.N.*, 1st NOVEMBER 1900. A tribute to Cornwall by the *Mining World*

31. *CORNISHMAN* 4th SEPTEMBER 1902

32. *IBID.*, 6th NOVEMBER 1902

33. See *IBID.*, 9th OCTOBER, 6th NOVEMBER and 4th DECEMBER 1902

34. *CORNUBIAN*, 28th NOVEMBER 1902. Inmates of the Redruth Union totalled 260 compared with 246 the previous year and out paupers 1,545 against 1,486. Total paupers 1,805.

35. *CORNISHMAN*, 18th DECEMBER 1902

36. *C.P.M.N.*, 13th OCTOBER 1898

37. Surprisingly enough Tom Mathews is not mentioned by Rowe, Rowse or Todd in their accounts of the Cornish in America.

38. *CORNISHMAN*, 15th JUNE 1893. Much of this information Mathews gave himself in an interview with the newspaper. See also Jack & Ray Simons *CLASS AND COLOUR IN SOUTH AFRICA 1850 – 1950 (LONDON 1983)* p.189 – 190

39. T.H.R. Davenport. *SOUTH AFRICA (LONDON 1979)* p.151. See also Norman Levy *THE FOUNDATION OF THE SOUTH AFRICA CHEAP LABOUR SYSTEM (LONDON 1982)*. According to Cornish Mine Captain J. Pryor, Cresswell was only a surveyor – not a Mine Manager – and he had worked for Pryor in South America so he was not surprised at his mistake. *C.P.M.N.*, 10th November 1904

40. See especially *C.P.M.N.*, Editorials *WHITE LABOUR ON THE RAND* , 2nd OCTOBER 1902 p.4 and *TRUTH ABOUT THE RAND*, 23rd OCTOBER 1902 p.4. The *POST* pointed out that the use of more rock drills would only enhance the risk of miners phthisis – see Chapter 8, *TO STRIKE IN THE LAND OF DEATH.*

41. *C.P.M.N.*, 23rd OCTOBER 1902

42. *CORNISHMAN*, 4th DECEMBER 1902

43. *C.P.M.N.*, 6th NOVEMBER 1902, Editorial: *Black Wages Raised.*

44. *CORNISHMAN* , 9th JULY 1903. For another equally depressing description see *IBID.*, 10th MARCH

45. *IBID.*, 23rd JULY 1904. A *bob* referred to a shilling which is now 5p in today's money.

46. *IBID.*, 3rd DECEMBER 1903

47. Hannan, *JOSEPH TUCKER – LETTERS* p.10

48. An experiment using Indian labour at the Kaffyfontein Mine ended in failure. Contracts were dissolved by mutual consent. *CORNISHMAN*, 19th FEBRUARY 1903

49. Cavalieri Rossi – the Italian Labour Commissioner – went to Johannesburg to negotiate terms. *IBID.*, 19th March.

50. Hannan, *JOSEPH TUCKER – LETTERS* p.11

51. *CORNISHMAN*, 12th FEBRUARY 1903

52. *C.P.M.N.*, 6th November 1902

53. *CORNISHMAN*, 9th APRIL 1903

54. *CORNUBIAN*, 3rd APRIL 1903

55. *IBID.*, 17th APRIL 1903. Lawson had 3,558 votes, Strauss had 2,869 votes.

56. *IBID.*, 17th APRIL 1903

57. Hannan, *JOSEPH TUCKER – LETTERS* p.29

58. *IBID.*, p.32

59. *C.P.M.N.*, 6th AUGUST 1903 p 4

60. One of the successes of Milner's regime was to have stopped drunkenness by closing down the Hatherly Distillery and preventing any further distilling, thus making the entire black work force on the gold fields more productive and efficient. See Charles van Onselen, *NEW BABYLON*, Chapter 2 for the full story.

61. *C.P.M.N.*, 6th AUGUST 1903 p.7

62. Hannan, *JOSEPH TUCKER – LETTERS* p.33

63. All extracts reported in the *Rand Daily Mail* 27th JANUARY 1903.

64. All extracts were included in the column *Topics of the Day C.P.M.N.*, 10th SEPTEMBER 1903 p.4

65. *RAND DAILY MAIL*, 27th FEBRUARY 1903

66. *CORNUBIAN*, 2nd OCTOBER 1903

67. *IBID.*, 5th DECEMBER 1903 p.2 and p.4

68. *C.P.M.N.*, 10th DECEMBER 1903

69. P. Warwick Ed. *THE SOUTH AFRICAN WAR* Chapter 15 Reconstruction in the Transvaal S.E. Katzenellenbogen p.357

70. *CORNUBIAN*, 5th DECEMBER 1903

71. Hannan, *JOSEPH TUCKER – LETTERS* p.35

72. *CORNUBIAN*, 1st AUGUST 1902

73. *IBID.*, 30th JANUARY 1904

74. Het Volk means The People. Established in 1905, its main aim was to win back self government for the Boer or Afrikaner nation.

75. Readers Digest, *ILLUSTRATED HISTORY OF SOUTH AFRICA* (NEW YORK 1988) p.267

76. *THE MINING JOURNAL*, 13th FEBRUARY 1904 p.177

77. *C.P.M.N.*, 3rd NOVEMBER 1904

78. *MINING JOURNAL*, 2nd APRIL 1904 p.384

79. *CORNISHMAN*, 25th FEBRUARY 1904

80. *CORNUBIAN*, 19th MARCH 1904

81. *CORNISHMAN*, 31st MARCH 1904

82. William Crooks (1852-1921) Labour M.P. for Woolwich 1903-21.

83. *C.P.M.N.*, 28th JANUARY 1904. See also *CORNUBIAN* 16th JANUARY 1904 p.4. For a reply to Crooks see Letter from J.S.V. Bickford *C.P.M.N.*, 4th FEBRUARY 1904 p.7 and Bickford's comments *IBID.*, 14th JANUARY 1904

84. *IBID.*, 23rd JUNE 1904

85. *IBID.*, 28th JANUARY 1904

86. *IBID.*, 4th FEBRUARY 1904 p.5

87. *IBID.*, 28th JANUARY 1904

88. *IBID.*, 7th JANUARY 190489. *IBID.*, 11th FEBRUARY 1904

90. *CORNISHMAN*, 21st JANUARY 1904 – MLC = Member of the Legislature Chamber.

91. *IBID.*, 23rd JULY 1903

92. *IBID.*, 13th AUGUST 1903

93. *IBID.*, 24th SEPTEMBER 1903

94. *C.P.M.N.*, 23rd JUNE 1904

95. *CORNUBIAN*, 2nd APRIL 1904

96. William T. Stead, (1848-1912) had been Editor of *THE PALL MALL GAZETTE*. (from 1883 to 1889) Milner had, in fact, been his assistant on the paper.

97. *C.P.M.N.*, 30th JUNE 1904. Stead in his list of places where Cornish miners could be found omitted Australia, Mexico, Bolivia and India – to name but a few others.

98. *IBID.*, 16th FEBRUARY 1905. See also Richardson, *CHINESE MINE LABOUR*, for how the Chinese were recruited, especially Chapters 4 and 5.

99. *CORNISHMAN*, 30th JUNE 1904

100. *C.P.M.N.*, 28th JULY 1904

101. *IBID.*, 1st SEPTEMBER 1904

102. *IBID.*, 1st SEPTEMBER 1904

103. *IBID.*, 6th OCTOBER 1904

104. *IBID.*, 20th OCTOBER 1904

105. *IBID.*, 20th OCTOBER 1904

106. *IBID.*, 3rd NOVEMBER 1904

107. *CORNUBIAN*, 30th JULY 1904

108. *IBID.*, 6th AUGUST 1904

109. *IBID.*, 22nd OCTOBER 1904

110. *C.P.M.N.*, 26th JANUARY 1905

111. *IBID.*, 30th JUNE 1904

112. *IBID.*, 8th SEPTEMBER 1904

113. *IBID.*, 15th DECEMBER 1904

114. *CORNUBIAN*, 28th JANUARY 1905

115. *C.P.M.N.*, 16th MARCH 1905

116. *IBID.*, 6th APRIL 1905

117. *IBID.*, 20th APRIL 1905

118. *IBID.*, 21st SEPTEMBER 1905

119. *IBID.*, 24th AUGUST 1905

120. *IBID.*, 13th JULY 1905

121. *CORNUBIAN*, 11th NOVEMBER 1905

122. *CORNISHMAN*, 8th JUNE 1905

123. *C.P.M.N.*, 27th APRIL 1905

124. *IBID.*, 28th DECEMBER 1905

125. *IBID.*, 30th NOVEMBER 1905

126. *IBID.*, 15th JUNE 1905

127. *IBID.*, 24th AUGUST 1905

128. *IBID.*, 27th JULY 1905

129. *IBID.*, 10th AUGUST 1905

130. *IBID.*, 29th JUNE 1905

131. *IBID.*, 19th OCTOBER 1905

132. *IBID.*, 13th SEPTEMBER 1906

133. *IBID.,* 10th DECEMBER 1908

134. *C.P.M.N.,* 31st AUGUST 1905

135. I thank Ken Sara for this story.

136. *C.P.M.N.,* 30th NOVEMBER 1905

137. *IBID.,* 12th JANUARY 1905

138. *CORNUBIAN,* 5th JANUARY 1905 p.5

139. *C.P.M.N.,* 1st JUNE 1911

140. Chilvers, *OUT OF THE CRUCIBLE* p.166

141. P. Rowland, *THE LAST LIBERAL GOVERNMENTS: THE PROMISED LAND 1905-1910* (LONDON 1968) p.24

142. *IBID.,* p.25

143. *CORNUBIAN,* 20th JANUARY 1906

144. *C.P.M.N.,* 11th JANUARY 1906

145. *IBID.,* 18th JANUARY 1906

146. *IBID.,* 18th JANUARY 1906 p.5

147. *IBID.,* 18th JANUARY 1906 p.7

148. *IBID.,* 30th NOVEMBER 1905

149. *IBID.,* 18th JANUARY 1906

150. *CORNUBIAN,* 13th JANUARY 1906

151. *C.P.M.N.,* 1st FEBRUARY 1906 p.7 The national result saw 377 Liberals, 53 Labour, 83 Irish Nationalists, 132 Conservatives and 25 Liberal Unionists. The new Prime Minister Campbell-Bannerman had an overall majority of 129. The result in the Mining Division was Dunn 4,614, Hewitt 2,384 and Jones 107. 7,107 voted, which was a record turnout for the constituency.

152. *CORNUBIAN,* 3rd MARCH 1906

153. *C.P.M.N.,* 8th MARCH 1906 p.7

154. *C.P.M.N.,* 25th JANUARY 1906 p.8. The article Hicks refers to is John Chinaman as a Diamond-Miner, His Way of Life in the Rand, by a Mining Engineer. It does say that Simmer Jack is a diamond mine and describes the Chinamen as lazy, riotous, dishonest, unable to respond to fair treatment, often drunk and says the problem of labour in S. African mines has not been solved by the arrival of the coolies. See *ILLUSTRATED LONDON NEWS* 23rd SEPTEMBER 1905 p.430

155. *IBID.,* 8th MARCH 1906

156. *IBID.,* 5th APRIL 1906

157. See for example the letter from W.S. Brokensha *IBID.,* 24 MAY 1906

158. *IBID,* 10th MAY 1906

159. *IBID.,* 26th APRIL 1906

160. *IBID.,* 31st MAY 1906

161. *IBID.,* 7th JUNE 1906

162. *IBID.,* 24th MAY 1906

163. *CORNISHMAN,* 28th DECEMBER 1905

164. *C.P.M.N.,* 27th DECEMBER 1906 – In August 1907 East Pool mine paid out its largest dividend since 1888.

165. *IBID.,* 8th FEBRUARY 1906

166. *IBID.,* 18th OCTOBER 1906

167. *IBID.,* 15th NOVEMBER 1906 Botallack mine was refloated with 400 share-holders. Rich deposits of tin were discovered and it continued to be worked until it eventually closed once more, in 1914.

168. *IBID.,* 27th SEPTEMBER 1906 p.4

169. *IBID.,* 15th NOVEMBER 1906 p.4

170. *IBID.,* 27th DECEMBER 1906

171. *CORNUBIAN,* 10th MARCH 1906

172. *C.P.M.N.,* 18th APRIL 1907

173. *CORNUBIAN,* 23rd JUNE 1906 p.2

174. *IBID.,* 23rd JUNE 1906 p.2. This point was also expressed in an article *Decline in Skilled White Miners* in the *MINING JOURNAL,* , 21st APRIL 1906 p.514. Creswell used a similar point in his *Address on the Economic Aspect of Chinese Labour.* See *MINING JOURNAL,* 10th FEBRUARY 1906 p.184. For a reply to Creswell, from R.W. Schumacher, see the *MINING JOURNAL,* 3rd MARCH 1906 p.276

175. C.P.M.N. 10th May 1906

176. *CORNUBIAN.,* 23rd JUNE 1906 p.2

177. *C.P.M.N.,* 8th NOVEMBER 1906 p.7

178. *IBID.,* 15th NOVEMBER 1906 p.7. See also *IBID.,* 20th DECEMBER 1906 p.4

179. *IBID.,* 31st JANUARY 1907

180. *IBID.*, 7th FEBRUARY 1907

181. *IBID.*, 28th FEBRUARY 1907

182. *CORNISHMAN*, 14th FEBRUARY 1907

183. *CORNUBIAN*, 21st MARCH 1907

184. *C.P.M.N.*, 5th DECEMBER 1907. See Richardson *CHINESE MINE LABOUR TABLE* p.119

185. *CORNUBIAN*, 21st NOVEMBER 1907. See also *C.P.M.N.*, 14th NOVEMBER 1907

186. *CORNUBIAN*, 28th JANUARY 1909

187. *C.P.M.N.*, 6th JANUARY 1910. there were two General Elections in 1910, the Liberal-Radicals won on both occasions. In the Mining Division the results were January – Dunn (Lib Rad) 5,027; Chamberlain (Lib Unionist) 2,587: December – F.D.Acland (Lib Rad 4,419 Dunn having resigned earlier) G.Coates (Lib Unionist) 2,326.

CHAPTER EIGHT

TO STRIKE IN THE LAND OF DEATH
1902-27

The Cornish miner never has been, nor is ever likely to become a trade unionist. His motto 'One & All' is quite sufficient protection for him in all labour questions.[1]

Mining Journal 15th April 1905

Their short coughs and wan faces were for many years as familiar as the wheezing of the old beam engines and the long shadows of the gaunt chimneys.[2]

Cornish Engineers — Hollowood.

In April 1902 the *Cornishman* presented a most damning statistic on the mining industry, concerning the migration of Cornish miners to South Africa:

Out of 30 miners who came home from the Rand 3 years ago in one ship to the Mining Division for the benefit of their health 29 had passed away. On Saturday Mr. Bartle of Crowan died. All were victims of the boring machine.[3]

The phrase 'wholly disabled from miners' complaint', according to the *Cornishman,* was heard at every meeting of the Redruth Board of Guardians, and at Camborne many formerly robust men had to be supported by the parish rates.[4] Referring to the miners who returned to Cornwall during the two and a half years of war, the Chamber of Mines stated that no less than 600 of these fine stalwart men had died from miners' phthisis.[5] A much later report in 1906 stated that the Redruth Union had 330 paupers whose pauperism was due directly to miners' phthisis.[6] The *Cornishman* said:

In this district, in fact right through the Mining Division, can be seen comparatively young men, walking about slowly, with sunken eyes, pale thin features, a difficulty to breathe and a hollow cough. It's a sad sight but they can frequently be seen... It's has been said that we as a County have been greatly benefited by Africa. Perhaps... but the general opinion is that it has been the means of raising the rates.[7]

Phthisis was a known disease amongst miners, especially those involved in the mining of gold, tin and copper. It was a disease which attacked the lungs and was caused by inhaling fine dust containing silica – hence silicosis – the modern term for 'miner's phthisis.' Burke and Richardson have discussed miners' phthisis in an article *The Profits of Death: A Comparative Study of Miners' Phthisis in Cornwall and the Transvaal, 1876-1918.*[8] During a visit home in 1902 Francis Oats was so concerned that a number of men had died unnecessarily that he paid a visit to Dr. Permewan, the Redruth Medical Officer of Health, asking him to investigate the number of deaths from phthisis. Permewan agreed to tabulate statements on behalf of the Rural District Council of the deaths from phthisis during the last two years and to send this to Oats,

> who was going to South Africa and would press the matter on the responsible parties and see what could be done. The deaths of so many miners, the result of working boring machines, was a very serious matter. Up to now the authorities in South Africa had not realised what had happened. The deaths did not occur in South Africa among the men but occurred when they came home.[9]

Oats left for South Africa in August, and in the following month the *Post* recorded:

> Men have come to Camborne from points as remote as Liskeard and St. Just in the hope that the 'shortness of breath' which troubles them may be found curable. It is always the same discovery – the lungs irretrievably injured by the fine particles of South Africa quartz, no possibility of renewing the lungs, the only prospect ahead being a few months', in rare cases a few years' rest from labour, with the certainty of a painful illness and premature death. We have looked forward to the reopening of the Rand with the hope born of empty pockets and long idleness. Now we have the prospect of work and money – and the dread of death ever before our eyes.[10]

The effect of the machine rock drills upon the rate of mortality amongst Cornish miners was discussed by the Redruth Urban Council in the same month, but a difficulty was fact that no figures for death from phthisis existed before the miner went to South Africa. However, it was acknowledged that the average age of death for a miner had been 55 years but most of the South African cases were under 40 years and too large a proportion were under 30 years.[11] As one Cornish writer claimed, the goldfields,

> attracted hundreds of the best Cornish miners, many of whom died of 'miners' complaint' in their early thirties, as it is borne testimony in many a churchyard in the west country.[12]

Fortunately for the miners by the end of 1902 came the welcome news that two Commissions, to investigate phthisis, were to be set up. The one in Cornwall was to be headed by Dr. John Haldane, R. Arthur Thomas, the Manager of Dolcoath mine, and the Inspector of Mines. In South Africa the Commission consisted of some eleven Commissioners of whom J. Harry Johns represented the Mine Managers and another Cornishman, E. Perrow, represented the Miners' Association. Even as the two Commissions sat, the deaths from miners' phthisis continued. James Hodge Williams of St. Erth died, aged 28 years, in Cornwall[13] and John Henry Oliver of Illogan, age 31 years, died in South Africa.[14] In June, the same week that the death of Oliver was announced, the Cornubian said that 13 miners with their families had returned home to Cornwall from South Africa due to the fear of death and on the last two Sundays 6 miners had died leaving behind families, the public verdict being death from millionaire economy.[15] Many would have agreed with the miner who said:

> *the miner wants to get money, the manager wants to get speed, the shareholders want dividends and the gravestones tell the rest of the story.*[16]

Or as another miner put it:

> *even if the Chinaman was to usurp the white man – it would be more than a blessing in disguise as it would materially help in staunching the great sacrifice of life made by so many of our young Cornishmen.*[17]

When the Commission in South Africa reported, in 1903, that the average life span of a miner was only 35. 5 years the *Cornishman* commented "we are paying a terrible heavy price for the Croust-bag full of nuggets of foreign gold."[18]

Money in the shape of a remittance home to his family was all-important to the ordinary miner – just how important is clearly shown in the letters written by Joseph Tucker to his son. From them we learn that his wife, to gain some financial control, put some of the money he sent into the Co-operative Society, but in her own name. This led Tucker to relate:

> *there was a man on the North Randfontein mine that was treated just as I was, only he had more money – when he got home when the war broke out he found his wife had it all in her name and she refused to let him have a shilling. He... borrowed money and came out to this country and he has not sent the scratch of a pen to his wife since and she has been advertising for him in the papers here.*[19]

Tucker was sending home £12 per month during 1902-13, pointing out that if he had been home he would be earning less than £8 a month which both he and his wife would have lived on. In another letter he said that from October 1902 to July

1903 he sent his wife £108 and asked his son if there was there any room to grumble at what he had sent? Apparently there was, and the subject of money reared its ugly head on many an occasion, causing a strain on their marriage.[20]

Trying to arrive at the exact total of remittances that the Cornish miners sent home from South Africa is extremely difficult. Even if the *Post* was correct and there were 7,000 Cornish miners on the Rand in 1905 and they each earned £300 per annum and were able to send home half their wage making a total of close to a million pounds then it can still only be a very rough estimate.[21] Sending home £10 a month seemed the norm, according to the newspapers,[22] but against this, of course, is the number of men who behaved like those dealt with by the Guardians – or like the man mentioned by Tucker.

The fact that many families in Cornwall lived off such remittances is still remembered today. The homecoming mail boats used to anchor in Mounts Bay and off-load what was known in Penzance as the Cape Mail. This was rushed to the Post Office at Penzance where it was immediately sorted, every available Post Office sorter being brought in, be it day or night, weekend or Sunday, so the money enclosed in the mail could be delivered as quickly as possible to the families in St. Just or Pendeen who were largely dependent on it. Mrs. White, Pendeen's first Post Mistress said she hated going in Cairn View Terrace as everyone would be out at the doors or windows and felt embarrassed for those for whom she had no letters with remittances.[23] At least one travel writer has commented on the weekly remittance which never failed to come.[24] Records of drafts home via the Post Office, like the emigration records, recorded names as British and not Cornish. What information there is at the Post Office has so far been of little relevance.[25] Then there are the remittances to be accounted for from places such as India, Australia and America – North Central and South. The *Post*, for example, estimated that in 1905 wages paid in Montana totalled £2,500,000, of which a large proportion would have come Cornwall's way in the shape of remittances.[26] Rowse says by 1869 Camborne men in California and Nevada were faithfully sending home some £15,000 to £18,000 a year.[27] Perhaps a true figure will never be reached, especially as the Cornish newspapers seem to provide the sentiment but rarely the fact. What is not in dispute is that Cornwall was living off the Rand, but at a very high price.

In March 1903 the Medical Officer of Health for Redruth recorded the largest number of deaths in one year from South African phthisis; out of the 21 deaths, 11 men had returned from South Africa and all but one were under 37 years of age:

> *the striking fact has also shown itself in no less than four or five of the*
> *eleven cases... the men have arrived home in the best of health, robust,*
> *fat, wind and limbs sound and have appeared home in first class health*
> *for eighteen months to two years when wasting, weakness and marked*

*shortness of breath more or less suddenly become apparent. Therefore from this point things go progressively from bad to worse until the end comes.*28

In South Africa miners' phthisis continued to take its toll. Joseph J. Richards died from it after a long and painful illness in the Johannesburg hospital, as did Thomas Pearce, a foreman at the Crown Reef mine. Richards was the cousin of Joseph Richards (the late Manager of the Ferreira Deep and Manager of South Crofty before leaving for Bolivia) whilst Pearce had a brother who had died from phthisis only the year before.29 Even Tiddy remarked:

*here death seems a more frequent and cruel visitor. Here his principle is to cut down the young and the strong – funerals of Cornishmen in the flush and hey day of life are weekly events – rock drill work is suicide at a price.*30

One of the authors in a book about Benoni, which was on the Eastern Rand and had a large Cornish population working in mines such as Van Ryn and New Kleinfontein, claims that one of his earliest memories was

*the long procession of mourners following poor Cousin Jacks to their rest. It was a point of honour with the victim's fellow workers to take part in the long procession looking very uncomfortable in their Sunday best. An incongruous feature was the fact that some of them smoked as they followed the hearse, probably quite unconscious of what they were doing.*31

Meanwhile in Cornwall in 1904 an important Home Office Inquest was held at Truro on William Cornish, aged 60 from Gwennap, who had died from phthisis. Cornish had worked a rock drill for only two months in the Transvaal before returning to Cornwall some four and a half years ago during which time he had not done any mining. The post-mortem examination revealed both lungs of the deceased being absolutely black from dust and smoke inhaled. Working a rock drill was seen to be inviting death – and an early death at that. A juror on the case, A. Pengelly, who had extensive experience in Cornish and Transvaal mines said:

*rock drilling was more dangerous in the Transvaal because the men were working on contract, and were anxious to get back to their work immediately after the blast, no matter how thick the dust was. That was not the case in Cornwall however, (laughter). In the Transvaal he had driven men away from their work immediately after the blast because he thought the dust too thick for them to be in. He believed in the water jet.*32

It turned out that Cornish had also worked in California, so the jury returned a verdict of death from phthisis caused by the inhalation of stone dust during work as a miner in Cornwall, America and the Transvaal. It was also revealed at the Inquest that when rock drilling was first introduced in Cornwall and the Transvaal, water jets were used to keep down the dust, but incredible as it now seems they were not widely used. The men were also unwilling to wear respirators because it prevented them from talking.[33] A similar Inquest was carried out within the week on another Cornish miner, William Heather, aged 46 from Barripper. He had worked five years at Dolcoath and before that had been a timberworker and pump worker at the Simmer & Jack in South Africa and New Lucy mine in Oregon, North America. Although he had not worked a rock drill in either South Africa or North America nonetheless he had died from phthisis; for it was agreed a miner could inhale dust by standing near a rock drill.[34] After both Inquests it was urged that legislation be introduced to prevent the inhaling of dust by miners. A month later the publication of the Haldane Report confirmed that conditions under which rock drill work had been carried out was far more detrimental to health in the Transvaal than in Cornish mines.[35] It probably came as no surprise, either, that Haldane's Commission recommended the use of a water jet in connection with rock drilling but unbelievably it was to take another sixteen years before a Committee in South Africa finally ordered, in 1919, dry drilling to stop. That piece of legislation was far too late for the majority of Cornish miners and in 1904 it was said that nearly every village in Cornwall possessed a considerable number of men on the youthful side of the prime of their life, cursed with this affliction.[36]

James Henry Paull died from phthisis at Redruth, and although he had been to South Africa on a number of occasions he was only 33 years old.[37] John Blamey – aged 30 – died from phthisis at Gwennap[38] and when William Thomas Bennets, Landlord of the Railway Hotel, Camborne, died from phthisis – he had spent some ten years in South Africa – it was reported:

> *It is an awful fact that 15 men who worked as rock drill 'pare' in the Germiston mine have all died from miners' phthisis. Mr. Bennets being the last to succumb – only 37 – returned from the Transvaal 7 years ago... Like so many other rock drill miners who return from South Africa Mr. Bennets at first appeared to possess good health and strength but for a year or two the unmistakable signs of phthisis were evident and for two or three weeks prior to the end, the decline was of a very rapid character.*[39]

In South Africa, William Jenkin at Roodepoort died from phthisis the very night he was to depart for Cornwall. The bearers at his funeral were fellow Cornishmen from his home village of Chacewater.[40] Another young Cornishman who died from phthisis had actually served as a Sergeant all through the Boer War, seeing action first with Lord Roberts' Horse and then Lord Methuen's Horse Company. Robert

Keskeys, formerly of Germoe, was still only 29 years old when he fell victim to the dread disease.[41] In the same month – February 1907 – it was announced that there had been a large increase in the number of rock drills being used on the Rand, from 1,357 in 1905 to 2,345 in 1906.[42]

Unfortunately the Transvaal Miners' Association, which perhaps should have been putting all its energies into getting better working conditions for the health of its members, was more concerned between 1904-06 with the Chinese question.

Then, in 1907, what faced the Cornish miner was a crisis which would have a far greater effect on his future than the Jameson Raid, Boer War or Chinese labour ever had. It began with the election which, on 20th February, saw the victory at the polls for the Het Volk Party over the Progressive Party (which was seen as the mouthpiece of the mine owners) and the much smaller Independent Labour Party, which mainly represented the mine workers.

Following the election result there was a mixed feeling among Cornishmen. William Hosken, who was returned as a Progressive Member, thought it not surprising to find the new Transvaal Parliament dominated by Boers.[43] Sir Lewis Michell believed the Empire stronger with self government in the Transvaal; he welcomed the part to be played by the Dutch and thought all racial feeling was dying down.[44] Not all Cornishmen agreed, as Tiddy remarked in typical fashion:

The Boer majority was expected by our own race, plus the Jews helping them to win the war against the real British Party. If Britain alone had the decision the Progressives would be overwhelmingly the strongest. As it is Australians, Jews and Dutchmen will furnish the majority of Het Volk.[45]

The white miner, fearing that Chinese or natives would eventually be employed as skilled machine men by the mine owners, had turned to Het Volk and Afrikaner nationalism, which was ready to protect itself by discriminatory laws. With the introduction of the new smaller, stoping drill the *Mining Journal* had prophesied that unless it was supervised exclusively by white labour then the result would be the greatest fight between labour and capital[46] that South Africa had ever seen. The prophecy came true. The actual battle was to be fought, not over exclusive supervision of the drills, but over the actual number of the drills the white miner was to supervise. When men at the Knights Deep mine were told to supervise three drills instead of two, they went on strike on 1st May 1907. One Cornish miner asked if the average machine man's life was six years with two machines, what was the average of his life with three? He claimed one extra machine was equal to a reduction by one third of white men employed.[47]

The all-important rock drill had revolutionised the whole nature of mining and, worse it had de-skilled the Cornish miner. As early as 1872 the *South African Mining Journal* had commented:

we state the fact and we challenge its disapproval that miners upon the Witwatersrand Fields have acquired the habit of shirking work themselves by delegating their duties to the Kaffir labourers, with which they have been in the past far too prodigally supplied, and that even today it is hard to find instances of drill holes put down by hand by white miners. [48]

With the introduction of the rock drill it had been the custom for a white miner to run one machine with the help of two or three natives. When the two-machine system became operative – a white miner supervising two machines and five natives – the customary payment of £1 per shift was increased to a minimum 25 shillings a shift. From being a skilled-hand driller the position of the white miner had been elevated to that of supervisor, being in charge of all blasting operations – a blasting certificate being denied to any native or Chinese labourer. The strike slowly gathered momentum, spreading from 5 mines – with 400 men out – to over 50 mines, with 4,000 miners involved. In Cornwall the *Post* said the news of the strike... will cause some uneasiness at home.[49]

The leader of the Strike Committee, which consisted of 18 men, was Cornishman Tom Mathews, who said he didn't want a class war but,

the interests of the capitalistic class were not any more important in the case of the welfare of a country than the interests of the workers – any man who could find it in him to blackleg was a traitor to his class.[50]

The Committee even sent a request to the *Post* asking for the names of Cornishmen considered to be scabs and blacklegs to be published but the *Post* refused on a point of legality.[51]

The success of the strike hinged on the engine drivers who were under no obligation to support the miners when out on strike. One Cornish engine driver – Charles Courtney of St. Austell – made the position quite clear when he said that the drivers had no grievance – for when in the past they had supported them the miners had not.[52] Although in sympathy, the drivers' decision to carry on working certainly weakened the strike as did the fact that at some mines, such as the Robinson Central Deep, the men refused to down tools. The reason for this was that on some of these mines the miners had already been working three machines.[53] Very early on during the strike a revolver was drawn by one mine manager, leading Mathews to claim that this was a poor substitute for argument.[54] Mathews himself faced embarrassment when the men at the Ferreira Deep – a mine employing a large number of Cornishmen – voted not to strike, despite a direct appeal to the men from Mathews himself. Hedley Chilvers has considered Tom Mathews to be the dominant figure in the 1907 miners' strike describing him as:

Robinson Deep gold mine No. 1 shaft headgear.

*an outspoken, fearless, and often mistaken Trade Unionist who, in an age
not altogether remarkable for its ideals, was essentially an honest man.
He was a bluff, earnest but somewhat breathless orator; earnest because
he had the cause of the miners so passionately at heart; breathless
because he had dust on the lungs and the Great Reaper stood ever closely
at his elbow... the Miners professed many grievances, and Mathews
voiced them all eloquently from one end of the Reef to the other;but,
although the men were enthusiastic at first they presently began to waver,
and strike support weakened and finally collapsed.*[55]

As mass meetings of striking miners took place the mine owners declared the
strike a lock-out, dismissed the strikers and took on Afrikaaners in their place – the
places of strikers being filled at Knights Deep mine within days of the strike being
called.[56] The strike was also to show that many of the mines had, in fact, been
overstaffed for, despite having men out on strike, they continued to work normally.
Newton Lauder, the Cornish Manager of the Rose Deep mine, said that despite
having a smaller staff the mine managed to keep up its output.[57] In other mines the
native and Chinese labour carried on working, with less supervision. For the
Cornish miner the strike was a disaster. Thomas Collingwood Kitto, the much
respected Cornish Mining Inspector and Engineer said, that in the history of
mining there had never been less cause for a strike[58] and claimed the men were
being duped, tricked and hounded on to destruction, pointing out that it was an
insult to mining to suggest a man was a skilled miner because he could operate a
rock drill, adding that any fool could run a drill after a fortnight's practice.[59]
Earlier in the year Kitto had addressed the miners at the Ferreira Deep, in which he
said he saw the miners as partners, not hirelings and that the miners and the
proprietors had a mutual interest in the mines.[60] Could this have been the reason
why the miners here had refused to go on strike? Many Cornishmen obviously
took notice of what he said, for by the end of May they had left for Cornwall,
being somewhat disgusted by the Strike Committee. It was said that they did not
intend to assist men who only want to work with their jaws.[61] In reply to the
suggestion that the strike was the work of labour agitators, Mathews said they had
only one paid man in the Union.[62] During the strike Mathew Trewick, a
Cornishman and Secretary of the Miners' Association had been approached by
some 200 Vrededorp Afrikaners asking for a guarantee from the Union that if they
did not take the place of strikers would the Afrikaner in future have an equal
chance with other miners to obtain work on the mines.[63] Trewick sent a letter back,
giving the Strike Committee's assurance. George Albu, an important Randlord,
predicted:

*the average mine would be run with fifteen to twenty per cent fewer high
paid labourers... after a thousand white men had vacated their*

positions... the stamps were running merrily as ever... A prolongation of
the strike would result in the men's places being filled by Afrikaanders...
and in the retention in the country of wages which were at present
*remitted overseas.*64

Although rowdyism marked the introduction of Afrikaners at Langlaagte Deep
mine, the day of the Afrikaner miner had arrived.65 Jacobus Oosthuizen testified
that the first time he worked as a miner was when he was employed as a strike
breaker on the Rose Deep for 8s a day where with other Afrikaners he was taught
how to drill and blast by Chinese.66 So-called racism between Boer and Britisher
existed in a more accentuated form among the miners themselves insofar as on
certain mines only Cornishmen were allowed to obtain employment.67 The
advantage had certainly passed to the Afrikaner, for the *Post* noted:

> *the places of the strikers, who are mainly Cornishmen are being filled by*
> *Dutchmen while those engaged in recruiting for the mines are refusing all*
> *British workers and engaging only Boers or Afrikaner*68

The strike certainly marked a turning point in the history of Rand mining for the
Cornish miner. South Africa no longer seemed attractive. The time when a Cornish
miner could earn as much as £120 – £150 a month was over and it was believed
that it was better for a Boer to earn £30 a month underground and spend it in the
Transvaal than for a Cornishman to earn £100 and send the bulk of it to his family
in the West of England.69 This view was echoed by Prime Minister Botha himself
when he said:

> *It is time South Africa began to raise her own skilled workers... in this*
> *vast, amply rich country with its army of imported artisans, with its*
> *perpetual stream of postal orders flowing to Cornwall.* 70

Near the end of May the strike turned violent, as the situation for the strikers
became desperate. Reports of terrorism and outrage appeared, and on some mines
savage blows and heavily shod boots had their effect. The striking miners were
accused of using brute force to accomplish what they could not do by persuasion.71
Against them was a determined Government which decided to send in the military.
The Riot Act was read and the order given to the 2nd Dragoon Guards and
Cameron Highlanders to draw swords and fix bayonets.72 A number of the strike
leaders were arrested; the strike committee sent a letter to Ramsay Macdonald and
the British Labour Party seeking support for the strike, but it was to no avail.
While Mathews turned to the argument that working more drills would lead to
more accidents plus an increase in deaths from phthisis, the miners began to drift
back to work. In the *Transvaal Leader*, under the heading 'Leading Cornishman's
Views', another letter from Kitto urged the men to abandon what he termed a

causeless strike,[73] whilst the Strike Committee met Prime Minister Botha along with the Minister for Mines, and Mathews asked them to intervene and set up an arbitration court, handing over a petition signed by 3,271 miners.[74] The death blow to the strike, however, came on 6th June when it was announced that no more hands were required and some 2,000 men had been taken on to fill the strikers' places.[75] Although many striking miners, whose places were now filled, left for Kimberley and Rhodesia, some were re-engaged on contract work.[76] Meanwhile the strike dragged on; there were still mines with men out on strike. When the Miners' Association finally admitted defeat in July, the failure of the strike was attributed to the weakness of organisation and a surplus of skilled men.[77] The *Cornubian* lamented:

> *In Cornwall, perhaps more than in any part of England, interest is felt in the state of affairs in the Transvaal, among the working people. We have in Cornwall and more particularly in Camborne and Redruth endured a great deal through South Africa.*[78]

Even the *Post* was to comment:

> *If hundreds of Cornishmen, who had been lured to Africa by the high wages had remained at home, their dust would not now be lying in the graveyards of those distant lands...*[79]

Referring to the monopoly of the Cornish miner the *Mining World* had said earlier:

> *That monopoly exists no longer. It has been dispelled by the Cornishmen themselves... until recent times it would have been difficult to replace them but it is not so difficult now... young Afrikaanders are coming to the front... 5,000 of these in Johannesburg... a school for their instruction has been started and in time, like the Cornishmen in the past, will have the monopoly of it.*[80]

For the members of the Strike Committee and other leading strikers their sacrifice led to victimisation. Mathews himself testified to a Mining Industry Commission[81] to show that many skilled miners could not find work due to having been strikers. He produced a letter from fellow Cornishman Captain Michell, Manager of the Ferreira Deep mine, which showed despite Mathews being a well-qualified miner who produced his best and no fault being found with his work, he was not being reinstated through his connections with the Union. It was regretted that Mathews should be connected in any way with people who had been instrumental in placing the miners in such a calamitous position. In Michell's opinion Mathews could obtain a better living as a miner than in preaching uneconomic principles.[82] Mathews had proved that he was being ostracised on account of the strike, and although the Committee agreed with him he was not reinstated. The plight of the ex-strikers received a boost when money for food was provided by the Government following a deputation led by Mathews and Trewick to Prime Minister Botha. Mathews was then put in charge of a so-called relief scheme where he and 25 miners were to work some surface tin areas in the Northern Transvaal – at 7s 6d a day with food.[83] The *Cornishman* said:

> *Tom, who is a man of great natural gifts as a speaker and who is much liked and trusted as a man deserves the good will of all good men of whatever party in politics for this latest attempt at making a poor man's mining field where a mitigated form of Socialism may be tried... so here's success to the old Newlyn boy as he fares forth.*[84]

Surface plant thought to be a compressor providing air for rock drilling at Geldenhuis Deep gold mine.

The Miners' Association turned its strategy once more to the health and safety of miners again trying to prevent the introduction of three machines claiming this to be a health hazard. It gained no support from fellow Cornishman J. Harry Johns, who told the Mining Industry Commission it was an absolute lie that men's health would suffer by using three machines. Asked about unions, Johns said he had never been a member at which the Commission's Chairman, Peter Whiteside, said "this is your misfortune. You would know more about the Union if you had".85

One sensation of the strike had been the murder of a Cornish miner, William Webb Richards of Four Lanes, Redruth, a shift boss at the New Comet mine. He had been on strike throughout May 1907 but apparently by June, along with many others, had returned to work. It was believed he had been attracted back by the offer of the post of shift boss at the Comet mine – the former shift bosses also being Cornishmen, one named James from Penzance, the other named Puckey, from Lanner. Richards lodged at a house owned by a Cornish family called Nile – also from Four Lanes – and shared a room with another Cornish miner – Joseph Rule of Roskear Fields, Camborne. Richards and Rule were both asleep when, during the night of 15th June, Richards was apparently awoken by the smell of burning. It was whilst they were investigating the source of the burning that dynamite, placed on the verandah outside the bedroom window, exploded and Richard's body was penetrated by splinters. Richards died the following day from his injuries. Rule had also been seriously hurt but the Nile family, who slept at the back of the house, escaped injury. Richards, who was 24 years old, had been married for four years and left behind in Cornwall a widow and three children.86

Five miners were later arrested and the trial that followed a year later was given full coverage by the Cornish press including details of meetings by night, buried revolvers and the attitude of the strikers towards non-strikers. It turned out that a third Cornish miner – Joseph Hart of Camborne – was also in the room with Richards and Rule, all three men having been judged blacklegs by the strikers. Hart had already been accosted by the strikers some days before and told to persuade Richards and Rule not to go to work. When asked if he had himself ever been on strike Hart rather surprisingly claimed there were no strikes in Cornwall. The case against the five accused eventually broke down and they were discharged.87

There seemed no doubt that a combination of the election, the violent strike and the increase in death from miners' phthisis (through the increasing use of the rock drill) all had a demoralising effect on the Cornish miner. For at least one miner writing in the *Transvaal Leader*, the fact that a number of Cornish miners could no longer find employment was rather amusing, as he considered the arrival of Cousin Jack on these fields a greater calamity to Johannesburg than the advent of the Chinese and thought the one good result of the strike had been to break forever the power of Cousin Jack on the Reef.88.

Despite the strike the Cornish were still prominent on the Rand, although their reputation had received a blow. They were now condemned as less energetic and less efficient and their wages, which were claimed to be far too high for what they actually did, were reduced. Those who had returned to Cornwall were also to be disappointed, for their future looked none too bright either. The signs of progress which heralded 1907 with a boom ended in a lull.[89] The following year was a depressing one for miners all round:

> *Every mining camp in the world is unsettled. Johannesburg has no room for more miners – the great De Beers Mine at Kimberley has discharged thousands of white men. Hundreds are out of work in various camps in the States.*[90]

Conditions eventually improved although Cornwall would not have been pleased with the news that the Cornish Chersen Drill had been beaten by the American Gordon Drill in a rock drilling competition run by the Transvaal Government; this led to 200 Gordon drills being installed by Ecksteins in their mines.[91] Such was the threat of the rock drill to any security of employment (and a high wage) that the Miners' Association issued a notice at Johannesburg that anyone taking on a machine under £1 a day would be considered a scab.[92] Although it was claimed the strike had reduced the number of white miners employed on the Rand by ten per cent – a Government Mining Engineer's Report for the year ending June 1907 having shown a decrease of 606 whites employed in the mining industry[93] – by 1909 official statistics from the Transvaal Mines Department showed the highest number of whites (20,924) ever employed on the mines.[94] In September 1909 W.H. Dawe, Vice President of the Chamber of Mines, announced that increased labour supplies were anticipated.[95]

The Cornish, it seemed, were still very much in demand on the Rand, for it was noted by the *Cornishman* in April 1910 that they had replaced Americans in many of the mines. J. Harry Johns was the Consulting Engineer to the Barnato group which employed many Cornish miners, while the largest single mining co-operation – the East Rand Proprietory Mines – with Sir George Farrar at its head, boasted that it employed 3,000 whites – out of which 750 were from Cornwall and the joint General Manager was Mr. Penlerrick of Perranwell.[96]

Despite the many attempts to prevent the spread of dust by methods such as using water sprays during the drilling process – the Stephens Climax Rock Drill Factory of Carn Brea Cornwall produced a Dust Allayer machine – deaths from miners' phthisis sadly continued. John Phillips, William Opie (both Redruth), Joseph Annear (St. Day), William Henry Christophers (Helston), Edward Trevarthen, James Trevarthen, Thomas Brewer, John Glanville (all Camborne), Ben Jacka (Troon), Clement Peters (Illogan) and John Tonkin (Chacewater) and many others died in South Africa between 1906-13. Thomas Henry Rogers (Illogan), William Hocking (Poole), William Rowe (St. Columb) and John Perry Trewhella returned home from South Africa only to die. J. H. Williams a Cornish mine Captain (New Primrose mine) died from phthisis in South Africa,[97] whilst John Thomas, who had been a miner at Carn Brea and Tincroft before going to

South Africa and Mexico, died within two years of arriving back in Cornwall, having taken up the position of Manager of a mine at Blisland near Bodmin.[98] John H. Treloar, known as Jack, died at Boksburg, South Africa, having spent some years in Australia, where his parents still lived,[99] and John Bray Whitburn was another Cornish miner who died from phthisis on the Rand but left behind a family in Australia.[100] Some having worked in South Africa, were to die in the other mining regions where the Cornish could be found – Australia, Mexico and the United States – whilst not all those who returned to England were to die in Cornwall. When Joseph Tucker went home to die in 1910 it was just one more reminder of the large Cornish community to be found in the North of England, centred on Barrow-in-Furness.[101]

Burke and Richardson have clearly shown that the mortality figures for miners' phthisis were appalling, with a higher percentage of deaths in the Transvaal than in Cornwall.[102] Equally appalling were the reports in the newspapers of Cornish miners who were killed by the other hazards of mining – flood, fire, rock-fall and explosion. Floods in the mines on the Rand were very rare but in January 1909 the Post reported that Walter White (St. Just) and James Whitford (Lanner) had both been drowned when seven inches of rainfall in 24 hours caused a dam to burst and flood the Knights Deep mine. Another Cornishman, named Williams, had a marvellous escape remaining 10 hours chin deep until rescued.[103] Credit went to William Morris Prout (Redruth), the Manager of the mine, and his assistants who never relaxed their efforts to rescue miners below, the rescue team including the wives of Mr. Prout, Dr. Perkins – Mine Doctor – and Mr. Matthews – mine Captain – who accompanied their husbands with the rescue party underground.[104] Fires were fortunately also rare, and when one broke out at the Langlaagte Estate mine Hebberd, the Cornish Manager, gave praise to his employees, the majority of whom were Cornishmen, who did splendid work on the arrival of the Johannesburg Fire Brigade.[105]

Rock-falls and explosions were unfortunately more common. William F. Prout was killed instantly by a rock fall at the Central Deep mine, Roodepoort[106] and a week later the *Post* recorded the death of another Cornishman, Thomas Dillon Canyell (Flushing), who was killed at the Village Reef mine when a piece of rock fell on his head'.[107] A Cornish mine Captain named Hancock was killed along with two other whites and six natives by a rock fall at the Vagelstruis mine,[108] and Joseph John Herran was just one more Cornish miner who was killed by a fall of hanging ground.[109] Alfred Polglase (Porthleven) died at the Stubbs mine, Randfontein, when he was inspecting a ladder and a piece of falling timber landed on his head, also killing a native.[110] William Inch Harvey (Gwennap) met his death with five others at the Driesfontein mine following a sudden explosion of powder;[111] his brother John M. Harvey had died from fever only three months earlier.[112] The Manager of the Driesfontein mine a Cornishman named Richards

(Madron) was later awarded the Humane Society Medal for his bravery, having descended the mine shaft time after time to rescue the injured.[113] The King Edward Medal – first class – was awarded to Harry Bennetts (Camborne) for bravery following an explosion at the Randfontein mine when he with great courage and at imminent risk of his life, descended two winzes alone to rescue natives overcome by poisonous fumes.[114] Three other Cornishmen – Edward J. Dunn, William Arthur and Percy E. Evans (Helston) – on another occasion were mentioned as having performed acts of heroism when rescuing a number of miners following an accident underground.[115]

In January 1910 the *Post* reported that two St. Agnes miners (not named) had been killed by dynamite. Two years later an uncle and nephew from St. Agnes, both with the same name – Nicholas Lawry – were also killed in a dynamite accident.[116] At the North Randfontein mine, E. Pentecost drilled into a hole that had misfired and was killed by the delayed explosion,[117] along with a native working with him. John Welch (Redruth) was blown to death following another dynamite accident[118] but Percy Floyd (Camborne), a shaftsman at the Witwatersrand mine, was lucky he didn't lose his sight when a box of carbide exploded in his face.[119]

In some cases no details of the accident or cause of death were reported. When Elijah T. Harry (Perranporth), a foreman timberman on the Roodepoort Deep mine, met his death by accident it was noted he had been a successful breeder and importer of mastiffs as well as a Wesleyan local preacher, having been engaged in evangelical work in Johannesburg with the late Richard Thomas of Barripper.[120] For other Cornish miners who met their deaths, such as Thomas Harry Johns (cousin to J. Harry Johns), Thomas Curtis, T.H. Thomas, John Marks, John Holman, and Alfred Bawden (St. Day) there were no details. Disease also accounted for a number of deaths, with enteric fever one of the most common, killing James White, Clarence Tippett and William Hosking – all from St. Just. Consumption killed George Edwards (Lanner)[121] whilst Sam Quick (Tuckingmill) died after an operation for appendicitis at the Randfontein Hospital[122] and William Edward Archibald Blackney (St Agnes), who worked at the Wemmer Mine and played in the brass band, also died from appendicitis.[123] Finally James Knuckey (Four Lanes) died at Johannesburg following an accident whilst motor cycling.[124]

Death from phthisis, however, overshadowed all other causes and appeared with a regular monotony in the columns of the Cornish newspapers. Dr. R.E. Permewan speaking in Cornwall at a meeting of the Redruth Council in March 1911 said:

> *South African miners' phthisis has been a terrible scourge to this and neighbouring districts – the tremendous loss in lives and money in this district for which rock drilling in the Transvaal has been responsible and the minor effect of a like kind resulting from similar work in the mines of our own locality.*[125]

By 1911 there were signs that phthisis in South Africa was being tackled by Government legislation. A deputation to the Transvaal Government in 1908 consisting of Mathews, Trewick and J. Coward from the Miners' Association had led to the Government setting up two Commissions to look into phthisis, but had not been prepared to legislate until it had obtained full reports. Two years later an article in the *Cornishman* entitled 'Is the Game worth the Candle?' brought mine life in Johannesburg under close scrutiny, and with Cornish miners on the Rand receiving lower wages and facing greater risks – the average miner's life on the Rand was now being considered as no more than four years – it was asked how many widows and orphans were there left in Cornwall to mourn men who had died from phthisis attributable to working in the gold mines of Johannesburg.[126] A few months later in the *Post* a letter from South Africa commented once again on the large number of Cornish miners to be found in the Johannesburg Hospital suffering from phthisis who were doomed never to leave that institution again.[127]

Despite the defeat in the 1907 Strike the morale of the Miners' Association was boosted by the arrival in South Africa of Tom Mann, one of the heroic figures in trade unionism. Mann had come to prominence in Britain for his role in the great Dock Strike of 1899, leading the fight for the eight-hour day and becoming Secretary of the Independent Labour Party. Between 1901-10 he was in New Zealand and Australia but on his way back to Britain he disembarked at Durban on 21st February 1910 and went direct to Johannesburg, where he met Tom Mathews. Mann found him

> *an exceptionally well informed man and an ardent worker on behalf of the members of his union. He was fully primed with information on the subjects that directly affected the miners' welfare. He supplied me with many facts and statistics, particularly in relation to phthisis.*[128]

At a public meeting in Johannesburg, Mann clearly showed that the miner's lot on the Rand was by no means an enviable one, claiming that the average life of a miner was not more than seven years. Those who used or supervised the use of rock drills were, he said, being brought to the grave in less than the time named and men were working in death traps to get big cheques. Mann considered the industrial magnates as ignorant as pigs, troubled with excessive greed and having little refinement.[129] Sir George Farrar, the leader of the Progressive Party, took exception to the remarks made by Mann concerning the health conditions;he called into question the claim that the average miner's life was less than seven years. It turned out that Mann had based his figures on the *Cornishman* reports which had been supplied by Mathews. Despite a Parliamentary Commission being appointed to investigate and report, the Attorney General of Transvaal had to admit that the figures were correct.[130] Together Mann and Mathews won concessions such as improvements in ventilation, the eight-hour day for the underground miner working a rock drill and compensation in some cases for miners unable to work. However, by the middle of April, Mann, after visiting Kimberley, was at Cape Town, from where he sailed for home. Mathews was left to carry on the struggle.

In the 1910 election in South Africa Mathews stood as the Labour Candidate for Georgetown against Sir George Farrar. Although phthisis was used as an election ploy receiving consideration from all classes and shades of politicians it was felt by the *Cornishman* something more had to be done to protect this annual slaughter of honest Cornish and other miners.[131] Mathews was unsuccessful in the election, which brought together Cape Colony, Natal, Transvaal and the Orange Free State to create the the the Union of South Africa on 31st May 1910. Louis Botha was the new Prime Minister. Although Boer and English may have ended their fight the battle between capital and labour went on.

Despite a bout of pneumonia Mathews was soon back leading the struggle, especially when it seemed the Government was about to reverse its policy with regard to compensation for miners' phthisis. In 1911 a proposed Miners' Phthisis Bill would have given a miner with phthisis £250 compensation (£500 in all, when associated with tuberculosis). Amendments were introduced which not only regulated the amount payable by each mine according to the number of white miners employed – a move which Mathews and the Association believed would limit the number of white men being employed by each mine – but the money granted for compensation was now to be in the form of dole and not in a lump sum.[132] With the miners claiming this to be a breach of faith, the Cornish Labour leaders went into action. Mathews advocated a general strike and William J. Carbis (St. Day), the Association's Organising Secretary, advised the men to down tools. The 1911 strike, however, was more of a skirmish than the battle, which was yet to come. The first Miners' Phthisis Act which followed was an important step towards improving mine conditions and went some way towards compensating those miners who had contracted the deadly disease. When the Chamber of Mines reduced the men's wages from £35 a month to £25 a month Mathews took this to be a ploy by the Chamber to pay for the phthisis compensation.[133] Cornish miners in particular were angered by the insensitive remarks made by O.K. Webber, the President of the Chamber of Mines regarding phthisis, when he referred to Cornishmen coming to South Africa with the germs of disease in their systems. The *Cornishman* was quick to point out that Dr. Haldane's report for 1910 showed that only eight deaths notified were traceable to miners' phthisis in Cornwall during that year.[134] A new Miners' Phthisis Act introduced in 1912 gave a miner whose work was impaired £8 per month not exceeding one year to dependants and £400 where the miner had died from phthisis but the miner had to have been employed underground for a period or periods amounting to at least two of the four years immediately preceding his death.[135] Mathews was soon berating the Phthisis Board (set up to deal with compensation claims) which, according to Mathews did

Chudleigh Brothers store in Johannesburg 1913. This was a rebuild of the 1896 store.

not seem to realise the urgency of some of the cases; claiming that there were men on the verge of starvation having been stopped by doctors from working underground. He gave the instance of a miner who threatened to commit suicide as he was penniless, adding they were helping some of them from T.M.A. funds but could not continue to do so.[136]

In January 1913 it was reported in the *Post* that since the passing of the Miners' Phthisis Compensation Act three years previously, between nineteen hundred and two thousand applications for benefits had been received. The Government, however, had instructed that claims where the deceased miner had died four years before the date of application were not to be accepted, which Mathews considered was unsatisfactory as there were supposed to be no time limits; and thus would cause much disappointment and pain to probably hundreds of families in Cornwall. Indignation was also expressed by Cornish miners who, suffering from phthisis, were being prevented from returning to Cornwall because the boat companies were demanding from £10 to £12 per man for anticipated special doctor's attendance. Amongst those who were refused passage were W. Morgan, a recent President of the Miners' Association, and Mr. George Blight of Camborne.[137]

It was in 1913, with feeling against the Chamber of Mines running high, that battle between labour and capital finally commenced. In May five men at the New Kleinfontein Mine were dismissed for refusing to work extra time. Mathews called the men out, demanded reinstatement of the men and recognition of the Association as a Union. The Kleinfontein incident was really the spark that ignited long term smouldering grievances, for as Tiddy was soon to comment, the failure of the 1907 Strike lay at the root of the trouble.138 The 1913 Strike culminated in the worst violence seen in Johannesburg as miners and police along with soldiers fought pitched battles in the streets after which more than a hundred strikers and innocent bystanders lay dead.

Thousands of miners had gathered in Market Square to attend a meeting but when Mathews tried to disperse the crowd the miners refused and the police charged. The strikers stopped the trams and trains from running – Central Station was set on fire – and no newspapers were published – the premises of the *Star* newspaper were razed to the ground. With the electric power station also taken over by the strikers, Johannesburg had not only come to a halt but had also been plunged into darkness. The next day – Saturday 5th July – saw all control of the town by the civil authorities gone and Imperial Troops brought in to enforce law and order. The windows of Chudleigh Brothers were smashed and Charles Chudleigh was himself lucky to escape death or injury when the strikers rushed the Rand Club, the usual haunt of the mine owners. Someone fired a rifle from the balcony of the club killing at least two strikers and Chudleigh, who had been eating at the club, was wrongly identified as the man with the rifle. Interviewed by the *Rand Daily Mail,* Chudleigh said he heard that his premises were wrecked because he had used a rifle at the Rand Club and shot his fellow mortals which was an infamous falsehood.139

The violence outside the Rand Club only ended when Mathews himself arrived carrying a white flag and arranged a cease fire. The mine owners faced with a possible scenario of flooded mines, rioting natives in the compounds, and the total collapse of the mining industry, which would take many months to restore to normal, persuaded Botha and Smuts to negotiate a settlement on their behalf. A meeting between the Government and Mathews and other Strike leaders at the Carlton Hotel led to one of the key demands – that of reinstating the five men – being immediately agreed upon, with a promise from the Government that other grievances would be investigated. From the balcony of the Carlton Hotel Mathews announced the strike was over.

The strike may have been over but the situation remained tense, especially during the next few days, with the funerals of those strikers who had been shot down by the police and military. Eighteen were buried on Monday 7th July with over thirty thousand people in attendance, the bodies carried on trollies draped in red, the strikers carrying banners inscribed 'In Memory of our friends, murdered

by the Capitalists'.140 The *Transvaal Leader* praised Mathews in particular saying:
*Tom Mathews – was the man who did more than any other to save the
situation. After the Rand Club battle, when passion had been worked up
to fever pitch, when the sight of blood had infuriated the mob, he played a
mans part. He took his life in his hands as he moved about the streets
before even the military were fully aware of the proclamations of an
armistice, and it was largely due to his efforts that after the conference
between the Strike Committee and Generals Botha and Smuts peace was
restored.141*

Although the battle was over very few believed it was the end of fighting
between labour and capital. In Cornwall the news of the strike had been received
with dismay, and the sudden stoppage of the mines was seen as the heaviest blow
which Cornwall had experienced for many years; a halt in remittances was
expected to bring the usual hardship all round. During the strike the *Daily News*
was reported in the *Post* as saying that the Miners Phthisis Board was dealing with
eleven fresh cases of phthisis a day, including Sundays.142 Phthisis was the subject
of an editorial in the *Chronicle*, again reprinted in the *Post,* pointing out that some
ten years earlier – in 1903 – J. Harry Johns, the Cornish engineer, had told the
Chronicle's Editor that the white miners of pre-war days were all dead of
phthisis.143 Although this was a slight exaggeration, it was close to the truth. One
pre-war Cornish miner still alive was Edwin Mill from Pool, a popular shift boss at
the Ferreira Deep, being one of the few men still alive who had a hand in cutting
the first sod and sinking the first shaft. Mill had recently been given surface work
but in September died of phthisis accelerated by heart failure leaving a widow,
Annie née Hart (Tuckingmill) and six children.144

No Cornish miner had died during the strike – even though G.S. Cara of
Penzance had a narrow escape when a bullet grazed his jacket 145 but the strike had
been too much for some. Fred Shackles had seen five men shot dead near him
during the street fighting, and on board the vessel on which he returned home there
were scores of Cornish miners who, like himself, had had enough of the Rand with
Dutchmen taking their places.146

In January 1914 a strike by railway men was effectively crushed by Smuts who
not only arrested the Union leaders including two Labour M.P.s – one of whom
was Frederick Creswell – but had nine of them deported. In April two of the nine
were able to explain the circumstances to a Cornish audience assembled at the
Rechabite Hall, Penzance. Both Waterson and McKerell said 3,000 out of 11,000
miners died from phthisis each year and only proper ventilation would do away
with phthisis but the Chamber of Mines would not allow a new system of
ventilation and the Chamber of Mines was the Government of South Africa. At the
end of the meeting a resolution deploring the deportations and demanding their

Tom Mathews, trade union leader.

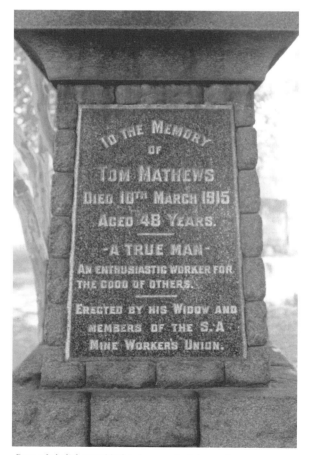

Base of obelisk over Mathew's grave in Johannesburg

readmission to South Africa was carried unanimously.[147]

Out of the eighteen men who had formed the 1907 Strike Committee, by 1914 only four – Mathews, Trewick, Johns and J. Clough – were still alive in South Africa. One had been killed in a mine accident, another had gone to live in Canada and miners' phthisis had claimed the lives of the other twelve, as it was to take that of Mathews.

Despite being blacklisted by the mine owners for his handling of the 1907 Strike, Mathews had been very much a moderate socialist. During the 1913 Strike he was criticised by two of the more radical leaders – Mary Fitzgerald and Archie Crawford – who complained that the Government assassins had yielded nothing except promises of useless inquiries. Mathews considered that what Fitzgerald and Crawford were really after was for the defeat of the Government to become a revolution. Mary Fitzgerald was apparently so angry with Mathews that she wanted the crowd to hang him on a lamp-post. Mathews controlled the situation by letting it be known that he was quite ready to use a revolver he was carrying and not just upon rebellious colleagues either. When in conference with Botha and Smuts at the Carlton Hotel the police appeared. Mathews said afterwards, if one shot had been fired on his people, those two would have been killed.[148]

Mathews has been described as the Cornish Transvaal Champion of the Rights of Man,[149] and not just for the white miner. His attitude towards the native was quite clear, for as he said he would

> *treat the native as well as anybody else. I am socialistic, and perhaps too idealistic, but I believe in treating the Kaffir as a white man. Let him have decent surroundings, fresh air, decent compounds, and treat him underground as he ought to be treated.*[150]

Mathews' greatest service to labour was that throughout his working life he went to great lengths to bring about awareness of the ever-rising death toll from miners' phthisis. The *Transvaal Leader* described Mathews as the true friend of the workers and said it would not forget

> *the gaunt stooping figure, the wild, impressive gesticulation, the tender eyes and voice – growing huskier as the fell disease gripped him fast and faster – yet soft with the sense of tears which made his oratory so compelling and so human.*[151]

Too ill to take part in the 1914 Strike, Mathews died the following year, 10th March 1915, at his home in Johannesburg at Pritchard Street East. He was only 48 years old and left behind a widow, several children and two brothers. At his own request Mathews was buried in the grave of his third brother, who had been killed in a mining accident before the Boer War. His funeral drew vast crowds and a picture of the funeral cortege shows a large carriage pulled by two black horses.[152] *The Rand Daily Mail* said Mathews had been exceedingly well known as a speaker in the causes of Socialism, Trade Unionism and free thought and that he was forever frank, outspoken and forceful.[153]

Before he died, Mathews said, "I have served the Labour movement faithfully these twenty-one years, I hope it is satisfied".[154] It was, and showed it by erecting a memorial for him in Brixton Cemetery, Johannesburg. Apparently just before he died, Mathews, said with a smile, "I'm afraid boys, my heart has gone on strike".[155]

After the First World War 1914-18, during which time the miners had succeeded in obtaining shorter working hours, the price of gold fell but production costs rose. Many mines on the Rand were operating for the first time at a loss. In 1921 white wages were reduced by 3 shillings a shift[156] but it was not enough, and the Chamber of Mines, in order to cut production costs further, set about persuading the Government to remove the legislation which prevented natives from doing many of the semi-skilled jobs. If the President of the Chamber of Mines, Lionel

Phillips and Jan Smuts (who had become Prime Minister following the death of Botha in 1919) had anything in common it was a single desire to break the power of the miners' union. By 1922, when restrictions on semi-skilled jobs for natives ended, and with the coal industry planning to reduce men's wages, the scene was set for yet another major battle between capital and labour. The 1922 Strike came as no surprise. It began on New Year's Day when the coal miners downed tools, to be followed by the white mine workers less than two weeks later. Violence soon became the order of the day and once again a Cornishman played a prominent part in what one Cornish writer calls the most bloody episode in South Africa's industrial history.[157] The 1922 Strike was in many ways hi-jacked by Afrikaner militants, for unlike the two previous strikes of 1907 and 1913 the rank and file miners were mainly Afrikaners with Cornishmen having little influence, except for one – Percy Fisher. Having gone to South Africa in 1914 to avoid conscription at the outbreak of war, Fisher was as extreme as Mathews had been moderate. He had already been behind a strike at the City Deep mine in 1919 and taken part in another at the Consolidated Langlaate mine in 1921, after which he was fined £50 and barred from holding office[158] by his own Union Executive for not having followed union discipline. Percy Fisher was also a Communist, but rather than break with the Union, he and other militants set up a Miners' Council of Action, with Fisher advocating the use of force and violence.[159] He and other strike leaders were arrested. While miners marched through Johannesburg under a banner proclaiming 'Workers of the World Fight and Unite for a White South Africa', elsewhere, at Boksburg for example, a number of strikers were shot dead by the police. The violence escalated and Smuts declared martial law. At Fordsburg the first of many clashes between whites and blacks occurred. With Johannesburg under control of the strikers, Smuts turned to the armed forces equipped with aircraft, artillery and tanks to defeat what was to all intents and purposes an attempt at revolution. Fisher had earlier been released on bail and with the other Council of Action members (including another Cornishman, H. Spendiff) and he prepared to make a stand at their headquarters in Fordsburg. The end of the 1922 Strike came as police and troops restored order and Fisher and Spendiff, rather than give themselves up, died, either at their own hands as the police alleged, or were killed by the troops after the surrender.[160] The strike had lasted some two months and resulted in 153 dead, 534 wounded, 4,750 arrests – including 62 women and 4 children – 650 persons appeared before the courts, 18 were sentenced to death and 4 hanged.[161] It was a far cry from the days of Mathews and negotiated settlements. The strike had not only been a victory for the Government but was also a success for the Chamber of Mines as well. Within a few months the *Cornishman* was already reporting that there were 3,000 fewer whites employed on the Rand mines than before the strike and wages had dropped 30 per cent.[162]

In 1922 the South African Mining Industry Board found that the flow of overseas miners had practically ceased, owing mainly to the fear of miners' phthisis and to the need to pass a strict examination for physical fitness by the Miners' Phthisis Medical Bureau before being permitted to work underground.[163]

The days of the Cornish miner on the Rand may have been over, but the legacy of miners' phthisis remained. In 1926 came welcome news to many mining families in Cornwall. A year earlier the Miners' Phthisis Consolidating Act in South Africa had not only brought together all existing miners' phthisis legislation but had made additional provisions for compensation. Two delegates from South Africa, Williams and Martienssen, arrived in Cornwall to check those entitled to make a claim for compensation. Unfortunately the Act once more set a date – August 1st 1910 – before which claims could not be made, leading to a campaign led by Herbert Thomas, the Editor of the *Cornishman* and *Cornish Telegraph*, to persuade the Transvaal Delegates to take back to South Africa some definite data with regard to families who could prove (first) their genuine poverty, and (second) that their bread-winner was one of the deserving Pioneers who died before August 1st, 1910, and could be proved to have died from the disease contracted in the Transvaal Mines.[164] Thomas sought the support of Joseph Cock, ex-Chairman of Camborne Urban Council, who had worked on the Rand for a number of years and was therefore considered to have some influence over the Transvaal Delegates. Cock, in a letter to Thomas, agreed to do all he could and pointed out that although there was no legal claim, a claim on humane grounds was irresistible, for the Act left out those most deserving and who according to Cock perhaps had, the greatest moral claims namely the dependants of those who from 1888 led the way by sacrificing health and life to the dreaded scourge – gold miners' phthisis.[165] Cock, then appealed for all those families who still held blasting certificates – the proof of an underground miner – to send a copy to him. In no time he received a small avalanche of letters and documents showing that in Cornwall there were still many distressed and deserving people whose breadwinners perished from the dreaded scourge.[166] It was all to no avail for there was to be little if any compensation for those families whose husbands, sons and brothers had died of phthisis before 1910. In 1927 A. K. Hamilton Jenkin's, *The Cornish Miner*, was published and in one memorable passage he paid tribute to all those Cornishmen who died:

> *The name 'South Africa' is cut deep in the heart of mining Cornwall, not so much engraved with an instrument of steel but as jagged and ghastly as the malignant quartz that hid the gold and filled the lungs of the Cornish Pioneers.*[167]

Porthledden a house built at Cape Cornwall, St. Just by Francis Oats.

NOTES – CHAPTER EIGHT

1. *MINING JOURNAL*, 15th APRIL 1905 p. 414

2. Hollowood, *CORNISH ENGINEERS* p. 54

3. *CORNISHMAN*, 24th APRIL 1902

4. *IBID.*, 7th AUGUST 1902

5. *C.P.M.N.*, 23rd OCTOBER 1902

6. *CORNISHMAN*, 30th AUGUST 1906. In 1902 the Redruth Union had 260 inmates against 246 of last year and out paupers 1, 545 against 1, 486 the previous year – giving the total number of paupers as 1, 805. See *CORNUBIAN*, 28th NOVEMBER 1902

7. *CORNISHMAN*, 11th SEPTEMBER 1902

8. Gillian Burke and Peter Richardson, *THE PROFITS OF DEATH : A COMPARATIVE STUDY OF MINERS' PHTHISIS IN CORNWALL AND THE TRANSVAAL, 1876-1918*. A paper given to the South Africa Seminar at Queen Elizabeth House, University of Oxford, in November 1977.

9. *C.P.M.N.*, 24th JULY 1902

10. *IBID.*, 4th SEPTEMBER 1902

11. *IBID.*, 11th SEPTEMBER 1902

12. Letcher, *GOLD MINES OF SOUTHERN AFRICA* p. 130

13. *CORNISHMAN*, 5th FEBRUARY 1903

14. *C.P.M.N.*, 4th JUNE 1903

15. *CORNUBIAN*, 5th JUNE 1903 p. 4

16. *C.P.M.N.*, 14th MAY 1903

17. *IBID.*, 4th JUNE 1903

18. *IBID.*, 17th SEPTEMBER 1903. The 11 Commissioners examined 187 miners certified as suffering from phthisis – 91 per cent had been working rock drills – the majority had worked 6. 4 years on the machines. It was pointed out that accurate figures were almost impossible regarding native labour. *IBID.*, 10th SEPTEMBER 1903.

19. Hannan, *TUCKER – LETTERS* p. 8

20. *IBID.*, p. 29 According to the *POST* in 1905 it cost an unmarried miner £15 a month to live on the Rand and a married miner with three children £24 a month. *C.P.M.N.*, 27th APRIL 1905

21. *C.P.M.N.*, 28th DECEMBER 1905

22. *IBID.*, 31st MARCH 1904

23. Information about the mail boats and life at Pendeen comes from correspondence with Hugh Miners of St. Just. His father was a Post Office sorter at the turn of the century.

24. Norway, *HIGHWAYS AND BYWAYS OF DEVON AND CORNWALL.* p. 317

25. The staff at the Post Office Headquarters, St. Martins Le Grand, were most helpful, but searches for remittances to Cornwall were barren.

26. *C.P.M.N.*, 28th DECEMBER 1905

27. Rowse, *THE CORNISH IN AMERICA* p.166

28. *C.P.M.N.*, 12th MARCH 1903

29. *CORNISHMAN*, 3rd NOVEMBER 1904

30. *IBID.*, 20th APRIL 1905

31. D. Humphries & D. G. Thomas, *BENONI SON OF MY SORROW, (1968)* p. 34

32. *CORNUBIAN*, 14th MAY 1904. A. Pengelly was most likely the late Manager of the New Kleinfontein mine – he retired in 1898 and returned to Cornwall.

33. This was confirmed by at least one miner see *C.P.M.N.*, 14th MAY 1903. Hannan in a postscript to Tucker's, *LETTERS*, puts forward the interesting theory as to why Tucker grew a moustache – that it helped prevent dust entering the throat – a theory put forward earlier by a Fellow of the Royal College of Surgeons at an Inquiry held in 1862 at St. Austell.

34. *C.P.M.N.*, 19th MAY 1904

35. *IBID.*, 16th JUNE 1904

36. *THE SOUTH AFRICA MINERS, COMMERCE & INDUSTRIES JOURNAL,* 21st MAY 1904 p. 226

37. *C.P.M.N.*, 5th JANUARY 1905

38. *IBID.*, 9th FEBRUARY 1905

39. *IBID.*, 5th APRIL 1906

40. *IBID.*, 27th APRIL 1905

41. *CORNISHMAN*, 14th FEBRUARY 1907

42. *IBID.*, 21st FEBRUARY 1907

43. *C.P.M.N.*, 28th SEPTEMBER 1907 Emily Hobhouse had been in South Africa since 1905, living in the Transvaal. She had considerable political influence among the Boer leaders, for not only was she a close friend of the ex-President of the Orange Free State (M. T. Steyn) and his wife but she was also a constant visitor to Jan Smuts and his wife at Pretoria. When the Het Volk Party won the election it appeared that Sir Richard Solomon was the main choice for Prime Minister until ex-President Steyn sent Emily to see Louis Botha and she cajoled and persuaded him into accepting nomination. See Fry, *EMILY HOBHOUSE*, p. 250

44. *CORNISHMAN*, 21st FEBRUARY 1907

45. *IBID.*, 14th MARCH 1907 There were over 5, 000 Australians living along the Rand in 1904 – bringing with them a strong Trade Union tradition and marked antipathies to Asians and Coolie labour. They came to play an important part in the history of South Africa's Trade Unions and Labour Party. See Brian Kennedy, *A TALE OF TWO MINING CITIES: JOHANNESBURG AND BROKEN HILL 1885-1925* (MELBOURNE 1984) p. 2

46. *C.P.M.N.*, 7th FEBRUARY 1907

47. *CORNISHMAN*, 6th JUNE 1907

48. *SOUTH AFRICAN MINING JOURNAL*, 3rd SEPTEMBER 1892 . p. 862

49. *C.P.M.N.*, 16th MAY 1907

50. *TRANSVAAL LEADER*, 4th MAY 1907

51. *C.P.M.N.*, 20th JUNE 1907

52. *IBID.*, 4th JULY 1907

53. *TRANSVAAL LEADER*, 8th MAY 1907

54. *IBID.*, 4th MAY 1907

55. Chilvers, *OUT OF THE CRUCIBLE*, p. 188-189

56. *TRANSVAAL LEADER*, 21st MAY 1907

57. *CORNISHMAN*, 22nd AUGUST 1907

58. *TRANSVAAL LEADER*, 18th MAY 1907, THE AFRICAN WORLD claimed Kitto had inspected over 2, 000 mines and was known and respected throughout the length and breadth of the Rand. *CORNISHMAN*, 28th FEBRUARY 1907

59. *TRANSVAAL LEADER*, 28th MAY 1907 see also *CORNISHMAN*, 13th JUNE 1907 It was claimed by one miner any man with one horse-power brain can learn to work a rock drill in three months. However, in an article called Training Rock Drillers, training apparently took two years. See *C.P.M.N.*, 18th JULY 1907

60. *CORNISHMAN*, 28th FEBRUARY 1907

61. *TRANSVAAL LEADER*, 28th MAY 1907

62. *IBID.*, 13th MAY 1907

63. *IBID.*, 21st MAY 1907

64. *CORNISHMAN*, 6th JUNE 1907 George Albu became Sir George Albu in 1912 – he died in 1935

65. *TRANSVAAL LEADER*, 18th MAY 1907

66. Elaine N. Katz, *A TRADE UNION ARISTOCRACY, A HISTORY OF WHITE WORKERS IN THE TRANSVAAL AND THE GENERAL STRIKE OF 1913* (Johannesburg 1976) p. 137

67. *TRANSVAAL LEADER*, 21st MAY 1907

68. *C.P.M.N.*, 30th MAY 1907

69. *IBID.*, 27th JUNE 1907

70. *TRANSVAAL LEADER*, 24th SEPTEMBER 1907. Boers were also appointed rapidly to posts in the Customs, Post Office and Police see *CORNISHMAN*, 10th SEPTEMBER 1908

71. *TRANSVAAL LEADER*, 23rd MAY 1907

72. *IBID.*, 25th MAY 1907

73. *IBID.*, 28th MAY 1907

74. *IBID.*, 4th JUNE 1907

75. *IBID.*, 6th JUNE 1907

76. *IBID.*, 19th JUNE 1907

77. *IBID.*, 16th JULY 1907

78. *CORNUBIAN*, 13th JUNE 1907

79. *C.P.M.N.*, 1st AUGUST 1907

80. *IBID.*, 11th JULY 1907

81. The Commission consisted of P. Whiteside (Chairman), F. H. P. Creswell, M. Franche and C. H. Spencer.

82. *TRANSVAAL LEADER*, 14th AUGUST 1907

83. *IBID.*, 14th SEPTEMBER 1907 Employment was also given to miners by the Johannesburg Town Council to connect houses to the sewage scheme. Twenty gangs of six men on piece work. *CORNISHMAN*, 17th OCTOBER 1907. The scheme plus relief work was finished by April the following year. *IBID.*, 9th APRIL 1908

84. *CORNISHMAN*, 10th OCTOBER 1907

85. *TRANSVAAL LEADER*, 9th OCTOBER 1907

86. C.P.M.N., 20th JUNE 1907, *IBID.*, 27th JUNE 1907. This issue also reported that another Cornishman from Four Lanes had hidden from strikers but been taken ill and died as a result. He was not named. *CORNUBIAN*, 4th JULY 1907. Josiah Angove in *TRANSVAAL SPECTATOR* suggested that the death of Richards was the work of Chinese coolies who took advantage of the strike to take revenge for some injury done to them . See *C.P.M.N.*, 1st AUGUST 1907

87. *CORNUBIAN*, In 1905 William Hosken had learned just how lucky he had been to escape with his life prior to the Boer War. It was discovered when repairs were being carried out on his former house Trelawny at Jeppestown, that the house had been undermined with four dynamite cartridges. It was only the failure of the fuses – one

fuse had burned right down to the cap – that had prevented the house from being blown apart.

88. *TRANSVAAL LEADER*, 28th AUGUST 1907. This ill-feeling towards Cornish miners could also be found in the States. Only two months earlier, following a strike in Montana, the *TRIBUNE REVIEW*, of Butte City claimed that it had been a mistake not to clear out the Cousin Jacks. *CORNISHMAN*, 13th JUNE 1907

89. *C.P.M.N.*, 2nd JANUARY 1908

90. *IBID.*, 6th AUGUST 1908

91. *IBID.*, 9th JANUARY 1908. The Gordon Drill was made by the American firm Ingersoll – Gordon Drills used at the Ferreira mine, however, proved faulty. See *MINING JOURNAL*, 6th JUNE 1908

92. *CORNISHMAN*, 8th AUGUST 1908

93. *C.P.M.N.*, 2nd JANUARY 1908

94. *CORNISHMAN*, 7th JANUARY 1909

95. *IBID.*, 30th SEPTEMBER 1909

96. *IBID.*, 14th APRIL 1910

97. *C.P.M.N.*, 17th MARCH 1910

98. *IBID.*, 23rd FEBRUARY 1911

99. *CORNISHMAN*, 23rd JANUARY 1918

100. *C.P.M.N.*, 8th NOVEMBER 1906

101. See Hannan, *TRAVELS AND HEARTACHES OF A MINING FAMILY* for full story.

102. Burke & Richardson, *PROFITS OF DEATH* p. 163. Rowe has also shown the effect of phthisis on Cornish miners in America, quoting the Editor of the Butte City *TRIBUNE REVIEW* who claimed in May 1908 that a dozen or more had died and added that men were dying of it almost daily. Rowe, *THE HARD ROCK MEN* p 243

103. *C.P.M.N.*, 28th JANUARY 1909

104. *IBID.*, 4th FEBRUARY 1909

105. *IBID.*, 24th NOVEMBER 1910

106. *IBID.*, 15th APRIL 1909

107. *CORNISHMAN*, 5th JANUARY 1911

108. *IBID.,* 24th MARCH 1910

109. *IBID.,* 15th MAY 1913

110. *IBID.,* 28th AUGUST 1913

111. *CORNUBIAN,* 25th APRIL 1907 – the account in the *POST* – published the same day differs slightly, claiming it was Harvey's last shift before leaving for Cornwall.

112. *C.P.M.N.,* 21st FEBRUARY 1907

113. *IBID.,* 2nd MAY 1907

114. *C.P.M.N.,* 23rd JUNE 1910. There followed some confusion afterwards, when another miner with the same name returned to Camborne and died. There was much publicity when the Harry Bennetts who had been awarded the medal turned up in a South African press office, very much alive!

115. *CORNISHMAN,* 2nd FEBRUARY 1911

116. *IBID.,* 11th JANUARY 1912

117. *C.P.M.N.,* 9th JANUARY 1908

118. *CORNUBIAN,* 30th MAY 1907

119. *C.P.M.N.,* 3rd AUGUST 1911

120. *CORNISHMAN,* 29th FEBRUARY 1912 For more on Richard Thomas see Chapter 9 *ONE & ALL in SOUTH AFRICA.*

121. *C.P.M.N.,* 28th SEPTEMBER 1908

122. *IBID.,* 9th MAY 1912

123. *IBID.,* 11th DECEMBER 1913

124. *CORNUBIAN,* 25th MAY 1911

125. *C.P.M.N.,* 9th MARCH 1911

126. *CORNISHMAN,* 3rd FEBRUARY 1910

127. *C.P.M.N.,* 9th JUNE 1910

128. Tom Mann, *MEMOIRS,* (LONDON 1967) p. 197 – When Keir Hardie had arrived in Johannesburg two years earlier he had been pelted with rotten eggs due to his anti – Chinese Slavery views. *TRANSVAAL LEADER* 18th FEBRUARY 1908

129. *CORNISHMAN,* 12th MAY 1910

130. *IBID.,* 19th MAY 1910

131. *IBID.,* 28th SEPTEMBER 1910

132. *IBID.,* 11th MAY 1911

133. *IBID.,* 21st MAY 1912

134. *IBID.,* 6th JUNE 1912

135. *IBID.,* 15th AUGUST 1912

136. *TRANSVAAL LEADER,* 10th AUGUST 1912

137. *C.P.M.N.,* 2nd JANUARY 1913

138. *IBID.,* 17th JULY 1913

139. *CORNISHMAN,* 7th AUGUST 1913. A. P. Cartwright says it was a completely unfounded rumour that Mr Chudleigh .... had killed Mary Fitzgerald, one of the strike leaders but because of that his shop was destroyed. See Cartwright *THE GOLD MINES* p. 168.

140. *C.P.M.N.,* 10th JULY 1913 A telegram received by the paper claimed that no Cornishmen had been killed or wounded in the Rand Strike. The following weeks paper confirmed this. See *IBID.,* 17th JULY 1913

141. *TRANSVAAL LEADER,* 11th MARCH 1915

142. *C.P.M.N.,* 10th JULY 1913

143. *CORNISHMAN,* 7th AUGUST 1913

144. *C.P.M.N.,* 11th SEPTEMBER 1913

145. *CORNISHMAN,* 31st JULY 1913

146. *C.P.M.N.,* 28th AUGUST 1913

147. *CORNISHMAN,* 30th APRIL 1914

148. *I.B.I.D.,* 30th APRIL 1914

149. *TRANSVAAL LEADER* 13th MARCH 1915

150. Katz, *A TRADE UNION ARISTOCRACY* p.271-272

151. *TRANSVAAL LEADER,* 15th MARCH 1915

152. *I.B.I.D.,* 13th MARCH 1914

153. *C.P.M.N.,* 22nd APRIL 1915

154. Simons, *CLASS AND COLOUR* p.189

155. *TRANSVAAL LEADER,* 11th MARCH 1915

156. *CORNISHMAN,* 21st JUNE 1921

157. Blackwell, *FROM A DARK STREAM* p.157

158. Simons, *CLASS AND COLOUR,* p. 273

159. *IBID.,* p. 286

160. *Ibid.,* p. 296 A Cornishman Charles
Blackwell was one of a number of
volunteers to guard the Johannesburg
Power Station – see Blackwell, *FROM A
DARK STREAM* p. 158-159

161. Lacour-Gayet, *A HISTORY OF SOUTH
AFRICA.* See also Simons, *CLASS AND
COLOUR* p. 296 – the figures vary slightly
but are in more detail.

162. *CORNISHMAN,* 16th AUGUST 1922

163. Knowles, *ECONOMIC DEVELOPMENT
OF THE OVERSEAS EMPIRE VOL. III* p.
239-240

164. *CORNISHMAN,* 3rd FEBRUARY 1926

165. *IBID.,* 3rd FEBRUARY 1926

166. *IBID.,* 17th FEBRUARY 1926

167. Jenkin, *THE CORNISH MINER* p.330. A
similar phrase was first used by H. Pascoe
(Truro) who gave a lecture at Redruth in
1924. See *CORNISHMAN & CORNISH
TELEGRAPH* 30th JANUARY 1924.

CHAPTER NINE

ONE AND ALL IN SOUTH AFRICA
1902-40

The fine motto of the Duchy of Cornwall – 'One & All' – should be the
watchword of the people of South Africa.[1]

J. Thompson.
(Mayor of Johannesburg 1908)

As the gold mines dominate the Rand, so the Cornish once dominated Johannesburg. With a strong community spirit it was not surprising that the Cornish Association on the Rand, which had folded with the advent of the Boer War, was reformed. The two main architects of the revival were Harold Spencer (Falmouth) and William Tonkin (St. Mary's Scilly Isles) who became the new President. Following a meeting held in the Grand National Hotel, Johannesburg, in October 1905 the Cornish Association of South Africa set about carrying on from where it left off – organising social events, calling on the sick and needy and preserving a Cornish identity.[2] It was to grow into a much larger Association than the one that existed before the Boer war.

The Cornish Association on the Rand became a recognised society once more when it celebrated its first Annual Dinner at the Wanderers Hall, Johannesburg in March 1906. Over 400 Cornish people attended. The aims of the Association were to promote social intercourse between Cornishmen on the Rand, to relieve any genuine cases of distress and to protect the interests of Cornish on or visiting the Rand.[3] The Association consisted of a number of local branches which included Fordsburg, Germiston, Roodepoort, Krugersdorp, Randfontein, Benoni, Denver and Johannesburg.

Fordsburg was very much a focal point for the Cornish on the Rand especially as the Ferreira mine was in its vicinity. One newspaper report said:

Residing in the neighbourhood of Fordsburg one is struck with the large number of people who have come from St. Just and Pendeen and are residing in this district, the majority of married men having their wives and families out with them.

On one mine there are three shift bosses from Pendeen, the mine Captain and Underground Manager are both Cornishmen. The underground man at the Robinson gold mine is a Cornishman, as is that at the Ferreira – scores of other instances could be given.[4]

Anyone seeking confirmation of past relatives residing at Fordsburg would do well to consult Dickason's *Cornish Immigrants to South Africa* in which he has identified nearly fifty Cornish people residing at Fordsburg in 1908 and over eighty more who were residing there in 1909. The Fordsburg Cornish Association was the only branch, it appears, to build its own club house, the opening ceremony in 1909 being attended by Tom Mathews and William Hosken, who was President of the Cornish Association that year.[5]

One Cornish tradition in Johannesburg that had survived the war was the gathering of a Cornish choir at Christmas. In 1902 it was well-celebrated by the Cornish miners at the Ferreira Deep mine, who spent Christmas morning at the mine singing T. Merritt's well known carols and the afternoon in Johannesburg at the Forfarshire Boarding House which was run by Mo May of Pool.[6]

In 1904 Tiddy remarked how a newly arrived Cornish miner in Johannesburg on walking down Pritchard Street could easily have been forgiven if he had thought for one moment he was in Trelowarren Street, Camborne. Standing under Chudleigh Bros balcony he would have heard the Fordsburg Cornish Carol singers, led by Andrew Birch (Penzance), which had earlier sung outside a number of houses belonging to Cornish people in the suburbs of Jeppestown and Fordsburg.[7]

On Christmas Day 1906 it rained all day in Johannesburg but not enough to dampen the spirits of the Cornish choir which once again sang in Pritchard Street, the long and wide street being packed by thousands of persons. This time the choir was conducted by Andrew Stevens (St. Erth). Carols sung were again selected from Thomas Merritt's popular collection including *Angelic Hosts, Hail Sacred Day, Hark the Glad Sound* and *Come let us all with one accord.* The singing apparently brought the highest commendations from the most critical of Johannesburg's musicians. On Christmas night the choir sang at the President Wesleyan Church, on Boxing Day at the Village Main Wesleyan Church and on Saturday night at Anderson Street Wesleyan Church. At the first and last venues the churches were packed but the audience was smaller on the Boxing Day evening due to incessant rain which began in the afternoon and continued until midnight. The report in the *Cornishman* entitled *How Rand Cornishmen spent Christmas* had been compiled by Richard Williams, a reporter who had worked both with the *Post* and *Cornishman* for thirteen years before moving to South Africa in November 1905 to join the Johannesburg newspaper *The Star*.[8]

Cornish musicians were very much to the fore. Arthur Richards was a celebrated trombone player and a former member of the Camborne Town Band; on a least one occasion he was mentioned as having raised money in Johannesburg for the Band enabling them to buy new uniforms.[9] In another newspaper report Richards and Harry Phillips, a cornet player and former member of Truro Town Band, were listed as being members of South Africa's Imperial Band.[10] William Matthews, won a prize as boy soprano at the Johannesburg Eisteddfod in 1907 and went on to carve a career for himself as a singer, musical comedy star broadcaster and an actor of note under the name of Billy Matthews.[11] Two other popular musicians at this time were Aldrovand Maynard and Anna Levington-Vincent. Maynard was an amateur tenor singer from Tuckingmill, his grandfather had been a Mine Captain at East Pool. Having obtained a reputation as a fine solo singer with the Wesleyan church choir at Tuckingmill Maynard left Cornwall for South Africa in 1902, singing first with the Observatory Wesleyan Choir at the Cape and then in Johannesburg, becoming a member of the Fordsburg Wesleyan Choir and later the Pretoria Wesleyan Chapel Choir, the Precentor of which was Mr. Tregarthen of Perranporth. Although Maynard was to return to Cornwall in 1906 where he delighted large audiences in Cornwall and Devon, he later returned to South Africa where his services were in constant demand, not only by Cornishmen but by every section of society.[12]

Anna Levington-Vincent came from an old and respected Cornish family – Williams of St. Ives. When only sixteen years old Anna Williams possessed a soprano voice of unusual power and tone. She was a member of the St. Ives Choral Society and St. Ives Wesleyan Band of Hope choirs and her name became a household word not only in Cornwall but in the West of England. In 1896 she joined her husband George Levington-Vincent who was then an engineer at the Salisbury & Jubilee mine. Within two years she won first prize at an Eisteddfod held at Johannesburg.[13] During the Boer War, Anna Levington-Vincent was the principal singer at all the leading theatres and public halls in Durban and especially during the period of rejoicing after the war. Her services were constantly sought after by the churches and charitable institutions, and they were always given free. With her husband an active member of the Johannesburg branch of the Cornish Association her voice was often heard at the miners' concerts all along the Reef, as well as at Masonic gatherings and public functions, many of which were held at the Carlton Hotel.[14]

Robert Hainsworth Heath a well known musician on the Rand died from pneumonia in 1912. An organist of St. Mary's Church, Johannesburg, he was best known for his work on Cornish carol music and for having composed the song *Kitty Cornish*.[15]

As in music so too in sport did the Cornish excel. Rugby has always been very much Cornwall's forte and therefore it is not surprising that along with their mining skills the Cornish took the game with them to South Africa. Goggan, Davey, Thomas, Pearce and Hosking were all notable rugby footballers, most of them playing for the Mines Rugby Football Team. The Captain of the Mines team was Jimmy Davey, who had been 16 years old when he played in Redruth's First Team during the 1898-99 Season. He gained his County Cap and played regularly for Cornwall for four seasons before he went to South Africa in 1902, a move which many believed lost him the chance of winning an international cap. In 1904

Cornish Association of Transvaal carol book c.1908.

he was appointed Captain of the Mines Team, leading it to victory in the 1905 Grand Challenge Cup. On being selected to play for the Transvaal in the Currie Cup Tournament at East London it was said that if he had been in the country for more than five years he would have been selected to play for South Africa itself.[16] Playing alongside Davey in the Mines Team were A. Thomas, (known as Spud),

Eathorne, Rich, Job, Pearce (all Redruth), Odgers, Rodda and Peters (all Camborne). If Davey was considered to be the best half back in Transvaal rugby then Peters was without a doubt the best forward. Jack Peters had played rugby, first for his home town Camborne, where he worked as a fitter for the Climax Rock Drill Company of R. Stephens, and then, on moving to South Africa, for the Crown Reef Mine rugby team. Peters and Sam Hosking were part of the Crown Reef team that won the Blane Cup in 1899. Peters, who served in the Imperial Light Infantry during the Boer War, returned home to play rugby once more for Camborne and Cornwall. In 1903 he was back in South Africa playing for the Mines Team and he, like Davey, was selected to play for Transvaal in the Currie Cup Tournament. After the 1905 season he married and returned home once more playing rugby for Camborne, Devonport Albion and for Cornwall against New Zealand. Returning to South Africa he was again selected to play for Transvaal in the Currie Cup Tournament being then considered the best forward in the Transvaal. Unfortunately in 1907 he died following an operation for appendicitis at the Modderfontein Hospital.[17]

Rugby was very much on the minds of the Cornish during Christmas 1906 because the South African rugby team was in England and scheduled to play Cornwall. News of the result of the match came during a social evening organised by the Germiston Cornish Association on 22nd December, at the Church School Hall in Victoria Street. When the Germiston Chairman H.J. Tonkin read out the message from Cornwall giving the final result of the Cornwall v South Africa match at Redruth as 9 points to 3 in Cornwall's favour all order was forgotten for a time, everyone cheering the Cornish and South African teams as true sportsmen.[18] The result of the match was also posted in the Central News Agency, Commissioner Street at about 9-30pm the same evening and the cheering from hundreds of Cornishmen who had assembled was deafening. The Cornish Association sent a telegram to Cornwall addressed to Thomas, Dolcoath Mine, Camborne giving their congratulations on the result of the match.[19]

Other notable Cornish rugby players in South Africa at this time were John Hosking (Redruth) who played for the City and Suburban Mine Team, A. Lawry, a Redruth and County rugby forward who played for the Randfontein team and T. Richards, A. Edwards, Fred Rodda, B. Thomas and W.C. Beckerleg who were all members of Randfontein United, and winners of the Dewar Cup and Shield in 1909.[20] In 1912, the team, now known as the Randfontein Cornish Association Rugby Football Club, was again winner of the Dewar Shield and Sir Abe Bailey Cup. Captain of the team in 1913 was Harry Rich, who along with his brother Nick had played for Cornwall before coming to South Africa in 1905. Unfortunately, two weeks after leading his team to the Bailey Cup Final he died from pneumonia, his funeral being one of the largest ever seen at Randfontein.[21] The previous year it had been considered:

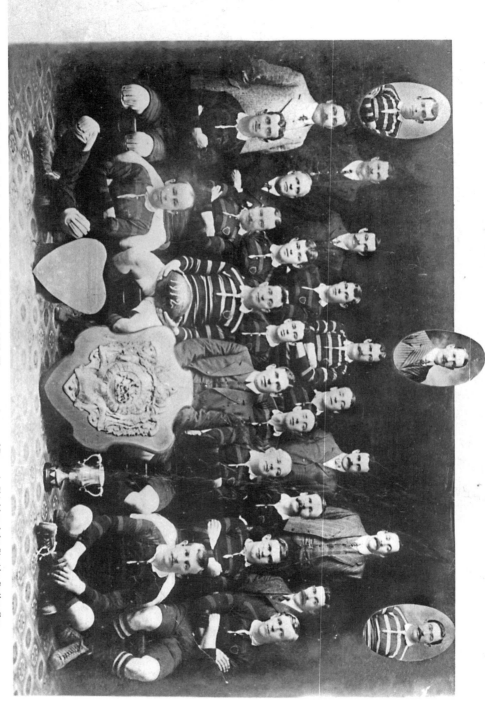

Randfontein Cornish Association Rugby Football Club 1912. They were winners of Dewar's Shield and the Sir Abe Bailey Cup.

*it would not be an exaggeration to state that the proud position at present occupied by South African Rugby Footballers has been attained to not a considerable degree by the assistance of Cornish players. Previous to the war and since the names of Thomas and Davey (halves) of Redruth; Eathorne (back) of the same town, the Roddas and Odgers of Camborne, Brays of Penzance etc., were on the lips of every footballer and supporter of the Rugby code in this country. Those undoubtedly did excellent work for Rugby Football in the Transvaal and their names will for a long time to come be associated with the advancements of the game in this country. Today we have amongst us, playing for the East Rand Proprietary Mines, a Cornishman Tommy White of St. Just. He is stand off half for the E.R.P.M who are the champions of the Transvaal.*22

When not playing rugby the Cornish could be found playing cricket and rivalry was strong between the miners, each of the Mines teams having a good quota of Cornishmen as reports in the newspapers testify.

At Cape Town Sid Smith (Gwinear), a Cornish jockey, won £800 in a steeplechase with a raw horse finding the obstacles trifles when compared with the banks and ditches of rugged old Cornwall. Smith afterwards was struck down with dysentery leaving for Cornwall a skeleton and claiming South Africa was not a white man's country. He added, rather dolefully, that with health a man could make money on the track.23

All Cornish in South Africa, and indeed in Cornwall, were no doubt proud when the heavyweight wrestling championship of the world was won by a Cornishman at Fordsburg in 1904. A crowd of some 200 people saw 49 year old Bill Irwen, veteran from Tavistock, dressed in the picturesque Cornish costume lose after 90 minutes to Phil Mitchell from Redruth, the match coincidentally taking place in the Redruth Hotel.24

Wrestling was very much a Cornish sport and in 1905 the *Transvaal Leader* noted that it had been indulged in before the Boer War and was now being resuscitated along the Rand, the reason being that a number of the best known exponents of the Cornish style had returned from a holiday trip to the old country where they had been adding to their reputations.25 A Wrestling Tournament was held at the Stars & Stripes Hotel, Fordsburg, now owned by two Cornishmen – Trezona and Gendle. Fifteen wrestlers took part under the supervision of a Committee consisting of W. Martin, John T. Bray and T. Peters. William Oliver (Lanner) was referee, assisted by two sticklers, R. Nankervis and W.C. Oats. James Triggs (Redruth), who had won the County Championship at Penzance, lost to an American. However, a year later in another tournament at the same venue, he regained his position as Heavyweight Champion of South Africa.26 Triggs had worked as a miner in Colorado, Michigan and Arizona before coming to South

Africa to work at the Boksburg mine and Robinson Deep, where, another Cornish wrestler – George Trudgeon (St. Austell) worked.[27] Wrestling tournaments were also organised at the Port Elizabeth Hotel by Martie Dunstan, the former owner of the Stars & Stripes and a report in October 1906 told how Tit Wills (Lanner) won a belt and £40 in a competition which the year before had been won by J. Rudd, who because he had returned to

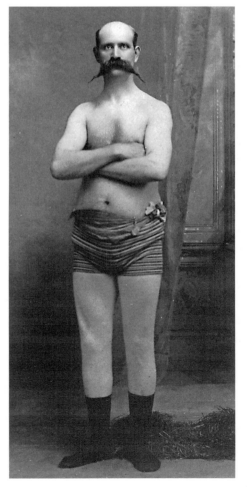

Cornish Wrestlers. Above, Bill Irwen from Tavistock, left, Phil Mitchell from Redruth.

Cornwall was unable to defend the belt.[28] Christmas Eve 1906 saw an eagerly-awaited contest between Tit Wills and Tom H. Thomas of Camborne. The referee on that occasion was Almond Giles, the champion lightweight wrestler of England, America and South Africa. Two other famous Cornish wrestlers, R. Jackson and Lukies acted as sticklers and the contest, which lasted well over an hour, was hard fought with Thomas eventually winning.[29] Other famous Cornish wrestlers in South Africa were A. L. Knuckey, P. Mitchell, W. Irwin, J. Murton and S. Pedlar, and although there are very few accounts of wrestling matches to be found in the newspapers, in 1910 a report claimed that Cornish wrestling on the Rand was as popular as it ever was.[30] W. Littlejohn (Gunnislake) was then the Heavyweight Champion of South Africa and Sam Ham (Condurrow) the Middleweight Champion. Ham was eventually beaten, not once but twice by Alfred (Barney) Williams, a young Cornish miner from Beacon.[31] Referee, William Oliver, who had originally worked in Butte City, Montana, before going to South Africa, eventually returned home to Cornwall where for a time he ran the Six Bells Hotel, Helston. When he died in 1907 he was described as one of the few survivors of the old school of Cornish wrestlers.[32] He left behind a widow in Cornwall, a son in South Africa and three daughters, at least one of whom was living in Butte City, U.S.A.

With the 1907 Strike and the animosity between labour and management, as well as the large number of Cornish miners who returned home that year, the Cornish Association on the Rand experienced a marked fall in membership. However, the concert, put on by the Germiston Branch of the Cornish Association at Christmas 1907 was well attended. Richard Hoskens' excellent voice singing *Trelawny* and *One & All* brought down the house. Hosken's rich baritone voice was considered to be of the best.[33] Unlike his brother William he had refused to enter politics although as a member of the Victorian Wesleyan Church, Jeppestown, he had filled every important position open to a layman, including that of circuit steward. As well as being Chairman of Johannesburg's Philharmonic Society he was also keen on shooting, often disappearing for a week's shooting expedition. Hosken was also a keen tennis player and like many Cornishmen could be frequently seen on the Wanderer's ground on Saturdays watching the Rugby.[34]

The youngest of the three Hosken brothers – Samuel or Sam as he was better known, – as well as being a member of the mining and commercial firm of Messrs. Wm. Hosken & Co was also a staunch Wesleyan and had a rich baritone voice Like his brother Richard he often performed songs at social functions. He was a prominent figure at the various Cornish Association meetings.[35] Sam was also a member of the Witwatersrand Agricultural Association. Even more prominent in agriculture was Sam's cousin and namesake – Samuel Hosken. When he first joined his cousins in South Africa, Samuel managed Sam's farm – Grasmere – for a while before farming his own land at Balfour Farm, Transvaal, where he became a successful maize grower. The *Cornishman* in June, 1908, reported that he had been personally congratulated by Premier General Botha and that his farm was to be observed by the Agriculture Department for two years to analyse the methods of so successful a farmer. At the local Heildelburg show that year his seventeen exhibits had won some fourteen prizes,[36] and another report in 1916 stated that Hosken had practically swept the board in the low veldt section of maize growing at the Witwatersrand Show.[37] The Championship prize for mealie growing went to another Cornish farmer S.J. Moon. who had emigrated to South Africa in 1880 from Connor Downs. At first he managed a 40,000 acre farm for a Joseph Baynes but when William Hosken, who had purchased Thorner Farm in the Camperdown Magisterial District in Natal, decided to let it, Moon took on the lease. He later bought the 1,200 acre farm from Hosken and added to it a further 1,200 acres – it was then valued at £20,000. Moon was a member of the Natal Royal Agricultural Society being on the Society's Executive Committee and serving as its Vice President. He was President of Camperdown's Agricultural Society and was reckoned to be one of the authorities on mealie growing in South Africa, often

being a judge at the agricultural shows where his mealie expertise was much in demand. Moon was a Justice of the Peace and was considered a man of integrity and honour and a credit to the country that gave him birth.[38]

The most successful Cornish farmer in South Africa without a doubt was Hugh Lanion Hall. He built up one of South Africa's largest family farming enterprises. Today the firm of H. L. Hall & Sons Ltd., which celebrated its centenary in 1990, is a leader in citrus and sub-tropical fruit processing and employs some 7,000 people on their farms on which the company has established schools, clinics and houses for its workforce. Hall celebrated his Golden Wedding in 1938 and before his death in March 1940 wrote his autobiography entitled *I've Reaped My Mealies.*

Hugh Lanion Hall, Farmer (1858-1940)

At Kimberley, after Michell, Francis Oats was the most important Cornishman. As a Life Director of De Beers, Oats had presided over many meetings of the De Beers shareholders and in politics, as M. P. for the Namaqualand region, was on equal footing with Michell. Oats, unlike Michell but like Rhodes, had the kudos of having remained throughout the Siege of Kimberley. Rhodes (along with his partners Beit and Barnato).[39] had also held Oats in high regard. After the war Oats, on behalf of De Beers, made a visit to British New Guinea and the Brazilian Diamond Fields during which, unfortunately, he was struck down with malaria.[40] It was this which prevented him from attending the 13th Annual Cornish Dinner at the Gladstone Hotel, Kimberley, on New Year's Eve 1902. The Dinner was chaired by Kimberley's other notable Cornishman – Thomas Quentrall.

In 1903 at the 15th Annual General Meeting of De Beers, following a motion put forward by Francis Oats, £10,000 was granted for higher education in the Cape Colony: £5,000 each to South Africa College, Cape Town and Rhodes University, Grahamstown.[41] During the same year, on the initiative of Julius Wernher – himself a Life Governor of De Beers – £5,000 was voted to Francis Oats for his services in various fields, notably in Namaqualand copper, Rhodesian gold, the Wesselton Diamond Mine and Natal coal.[42] However, in Cornwall, where he was the largest shareholder in the Levant and Basset Mines, Oats' reputation was perhaps not so high. A few years earlier whilst on a visit to Cornwall he delivered a three hour address to the shareholders following which the *Post* considered his comments on the Cornish tin industry as 'scrappy and inaccurate', but put it down to his absence from the county.[43]

1908 was quite an eventful year for the Cornish in South Africa. The question which everyone asked was whether diamonds could be manufactured. According to a Frenchman Henri Lemoine the answer was yes and he claimed he could produce artificial diamonds in his Paris workshop. The threat to Kimberley's diamond industry was such that one of De Beer's leading Directors – Julius Wernher – was sent by the company to investigate. To his horror Wernher saw with his own eyes Lemoine produce a flawless diamond. Before panic set in, however, another De Beers Director – Dr. Jameson – who was also the Cape Prime Minister, requested that Francis Oats be sent to Paris:

> *Oats was one of the oldest and wisest of Kimberley hands, a Cornish miner who had worked his way from mining engineer to director of De Beers. He watched the astonishing process and then examined the diamond which the furnace produced. It was too good to be true: a fine Kimberley stone. Lemoine was a skilful fraudsman but he met his match in Oats, who by his own sleight of hand proved that the 'furnace' was a nonsense.*[44]

Perhaps it is not surprising that when De Beers faced a collapse in the diamond market, especially in the U.S.A. (which accounted for some seventy per cent of sales) the Company turned again to Oats and appointed him Chairman in June 1908. The *Diamond Fields Advertiser* thought that he would be a strong Chairman and that the interests of the company would be safe in his hands.[45] Oats certainly had to take some tough decisions covering the slump. De Beer's mine stopped working for a time with 200 white men and 1,200 natives being discharged. Output was reduced in order to restore confidence in the diamond trade. It was to be a long haul. Kimberley was hit so severely by the depression that it was even considered inappropriate to hold the Annual Cornish Dinner. Thus the 18th Annual Cornish Dinner held at Kimberley's Central Hotel early in January 1910 came after an interval of two years, but it was revived with the greatest possible success and Oats himself acted as Chairman.[46] In 1913 the *Cape Argus* reporting on De Beers claimed:

> *It is greatly to the credit of the present Chairman (Mr. F. Oats of St. Just) and his colleagues – that they have proved fully equal to the demands made upon them. The lessons of the crisis of 1907-08 have been taken to heart... the company is now in a position of greater financial strength.*[47]

One writer has suggested that Oats, as Chairman of De Beers, was exceedingly unpopular and that his rough and dictatorial manner was not acceptable.[48]

Francis Oats c.1908 Onetime Chairman of the De Beers company.

However, this could hardly have been the case, as he was annually voted Chairman until his death in 1918.

It is perhaps ironic that the two most influential Cornishmen in South Africa, Oats at Kimberley and William Hosken at Johannesburg, became involved in an amalgamation struggle. Hosken was one of the original directors of the British South Africa Explosives Company which had its factory at Modderfontein just north of Johannesburg. Oats had been involved in setting up the Cape Explosives Works at Somerset West in 1903 for De Beers. During the diamond slump Hosken's company made a bid to take over the Somerset West Factory but Oats turned down the offer. A third Cornishman became involved as Warrington-Smyth, Secretary of the Department of Mines, considered such an amalgamation an attempt to revive the old monopoly and this the Government would not tolerate.[49] A.P. Cartwright considered Hosken to be

> *completely uncrushable, almost unsnubbable. Whatever turn the*
> *argument took, whatever point made against the British South Africa*
> *Explosives Company Hosken had a reply ready the next day. And he had a*
> *peculiar gift of making any action taken in the face of his arguments seem*
> *like mean treatment of an upright man. He was regarded as a somewhat*
> *stern character but everyone gave him his due for the dogged-does-it-*
> *spirit in which he served his company's interests.*[50]

Cartwright's view of Oats was that he was not a man to mince his words and was feared for his outspokenness but was basically an honest and courageous man who served both De Beers and the Cape Explosive Works faithfully for many years.[51] Neither man was involved in the eventual amalgamation of the explosive companies following the Great War, for Oats had died and Hosken had resigned as Director of his company in 1914, due to illness.

When Oats had been a member of the Cape Parliament he had obviously spent some time at Cape Town, and it was mainly due to his influence there that a West of England Association – consisting of people from Cornwall, Devon, Somerset, Dorset and Gloucestershire – was formed.[52] Such was Oats' standing that even though he was unable to attend the Association's 3rd Annual General Meeting at the Royal Hotel, Cape Town in 1907 he was again re-elected as its President.[53]

It was Oats who first recognised the potential of asbestos specimens and it was his interest that led to a syndicate being formed which purchased a number of farms in the Prieska region along the Orange River where the mineral was found. The Cape Asbestos Company was formed in December 1893 with Oats as one of the two Directors. Thus:

> *Francis Oats contributed another page to Cornish mining history. He dug*
> *his fire-resistant hole in the groundwork of building and industrial*
> *development and struck gold.*[54]

Being Chairman of De Beers led to many other appointments. At one time or another as well as being Chairman of the Asbestos and Explosive Companies he was Chairman of Rhodes Fruit Farms Ltd., South African Marine Fire and General Insurance Company, South African Collieries Ltd., and the Imperial Cold Storage Company; he was also a Director of the Swaziland Tin Mines and various other mining companies. Oats had been very much the Pioneer prospector; always ready to make a personal investigation. His practical knowledge of mining was unrivalled. He had certainly come a long way since attending the village school in St. Just. De Beers dominated Kimberley, and Oats as its Chairman was very much the most influential figure, his expertise in civic matters being as wide ranging as that in mining. Not only was he President of the Northern Districts Agricultural

Society, Chairman of the prestigious Kimberley Club and Chairman of the Kimberley Boy Scouts Association but he did

> *a great deal to promote education being a strong believer in boys showing good manners and behaving in public as gentlemen. He took a keen interest in the coloured and native peoples and in questions affecting their welfare and rights adopted a broad minded attitude... he was at all times a liberal supporter of every charitable appeal and made many donations.*[55]

At the end of 1913 at a cost of £20,000 to De Beers, Oats decided that the European employees at Kimberley should be able to get away from the heat and the dust and would pay them two weeks'wages to let them go to Europe if they wished.[56] This enabled many a Cornish miner to visit his family back in Cornwall.

Above all was Oats' leadership of the Cornish community in Kimberley. At the Twentieth Annual Cornish Dinner held on 13th January 1913 the chief guest Ernest Oppenheimer,[57] the Mayor of Kimberley, reminded those present of the debt the diamond industry and especially De Beers owed to Oats for, due to the careful policy of limiting the output to the demand, De Beers had risen Phoenix-like from the ashes more wonderful than before. Oppenheimer also related how he had pleasure, as the guest of Mr. Francis Oats, of touring in Cornwall and had enjoyed there a drive which for grandeur of scenery was unequalled in the world, drawing loud applause. Oppenheimer also reminded his audience that in South Africa mining is inseparable from the Cornishmen and they had rendered excellent service in De Beers Consolidated Mines as directors, managers and miners.[58]

The following year the 21st Cornish Dinner, described as the Kimberley Society's coming of age celebration, in fact turned out to be the last one. It was a combination of the First World War and the deaths of the leading personalities which brought an end to the Annual Cornish Dinner at Kimberley. The war was hardly a time of celebration especially with many men away at the front, either in German South West Africa, German East Africa or Europe. Oats, as Chairman of De Beers, immediately curtailed the company's operations. With no diamonds being sold many employees were laid off while others worked on half pay. Financial inducement was even offered to employees to go elsewhere.

On 6th November 1914, two months after South Africa entered the war Thomas Quentrall died at Kimberley Hospital – he was 63 years old. Amongst the many mourners at this funeral were Oats, Oppenheimer, Sir David Harris M. P., the Tredrea brothers and a large number of Cornish miners. *The Diamond Fields Advertiser* described Quentrall as having been quiet but genial with a companionable disposition having had a host of friends and never having made a single enemy during his long career in Kimberley.[59]

Before the war ended, Oats – the true citizen of Kimberley – had also died. Feeling ill, he had left Kimberley on 7th August 1918 to go to stay with his daughter at Port Elizabeth. He never recovered from his illness and died there 1st September 1918. In his obituary the Diamond Fields Advertiser announced:

> *In the death of Mr. Oats, Kimberley loses one of its best most public spirited and most respected citizens whose memory will be long cherished. He will be sincerely mourned by a wide circle of friends in all walks of life throughout South Africa.*[60]

In June 1919, De Beers granted a sum of £15,000 to the Kimberley School Board which was put towards the cost of erecting a boys' hostel.[61] It was named the Francis Oats House – a worthy monument to a very able Cornishman, ambitious, somewhat pugnacious and masterful but a born Captain of Industry.[62] At the De Beers A.G.M., David Harris M.P., paid a touching tribute to the memory of Francis Oats who had presided with such conspicuous ability at the meetings of the Company since 1908.[63] It was the end of an era for the Cornish at Kimberley.

At Johannesburg the Cornish Association continued to thrive. William Hosken had become President of the Cornish Association in 1908 and with Charles Chudleigh elected as the first Cornish Mayor of Johannesburg, shortly after Oats had become Chairman of De Beers, the Cornish in South Africa must have thought there was no position to which they could not aspire.

Charles Chudleigh. Mayor of Johannesburg 1908.

The Cornish Association on the Rand was not just responsible for organising banquets, concerts and carol services – important as these were. It was a lively body, a result of the enthusiasm and hard work of its officers which made the Association more than just a social club. In 1909, William Francis Trevithick Harvey became President of the Association and it was said of Harvey that no one has done more to make it the strongest of any similar Association on the Rand.[64] It was Harvey's idea that the Association should have an Organising Secretary and W.G. Tickell of Bodmin was appointed. Together Harvey and Tickell transformed the Cornish Association. It was said Harvey's election was an honour richly deserved and that fresh life had been infused into the whole of the existing branches mainly through Harvey's dynamic attitude.[65] It was Tickell's organising skills that had led to the success of the 1908 Cornish United Carol Service which he, in that year, inaugurated and the formation of the Cornish Sick and Benevolent Fund which received the receipts of the first united carol concert.

With Tickell's driving force and abundant energy the Cornish Association provided the means to relieve the distress of Cornish widows and orphans residing in the Transvaal; for this Tickell deserved full credit. On 29th January 1910, Harvey presented Tickell with a gold sovereign piece on behalf of the Association for his great effort in making the United Carol Concert of 1909 an unqualified success.[66] Tickell had arranged virtually the whole concert.

A third officer of the Association who was held in great respect was the Treasurer Henry Arthur Young J.P. from St. Ives. On leaving Cornwall, Young had first worked for the Standard Bank in London before being transferred to Durban in 1889. In 1892 he had joined a large mercantile firm in Cape Colony, during which time he had travelled extensively throughout South Africa. In 1907 he moved to Johannesburg, becoming the Secretary of Companies to the Liquidator of Estates. The *Post* noted:

> *Mr. Young, in his professional capacity at present has charge of a great number of estates of deceased Cornishmen. His duties are to realise the assets and remit to the relatives at home, and more particularly to see that the dependants of Cornishmen killed in the Rand mines get the full amount due to them under the Workman's Compensation Act… since he has taken upon himself to see that justice is being done to the poor widows and orphans in Cornwall, he has sent thousands of pounds to the dear old country for distribution through his solicitor Mr. T. J. Chellow of St. Ives for whom he has nothing but praise.[67]*

In April 1910, Young said he had remitted to friends of Cornishmen at home during the past year over £31,000[68] which in the main was compensation owing to the relatives of those who had met fatal accidents.

Another innovation set up under the Association's triumvirate of Harvey, Tickell and Young was the establishment of a Labour Bureau which opened in March 1910. Its purpose was to help Cornishmen on the Rand find work, and new arrivals on the Rand were encouraged to call and see Tickell at the Association office on the corner of Russek and Commissioner Streets in Johannesburg. The Fordsburg Branch of the Cornish Association provided some furnished rooms at its new clubhouse for those coming from Cornwall who had yet to find accommodation or employment. Unfortunately, by August the Labour Bureau was warning men not to come out to the Transvaal there being little chance of employment for miners, carpenters and bricklayers. Since April the Bureau had given £28.5s.6d in loans to men to assist them in buying tools, of which £15 had been repaid. At the same time the Association was actively at work endeavouring to find some method of alleviating the condition of miners on the Rand suffering from phthisis.[69]

Although the constitution of the Cornish Association prohibited the introduction and discussion of politics at meetings, during the 1910 election, which saw the formation of the Union of South Africa, the leaders of the Progressive Party took a deep interest in the Association. It was hoped, however, that no political deal would be made with the Progressive Party.[70] Lionel Phillips, a leading light in the Unionist Party became an honorary member of the Cornish Association which showed just how influential the Association was considered.[71] The Labour Party was strongly supported in the Fordsburg district and a number of Cornishmen were involved in its organisation, in their capacity as union leaders. As well as Tom Mathews the work of W.C. Angwin (St. Just) was considered as deserving the highest praise while S. Woolcock (Helston) was presented with a medal as an appreciation of his work in the labour movement.[72]

Another role of the Cornish Association was that of a clearing house where enquiries could be made to find the whereabouts of missing friends and relatives. At branch meetings such topics as provision of hospitals, suitable housing accommodation for miners wishing to bring their families to the Transvaal and other issues concerning the general welfare of the Cornish on the Rand were constantly on the agenda. One question that was never successfully answered was why miners were reluctant to bring out their wives and families to the Transvaal. The explanation by the *Cornishman* that it was due to uncertainty of employment and political instability in the country itself goes but part way to providing an answer. [73]

At Easter 1910 the Cornish Association inaugurated another social function – the Good Friday Picnic – which, like the Christmas Carol Concert, was to become an annual event. Good Friday was one of the few days in the year when all the mines shut down. The first picnic was declared to be one of the greatest successes in connection with the Association. Special trains were run to Vereeniging where over 800 Cornish had a splendid day and were loud in their praises of the excellent arrangements which included boating and motor launch trips in the morning and sports after lunch, including Cornish wrestling.[74]

Dr. Tucker (Tintagel) Chairman of the Fordsburg Branch considered that the success of the Cornish Association could be measured by the fact that although seventy Cornishmen had been admitted to hospital since February and nine had died from phthisis, one from appendicitis, one from an accident, one from cancer and one from asthma, not one Cornishman was buried as a pauper.[75] Out of 51 applications for work the Association had found employment for 31 men whilst 21 out of 27 enquiries into missing relatives had been successful.

Past Presidents and officers of the Cornish association of the Transvaal about 1910.
1. M. Rodda (Chairman, Fordsburg Branch); 2. G.E. Symons (Hon. Treasurer); 3. Dr. A.B. Tucker (President); 4. W.G. Tickell (Hon. Gen. Secretary); 5. J. Job (Chairman, Benoni Branch); 6, H. Warrington-Smythe (past Pres.); 7. W. Hosken; 8. W.F.T. Harvey; 9. E. Sims (Chairman, Roodepoort Branch); 10. J.Mallet (Chairman, Krugersdorp Branch); 11. G.L. Vincent (Chairman, Johannesburg Branch); 12. S. Ustick Pearce (Chairman, Germiston Branch); 13. W.W. Strong (Chairman, East Rand Branch).

Links with Cornwall were strengthened by the Association following a conference of 50 delegates chaired by Dr. Tucker at the Grand National Hotel, Johannesburg, in July 1911. There was an overwhelming desire by delegates to see that miners kept their obligations towards their wives and families in Cornwall.

Resolutions were passed urging:

> *That pressure be brought to bear by members upon those who do not support their families with the object of inducing them to do so,*

and:

> *that owing to the fact of there being a number of men in this country who have a wife and family depending on them at home and are failing to remit money the Association take the necessary steps to bring them to their sense of responsibility.*[76]

In Cornwall John Penberthy (Crowlas) was the Association's Home Secretary. He was well-versed in South African affairs, having recently returned home to Ludgvan from the Rand, where he had been working since 1895 at the Robinson mine. He was a prominent Wesleyan and Sunday School teacher, and during the elections he had worked hard for the Progressive Party. His son E.J. Penberthy was still in South Africa working at the Robinson mine as a timberman.[77] In a visit to the Penzance Board of Guardians, November 1911, John Penberthy gave evidence of cases where intervention by the Association had led several gold mining companies to deduct money from men's wages and send it direct to their wives and families in Cornwall. The Association was applauded by the Penzance Board of Guardians who donated £5 to the Association hoping it would encourage other Boards to do the same. Penberthy also said missing husbands had been found for families in Hayle, Truro, Tuckingmill and Redruth.[78]

Although the resolutions at the July Conference were passed in good faith, in the long run they were unpopular. As Dickason rightly points out:

> *many a branch had ruffled the feathers of the independent spirit when interfering in matrimonial matters. To a man the miners ruled this was outside the province of the association. But the association had strong thoughts on the matter. In a misguided attempt to appear socially and morally representative of the Cornish community, the more the associations interfered, the more financial support waned.*[79]

Tickell himself had been praised for his untiring efforts in pioneering this positive action by the Association the previous year[80] and a few months later, during a Ladies' Social held by the Association in the Masonic Hall, Johannesburg, the loudest cheers followed an announcement by Tickell that no less than 28 enquiries within a twelve month period had resulted in money now being regularly sent home to families which had previously not been receiving a remittance.[81]

In March 1912 the largest gathering of Cornishmen and women ever known to Johannesburg occurred when an At Home celebration at the Grand National Hotel was held in honour of Frank Harvey, the head of the Cornish engineering firm

Harveys of Hayle. Over six hundred Cornish attended the function which included whole families – sometimes as many as three generations. As expected the Association was at full strength. H.A. Young as President, George Levington Vincent as Treasurer and Tickell as Secretary were supported by Vice Presidents Charles Chudleigh, Sam and Richard Hosken, James Howard Vivian, and W.W. Strong. Also present were the Branch Chairmen – J. Tonkin (Germiston), M.A. Rodda (Fordsburg), S. Ustick Pearce (Roodepoort), M.H. Combes (Benoni), H. Olver (Randfontein) and J. Wevell (Johannesburg). Chief guests besides Harvey and his wife were Mr. & Mrs. J.K. Holman who were also visiting from Cornwall. Young commented on the large attendance, which he considered was the finest and most representative gathering of the Cornish Association that had ever been seen in Johannesburg and he paid tribute to the large number of ladies present which in itself was not surprising as much of the Association's work behind the scenes was done by them, especially the hospital visits.[82]

Although the occasion was ostensibly to honour Frank Harvey it became more of a tribute to Cornish women, and to one in particular – Anna Levington-Vincent. W.F.T. Harvey (Frank Harvey's eldest son) on behalf of the Association made a presentation to her, not only as a reward for her work on behalf of the Association, but as a token of the esteem in which she was held by the Cornish people of the Rand. William Hosken who, as always, was loudly applauded having spoken of his boyhood memories of Frank Harvey – both men coming from Hayle – also paid tribute to Anna Levington-Vincent, in particular the quality of her voice. It was left to Charles Chudleigh to close the speeches and, as one of the original members of the Association before the Boer War, he reminded them that in the past the Association had not encouraged women to take an interest; if the Association was to continue to be successful it needed the women's support. He pointed out that a future event – a Cornish Fair to be held in August – would only succeed with the women's support.[83]

In 1912 Lord De Villiers, Chief Justice and Acting Governor General of South Africa made his first public appearance when he opened the Cornish Fair in the Drill Hall, Johannesburg. Stalls were set out and decorated with gold and black and were named after old Cornish fairs – there was even a Padstow 'obby 'oss. De Villiers said:

> *but for the aid of the Cornishmen the Rand could not have been in its present prosperous condition. So many of you I hear come here and leave your wives overseas – bring your wives and children and make good South African citizens of them. One hears a great deal about a white South Africa. Unless people like you come and make your homes here, the country can never really become that.[84]*

Young's Presidential year marked a high point in the history of the Cornish Association in the Transvaal and it was claimed that his assiduous attention to the presidential duties had deserved the highest praise from those who watched his work on behalf of 'One & All'.[85] Young, who was also a Freemason, was responsible in 1910 for setting up the Masonic Lodge known as Lodge Cornwall which the *Cornishman* reported in 1912 was prospering in every sense of the word and looked upon as one of the best conducted on the Rand.[86] Many Cornishmen belonged to both the Freemasons and the Cornish Association. Young was the first Master of Lodge Cornwall and other Masters included, M.A. Rodda, C.H. Polmear, R.T. Leggo, W.J. Tregeare, R. Trevaskis and B. Trewavis.

The newly elected President of the Cornish Association in 1913 was William Henry Morcom. Born at Scorrier in 1865, by the age of 22 years he was mining in Minnesota, U.S.A. He was a typical roving miner, spending six years in Pachuca, Mexico before going to South Africa just prior to the Jameson raid. He was resident engineer at the Robinson, Randfontein Central Mine and had been Chairman of the Randfontein branch of the Cornish Association. In 1890 he had married Nanny Michell of St. Day and it was mainly due to her that, during Morcom's presidency, women were at last admitted as full members.[87] The strong links between Cornwall and South Africa were again emphasised when Thurstan Peter, the Clerk of the Redruth Board of Guardians was given the heartiest votes of thanks for the noble manner in which he had assisted the Cornish Association of the Transvaal. Peter had been instrumental in enabling miners' to claim compensation under the terms of the Phthisis Act.[88] Another link was that the Association was sending a regular sum of £40 per month to the Mining Division, to help destitute miners families.

After the 1907 and 1913 strikes the influence of the Cornish miner was on the wane, as the mining industry of the Transvaal became more of an Afrikander industry and less of a gathering ground for the bird of passage.[89] In 1908 the *South African Mining Journal* had reported that on the Rand one of the most important changes and probably the most far reaching in its effects on the mining industry was the alteration that had taken place in the personnel of the staff of the mines. It continued:

> *The Witwatersrand has proved a happy hunting ground for large numbers of Cornish miners and at one time there were large mines here that employed only Cornishmen as skilled labourers. A Cornish manager generally employed a Cornish Mine Captain. Often the manager was neither Cornishman nor a mining man, and he found the Cousin Jack mine captain indispensable. A Cornish mine captain invariably meant Cornish shift bosses, and that in turn, means Cornish workmen.*

The *Journal* then criticised the Cornish miner for maintaining a conservative spirit and being too slow to adapt to the onward march of science and engineering skill, claiming that the spirit of lethargy had done the Rand no good, and although the *Journal* recognised that Cornish miners were good workmen their spirit of clannish comradeship had hampered the progress of the Rand. The *Journal* concluded:

> *There are of course progressive Cornishmen... but we must say we regard it as a favourable sign that the old time Cousin Jack manager who reckoned the experience of his boyhood at Wheal Harriet his greatest educational asset is by no means so common as he used to be.*[90]

Evidence that what the *Journal* said was true and that change was inevitable, came in 1910 with the retirement of J. Harry Johns as Consultant Engineer to the Barnato Group. Many Cornishmen subsequently had to quit the group without the 'slightest reason' for such changes being assigned.[91]

Holman advertisement Cornish Port & Mining News May 1907.

Although the influence of the Cornish miner may have been in decline the same could not be said about Cornwall's export market in South Africa. Despite the success of the American firm Ingersoll Rand with the Gordon Hope Drill, Cornish firms also did well in the rock drill market. Names such as Little Hercules (Tuckingmill Company), Little Wonder (Stephens of Redruth) along with the Cherson (Bartles of Tuckingmill & Johannesburg) and Cornish Rock Drill (Holmans of Camborne) were in common use on the Rand as the many advertisements in the press during the 1904-1914 period show. One advertisement of Holmans in 1907 took particular pride in announcing that their rock drill had established no less than four world records. The first had been in 1904, the second in 1905 and then twice in 1907 – first at the Cinderella Deep and second at the Kleinfontein Deep.[92] Holmans gained further success and prestige when their Number One Rock Drill won joint first prize in the year-long stope drill competition organised by the Transvaal Government and the Chamber of Mines. The competition began in May 1909 and Holmans shared the £5,000 prize with Siskol Drills. Both had run at an average cost of just under 10d a foot, compared with an average cost of 13d for hand drilling with native labour.[93] Company representatives travelled between Cornwall and South Africa on a regular basis. William John Trythal was Holman's representative and Harry Glasson represented Stephens. One Cornishman – F.C. Eddy – was even a representative for Ingersoll Rand.[94] A presentation of a gold watch was made to Glasson for his supervision of the Little Wonder Drill in 1907. The drill established a world record having drilled between 9-45am and 3-45pm thirteen holes each averaging three feet.[95] Two years later the *Post* reported that Stephen's Climax Imperial Drill had obtained remarkable results in South Africa.[96] Sometimes the company chairmen travelled to South Africa to see their companies' products in action. William Stephens of Climax Rock Drill went in 1906[97] and Frank Harvey in 1910. James Oliver Bartle was on the Rand full time, having established a branch of Bartles which was one

Bartles Scales Dept. at Johannesburg 1914.

of Johannesburg's leading merchants.[98] Another business connected to mining was that of the Old Rand Foundry run by Cornishman James Jenkin Rowe and Henry Jewell. Rowe (St. Just) arrived in South Africa in 1893 having been previously employed by Holmans. Jewell, who came from Camborne, had spent some time in Australia before coming to South Africa and entering into partnership with Rowe. When Rowe retired in 1908 Jewell became the sole proprietor but still traded under the name Rowe and Jewell. The foundry employed many men from Hayle, Redruth, Camborne and St. Just.[99] In September 1910 William Hosken claimed:

> *The greatest market ever opened in the world for things manufactured in Camborne was South Africa... Two thirds of the rock drills that come to the Transvaal come from that immediate neighbourhood... Three fifths of the fuse used in the Transvaal come from the neighbourhood of Camborne... there were 23,000 white people employed in the mines and it was estimated that 7,000 of that number were Cornish.[100]*

Two years later, at the welcome for Frank Harvey, Hosken again commented on how Cornwall and South Africa needed each other. Although Hosken considered the decline of the Cornish mining industry a natural disaster he remarked that on the Rand the county of Cornwall took two thirds of the safety fuse business.[101]

To Cornwall's further credit came news that T.H. Blackney (St. Agnes) a foreman smith at the Ferreira gold mine had invented a device to assist in the sharpening of drills. His invention meant a saving of £59 in native labour and fuel was effected in one month.[102]

Probably of more interest to the layman, who may have had little idea of the complicated machinery at work in a gold mine, was the human story concerning the bravery of some seventeen Cornish miners. Following a fire in the Salisbury mine Geo Matthews, W. Christophers, John Webb, James Moon, John Moon, W.H. Sandoe, F. Dunston, R. Lanyon, J.H. Axford, E.J. Craze, W. Bawden, Stephen Bennetts, J.H. Pascoe, Jas. Harris, J.H. Whitford, C. Angwin and W. Polgrean were praised for

> *The noble manner in which you all behaved on the night of June 21st in rescuing many of our native labourers from what might have been a ghastly death.[103]*

The Cornishmen were each given money plus a silver watch, which had the man's name and an inscription from the mine's owner – Wemmer & Company.

The period 1904-14 was a violent one for the Cornish on the Rand and not simply because of the strikes or clashes with the Chinese. William Blewett (St. Day), was shot in the head and robbed of £22 by an unknown assailant,[104] and William Jones (Camborne) was murdered at Roodepoort.[105] N.T. Martin (St. Day) was murdered for his watch and chain, his body being found in a dam near

Fordsburg,[106] whilst Thomas Alfred Donald, a 28 year-old Cornish grocer at Roodepoort was shot dead by one of his own employees, according to the *Cornishman*.[107] The murder which caused the biggest sensation, both in the Transvaal and Cornwall, was that of one Cornishman by another. Called the *Veldt Tragedy* by the press, the murder of Alfred Jennings on 15th July 1909 by James Hambly of Illogan involved 'a web of immorality'.[108] *The Transvaal Leader* called the subsequent trial one of the most sensational – in the criminal annals of the country.[109] Hambly had been living with Jennings and his wife and three of her six children were his. Jennings was a violent man and Hambly – who had shot Jennings three times – said at his trial "I did it in self defence as I would have been a dead man otherwise".[110] On hearing the news that Hambly had been sentenced to death, his mother in Cornwall died from shock.[111] A series of letters and articles, all in Hambly's favour, appeared in the press[112] although the Cornish Association, of which Hambly was a member, and the Wesleyan Methodists seemed unwilling to become involved and take up his case, causing anger and outrage.[113] Tiddy wrote that Hambly was not any longer being tried for murder but for morals,[114] and it was said many were glad to see that Mr. Tiddy had started to work and get the sentence passed on young Hambly reduced to life at any rate.[115] It was not to be; despite Tiddy's tremendous effort plus the support of William Hosken, who organised a petition,[116] and a committee of leading churchmen and businessmen adding their weight. Just before Hambly was executed he admitted that he had not been attacked first by Jennings as he had been said at his trial, but that he was goaded to desperation and in a moment of frenzy had started shooting at Jennings.[117] At Hambly's interment there was no official religious ceremony due to an apparent misunderstanding, so the Rev. W.B. Allcock acted upon his own responsibility and conducted a short burial service at which another minister and Hambly's brother were the only people present.[118] Within a few months another Cornishman – Thomas Richards – was lucky to escape a charge of murder when he accidentally shot a native child whilst taking part in revolver practice.[119]

A number of prominent Cornish Pioneers died during the period 1904-36; not all of these were connected to mining. The deaths of William F. Stuttaford (1911)[120] and his brother Samson Rickard Stuttaford (1914)[121] were a reminder of one Cornish family which had established a retail business with outlets throughout South Africa. Five years before Samson's death he gave a number of shares in Stuttafords to a college in Cape Town to finance the building of a library. Later the college became the University of Cape Town. With the death of Samson the company passed into the capable hands of his eldest son – Richard Stuttaford (1879-1945).[122]

One of the most prolific Cornish newspaper proprietors in South Africa, Charles Deecker, died in 1912. With the Boer War and his obvious anti-Boer stance, Deecker had quickly to abandon his newspapers the *Krugersdorp Times* and the

Roodepoort Mail and leave the Transvaal. Staying at Delagoa Bay he became English Editor of the Portuguese newspaper *O'Futura*. His appointment had lasted barely a year before he had suffered from a number of malarial attacks, and so for the benefit of his health he and his wife moved to Cape Town. There, at nearby Muizenburg, he published the *Seaside News* but with the end of the war he returned to the Transvaal. With his newspaper plant at Roodepoort having disappeared (and with it the chance of any financial compensation) he could only lease – with the support of his wife's money – the *Heidelberg News* for two years, and then the *Hay & Herbert News* at Douglas. He then transferred the paper first to Griquatown and then Prieska, where the paper became the *Northern Press*. Deecker died after a short illness and his obituary claimed that Deecker

While a true and loyal Imperialist, was at the same time very broad minded, and liberal in thought. Wherever he has lived and worked the interests, welfare and progress of his community where he has found his work has always been his aim regardless of creeds, nationality or politics...[123]

The other prolific newspaper man Josiah Angove Jr. had been a Pioneer at Kimberley where he had established his first newspaper. He then went on to establish others at Vryburg, Johannesburg, East London, Port Elizabeth, and at Cape Town the *Looker On*. In May 1905 the *Cornishman* announced that the last issue of Angove's *Looker On* had been sold and in October the same year it was apparent from another report in the *Cornishman* that Angove was once more back in the Transvaal and had begun publication at Potchefstroom of yet another newspaper – *The Transvaal Express*.[124] It was to be by no means his last. In 1913 he returned to Port Elizabeth to resurrect the *Looker On*. Two years later he moved to Knysna to establish the *Knysna Mail* and finally in 1924 he purchased the *Middleburg Echo*, the paper of which he was the proprietor at the time of his death.[125] All of Angove's newspapers were published under the motto "Without fear, favour or prejudice".

Although Angove and Deecker were the most prolific of the Cornish newspapermen in South Africa – Angove published more newspapers in South Africa than anyone else – they were not the only Cornishmen to establish newspapers. Charles Veale Bate established three newspapers in a journalistic career that spanned over fifty years. Bate arrived in South Africa from Cornwall in 1902, aged 24 years. He first enlisted with the Rand Rifles and then worked for a short while with Lionel Curtis, Johannesburg's first Town Clerk. Bate then moved to Potchefstroom, the oldest town in the Transvaal, and restarted the old *Potchefstroom Budget*. The newspaper had originally been published at Kowie as the *Port Alfred Budget* so the old printing plant had to be brought from there by ox-wagon. In 1908 Bate purchased the defunct *Potchefstroom News* and changed its name to the *Potchefstroom Herald*. Bate later recalled:

> we worked at night with candles and oil lamps and the ancient machine –
> on which The Star was first printed in Johannesburg – was turned by two
> perspiring Natives.
> The Christmas issue that year was printed in two colours. I don't know
> how we managed it.[126]

Bate's memories included the days of turmoil at Potchefstroom council meetings, the council having an official 'chucker-out', a local prize fighter, an aggressive-looking fellow in gaiters, breeches and green-braided frock-coat. According to Bate, his greatest achievement was in 1915 when he established his third newspaper – *Die Westelike Stem* – claiming "I'm the only Englishman who ever started, maintained and brought to success an Afrikaans newspaper in South Africa".[127] Bate, like many Cornishmen, was not only a Methodist but a great benefactor. For many years he took a leading part in the distribution of Christmas presents to the needy, and as Deputy Mayor of Potchefstroom he saw to the presentation of gift parcels of meat to old and infirm non-Europeans. During the depression in the early thirties Bate was responsible for a children's playground being laid out in the town park and subsequently named after his first wife – Elizabeth Bate. With Bate's death on 10th July 1961 the *Potchefstroom Herald* reminded its readers:

> his humanity extended also to those people who had been in his service
> through the long years of his association with the Herald Newspaper and
> Printing Works. It is said he never dismissed a worker and he is
> remembered with affection by those who served under him.[128]

Bate had been a leading figure in the Newspaper Press Union of South Africa, and another Cornishman – James Savage (Penzance) – before he died in 1941 had been one of the oldest members of South Africa's Typographical Union. Savage had originally worked for the *Cornish Telegraph* before going in 1895 to South Africa, where he worked on a number of South African newspapers including the Johannesburg *Times*, Kimberley *Diamond Fields Advertiser* and the *Rand Daily Mail*. He died in 1941, aged 66 years.[129] Another Cornish journalist who died the same year was Richard Williams, originally a reporter with the *Post* before moving to Johannesburg to work for a number of newspapers. He had sent the *Post* a regular column entitled *Our South African Letter*. His death was regretted both in Cornwall and South Africa.[130] One other Cornish newspaper man who deserves mention is Albert Mitchell (Penzance). Having trained as a journalist with the *Cornishman* he went to South Africa in 1902 and joined the staff of the *Transvaal Leader* at Johannesburg. He spent a brief spell as sub-editor of the *Rhodesian*

Herald at Salisbury (now Harare) and then moved back to South Africa to work for the *Cape Argus*. During the First World War he served with the South African Heavy Artillery returning to the *Cape Argus* when the war was over. In 1920 he became Editor of the *Natal Times* but resigned two years later to become Assistant Editor and special writer for the *Natal Mercury*. Mitchell was a founder member of the South African Society of Journalists serving on its council for many years.[131] In 1925 he became Secretary of the Durban Chamber of Commerce, but he was also remembered for his fine singing voice, winning a gold medal as a tenor at one of the South African Eisteddfods. He died in 1942 at Durban.[132]

A Cornishman who took a keen interest in the activities of the Typographical Union – as well as having links with Kimberley – was James Farquharson Trembath If Tom Mathews came to represent the working man in Johannesburg, then in Kimberley it was Trembath. Like Mathews he was a Pioneer of the Labour Movement in South Africa. Trembath had been an apprentice compositor with the *Cornishman* newspaper – first at Penzance, where he was born in 1874, and later at St. Ives. Having spent a short time working in London he left for South Africa in 1897. Described as a man of distinct personality, from the very beginning Trembath had associated himself with political and social matters and more particularly the Trades Union movement. On arrival at Cape Town he joined the Typographical Union and he soon became one of its officers. Trembath assisted in the formation of the first Cape Town Trades Council in 1899, before moving to Kimberley shortly after the siege of 1900. From 1904-11 he was the Secretary of the Kimberley Trades and Labour Council, during which time he was to have an uphill struggle against the formidable power of the De Beers Company which dominated the town. Having been unsuccessful in his attempt to secure a seat for Kimberley in the First Union Parliament, he moved to Durban where, in 1914, he became Chairman of the Durban District Committee of the South African Labour Party, a position he held for many years. Trembath actually died at Cape Town, where he had gone to visit a sick member of the Union. His funeral on 3rd May 1932 was attended by many politicians and union officials including Colonel F.H. P. Creswell, Minister of Labour and H.W. Sampson, Minister of Posts and Telegraphs who said Jimmy Trembath never sought position or power except to promote the welfare of workers.[133]

The deaths of two Cornish Pioneers were indeed tragic. One was that of Frederick J. Tiddy, who had provided many pen portraits for the *Cornishman* and who was well known in and around Johannesburg. He had returned home to the Scilly Isles in 1920, in ill health and died from a gunshot wound in the head which an inquest found to be evidently self-inflicted whilst of unsound mind after years of suffering. His funeral was attended by two representatives of the Cornish Association, Mr. J. Gould and Mr. J. Davis.[134] The second death – that of Thomas Collingwood Kitto – was shrouded in some mystery. He died in Cornwall apparently from a heart attack whilst at the Plume & Feathers Public House following a visit to his parents' grave at Redruth. There was speculation at least in two Cornish newspapers that one of the finest mining engineers in the world had somehow committed suicide.[135]

A number of Cornishmen in South Africa had been successful builders. Albert C. Wallis (St. Buryan), was considered to be one of Johannesburg's successful builders and contractors,[136] and another was E.J. Rowe (St. Just) at Benoni; in 1935 he was elected President of the Transvaal Cornish Association.[137] William Bawden (Ludgvan) had a building business in Johannesburg and was also from 1933 until his death in 1947 member of Parliament for the Langlaagte district and Deputy Mayor for Johannesburg 1931-32. Bawden was also a Johannesburg City Councillor, claiming that he had the honour of introducing the bill which made Johannesburg a city. Bawden Park in Booysens, Johannesburg is named after him.[138.] Charles Williams (St. Just), after a period spent mining on the Rand, established his business in Durban.[139]

Perhaps the two most notable Cornish builders in South Africa were Albert C. Collins and William Mountstephens. The legacy these two Cornishmen left behind was the establishment of St.Stithians College. Although both Collins and Mountstephens believed that education was a duty of the State and not a matter for private enterprise they later became critical of State schools, which they saw as being

> *devoted almost exclusively to academic studies, while they themselves favoured a greater emphasis on the teaching of Christian principles and thought that more should be done within the schools to develop leaders in social matters.*[140]

For that reason both men stipulated in their Wills that the school must be under the control of the Methodist church. Collins had led a most frugal life, but when he died at Johannesburg in 1938 aged 81 his estate was valued at £550,000, out of which he had left £110,000 to more than 100 charities in Johannesburg and England barring no colour, class or creed.[141] Both Collins and Mountstephens had been extremely generous. In South Africa a number of children's homes received support and they built Mount Collins for the Rand Aid Association which looked after the elderly. They also financed the building of a clinic in the Alexandra township. In Cornwall the Falmouth Seamen's Mission, the National Children's Home and St. Dunstans for the Blind all received donations, but the largest gift was a fully-equipped hospital for the people of Falmouth and District, at the time the most modern hospital in England. In 1936 they added a second storey to the building which earned both men the Freedom of the Boroughs of Falmouth and Penryn.[142] Mountstephens died in 1943 aged 86, leaving £146,800 to charity which included £7,000 to the Methodist Epworth Children's Home, £3,500 to the

Salvation Army, £4,000 to the Y.M.C.A., £1,500 to the Cornish Association of the Transvaal, £5,000 to the Johannesburg General Hospital, £4,000 to the Rand Aid Association (the first approved Welfare Organisation on the Rand, founded in 1903) and £2,000 to the Alexandra Health Clinic. In Cornwall the Falmouth and District Hospital received £10,000, the Royal Lifeboat Institution £3,000 and many bequests to institutions in Falmouth, Cornwall where Mountstephens was born.[143]

The money the two men left for the school was put into a trust, and although Mountstephens was present at the first Trust meeting in 1941, (which on Mountstephens' suggestion was named the St. Stithians trust) neither man was to see the school which they founded. St. Stithians was eventually adopted as the name for the school, officially opened in January 1953. Situated on a 300 acre site in Ferndale, Randburg and built at a cost of £250,000, St. Stithians College is a lasting monument to Collins and Mountstephens. The ethos of the school is a liberal education with Christian teaching and boarders at the school live either in Collins House or Mountstephens House. The school shield became a modified version of the Cornish shield,

Shield from the St. Stithians College prospectus 1987

> *having a dark blue border along the outside edge of the shield with the fifteen gold bezants arranged equally along either side on the blue border. This leaves an inner silver shield on which the red cross stands out boldly to signify the Christian foundation of the college. No better motto for a school can be found than that of Cornwall, 'One and All.'*[144]

One other Cornish builder on the Rand of note was Herbert Alexander Berriman (most likely a relative of William Berriman, the St. Ives man who built Maritzburg). H.A. Berriman came to South Africa in 1899 to work on the railways but then became a building contractor at Johannesburg, where he was responsible for the building of St. Mary's Cathedral and the Johannesburg City Library. He died in 1955.[145]

From August 1914 onwards the First World War was to have a devastating effect not only in Cornwall but in South Africa too. A number of Cornish-South Africans were killed during the war. South Africa entered the war on 8th September and unlike many countries that came to Britain's aid, South Africa actually faced the enemy on her very own border. Noel Carter (St. Erth), Philip Lloyd Davey (St. Just) and Tom Rickard (Camborne) all died in 1917 whilst on active service in German East Africa. M.A. Rodda, the former Fordsburg Chairman, was killed there a year earlier.[146]

John James (Gulval) was just one of many Cornish-South Africans to be killed on the Ypres Salient. Another was William Stanley Harris (Trevallas, St. Agnes) a former Shift Boss at the City Deep mine. His brother, John Clifton Harris (also Trevallas), was in the same sector but never saw him and was lucky to survive the end of the war.[147] For all too many, however, the only record is a name on a war memorial somewhere.

The Cornish Association had no doubt where its loyalties lay. During the annual Christmas dinner in 1914 they proclaimed in a rare burst of patriotic fervour, for Country, for Cornwall and for Empire.[148] Throughout the war the Association held a number of functions in support of war relief. Thomas Blewett (Newlyn) had replaced George Levington-Vincent as President of the Cornish Association in late 1914, and one of his first actions was to turn the Benevolent Fund over to War Relief.[149] With a falling membership Charles Rowe believed the Association was being taken for granted and urged more support.[150] The Association still had influence for when it transpired that a number of men had come to South Africa from Cornwall, for the purpose of escaping military service, the Association quickly expressed its disgust at such behaviour on the part of the fellow countrymen, adding:

> *It seems incomprehensible to us that young able bodied men should desert their country at a time when it is fighting for its very existence. The Association intends if the offence continues to approach the Chamber of Mines and invite them to refuse any employment to eligible men arriving in that country from England and have every reason to believe that the Chamber will comply with their request.* [151]

The First World War was only a year over when the St. Just neighbourhood was suddenly plunged into gloom and despair. On Monday 20th October 1919 a tragic mining disaster occurred when the man-engine at the Levant Mine collapsed, killing 31 men and injuring 12 others. Its effect was felt world wide:

> *a shudder went like an earth-tremor to Johannesburg and Butte City, to Broken Hill and Pachuea to Grass Valley and Ballarat and many other abodes of Cornish exiles and their descendants.*[152]

The families who suffered, many of whom had South African connections, included Angwin, Eddy, Grenfell, Oats, Pascoe, Rowe, Tregear and Trembath.[153] One of the dead miners – John Wearne – had spent six years in South Africa and had only been 3 months back home in St. Just.[154] Not surprisingly sympathy was expressed by the Cornish communities overseas, but perhaps of more importance were the many donations sent to the bereaved families. From De Beers, Kimberley – which always had close links with St. Just – a sum of £775 was sent which was the largest single donation to come from South Africa.[155] The Cornish at Kimberley set up a Kimberley – Levant Relief Fund. When the fund was finally closed, over £1,000 had been raised and sent to St. Just. The committee received a letter of thanks from Major F.F. Oats, who, since the death of his father had as the largest shareholder, become the Manager of the Levant mine.[156] At Johannesburg sympathy from the Rand Cornish was expressed at a special memorial service for the Levant mine disaster held at the Fordsburg Wesleyan Church on 21st December 1919. Cornishmen J. Eddy of Crown Mines and T. Bulger of Roodepoort both made speeches and the Rev. F.E. Barrit, the Fordsburg minister, sent a letter to the Rev. T. Little of St. Just Wesleyan church in which he said:

> *This congregation largely composed of Cornish folk and representative members of the Cornish Association... desire to express their reverent and prayerful sympathy and condolences with the relatives and friends of the brave men who so tragically and suddenly lost their lives in the Levant mining disaster, St. Just, Cornwall.*[157]

Unfortunately the Levant man-engine was not the only collapse in Cornwall. During the First World War a number of mines in Cornwall – Dolcoath was one – due to a continual fall in the price of tin had been forced to curtail production. Other mines, such as Botallack and Wheal Jane shut down altogether. Even Hall's, Redruth and Chacewater Railway closed in 1915, and before the war was over further mine closures included West Kitty at St. Agnes and the Basset Mines at Camborne. Immediately after the war the tin industry experienced a boom; the tin price – which had been £139 per ton in 1914 – reached £396 per ton in February, 1920.[158] Then came a collapse in the price and the result for Cornwall and in particular the Mining Division was a disaster of a greater magnitude. The hardest news for many to take was the headline in June, 1920, which simply said, 'Dolcoath to be Scat'.[159] For Cornwall's premier mine – the pride and glory of Cornwall's mining industry – actually to close, with some 600-700 miners losing their jobs, was a shock indeed and the closing of Dolcoath marked the end of an era in Cornish history.[160] Worse was to follow. Following two deputations to London, seeking Government help which was not forthcoming, Cornwall received its knockout blow.[161] By the end of July 1920 with all underground miners discharged at the Grenville mine, hundreds of unemployed Camborne and Redruth miners were said to be living on hot chips.[162] The advice given by the Redruth Board of Guardians was to the point. The miners would have to do what the people of Gwennap did forty years ago – emigrate.[163] South Africa, however, had little to offer. Mines on the Rand had also closed following a post-war depression. Wages had been reduced as the price of gold had fallen, but production costs rose. The frustrations of the work force culminated in the 1922 Strike although it had been pointed out before the strike that the Transvaal could not be relied upon to furnish openings for unemployed Cornish miners who might be able and willing to emigrate.[164]

As if St. Just had not suffered enough, in August 1920 there was another mining disaster at Levant when an explosion underground killed four more Cornish miners and injured several others.[165] By January 1921 Levant itself had been forced to reduce its workforce and with the neighbouring mine of Geevor lying idle there was distress throughout the West Penwith peninsula. In February the Camborne-Redruth district suffered the same fate. The Tresavean mine at Lanner,[166] one of the mines to re-open in 1907, discharged 200 men and the first of many marches by the unemployed miners began. A march by some 70 Camborne miners to the Redruth Workhouse was described as a sad spectacle to watch as the men cried out "Our children are suffering through lack of food".[167] Before the month was out 1,000 miners had been discharged from the two most productive mines in the district – East Pool & Agar and South Crofty. In May the amalgamated Tincroft and Cooks Kitchen mine finally closed, bringing to an end work at the mine which had been carried on for a hundred years or more. With Levant, East Pool & Agar, plus South Crofty virtually at a standstill:

> *Throughout the mining districts, the abiding roar and rattle of stamps came to an end, a sound that – distant or near at hand – had been a ceaseless accompaniment to life in the Mining Division of West Cornwall for many decades. Disturbing this unaccustomed silence was only the thin whistle of wind through head gear and the broken window panes of silent engine-houses.*[168]

From all the Cornish mining districts came appeals for food especially for miners' children. It became very reminiscent of the 1870's and 1880's, as soup kitchens were set up and Unemployed Relief schemes began to distribute food and clothing. With the number of unemployed in June 1921 having reached 7,000, the first of many contributions towards the relief fund arrived from South Africa. The Benoni branch of the Cornish Association sent £50 – two thirds for Camborne-Redruth and one third for the St. Just area. [169] When larger amounts began to arrive from America – over £300 from Grass Valley, California and £800 from Calamut, Michigan, the *Cornishman* asked "What might be expected from Africa?"[170]

Charles Rowe, a former President of the Cornish Association in South Africa 1918-19, although being on holiday in Cornwall was recruited as a member of the Relief Committee. Rowe had the right connections; not only was his wife Ellen the daughter of Charles Thomas, a previous manger of the Cooks Kitchen mine, but Rowe himself was known throughout South Africa. His father – also Charles Rowe – had taken him to Namaqualand at the early age of 3 years (Rowe senior had been instrumental in having churches built at Port Nolloth and O'okiep). Rowe had been a foreman at the Ferreira mine. Like his father he was best known for his work as a Methodist preacher, it being reported that there was no pulpit in the

Methodist churches of the Reef where Mr. Rowe was not welcomed as a preacher of intellectual and spiritual force and grace.[171] Despite seeing for himself the extent of the hardship brought about by the wholesale closure of the Cornish mines, Rowe, nonetheless, warned:

> *If you get £500 from the Transvaal I think you will do well. There is considerable unemployment on the Reef at the present time, about 2,000 men being idle. Efforts are being made for these men's assistance and you cannot blame the Cornish folk in the Transvaal if they do not reach the high level attained on the occasion of the Levant disaster.*[172]

While Cornwall waited for a South African response a Cornish Miners' choir began to tour the country to raise funds, as the distress within the mining community became even more acute. Two hundred miners marched to the Redruth workhouse, hoping to obtain outdoor relief.[173] Even Holmans future began to be in doubt as the company began to discharge men and put others on short time work. The Holman choir also set out to raise funds – the two choirs between them raising £2,000 for the relief fund by touring Cornwall and Devon. Meanwhile in South Africa a relief fund was set up on the Rand under a committee chaired by H.A. Young with R. T. Leggo as Treasurer. A cheque for £400 was sent by October.

Most at risk were the Cornish children. Cornwall's Education Committee had since March issued half a pint of milk and a bun each morning to necessitous children of the Camborne schools.[174] There was an appeal for clothing for the destitute St. Just children. Questions were asked in Parliament and 78 per cent of rate payers in the Cornish mining district were said to be out of work and living on charity.[175] Just before Christmas a splendid Christmas gift arrived from South Africa. The Secretary of the Cornish Association in the Transvaal sent a cheque for 1,000 guineas to the Lord Lieutenant of Cornwall, J.C. Williams, with the instruction that the money be used for the Cornish children in order to provide a Christmas treat for every scholar in the elementary schools of the distressed areas of Cornwall.[176] A further sum of £43 for the same purpose was received from the Kimberley Cornish. The newspaper reports for that Christmas and the New Year told of the many children's parties, entertainments and free visits to the cinema enjoyed by children at Camborne, Redruth and St. Just. The Cornish children could well be thankful to the Cornish in South Africa.

For two years the Cornish mining industry suffered virtual paralysis during which mining families were sustained on charitable funds, outdoor relief and remittances from bread-winners in South Africa, America and elsewhere. At its highest level unemployment in the mining industry reached just over 9,000, in January 1922. On the other hand the relief fund totalled £80,000, of which £20,000 was subscribed by the Cornish police force. The Chief Constable, Colonel H.B. Protheroe Smith, himself a Boer War Veteran, raised £10,000 often begging personally or by letters.[177] Just how many miners emigrated during the 1921-23 period is difficult to gauge, although the *Cornishman* estimated that about 1,000 had filtered away from the district.[178] Exact figures are not available although most went to America. For example 100 miners left Cornwall to work in the Hollinger Gold Mines in Ontario, Canada – the British government paying two thirds of their expenses – and the miners of Calumut, Michigan, U.S.A. offered to lend the passage money to some 25 miners.[179] Very few individuals seem to have gone to South Africa, especially during the period of the 1922 Strike.

One casualty of the First World War had been the Namaqualand copper industry closed mainly due to difficulty with supplies and the constant interruption of the market. The Kimberley diamond mines closed in 1921 although the diamond industry prospered as new diamond discoveries were made, ironically in Namaqualand. The gold industry on the Rand, like the tin industry in Cornwall, recovered from the post war slump, although its future was far more long lasting. A combination of phthisis, the First World War, the collapse of the Cornish tin industry and the 1922 Rand Strike saw an end to the pre-eminent position once held by the Cornish miner in the land of gold and diamonds. Although in January 1923 the *Cornishman* could still remind its readers that thousands of Cornish homes were still dependent on remittances from South Africa[180] that number was becoming ever smaller. There had been a significant drop in the number of Cornish miners going to South Africa and the number of Cornish miners at Johannesburg and Kimberley had also diminished as many returned home; others never left South Africa, for they died and were buried there.

By 1923 there were encouraging signs that the depression in Cornwall was beginning to lift and the unemployment figures began to drop, not just because of emigration. Some Cornish mines, such as Levant, re-opened as the tin price slowly began to rise again. By May there were over 1,000 employed once more in the tin mines of West Cornwall. The best news came in October when it was proposed to sink a new shaft at Dolcoath – the raising of the necessary investment being helped by the Government providing half of the total £130,000 required.[181] Although by the end of 1924 Levant, Geevor, Tresavean, South Crofty and East Pool & Agar were back in normal production,[182] the unemployment Committee was not disbanded until 1927. It appeared, however, that once again the Cornish mining industry had survived.

After the war in South Africa although the news of Cornish miners was sparse a number of Cornish Pioneers had excelled in civic duties. W. Fox (Penzance) had worked for the South African Railways Durban Institute which he had joined in 1879. As there were no facilities for technical education, Fox started up evening classes which he ran as an instructor. When he retired in 1920 after 40 years as Foreman in the mechanical department he received a presentation as a Pioneer of the railway institute for technical education which commenced in 1885 in a shed belonging to the old Natal Government railways.[183]

Following in the footsteps of W.T. Hoal the Cornish Post Master General of the South African postal service, were two other Cornishmen – George Rees (Hayle) and Marwood French (Penzance). Rees had been Controller of Posts at Johannesburg, having held the position for 16 years before his retirement in 1922. Having first joined the Imperial Post & Telegraph Service at Penzance in 1880 he had transferred to the Cape Telegraph Service in 1889, being employed at Kimberley. He then moved to Cape Town's Central Telegraph Office and from there became Postmaster of Rondebosch. In 1896 he became Superintendent General of Cape Town's Post Office, a position he held until the Boer War during which he was loaned to the Imperial Army's Postal service. After the war he reorganised Transvaal's civil postal service and for a time acted as Postmaster of Pretoria, before becoming Controller of Posts at Johannesburg.[184] Marwood French also began his postal career at Penzance before moving to Johannesburg, where in 1912 he became Chief Superintendent of Johannesburg's General Post Office. Before that he had been Postmaster at over twenty Post Offices within the Transvaal. At his retirement in 1931 the Postmaster General said he had never met an officer who has a higher conception of loyalty to the department and personal loyalty to his Chief.[185]

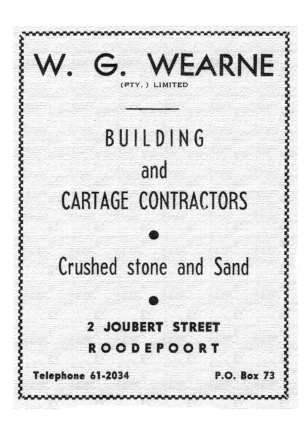

W. G. WEARNE
(PTY.) LIMITED

BUILDING
and
CARTAGE CONTRACTORS

●

Crushed stone and Sand

●

2 JOUBERT STREET
ROODEPOORT

Telephone 61-2034   P.O. Box 73

Rundle Olds (St. Just), a relative of Francis Oats, had been General Manager of the Cape Asbestos Company Headquarters at Kimberley for over 30 years when he retired to look after his large sheep farming interests in the Prieska district. In 1936 he was elected to the municipal council of the township of George.[186] William Olds – who was probably a relation – had been a lifetime councillor at Bloemfontein, until his death in 1935.[187] Charles Chudleigh the ex-Mayor of

Johannesburg had been one of the most prominent Cornishmen on the Rand in the world of commerce, and his four-storey building – Mounts Bay House – was not only a major landmark in Johannesburg but one of the largest and most up-to-date drapery and outfitting establishments in South Africa.[188] Although he died in 1924, leaving behind a widow and four married daughters, he was not the last Cornish Mayor in South Africa by any means.

In 1927 there were no less than three Cornish Mayors on the Rand; T. Stark, Mayor of Germiston, J. Stansbury, Mayor of Boksburg and W.G. Wearne, Mayor of Roodepoort. The Cornish Association held a special celebration in honour of the three men at the Grand National Hotel and over 200 people nearly all of Cornish birth or extraction heard Dr. William Terril of the Methodist Episcopal Church say:

> *We have met here tonight as sons and daughters of Cornwall to do honour as three sons of that county have risen to the highest offices their respective towns can bestow upon them.*[189]

Although little is known about Stark or Stansbury, William George Wearne (Wendron) and his wife, Alice, were Mayor and Mayoress of Roodepoort in 1926-27, 1927-28 and 1939-40. Wearne was a stonemason who went to South Africa from Cornwall in 1900. He worked on two mines – the Roodepoort Central and Durban Roodepoort – before setting up his own stone quarrying business – W.G. Wearne Pty. Ltd. In addition to being a member of the Roodepoort-Maraisburg Town Council Wearne took a keen interest in the Boy Scout movement and during his time as Mayor he met Baden Powell. In 1930 Wearne became President of the Cornish Association and in 1938 made a visit to Cornwall to stay with relatives at Porkellis and Carnkie, during which time he visited Trannock school where he was once a scholar and spoke to the children. When Wearne died in August 1946, the Benoni branch of the Cornish Association sent a letter of sympathy to his widow, saying he was a fine type of a Cornishman and loved by all.[190]

Other Cornishmen on the Rand who were elected Mayor included, W.R. May (Pendeen), Mayor of Randfontein 1936,[191] William Davey (Commonmoor), Mayor of Benoni 1952-53, who was mainly responsible for the creation of the African township of Daveytown at Benoni[192] and finally James Thomas Halse (Marazion), Mayor of Krugersdorp 1929-32 and the only Cornish Mayor in South Africa to die whilst in office. Halse's contracting business built hospitals at Dundee, Heidelberg, Roodepoort and Potchefstroom, two school hostels at Heidelberg, two at Potchefstroom, the Randfontein Town Hall, Government buildings at Mafeking and the Technical College at Krugersdorp, plus a large number of Government schools throughout the Transvaal. Halse was elected to the Krugersdorp Town Council in October 1918 and, except for two years, served until his death. Like Wearne he had been elected Mayor three times. The news of his death was received with deep regret by the Governor General of the Transvaal. The funeral of

Halse on 30th September was the largest ever seen on the Rand for he had been a great favourite of the poor, having started the Mayor's Relief Fund which was the salvation of over 200 unemployed men and over 500 families of the town who were helped by it. Amongst the mourners were Sir George Albu, nearly all the other Mayors on the Rand plus representatives of the Transvaal Master Builders Association, of which Halse had been a past President. Six ex-Mayors of Krugersdorp were pall-bearers and with the Krugersdorp Methodist church crowded with hundreds of people being unable to get in, plus over 200 wreaths on his grave it was a fitting tribute indeed to just one more Cornish Pioneer who had made his mark in South Africa.[193]

The revival of an ancient Cornish Celtic ceremony, re-enacted for the first time at the Bronze Age stone circle of Boscawen-un near Penzance on 21st September 1928, established the Cornish Gorsedd. Based upon the Welsh model it was the inspiration of Henry Jenner, R. Morton Nance and the Federation of Old Cornwall Societies. It became an annual event. Bards had to have made a significant contribution to Cornwall's culture, tradition and history, or demonstrated proficiency in the revised Cornish Celtic language. Jenner became the first Grand Bard of Cornwall and others who were created Bards in 1928 included Sir Arthur Quiller Couch, A.K. Hamilton Jenkin, Charles G. Henderson, Herbert Thomas and John Coulson Tregarthen.[194] Tregarthen's brother – William Coulson Tregarthen – was the first Cornish-South African to be made a Bard. It was he who had played before the Empress Eugenie when she was en-route to the scene of the Prince Imperial's death after the Zulu War. Tregarthen had then been organist and choir-master at St. Mary's Collegiate church, Port Elizabeth. He went on to make a very important contribution to the musical literature of South Africa introducing into the country the first musical examination. At President Kruger's request he harmonised for four voices the *Transvaal Volksleid* and also composed music for the national *Hymn of the South African Republic* with Dutch and English words and an air *Beyond the Night* to words in the ancient Bantu language by Herbert Price.[195] Tregarthen was responsible for drawing up the specifications for the organ at Kimberley Wesleyan church and at Queenstown he composed a march for the Queenstown Rifle Volunteers and presented 30 palm trees to form the Tregarthen Avenue leading to the local hospital.[187]

Richard Hall (St. Just), a Bard of Cornwall (Carer Kern) who died in 1932 at the residence of his son-in-law in Durban was probably the first Cornish Bard to die in South Africa.[196]

The world-wide depression which began with the Wall St. Crash in 1929, was mirrored in Cornwall with another collapse of the tin mining industry. In February 1930 there were 4,806 unemployed miners in the Camborne area alone[197] and by the end of the year, Levant mine had stopped production, with 200 miners discharged.[198] At Camborne both East Pool and South Crofty mines suspended operations, affecting some 600 men.[199] When Geevor mine suspended operations in October, affecting some 200 men, it was said to be the first time in history that mining operations in the parish of St. Just have been entirely suspended.[200] By November East Pool & Agar was the only mine in Cornwall to be carrying out any real work and the *Cornishman* stated at that time Cornwall could scarcely be called a mining area.[201] It was to be nearly a year before hopes were raised for the industry's future. In October 1931 South Crofty restarted operations and in January 1932 Geevor began once more to take on men. The mines of Levant, Wheal Kitty, Tresavean and the New Dolcoath, however, never re-opened

South Africa also experienced closure of some of its mines during the depression, including the Ferreira Deep on the Rand in 1929 and the diamond mines of Kimberley and Pretoria in 1932, which naturally affected many Cornishmen. In 1934 with the collapse of the diamond market the *Cornishman* reported that at Kimberley the very aspect of the town told of a severe depression,[202] and a few months later it commented:

> *Kimberley is the worst place in South Africa just now because the diamond trade is in the Slough of Despair. I do not think the mines there will ever be worked on the same scale as they used to be years ago, almost like the tin and copper mines of our beloved county.*[203]

Kimberley eventually recovered, with mines such as Dutoitspan and Wesselton re-opening by 1937. However, with the outbreak of the Second World War in 1939 the diamond industry received a further blow which sent it reeling once more, although the strength of De Beers and the expertise of the Oppenheimers helped the industry eventually to recover.[204]

Despite the First World War, the strikes and depression, the virtual collapse of Cornwall's mining industry and the end of large scale emigration from Cornwall to South Africa, the wane of Cornish influence at Kimberley with the death of Oats, plus the high rate of mortality amongst the Cornish miners, especially on the Rand, the Cornish Association in South Africa somehow survived, so that even after the Second World War it was still in existence and quite active. From all accounts it appears that this was due to Hedley Heath Sobey, who was very much the driving force behind the Association between the two World Wars. Ken Sara considered him a real gentleman, who was loved by many and respected by all, and remembered how Sobey did a tremendous job in keeping the Cornish miners united with their families in Cornwall, which was no mean feat, as in some cases the miners failed to send maintenance money to their families.[205]

The Cornish Association continued to organise a wide range of social functions with wrestling, whist drives, dances, picnics, carol concerts and annual dinners being as popular as ever, although reports in the Cornish Press were less frequent. In 1937 at the Association's Annual Dinner held at the Langham Hotel,

Johannesburg G.L. Symons was President and Sobey had resumed his office as Honorary Secretary. The guest speaker was J.H. Hofmeyr, the Minister of Mines, who believed that it was Cornishmen who had taught engineering to the Americans in the early days. Hofmeyr was no stranger to Cornwall for he had been a student at the Camborne School of Mines where he had found,

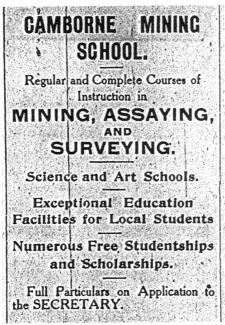

CAMBORNE MINING SCHOOL.

Regular and Complete Courses of Instruction in

MINING, ASSAYING,
AND
SURVEYING.

Science and Art Schools.

Exceptional Education Facilities for Local Students

Numerous Free Studentships and Scholarships.

Full Particulars on Application to the SECRETARY.

Camborne School of Mines advertisement of 1908.

warmth and sunshine in a place in England where I could get nearest to South Africa. I remember the Cornish pasties, cream and cider, and not quite so gratefully I remember the Cornish hills up which I sometimes had to push my bicycle in the rain... they could never forget what Cornishmen had done to build up the mining industry... we should never forget the price which many Cornishmen have paid for the building up of our mining industry. Even today there are in many Cornish villages sufferers from miners' phthisis contracted on the Witwatersrand.[206]

A lifeboat disaster at St. Ives, Cornwall early in 1939 showed that the Cornish in South Africa were as ready as ever to send their sympathy and financial support to their home county. The Cornish Association held a number of concerts and other events in order to raise money for the disaster fund.[207]

In 1936 the Rand celebrated 50 years. As at Kimberley, so too at Johannesburg, many of the early Cornish Pioneers had died or returned home to Cornwall. The *Cornishman* gave a three-column report on the Jubilee celebrations held at Johannesburg, although it bemoaned the fact that the South African newspaper accounts of the Jubilee made no mention of Arthur James of Redruth and his part in the cyanide process, or Professor J.G. Lawn, one time Principal of the Camborne School of Mines and technical advisor to Consolidated Goldfields, or Tom Mathews, of Newlyn who fought pluckily for what he considered the right of miners in those steamy days, or Moses Roberts of St. Agnes, Editor of the *Standard and Diggers News*, or J. Harry Johns – the list is long. There was some compensation, however, in that some newspapers carried portraits of William Hosken and Charles Chudleigh.[208]

No mention was made of Emily Hobhouse but then her death in 1926 had not even been acknowledged in the Cornish newspapers. Having handed over her spinning and weaving industries to the Transvaal and Orange Free State governments in 1908 she had returned to Europe preferring to live in Rome, rather than Cornwall, because of the warmer climate. In 1913 she was invited back to South Africa to unveil the Women's Memorial in Bloemfontein. Sadly after her arrival in the country her health deteriorated so that she had to return to the coast before the actual ceremony. A message from her was read out instead which said:

> *As your tribute to the dead, bury unforgiveness and bitterness at the foot of this monument forever. Instead forgive, for you can afford it, the rich who were over greedy of more richness, the statesman who could not guide affairs, the bad generalship that warred on weaklings and babies, forgive – for so only can you rise to full nobility of character and a broad and noble national life. For what really matters is character. History clearly teaches this.*[209]

It was during her visit that Emily met Gandhi, who had begun his non-violent campaign against the South African Government restrictions on the Asian community which had already earned him a spell in jail. According to one author it was this meeting that led Emily Hobhouse to adopt pacifism, a cause she championed for the rest of her life.[210] Therefore, when war broke out in 1914 and her beloved South Africa joined in, she denounced its involvement in no uncertain terms. Nor was she happy when her friends De Wet and De la Rey rebelled against her other close friends – Botha and Smuts. Her friendship with Smuts came almost to breaking point. Her decision to visit Germany itself in June 1916 earned her once more accusations that she was disloyal and unpatriotic. Emily's actions and motives were, as always, in the interests of peace and humanity. The fact that she had visited a British prisoner of war camp in Germany, in order to see that prisoners were not being ill treated, tended to be overlooked. It also ignored her work with the Save the Children Fund after the war – a fund which through Emily's connections received a large amount from South Africa (£12,000 raised privately in South Africa, plus a further £5,000 from the South African government). In Cornwall the only memorials to Emily Hobhouse are at St. Ive near Liskeard. A blue plaque by the door of the old Rectory reads 'Birthplace of Emily Hobhouse 1860 – 1926' while a small brass plaque on the wall behind the choir stalls of her father's church says:

South African stamp commemorating Emily Hobhouse in 1976.

To the memory of Emily, Youngest daughter of Reginald Hobhouse first Archdeacon of Bodmin and 50 years Rector of this Parish Born 9th April 1860 Died 8th June 1926

There is no mention of South Africa, and yet it is there that a more fitting memorial stands. For although Emily died in a London nursing home, she is buried neither in London nor Cornwall. Her body was cremated and her ashes were buried at the Women's Memorial in Bloemfontein which she herself had been unable to unveil some thirteen years before. At a special ceremony on 27th October 1926 Jan Smuts, then Prime Minister, said:

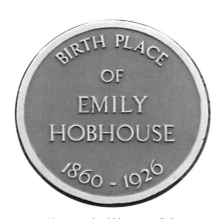

Plaque at the Old rectory, St Ive.

We stood alone in the world, friendless among the peoples, the smallest nation ranged against the mightiest Empire on earth. At the darkest hour, when our race almost appeared doomed to extinction, she appeared as an angel, as a heaven-sent messenger. Strangest of all, she was an Englishwoman.[211]

If Emily Hobhouse is to be best remembered for her humanitarian stance and for having the courage of her convictions – totally objecting to any segregation of people by race, colour or class – then her Cornish male equivalent is without a doubt William Hosken.

Hosken deserves above all to be remembered for his fight on behalf of the rights of Indians in the Transvaal. He was one of the very few politicians after the Boer War actually to be in favour of granting the municipal franchise to coloured persons. It was Hosken who led a deputation to Lord Selborne, the High Commissioner, who had replaced Lord Milner in 1905, making it clear to him that the treatment of the coloured races in the Transvaal since British occupation was worse than before. Hosken was the first signatory to petition on their behalf and "although it was a voice in the wilderness it was fearlessly in favour of justice and humanity" wrote Gandhi.[212] Hosken is praised time and time again by Gandhi for making what was often a lone stand against Indian discrimination, and in his memoirs, Gandhi pays tribute to Hosken's encouragement.

Mohandas Karamchand Gandhi, having studied in England, went to South Africa to practise law in 1893. During the Boer War Gandhi had led an Indian Ambulance Corps. consisting of around a thousand men. He thought that after the war the British would be very much in sympathy with the rights of Asiatics in South Africa but he could not have been more wrong. In 1903 the Asiatic Department which operated in the Transvaal began to introduce new regulations to restrict the Asiatic community, both Indian and Chinese. Gandhi said of Hosken:

> *he had always been free from colour prejudice but his interest in the Indian question deepened after the starting of Satyagraha.*[213]

Gandhi's idea of Satyagraha – truth force or love force – advocating non-violence – was more than just passive resistance. By 1906 all the frustrations and anger of the Indian community at being treated unfairly erupted in the Transvaal when it was announced that a new Act would compel all Indian men and women to be registered and fingerprinted. The Asiatic Law Amendment Act or Black Act was denounced by Hosken as "a Bill being appropriate only in Russia".[214] Although intervention by Gandhi managed to delay the Act, with the victory of Botha's Het Volk party at the polls in February 1907, the Act became law, being followed quickly by an Immigration Act which prevented any more Indians from entering the Transvaal.

Gandhi became the key figure in the resistance campaign that followed, writing letters to the press, meeting politicians, organising petitions, addressing meetings as well as founding a newspaper – *The Indian Opinion*. Refusing to register under the Act large numbers of Indians were arrested and put in jail, and some were even deported. In an attempt to get Gandhi and the Indian community to submit to the terms of the Act, and bow to the inevitable, Prime Minister Botha and the Colonial Secretary, Jan Smuts, sent William Hosken as their emissary to address a large meeting of Indians on 31st July 1907 at Pretoria. Hosken although in total support of the Indian cause still felt they should comply with the law and finished with the words:

> *To resist it will be to dash your head against the wall. I wish that your community may not be ruined in fruitless opposition or invite needless suffering on their heads.*[215]

Gandhi translated the speech and Hosken retired amidst cheers. Later he regretted ever having advised Gandhi and the Indian community to abandon such a great struggle and from that time never wavered in his support.[216] When Gandhi himself had been imprisoned for two months, Hosken said:

> *We can all take one lesson to heart. This is a notable day in the history of the Transvaal and South Africa because today several men have been sent to prison for conscience's sake. It is the bounden duty of every man and woman in this community carefully to consider what their duty is in these difficult conditions.*[217]

Hosken was in no doubt as to his duty. He had become Chairman of the European Sympathisers which mediated between the Satyagrahis and the Government. In March 1908, at a special dinner provided by the Indian community for the European Sympathisers, Hosken said on behalf of the whites:

> *I feel ashamed now to think that in July (1907) I had advised the Indian community to accept the law. I meant well. I felt it would prove to be futile to resist the Boer Government. But Mr. Gandhi told me that they did not depend on human help for their movement. They depended on divine aid. They were sure of help from him in whose name they had embarked on the movement. I see his words have come true. The courage shown by the Indian community has won for it increased sympathy from the whites, The Indian community has taught the whites a great deal... Whites and Coloured persons ought to live together amicably. The Indian community deserves praise for the unity, patience and humility it has shown.*[218]

A few days later at another dinner, this time provided by the Chinese community for the European Sympathisers, Hosken said:

> *There is very little I have done. I make no distinction between coloured persons and whites. The Asiatics have taught us a lesson. I think both your courage and your success are worthy of the highest admiration.*[219]

Gandhi considered Hosken to be one of the few men in South Africa who had the courage of his convictions, and claimed Hosken

> *was known all over South Africa to be the friend of the non white races at a time when practically every public man with the exception of Mr. Hosken seems to be opposed to the Indians.*[220]

On another occasion Gandhi wrote to Hosken that the Indian community was:

> *deeply grateful for the kindly interest you, as a lover of the Empire and a Christian gentleman take in the present bitter struggle that Asiatics are engaged in.*[221]

By 1910 Hosken's sympathies had become more concrete and he wrote to Smuts supporting Gandhi and the Indian community in their struggle. His letter angered Smuts who wrote in reply:

> *I very much regret your attitude – I can only express in reply my regret at your action which I feel is ill considered and mischievous. It is not you who will suffer in the end but the Indian community against whom the white population is becoming daily more exasperated and demanding even more stringent legislation.*[222]

The support Hosken gave to Gandhi and the Asiatic community probably cost him his seat in the 1910 Election. The *Transvaal Leader* and the *Pretoria News* were highly indignant at the non-election of this Cornish worthy while the *Leader* said:

> *the objection against Mr. Hosken on the ground of his so-called negrophilism is one which we could more patiently hear of if it came from men who have earned the right to voice it by public labours one-fifteenth as valuable as his; the News wrote it is difficult to write with patience at the rejection of Mr. Hosken as a Senator.*[223]

Hosken and his wife returned home to Cornwall, where such was his popularity that about 1,000 men attended the Tuckingmill Men's Brotherhood monthly meeting one Sunday afternoon to hear Hosken give a speech entitled Cornishmen in the Transvaal.[224]

On returning to the Transvaal, Hosken continued to speak out on behalf of Indians and in June 1911 the *Indian Opinion* contained a portrait of Hosken saying:-

> *We should like our readers to have the portrait glazed and to hang it up in their rooms – we earnestly hope that every Indian will have in his living room only the portraits of those who have us in their debt or whose memory we wish to cherish.*[225]

Despite Hosken having been the butt of cartoonists and being given nicknames such as *Biljee Oskendhi* and *Banana Bill* he stuck firmly to his principles.[226] When Gandhi made his farewell speech to his followers before returning to India in 1914 he said that Hosken had been the most influential of his helpers. When Hosken's wife died in 1915 many Indians attended her funeral at Johannesburg out of respect for Mr. Hosken, who has never failed to champion their cause when support was most needed.[227]

William Hosken himself died on 7th June 1925. He had been, without a doubt, the most influential Cornishman in South Africa and it was believed by one newspaper that he might have been Prime Minister, except that,

> *his candour, his regard for the native races, his religious fervour and the tenacity with which he held a belief in Free Trade probably robbed him of the leadership of the British electorate in the Transvaal.*[228]

Although he died in the Cape at Muizenburg, he was buried at Johannesburg. At the funeral, as his coffin was carried out of the Wesleyan Central Hall:

> *An Indian Military Officer in full uniform passed through to the front rank of the great crowd that was present. As the coffin passed he drew his sabre and gave the impressive sweeping salute of the swordsmen. He*

sheathed his weapon and then again as the last bearer passed him the glittering steel flashed once more – the final salute.

It was Jamadur Nawabkhna of the 1st Punjabs and the picturesque incident acted as a reminder to everyone who saw it as one of the most notable characteristics of the late Mr. Hosken. His work for Asiatics and for the natives was one of his leading interests and at his funeral there were scores of native men and women and many Indians for whom special transport to the cemetery was provided.[229]

1. *CORNISHMAN*, 18th JUNE 1908

2. *IBID.*, 29th JUNE 1899

3. *C.P.M.N.*, 24 JANUARY 1907

4. *IBID.*, 27th JULY 1905

5. *CORNUBIAN*, 25th FEBRUARY 1909

6. *C.P.M.N.*, 29th JANUARY 1903

7. *C.P.M.N.*, 26th JANUARY 1905

8. Williams died in 1941, his death being regretted both in Cornwall and South Africa. *IBID.* 9th JANUARY 1941

9. C.P.M.N., 31st MAY 1907

10. *IBID.*, 18th APRIL 1907

11. *DICKASON, CORNISH IMMIGRANTS* p.67

12. *C.P.M.N.*, 18th AUGUST 1910

13. James Warmington (Lelant) was another Cornish singer who won a prize at the event securing first honours for tenors.

14. *C.P.M.N.*, 18th MAY 1911

15. *IBID.*, 7th MARCH 1912

16. *IBID.*, 19th JULY 1906

17. *IBID.*, 26th DECEMBER 1907

18. *IBID.*, 7th FEBRUARY 1907

19. *IBID.*, 3rd JANUARY 1907

20. Blackwell, *FROM A DARK STREAM* p.212

21. *C.P.M.N.*, 2nd OCTOBER 1913

22. *CORNISHMAN*, 15th AUGUST 1912

23. *C.P.M.N.* 5th MAY 1904

24. *CORNISHMAN* 9TH JUNE 1904

25. *IBID.*, 9th FEBRUARY 1905. Cornish wrestling has little in common with modern wrestling. It goes back centuries – in 1415 the Cornish contingent at Agincourt carried a banner portraying two wrestlers in a hitch. Cornish wrestlers were again present at Henry VIII's Field of the Cloth of Gold.

26. *IBID.*, 1st FEBRUARY 1906

27. *CORNISHMAN*, 15th MARCH 1906

28. *C.P.M.N.*, 11th OCTOBER 1906

29. *CORNISHMAN*, 24th JANUARY 1907

30. *IBID.*, 15th SEPTEMBER 1910

31. See also Blackwell, *FROM A DARK STREAM* p. 212-213 for more about Williams.

32. *C.P.M.N.*, 19th NOVEMBER 1908

33. *CORNUBIAN* 16 JANUARY 1907

34. *IBID.*, 14 JULY 1910

35. *IBID.*, 24 NOVEMBER 1910

36. *CORNISHMAN*, 4th JUNE 1908

37. *C.P.M.N.*, 2nd NOVEMBER 1916

38. *IBID.*, 3rd JUNE 1915. See also *IBID.*, 2nd NOVEMBER 1916

39. *DIAMOND FIELDS ADVERTISER*, SEPTEMBER 1918

40. Chilvers, *THE STORY OF DE BEERS*, p. 284. See also *C.P.M.N.*, 5th SEPTEMBER 1901 – it was reported that Oats and his son left Georgetown on the 13th for Trinidad, whence they were to proceed to Venezuela.

41. *IBID.*, p. 284

42. *IBID.*, p. 148 – 149

43. *C.P.M.N.*, 25th APRIL 1901

44. Wheatcroft, *RANDLORDS*, p. 226 See also Roberts, *DIAMOND MAGNATES* p. 289

45. *CORNISHMAN*, 24th SEPTEMBER 1908

46. *CORNUBIAN*, 10th FEBRUARY 1910

47. *CORNISHMAN*, 13th FEBRUARY 1913

48. Paul H. Emden, *RANDLORDS* (LONDON 1935) p. 263

49. A.P. Cartwright, *THE DYNAMITE COMPANY* (CAPE TOWN 1964) p. 165

50. *IBID.*, p. 120

51. *IBID.*, p. 144

52. *C.P.M.N.*, 21st SEPTEMBER 1905

53. *IBID.*, 9th MAY 1907

54. *WEST BRITON* 31st DECEMBER 1953

55. *DIAMOND FIELDS ADVERTISER*, 2nd SEPTEMBER 1918

56. *C.P.M.N.*, 8th JANUARY 1914

57. *DIAMOND FIELDS ADVERTISER*, 4th JANUARY 1913 Ernest Oppenheimer was Mayor of Kimberley 1912-15 and became Chairman of De Beers 1929. He was a member of Parliament 1924-48 being knighted in 1920. He died in 1957 aged 73 years.

58. *DIAMOND FIELDS ADVERTISER*, 4th JANUARY 1913

59. *IBID.*, 2nd SEPTEMBER 1918

60 *IBID.*, 2nd SEPTEMBER 1918

61. Chilvers, *STORY OF DE BEERS*, p. 295

62. *CORNISHMAN & CORNISH TELEGRAPH*, 11th SEPTEMBER 1918

63. Chilvers, *STORY OF DE BEERS*, p. 217

64. *CORNISHMAN*, 19th MAY 1910

65. *C.P.M.N.* 19th MAY 1910. Tickell's first names were never recorded in the press Even when he fell down stairs – he suffered internal injuries and it was some days before he could resume his duties – he was referred to as Mr. Tickell. See *CORNISHMAN*, 25th AUGUST 1910.

66. *IBID.*, 10th MARCH 1910

67. *C.P.M.N.*, 5th MAY 1910

68. *CORNISHMAN*, 14h APRIL 1910

69. *IBID.*, 11th AUGUST 1910

70. *IBID.*, 12th MAY 1910

71. *IBID.*, 25th AUGUST 1910. Phillips even had a Cornish gardener. See *C.P.M.N.*, 4th MAY 1911

72. *C.P.M.N.*, 28th APRIL 1910

73. *CORNISHMAN*, 9th JUNE 1910

74. *C.P.M.N.*, 19th MAY 1910

75. *CORNISHMAN*, 3rd NOVEMBER 1910. An earlier report stated that hospital visitation was never neglected with over 30 visits having been paid to 60 Cornish patients between March-July with money being spent on fruit and flowers plus other necessities. *IBID.*, 11th AUGUST 1910

76. *CORNISHMAN*, 29th JUNE 1911. Miners' phthisis was also high on the agenda.

77. *IBID.*, 14th MARCH 1907

78. *IBID.*, 30th NOVEMBER 1911. The following year the Penzance Board of Guardians voted to give an annual subscription to the Association. See *IBID.*, 25th JANUARY 1912

79. Dickason, *CORNISH IMMIGRANTS* . p.72

80. *CORNISHMAN*, 7th JULY 1910

81. *C.P.M.N.*, 1st DECEMBER 1910

82. *CORNISHMAN.*, 13th JUNE 1912. For more information on Frank Harvey see Vale, *HARVEYS OF HAYLE*.

83. *CORNISHMAN*, 13th JUNE 1912

84. *TRANSVAAL LEADER*, 10th AUGUST 1912

85. *CORNISHMAN*, 26th SEPTEMBER 1912

86. *IBID* 4th JULY 1912

87. *C.P.M.N.*, 10th OCTOBER 1913. Morcom continued to *rove* – he died in Manitoba, Canada in 1940. See *STANDARD & WEST RAND REVIEW*, 2nd FEBRUARY 1940

88. *IBID.*, 14th NOVEMBER 1912. Peter was also a noted Cornish historian and antiquary. He died in September 1917.

89. Kennedy, *A TALE OF TWO MINING CITIES* p. 77. The proportion of South African born whites to other whites (American, Australian and Cornish) employed on the mines increased from 17. 5 per cent just before the 1907 strike to 24. 6 per cent during it.

90. *C.P.M.N.*, 14th MAY 1908

91. *CORNISHMAN*, 3rd NOVEMBER 1910. J Harry Johns went to live in Italy where in December 1932 he died. According to the *POST* Johns left property in his will worth £30, 960 see *C P M N.*, 8th April 1933.

92. *C.P.M.N.*, 16th MAY 1907

93. *CORNISHMAN*, 23rd JUNE 1910

94. *IBID.*, 21st MARCH 1907

95. *C.P.M.N.*, 21st FEBRUARY 1907 and *CORNISHMAN*, 17th OCTOBER 1907

96. *C.P.M.N.*, 10th DECEMBER 1908

97. *IBID.*, 15th FEBRUARY 1906

98. *IBID.*, 11th JANUARY 1912 Bartle died in January 1933 at Newquay where he had been resposible for the inception of Mount Wise recreation grounds, plus a new Constitutional Club for although being a consistent Wesleyan Methodist he had been an ardent Conservative.

99. *CORNISHMAN*, 18th JANUARY 1912

100. *C.P.M.N.*, 15th SEPTEMBER 1910

101. *CORNISHMAN*, 13th JUNE 1912

102 *IBID.*, 4th DECEMBER 1902

103. *C.P.M.N.*, 11th AUGUST 1904

104. *IBID.*, 10th JANUARY 1910

105. *IBID.*, 28th FEBRUARY 1907

106. *IBID.*, 26th MARCH 1908

107. *CORNISHMAN*, 16th SEPTEMBER 1909

108. *TRANSVAAL LEADER*, 3rd NOVEMBER 1909

109. *IBID.*, 4th NOVEMBER 1909

110. *CORNUBIAN*, 26th AUGUST 1909

111. *IBID.*, 2nd DECEMBER 1909. Hambly's sister also died – she had been suffering from tuberculosis, but it was believed the tragedy had accelerated her death.

112. See especially, *THE VELDT TRAGEDY – SHOULD HAMBLY DIE?* by F. J. Tiddy *TRANSVAAL LEADER* 3rd NOVEMBER 1909 also *IBID.*, 6th NOVEMBER 1909

113. *TRANSVAAL LEADER*, 8th NOVEMBER 1909 and *IBID.*, 10th NOVEMBER 1909

114. *IBID.*, 9th NOVEMBER 1909

115. *IBID.*, 5th NOVEMBER 1909

116. *IBID.*, 18th NOVEMBER 1909. Hosken kept the petition in his own office for people to sign.

117. *IBID.*, 23rd NOVEMBER 1909

118. *IBID.*, 24th NOVEMBER 1909

119. *CORNUBIAN*, 17th FEBRUARY 1910

120. *CORNISHMAN*, 3rd MAY 1912

121. Samson R. Stuttaford died in London April 1914. See also the *STORY OF STUTTAFORDS* (CAPE TOWN 1957).

122. *CAPE TIMES*, 20th OCTOBER 1945

123. *NORTH WESTERN PRESS*, 24th MAY 1912. See also *CORNISHMAN*, 4th JULY 1912

124. *IBID.*, 12th OCTOBER 1905

125. *THE EASTERN PROVINCE HERALD*, 10th SEPTEMBER 1926

126. Tom MacDonald, *TRANSVAAL STORY* (CAPE TOWN 1961) p. 32

127. *IBID.*, p. 33

128. *POTCHESFSTROOM HERALD*, 14th JULY 1961

129. *CORNISHMAN*, 21st AUGUST 1941

130. *IBID.*, 9th JANUARY 1941

131. *IBID.*, 30th DECEMBER 1925

132. *IBID.*, 24th DECEMBER 1942

133. *IBID.*, 26th MAY 1932

134. *IBID.*, 29th OCTOBER 1931. Tiddy was confined to bed in June suffering from severe internal bleeding. See *IBID.*, 25th JUNE 1931

135. See *CORNUBIAN*, 4th FEBRUARY 1909 and *CORNISHMAN*, 4th FEBRUARY 1909

136. *IBID.*, 5th JANUARY 1921

137. *IBID.*, 28th MARCH 1935 – Rowe died in 1954

138. *IBID.*, 24th MAY 1928. According to Dickason, Bawden became M. P. for Langlaagte in 1929 and represented that constituency periodically thereafter. See Dickason *CORNISH IMMIGRANTS* . p. 88. See also *CAPE ARGUS* 19th JULY 1947.

139. *IBID.*, 10th AUGUST 1939

140. Mears, *HISTORY OF ST. STITHIANS COLLEGE* . p. 4-5

141. A recollection by Benjamin Bennett – News Editor of the Cape Argus who once worked for the *STAR* as a young reporter. See also *THE STAR*, 22nd OCTOBER

1937 for a full account of the charities that benefited from Collins' will.

142. Mears, *HISTORY OF ST. STITHIANS COLLEGE* p. 4

143. An undated newspaper clipping supplied by Carol Botha.

144. Mears, History, p. 39

145. See Dickason, *CORNISH IMMIGRANTS* p. 88-96

146. *C.P.M.N.*, 17th MAY 1917

147. Information supplied by Ada Grassman

148. Dickason, *CORNISH IMMIGRANTS* p. 70

149. *CORNISHMAN*, 15th OCTOBER 1914

150. *IBID.*, 8th APRIL 1915

151. *C.P.M.N.*, 23rd DECEMBER 1915 – Many Cornish miners were drafted to the front – their tunnelling skills being such that a Cornish Tunnelling Corps. was created.

152. *IBID.*, 29th OCTOBER 1919

153. For a full list of the victims plus details of the disaster see Noall, *CORNISH MINE DISASTERS* and Noall, *LEVANT: THE MINE BENEATH THE SEA* (BRADFORD BARTON 1972). The effect that the mining disaster had on St. Just is best summed up by Raymond Harry, one of the lucky survivors who said, "The disaster at Levant put paid to St. Just as my generation knew it. It will never be the same because hundreds of young people in my generation who left there, went to America, South Africa, Australia, Canada. Really my generation is gone from there – there is a generation short in St. Just". Douglas Williams, *WEST CORNWALL IN THE OLD DAYS* (BODMIN 1985) p. 81

154. *CORNISHMAN*, 29th OCTOBER 1919

155. *IBID.*, 17th DECEMBER 1919

156. *IBID.*, 3rd MARCH 1920

157. *IBID.*, 4th February 1920

158. All figures for the tin prices come from either the *CORNISHMAN* or Barton, *A HISTORY OF TIN MINING AND SMELTING IN CORNWALL*

159. *CORNISHMAN*, 2nd JUNE 1920

160. Barton, *A HISTORY OF TIN MINING* p.61

161. *CORNISHMAN*, 7th JULY 1920

162. *IBID.*, 28th JULY 1920

163. *IBID.*, 2nd JUNE 1920

164. *IBID.*, 1st JUNE 1921

165. *IBID.*, 18th AUGUST 1920 See also Noall, *CORNISH MINE DISASTERS*.

166. According to Claude Berry the village of Lanner was built largely with remittances from Cornish miners on the Rand. Berry, *CORNWALL* p. 101

167. *CORNISHMAN*, 15th JUNE 1921

168. Barton, *A HISTORY OF TIN MINING* . p. 262-263

169. *CORNISHMAN*, 15th JUNE 1921

170. *IBID.*, 17th August 1921

171. *C.P.M.N.*, 10th SEPTEMBER 1914. Charles Thomas had two sons. William was Manager of Botallack, Fred was in South Africa mining. Charles Thomas died in 1931. See *CORNISHMAN* 20th AUGUST 1931

172. *CORNISHMAN*, 17th AUGUST 1921

173. *IBID.*, 28th SEPTEMBER 1921

174. *IBID.*, 26th OCTOBER 1921

175. *IBID.*, 16th NOVEMBER 1921

176. *IBID.*, 28th DECEMBER 1921

177. *IBID.*, 18th JANUARY 1922 – Smith served with the 6th Dragoon Guards, being at both the relief of Kimberley and Battle of Paardeberg – he received the Queen's Medal. In 1905 he commanded the Military Police in Egypt. He became Chief Constable of Cornwall in 1909.

178. *IBID.*, 25th APRIL 1923

179. *IBID.*, 4th OCTOBER 1922. Many of the miners who went to Canada drifted over the border See *IBID.*, 27th JUNE 1923. In 1928 there was a disaster at the *Hollinger Mine* – 39 miners lost their lives. Two Cornishmen were named – Charles E.

Richards and Harold Barrett. *IBID.*, 14th MARCH 1928

180. *IBID*, 3rd JANUARY 1923

181. *IBID.*, 10th OCTOBER 1923

182. Barton, *A HISTORY OF TIN MINING* p. 270

183. *CORNISHMAN*, 29th SEPTEMBER 1921

184. *IBID.*, 22nd FEBRUARY 1922

185. *IBID.*, 12th NOVEMBER 1931

186. *IBID.*, 2nd APRIL 1936

187. *IBID.*, 31st JANUARY 1935. Jane Olds his wife died in 1929.

188. *IBID.*, 25th JUNE 1924

189. *IBID.*, 5th JANUARY 1927

190. Information concerning W. G. Wearne – especially the letter from the Benoni branch of the Cornish Association and undated newspaper clippings was given by June Melville

191. *CORNISHMAN*, 17th DECEMBER 1936

192. Dickason, *CORNISH IMMIGRANTS*, p. 92. Dickason also mentions John Squire (1858-1937) Cornish Mayor of Simonstown Nr, Cape Town, also a builder. See *IBID.*, p. 106

193. *CORNISHMAN*, 27th OCTOBER 1932 – When Halse's only daughter – Mildred – was married to Robert Bolt in 1931 there were over 1, 500 guests at the wedding. *IBID.*, 2nd APRIL 1931

194. *IBID.*, 27th SEPTEMBER 1928. At the Cornish Gorsedd, which has links with the Gorsedds of Wales and Brittany, songs are sung in Cornish and the whole ceremony reminds those taking part of their Celtic past.

195. *IBID.*, 1st DECEMBER 1926

196. *IBID.*, 12th SEPTEMBER 1935

197. *IBID.*, 20th FEBRUARY 1930

198. *IBID.*, 9th OCTOBER 1930

199. *IBID.*, 16th OCTOBER 1930

200. *IBID.*, 23rd OCTOBER 1930

201. *IBID.*, 20th NOVEMBER 1930

202. *IBID.*, 27th SEPTEMBER 1934

203. *IBID.*, 13th DECEMBER 1934

204. See especially Roberts, *KIMBERLEY*

205. Letter to author dated 15th April 1989

206. *CORNISHMAN*, 16th DECEMBER 1937

207. *STANDARD & WEST RAND REVIEW*, 10th FEBRUARY 1939 – Seven out of the eight crew men of the St. Ives Lifeboat lost their lives in that disaster. When there was a fishing boat disaster at Porthleven ten years later the Transvaal Cornish Association sent the Mayor of Helston £56 for the Disaster Fund. See *CORNISHMAN* 6th JANUARY 1949

208. *CORNISHMAN & CORNISH TELEGRAPH*, 12th NOVEMBER 1936

209. A. Ruth Fry, *EMILY HOBHOUSE* p. 262

210. Brian Roberts *THOSE BLOODY WOMEN* (LONDON 1991) p. 269

211. Fry, *EMILY HOBHOUSE* p. 295-296 South Africa has honoured her by a stamp issued in her name in 1976 and strangely by having a submarine named after her in 1972

212. *THE COLLECTED WORKS OF MAHATMA GANDHI* (PUBLICATIONS DIVISION 1964) VOL. III . p. 295

213. M. K. Gandhi, *SATYAGRAHA IN SOUTH AFRICA* (MADRAS 1928) p. 174

214. Gandhi, *COLLECTED WORKS* VOL. II p. 151

215. Gandhi, *SATYAGRAHA* . p. 205-206

216. *INDIAN OPINION*, 17th JUNE 1911

217. *TRANSVAAL LEADER*, 11th JANUARY 1908

218. Gandhi, *COLLECTED WORKS* VOL. VII p. 149

219. *IBID.*, p. 163

220. *IBID.*, p. 343

221. *IBID.*, VOL. IX p. 59

222. *IBID.*, VOL. X Appendix XII p. 532

223. *CORNISHMAN*, 26th MAY 1910

224. *C.P.M.N.* 8th SEPTEMBER 1910

225. Gandhi, *COLLECTED WORKS* VOL. XI
     p. 110

226. See, *RAND DAILY MAIL* 12th JANUARY
     1910

227. *C.P.M.N.,* 25th MARCH 1915

228. *IBID.,* 20th JUNE 1925

229. *IBID.,* 11th JULY 1925. See also *IBID.,*
     4th JULY 1925

A CORNISH LEGACY

A forgotten large part of the population of Cornwall is overseas –
Pioneers in a great trek to mine fields and ranches that has
characteristically, seldom been recorded.[1]

Denys Val Baker.

The impact Cornwall had on South Africa, although largely neglected by historians – an injustice which hopefully this study goes some way towards correcting – was clearly important. Chronologically, South Africa is very much the high point of the Great Migration from Cornwall during the last century. South Africa, more than any other country in the world where the Cornish have migrated, made an impression upon Cornwall enduring to this day. The link between Cornwall and South Africa was so close that there seemed little physical distance between the two places, as expressed in the old adage about the old St. Just woman who, when asked where Johannesburg was, said, "I don't know zactly wheer'tis, but 'tis somewheer up beyond Redruth".[2] It can still be debated whether Cornwall gained more from its relationship with South Africa than South Africa gained from Cornwall, but there can be little doubt as to the important contribution of the Cornish Pioneers in South Africa. They were influential in all spheres of society as evidenced by the work of Oats, Johns, Kitto and Quentrall in mining; Hall in railways; Tossel in the police; Brokensha and Morcom in law; Michell in banking; Lyle, Lawn, Collins and Mountstephens in education; Heath in music; Angove, Deecker, Bate and Tiddy in journalism; Henwood, the Wevell brothers, Stuttaford and Chudleigh in commerce; Colenso in the church; Mathews, Trembath and Trewick in the trade unions; Tredrea, Higgo and Berriman in building; Hall, Hosken and Moon in agriculture; Davey, Bawden, Chudleigh and Halse in civic administration; Triggs and Peters in sport, to say nothing of the humanitarian stances taken by Colenso, Hobhouse and Hosken. Yet the majority of those Cornish who each in their own smaller way contributed to South Africa's early history is still relatively unknown.

The Cornish influence was paramount in the establishment of South Africa's mining industry. If Cornwall assisted in the birth of the Industrial Revolution in Britain, then its miners were carrying on that tradition when they brought about the births of South Africa's gold, diamond and copper industries, helping especially to nurture them through formative years and enabling South Africa to become the leading diamond and gold producer in the world. When his hard rock skills were in demand the Cornish miner could quite rightly be called an aristocrat of labour, but with the increased mechanisation of the mining industry, especially with the introduction of the rock drill, his hand drilling technique was superseded by his role of supervisor.[3] With the advent of the machine rock drill – the drills themselves becoming known as widow-makers – the Cornish miner often succumbed to the deadly miners' phthisis; at the same time he worried whether he was about to be ousted, first by skilled native labour and then by Chinese. It is therefore perhaps ironic that, having joined a Union for protection and security of employment against these two groups, it should be through that very Union carrying out a series of strikes that the Cornish miner was eventually replaced by his fellow white miner – the Afrikaner.

A disadvantage for the Cornish miner in South Africa was that he appeared content to remain a migrant labourer, a bird of passage, a roving miner. The roots of too many Cornish miners in South Africa remained firmly bedded in Cornwall. Reluctant to bring out his wife and family, the Cornish miner seemed satisfied to regard

> *the goldfields of South Africa as a sort of El Dorado or 'Tom Tiddlers' ground to which, when tired of cold pasties, an eight hour shift and 18s per week he might retire for a few years and where his voluntary exile might bring him anything from £20 to £30 per month.*[4]

Nothing was settled for the Cornish miner in South Africa. Often working on a 24 hour contract it required only a raid, a war, depression or a strike to see him move on elsewhere, or pack up and go home to Cornwall. After all it was not a question of politics with many a Cornish miner, but more a question of economics. If the diamond or gold mines closed then what was the point of staying on for many a Cornish miner saw Kimberley and Johannesburg as little more than mining camps, no different from the other mining camps such as Butte City, Grass Valley, Broken Hill or Pachuca. Once the work was no longer available then it was time to change camps – after all the family back home in Cornwall depended on the monthly remittance and what did it care if the money came from South Africa, U.S.A., Australia, Mexico or elsewhere.

There is no doubt the diamond and gold industries of South Africa cushioned Cornwall as its own copper and tin industries died a slow death, and families in Cornwall certainly benefited from the high wages earned in South Africa. However, the land of gold and diamonds claimed many more lives of Cornish miners than ever the Cornish mines did and Tiddy shows with poignancy the trials for so many Cornish mining families whose men were in South Africa when he wrote:

> *None of us know the amount of pain these gaps out of your united lives cause. We are sorry for these terrible breaks and wrenchings in the only world you know, you live in and that you care for. Some of these*

sweethearts shall never return; some of these husbands will go to their
'long home'; and on a sunny afternoon, the postman shall bring a letter
to that distant village, written in a strange hand and the sun shall cease
shining on one house and the blinds shall be drawn, while a woman's
heart breaks and the playshouts of the fatherless children are still heard
in the sun.
Death and distance are cousins when we love. And the miner on the Rand
suffers the death which is distance for those he loves.[5]

The question as to whether the price paid by Cornwall to South Africa was far
too high is surely answered by the army of Cornish miners who lie in lonely graves
in South Africa's cemeteries as silent witnesses.

Between the two World Wars came the final collapse of the Cornish tin industry
– except for a mere handful of mines. As the years passed there was to be no new
exodus of Cornish miners to South Africa. Tom Kendrick, who had been with the
Roan Antelope copper mine, Northern Rhodesia, and Underground Manager at
Cornwall's South Crofty mine, believed the tradition of home mining was lost with
the slump between the wars.[6] Added to this was a home government's reluctance
to invest in its own mining industry and one by one the few remaining mines have
all but one closed down, making Cornwall – as far as mining goes – one of the
most depressed regions in the country with large unemployment. As late as 1986
the *Western Morning News* told how Paul Newcombe, a graduate of the Camborne
School of Mines, had to find work in South Africa at the Palabora copper mine.[7]
By 1990 there were only three mines left in Cornwall. Geevor, near St. Just, which
closed in 1991 became a heritage centre. Wheal Jane – near Truro also closed in
1991 while at the time of writing the fate of South Crofty hangs in the balance. It
was ironic that hearing of the proposal to close South Crofty in August 1997 one
miner – George Trevaskis – who had worked at the mine for 14 years said, "I
might have to go to the gold fields of South Africa to find similar work".[8]

In South Africa there had been a number of changes after the First World War,
especially on the political front. Louis Botha who died in 1919 had been replaced
as Prime Minister by Jan Smuts, but the 1922 Strike did little to enhance Smuts'
reputation and in the 1924 General Election he was defeated by a combination of
the Nationalist and Labour Parties. General J.B.M. Hertzog became Prime
Minister and quickly set about advancing the spirit of Afrikander nationalism.
Within a year Afrikaans had become an official language and the country soon had
two flags, and two national anthems.[9] Those Cornish who were ready to make
South Africa their new home soon found their culture submerged beneath the
much stronger force of Afrikaner nationalism against which the Cornish
Association, with its non-political constitution, was impotent. The Het Volk party
considered it more important to be white in South Africa than to maintain a

Cornish identity and thus had little time for a minority group whose interest basically lay in a county overseas.

The Cornish Association may have been ineffective to a great extent in encouraging Cornishmen to bring their wives and families out to South Africa, but the welfare work it carried out on behalf of, and for, the Cornish in South Africa and Cornwall was invaluable. However, on the negative side the Association was unfortunately seen by some to be interfering in a man's private life; as Dickason has pointed out:

> *Times were hard, conditions in the mines rough. Moral remonstrance was not what Cornishmen wanted when they were already living under the harsh strictures of the times. They would adjust to them as they saw fit and as their own personal circumstances dictated.*[10]

Between 1942 and 1957 the Cornish Association of the Transvaal published its own magazine The *Cornubian*.[11] By the late 1950s it was obvious by looking at the contents of the magazine that the Cornish Association was a mere shadow of its former self. Events organised were on a small scale and branches had difficulty filling positions on Committees. Dickason was quite correct in that there were two main reasons why the Cornish Association did not survive on the Rand – one being a lack of interest as the Cornish integrated themselves into the new society or returned to Cornwall which led to the second – a lack of financial support.[12] Both reasons spelt doom for the Association especially when it was lacking new blood as evidenced by the difficulty the branches had in filling

Wemmer Villa, Illogan.

East Rand, Polgooth.

Ferreira, St. Just.
House names in Cornwall 1997.

their posts. Not surprisingly, as the membership continued to age and decrease individual branches folded. The Association entered its twilight years before its final demise in the mid-nineteen-fifties. Its last Chairman was Fred Bath.

For the Cornish on the Rand in addition to the influence of the Cornish Association and the Freemasons (Lodge Cornwall still exists but there are no longer any Cornishmen present as active members) there was the important influence of Methodism, which one writer – Claude Berry – believes gave direction and rhythm to the life of the Cornish miner.[13] Richard West, a writer who visited South Africa in the late nineteen-eighties, recounts in his book *The Diamonds and the Necklace* how a Methodist minister he met there said that whereas Methodism had once been strong in Johannesburg three Methodist churches had closed in central Johannesburg, and although the Methodist congregations were growing in some of the wealthy suburbs like Sandton the minister added that they were losing support from the people who created Methodism, the Cornish miners.[14]

The Natal Cornish Association, centred on Durban, was active up until the mid-nineteen-seventies when it, too, fell away with an ageing and diminishing membership. Although there have been attempts to revive the Cornish Association in South Africa they first met with little success. When Hugh Miners, a former Grand Bard of the Cornish Gorsedd, visited South Africa in Spring 1987 he met a number of Cornish exiles but found

> *the enthusiasm for some link with Cornwall was diluted for many by the political difficulties which existed between their country and Britain… I found similar feelings amongst Cornish descendants on the Reef at Johannesburg.*[15]

There have been further political changes in South Africa as the *Apartheid* system of government was brought to an end in May 1994 and Nelson Mandela became the first black President of South Africa.

Since the publication of the quarterly magazine *Cornish World* in June 1994, which is aimed at Cornish overseas, there has been optimism that a Cornish Association of South Africa will be revived and *Issue 7 (Dec./Jan./Feb./1995/6)* of the magazine carried the news that *Johannesburgs' up and running!* and told how Rob Harvey (St. Columb) and Graham Money (Truro) had successfully organised the first meeting of a new Cornish society at Sandton, Johannesburg. The next issue of *Cornish World* brought news that the new association had taken as its name the Cornish Association of Witwatersrand. Its aims and objectives were declared to be to create interest and renew ties between Cornish descendants and immigrants as well as to discover the history and contributions of our Cornish forebears. Whether it will turn out to be as successful as the first Cornish Association only time will tell.

Colenso Place, St. Austell.

Paardeberg Road, Bodmin.

Kimberley, Redruth.

Benoni, St. Just.
House and road names in Cornwall 1997.

Although Cornwall's legacy to South Africa lay with its mining industry, and perhaps to a lesser extent in commerce, there are other reminders. Even if the Cornish choir can no longer be heard singing carols along the Rand at Christmas or *Trelawny* at any other time, the presence of the Cornish is everywhere and not just in Methodism. Dickason has identified nearly a hundred Cornish place names in South Africa which include streets named after Cornish towns such as Falmouth, Helston, Launceston, St. Austell, St. Just and Truro, whilst the township of Alberton, just south of Johannesburg, has a suburb called New Redruth.[16] Many fine buildings built by the Cornish in Cape Town, Johannesburg and Durban are still standing – many being the pride of civic administration. Dickason has also identified a number of Cornish colloquialisms and expressions that have become standard South African English.[17]

As well as introducing into South Africa the sports of wrestling and rugby, from a culinary point of view Cornwall gave South Africa the staple diet of the miner – the Cornish pasty. In 1936 the South African travel writer Lawrence Green, having been down a gold mine somewhere along the Rand, wrote:

> *I followed my guide into a stope where the white miner and his crew of drill, spanner and timber boys were working the South Reef at a depth of 6,500 feet… I learnt that miners still take Cornish pasties to eat with their cold tea – a taste inherited from the old Cornishmen.*[18]

Another culinary delight that the Cornish gave to South Africa was the less well-known saffron cake:

> *It is said that in the early days of the Cornish emigration to the Rand the curiosity of the postal authorities at Johannesburg was aroused by the number of strange-smelling packets passing through their hands. At length an order was given that one of these should be opened. On inspection its contents were adjudged to be a rank poison, and the package was accordingly returned to the sender, accompanied by a stern warning pointing out the nature of the offence. The officials, however, were soon destined to learn more of the ways of Cornishmen, and twenty years later, when almost every family in the mining districts of Cornwall owned some member working on the Reef, the amount of saffron which yearly found its way to the goldfields must have been worth a small fortune.*[19]

In Cornwall there are a few visible reminders of Cornwall's once strong links with South Africa, other than those found in the graveyards. The odd house bearing a name of a South African mine such as Ferreira can still be found and Richard Lander's statue at Truro and Penn Symon's memorial at Saltash are evidence of the Cornish-South African connection.

The South African Boer War 1899-1902 affected Cornwall more than any other part of the British Isles. It made a deep impression upon Cornwall and it was claimed:

> *In 1939 the old men of St. Just and Camborne had a clearer memory of Ladysmith and Spion Kop than of that long terrible struggle on the Somme.*[20]

The largest memorial to those Cornish who fell in battle during the Boer War can be found in Truro Cathedral but there are others throughout the county such as Bodmin church (D.C.L.I. Depot town) and the lychgate at Madron church to name but two.[21]

With so many Cornish mines now closed their ruined engine houses, along with the world famous Camborne School of Mines, remain as a lasting testimony to Cornwall's once proud mining industry. Gone also are the Cornish newspapers – the *Cornubian* and the *Cornish Post & Mining News*[22] – whose columns were once full of news from the land of gold and diamonds, and long gone are the days in Cornwall when

> *the talk is all of the Rand, whose dust filled gold mines have sent more money home to Cornwall than any other camp in the world, though none has given more cause for dread to mining families, whose best and strongest have perished there.*[23]

Headstone for John Rogers, a Cornish prospector in Namaqualand.

1. Denys Val Baker, *THE SPIRIT OF CORNWALL* (LONDON 1980) p.16

2. *C.P.M.N.*, 16th JANUARY 1908

3. This role often brought adverse criticism from fellow Cornish miners working in other mining camps overseas – especially in the U.S.A. See *CORNISHMAN*, 13th JUNE 1907 and *C.P.M.N.*, 18th JULY 1907

4. *MINING JOURNAL*, 12th MARCH 1903 p.177 It was also said 'Before the war … Transvaal was an El Dorado for the Cornish miner, there under Kruger's beneficent despotism he could amass that competence on which he hoped to spend his later years'. See *CORNUBIAN*, 5th DECEMBER 1903

5. *CORNISHMAN*, 18th MARCH 1900

6. *IBID.*, 3rd APRIL 1952

7. *WESTERN MORNING NEWS*, 10th JANUARY 1986. See article 'Dig a hole in South Africa – and you are sure to find a Cornishman'. Paul Newcombe has since returned to Cornwall to work in the China Clay industry.

8. *THE DAILY TELEGRAPH* 8th AUGUST 1997

9. The flag of orange, white and blue was introduced in May 1928, the anthem *Die Stem Van Suid Afrika* (The voice of South Africa) was introduced in JULY 1936

10. Dickason, *CORNISH IMMIGRANTS* p.72

11. Lambert Truran provided a copy of the *CORNUBIAN*; No.55 May 1956. Despite much searching it seems it is the only one of the issues published to remain in existence. Issue No.1 was printed in August 1942 and the last issue – No.56 – in January 1957

12. Dickason, *CORNISH IMMIGRANTS* p.74

13. *KERNOWYON DRES OLL ANBYS – CORNISH WORLDWIDE – BLEDHEN NOWETH 1991 NYVERA 3* p.2 (published by the London Cornish Association)

14. Richard West, *THE DIAMONDS AND THE NECKLACE* (LONDON 1989) p.13 Ken Sara, disputes this by claiming that this is due to a great shift in population away from Johannesburg adding that there is certainly no decline in Methodism, but continual growth. Letter to author.

15. *IBID.*, p.2

16. Dickason, *CORNISH IMMIGRANTS*, p.81-82

17. *IBID.*, p.75-76

18. Lawrence G. Green, *SECRET AFRICA* p.271

19. A.K. Hamilton Jenkin, *CORNWALL AND ITS PEOPLE* p.403

20. *CORNISHMAN*, 5th January 1950

21. A Boer War memorial which led to controversy was one which was in the Morrab gardens, Penzance (See p.184). In 1933 it was claimed in one Cornish newspaper that the brim of the hat of the soldier – which was turned up on the left – should have been turned up on the right side in order that the sighting of the rifle should not be obscured by a flapping brim. This quickly brought a reply from a Cornish-Boer War Veteran, a trooper in the Matabeland Relief Force 1896 who had also seen action as a Corporal with the Diamond Fields Horse during the siege of Kimberley claiming that the left side was correct for it shades the right eye from the sun for sighting the rifle. This was supported by another D.C.L.I. veteran from St. Just who sent a photograph of some D.C.L.I. men at Pretoria, clearly showing their hats with the brims turned up on the left side.

22. The *CORNUBIAN* became the *REDRUTH TIMES & CAMBORNE ADVERTISER* in

1924 and the *CORNISH POST & MINING NEWS* was incorporated in the *CORNISHMAN* in 1944.

23. Hamilton Jenkin, *THE CORNISH MINER* p.20

BIBLIOGRAPHY

H.R. Abercrombie: *The Secret History of South Africa: Sixty Five Years in the Transvaal* (Johannesburg 1951)

John Angove: *In the Early Days* (Kimberley & Johannesburg 1910)

Denys Val Baker: *Spirit of Cornwall* (London 1980)

W.G.V. Balchin: *Cornwall* (London 1964)

Michael Barthorp: *The Zulu Wars* (Poole 1984)

Michael Barthorp: *The Anglo Boer Wars* (London 1987)

D.B. Barton: *Essays in Cornish Mining History* 2 Vols (Truro 1968 & 1971)

D.B. Barton: *A History of Copper Mining in Cornwall & Devon* (3rd Edition Truro 1978

D.B. Barton: *A History of Tin Mining and Smelting in Cornwall* (Exeter 1989)

D.B. Barton: *The Cornish Beam Engine* (Exeter 1989)

George Beet: *The Grand Old Days of the Diamond Fields* (Cape Town 1931)

A.L. Behr & R.G. Macmillan: *Education in South Africa* (Pretoria 1966)

Eversley Belfield: *Boer War* (London 1975)

W.H. Somerset Bell: *Bygone Days* (London 1933)

Claude Berry: *Portrait of Cornwall* (London 1963)

C.T. Binns: *The Last Zulu King: The Life and Death of Cetewayo* (London 1963)

Henry Cecil Blackwell: *From a Dark Stream* (Kernow 1986)

Frank Booker: *Industrial Archaeology of the Tamar Valley* (Newton Abbot 1971)

A.K. Bot: *Century of Education in the Transvaal 1836-1936* (Pretoria 1936)

Frederick Boyle: *To the Cape for Diamonds* (London 1873)

W.V. Brelsford: *Generation of Men* (Salisbury 1965)

Piers Brendon: *Hawker of Morwenstow* (London 1975)

E.H. Brooks & C. de B. Webb: *A History of Natal* (Natal 1965)

T.V. Bulpin: *Lost Trails on the Low Veldt* (Cape Town 1951)

T.V. Bulpin: *Storm over the Transvaal* (Cape Town 1953)

T.V. Bulpin: *The Golden Republic* (Cape Town 1953)

T.V. Bulpin: *To the Shores of Natal* (Cape Town 1953)

T.V. Bulpin: *Trail of the Copper King* (Cape Town 1959)

T.V. Bulpin: *To the Banks of the Zambesi* (Cape Town 1968)

T.V. Bulpin: *Lost Trails of the Transvaal* (Cape Town 1969)

Kate Caffrey: *Great Emigrations: The British to Southern Africa* (London 1973)

Dorothy E. Rivett Carnac: *Thus Came the English 1820* (London 1961)

A.P. Cartwright: *The Corner House* (Cape Town 1958)

A.P. Cartwright: *The Gold Miners* (Cape Town 1962)

A.P. Cartwright: *The Dynamite Company* (Cape Town 1964)

A.P. Cartwright: *The First South African : Life & Times of Sir Percy Fitzpatrick* (Cape Town 1971)

A.P. Cartwright: *The Old Transvaal 1834-1899* (Cape Town 1978)

Robert Cary: *A Time to Die* (Cape Town 1968)

H.A. Chilvers: *The Seven Lost Trails of Africa* (London 1930)

H.A. Chilvers: *Out of the Crucible* (London 1929)

H.A. Chilvers: The Story of De Beers (London 1939)

J. & M. Churchill: A Merchant Family in Early Natal (Cape Town 1979)

Randolph S. Churchill: Winston S. Churchill Youth:1874-1900 (London 1966)

Winston Churchill: The Boer War: London to Ladysmith (London 1989)

William St. Clair Trelawny: The Incurable Romancer (London 1977)

Mary Coate: Cornwall in the Great Civil War (Oxford 1933)

Patrick Coghill: Whom the Gods Love (London 1968)

J.W. Colenso: Ten Weeks in Natal: A Journal of a first tour of Visitation among the Colonists & Zulu Kaffirs of Natal (Cambridge 1855)

J.E. Cookson: Lord Liverpool's Administration 1815-22 (Edinburgh 1975)

Basil Cordeur: The Politics of Eastern Cape Separation 1820-1854 (Cape Town 1968)

Sir G.E. Cory: The Rise of South Africa 6 Vols (Cape Town 1964)

T.H.R. Davenport: South Africa (London 1979)

R.A. Davis: Fruit Growing in South Africa (Cape Town 1928)

Arthur Davey: The British Pro-Boers 1877-1902 (Cape Town 1978)

Donald Denson: A Grand Illusion (London 1973)

Graham Dickason: Cornish Immigrants to South Africa (Cape Town 1975)

Oswald Doughty: Early Diamond Days (London 1963)

A. Conan Doyle:The Great Boer War: A Two Year Record 1899-1901 (London 1902)

Daphne Du Maurier: Vanishing Cornwall (London 1972)

I.E. Edwards: The 1820 Settlers in South Africa (London 1934)

Frank Emery: The Red Soldier: The Zulu War 1879 (London 1977)

Paul H. Emden: Randlords (London 1935)

John Fisher: That Miss Hobhouse (London 1971)

Paul Kruger: His Life & Times (London 1974)

J.P. Fitzpatrick: The Transvaal From Within (London 1900)

J.P. Fitzpatrick: Jock of the Bushveld (London 1907)

J.P. Fitzpatrick: South Africa Memories (London 1932

Ruth Fry: Emily Hobhouse (London 1969)

W.D. Gale: One Man's Vision (London 1935)

M.K. Gandhi: Satyagraha (Madras 1928)

E. Gitsham & J. Trembath A First Account of Labour Organisation in South Africa (Durban 1925)

G.P. Gooch: Life of Lord Courtney (London 1920)

Dr. Ruth E. Gordon: Shepstone (Cape Town 1968)

George A.L. Green: An Editor Looks Back: South African and Other Memories (Cape Town & Johannesburg 1947)

Lawrence G. Green: Secret Africa (London 1936)

Lawrence G. Green: So Few Are Free (Cape Town 1946)

Lawrence G. Green: The Drums of Time (London 1956)

B. Greenhill: The Merchant Schooners (London 1988)

Kenneth Griffith: Thank God We Kept the Flag Flying: The Siege & Relief of Ladysmith 1899-1900 (London 1974)

Jeff Guy: The Heretic (London 1983)

Henry Rider Haggard: Days of My Life 2 Vols (London 1926)

H.L. Hall: I Have Reaped My Mealies (London 1935)

F.E. Halliday: A History of Cornwall (London 1959)

Norman Hannan: Travels and Heartaches of a Mining Family (Romford 1984)

Colin Harding: Frontier Patrols (London 1937)

John Harris: My Autobiography (London 1882)

J.R. Harris: The Copper King (Liverpool 1964)

David Harrison: The White Tribe of Africa (London 1981)

A.F. Hattersley: The Natalians (London 1940) The British Settlement of Natal: A Study in Imperial Migration (Cambridge 1950)

Robert Stephen Hawker: Cornish Ballads & Other Poems (London 1975)

J.A. Henry: The First Hundred Years of the Standard Bank (London 1963)

Norman Herd: The Revolt on the Rand 1922 (London 1966)

Peter Hinchliff: John William Colenso (London 1964)

C. Lewis Hind: Days in Cornwall (London 1907)

Emily Hobhouse: Report of a Visit to the Camps of Women and Children in the Cape and Orange River Colonies(London 1901)

Emily Hobhouse: The Brunt of War & Where it Fell (London 1902)

Emily Hobhouse: Tant Alie of Transvaal (London 1923)

Silas Hocking: My Book of Memory (London 1923)

H.E. Hockley: The Story of the British Settlers of 1820 in South Africa (Cape Town 1957)

Sydney Hudson-Reed: Hope Beyond: A Memoir of Treverton's First Twenty-One Years 1964-1985 (Treverton 1987)

Robert Hughs: The Fatal Shore (London 1987)

D. Humphries & D.G. Thomas: Benoni (Son of My Sorrow) (Benoni 1968)

S.P. Hyatt: The Old Transport Road (London 1914)

A.K. Hamilton Jenkin: Cornwall and its People (London 1945)

A.K. Hamilton Jenkin: The Cornish Miner (3rd Ed. Newton Abbot 1972)

David Jenkins & Dorothy Slebbing: They Led the Way (Cape Town 1966)

E. Morse Jones: Roll of the British Settlers in South Africa (Cape Town 1969)

Elaine N. Katz: A Trade Union Aristocracy: A History of White Workers in the Transvaal and the General Strike of 1913 (Johannesburg 1976)

Brian Kennedy: A Tale of Two Mining Cities: Johannesburg and Broken Hill 1885-1925 (Melbourne 1984)

Ian Knight: Brave Men's Blood: The Epic of the Zulu War 1879(London 1990)

L.C.A. Knowles & M. Knowles: The Economic Development of the Overseas Empire Vol. 3 (London 1936)

S.J.P. Kruger: The Memories of Paul Kruger (London 1900)

Robert Lacour-Gayet: A History of South Africa (London 1988)

Richard Lander: Records of Captain Clapperton's Last Expedition to Africa 2 Vols. (London 1830)

Emanuel Lee: To the Bitter End (London 1985)

Joseph Lehmann: The First Boer War (London 1972)

Owen Letcher: The Gold Mines of Southern Africa (London 1936)

Norman Levy: The Foundations of the South African Cheap Labour System (London 1982)

G.R. Lewis: The Stannaries: A Study of the Medieval Tin Mines of Cornwall & Devon (Truro 1965)

G.A. Leyds: A History of Johannesburg (London 1964)

Adele Lezard: Gold Blast (London 1936)

Elizabeth Longford: Jameson's Raid: The Prelude to the Boer War (London 1982)

Tom MacDonald: Transvaal Story (Cape Town 1961)

Roy Macnab: Journey Into Yesterday (Cape Town 1962)

Ben Maclennai: A Proper Degree of Terror (Johannesburg 1986)

Ralph Mann: After the Gold Rush: Society in Grass Valley & Nevada City, California 1849-70 (California 1982)

Tom Mann: Tom Mann's Memoirs (London 1967)

W.G.A. Mears: The Early History of St. Stithians College (Randberg 1972)

Arthur Mee: Cornwall (London 1943)

Sir Lewis Michell: The Life of the Right Hon. Cecil John Rhodes 2 Vols. (London 1910)

Donald R. Morris: The Washing of the Spears: The Rise and Fall of the Zulu Nation (London 1966)

Bruce K. Murray: Witwatersrand the Early Years (Johannesburg 1982)

L.M. Nesbitt:Gold Fever (London 1936)

G. Nicholson: Fifty Years in South Africa (London 1898)

John Nixon: The Complete Story of the Transvaal (London 1885)

C. Noall: Botallack (Truro 1972)

C. Noall: Levant: The Mine Beneath the Sea (Truro 1972)

C. Noall: St. Just Mining District (Truro 1973)

C. Noall: Cornish Mine Disasters (Redruth 1989)

Charles Norris-Newman: With the Boers in the Transvaal & the Orange Free State 1880-81 (London 1882)

Arthur Norway: Highways & Byways in Devon & Cornwall (London 1897)

Thomas Oliver: Autobiography of a Cornish Miner (Camborne 1914)

Charles Van Onselen: Studies in the Social and Economic History of the Witwatersrand Vol. 1 New Babylon Vol. 2 New Nineveh (London 1982)

John O'Reilly: Pursuit of the King (Bulawayo 1970)

Thomas Pakenham: The Boer War (London 1982)

Philip J. Payton: The Cornish Miner in Australia (Kernow 1984)

Philip J. Payton: The Cornish Farmer in Australia (Redruth 1987)

John Pearce: The Wesleys in Cornwall (Truro 1964)

Mrs. Lionel Phillips: Some South African Recollections (London 1899)

Ambrose Pratt:The Real South Africa (London 1913)

T.O. Ranger: Revolt in Southern Africa 1896-7 (London 1967)

Oliver Ransford: The Great Trek (London 1974)

Peter Richardson: Chinese Mine Labour in the Transvaal (London 1982)

Deneys Ritz: Commando: A Boer Journal of the Boer War (London 1983)

Brian Roberts: The Diamond Magnates (London 1972)

Brian Roberts: Kimberley: Turbulent City (Cape Town 1976)

Brian Roberts: Cecil Rhodes: Flawed Colossus (London 1987)

Brian Roberts: Those Bloody Women: Three Heroines of the Boer War (London 1991)

Barry Rohan: Forty South African Years (London 1923)

L.T.C. Rolt: The Cornish Giant (Richard Trevithick) (London 1960)

Eric Rosenthal: Gold! Gold! Gold! (London 1970)

Peter Rowland: The Last Liberal Governments: The Promised Land 1905-10 (London 1968)

John Rowe: Cornwall in the Age of the Industrial Revolution (St. Austell 1993)

John Rowe: The Hard Rock Men: Cornish Immigrants and the North American Mining Frontier (Liverpool 1974)

A.L. Rowse: A Cornish Childhood (London 1942)

A.L. Rowse: Tudor Cornwall (London 1969)

A.L. Rowse: The Cornish in America (London 1969)

A.L. Rowse: The Little Land of Cornwall (London 1986)

A.L. Rowse: Quiller Couch: A Portrait of Q (London 1988)

A.L. Rowse: The Controversial Colensos (London 1989)

John Rule: The Labouring Classes in Early Industrial England 1750-1850 (London 1986)

Gerald Sharp: The Siege of Ladysmith (London 1976)

Rev. T. Shaw: A History of Cornish Methodism (Truro 1967)

Jack & Ray Simons: Class & Colour in South Africa 1850-1950 (London 1983)

Sir Horace Smith-Dorrien: Memories of Forty-Eight Years' Service (London 1925)

L.S. Snell: A Short History of the Duke of Cornwall's Light Infantry (Aldershot 1945)

Shelagh O'Byrne Spencer: British Settlers in Natal 1824-1857 Biographical Register 2 Vols (Pietermaritzburg 1981 & 1983)

Peter Stanier: Cornwall's Mining Heritage (Truro 1988)

Gordon Le Sueur: C.J. Rhodes (London 1913)

E.C. Tabler: Pioneers of Natal & S.E. Africa 1552-1878 (Cape Town 1977)

Nigel Tangye: Voyage into Cornwall's Past (London 1978)

Nigel Tangye: The Living Breath of Cornwall (London 1980)

Nigel Tangye: Proud Seas and Cornwall's Past (London 1982)

J.B. Taylor: A Pioneer Looks Back (London 1939)

William P.Taylor: African Treasures: Sixty Years Among Diamonds & Gold (London 1932)

H. Thomas:Cornish Mining Interviews (Camborne 1896)

A.C. Todd: The Cornish Miner in America (Truro 1967)

A.C. Todd: The Search for Silver: Cornish Miners in Mexico 1827-1947 (Padstow 1977)

A.C. Todd & Peter Laws: Industrial Archaeology of Cornwall (Newton Abbot 1972)

Rex Tremlett: Road to Ophir (London – no date)

Eric W. Turpin: Basketwork Harbour (Cape Town 1964)

C.J. Unys: In the Era of Shepstone (Cape Town 1933)

E. Vale: The Harveys of Hayle (Truro 1966)

C.E. Vulliamy: Outlanders: A Study of Imperial Expansion in South Africa 1877-1902 (London, 1938)

Richard West: The Diamonds & The Necklace (London 1989)

Geoffrey Wheatcroft: The Randlords (London 1985)

Charles Wiliams: The Life of Lieut-General Sir Henry Evelyn Wood V. C. (London 1892)

Douglas Williams: West Cornwall in the Old Days (Bodmin 1985)

Gardner Williams: The Diamond Mines of South Africa (London 1902)

A. Wilmot: The History of Our Times in South Africa Vol. 1 1872-79 (Cape Town 1897)

Donald Woods: Asking For Trouble (London 1980)

William H. Worger: South Africa's City of Diamonds: Mine Workers and Monopoly Capitalism in Kimberley 1867-1895 (New Haven & London 1987)

EDITED WORKS

C.J. Beyers: Dictionary of South African Biography 5 Vols (Pretoria 1987)

Daphne Child: A Merchant Family in Early Natal Diaries and Letters of Joseph & Marianne Churchill 1850-1880 (Cape Town 1979)

Readers Digest: Illustrated History of South Africa: The Real Story (New York & Montreal 1989)

A.H. Duining & W.R. Guest: Fitzpatrick: South African Politician Selected Papers 1888-1906 (Johannesburg 1976)

F.E. Halliday: Richard Carew of Anthony 1555-1620 The Survey of Cornwall Etc., (London 1953)

Norman Hannan: Joseph Tucker: Letters of a South African Miner 1898-1904 (Romford 1981)

W.J. De Kock & D.W. Kruger: Dictionary of South African Biography 3 Vols (Cape Town 1968, 1972, 1976)

Mahatma Gandhi: Collected Works of Mahatma Gandhi (London 1964)

Crispin Gill:The Duchy of Cornwall (London 1987)

S. Marks & P. Richardson: International Labour Migration Historical Perspectives (London 1984)

S. Marks & P. Richardson: Industrialisation and Social Changes in South Africa: African Class Formation, Culture and Consciousness 1870-1930 (London 1982)

W.A. Maxwell & R.T. McGough: The Reminiscences of Thomas Stubbs (Cape Town 1978)

W. Rees: Colenso : Letters from Natal (Pietermaritzburg 1958)

Eric Rosenthal: The Southern African Dictionary of National Biography (London 1966)

Pamela Todd & David Fordham: Private Tucker's Boer War Diary (London 1980)

F.G. Van Der Riet & Rev. L.A. Hewson: Reminiscences of an Albany Settler: Rev. Henry Hare Dugmore (Grahamstown 1958)

Peter Warwick: The South African War/The Anglo-Boer War (London 1980)

PRIVATELY PUBLISHED BOOKS & PAMPHLETS PLUS UNPUBLISHED MATERIAL

G. Burke: The Cornish Miner and the Cornish Mining Industry 1870-1921 (Unpublished PhD thesis, University of London 1982)

D.D. Hall :The Story of a South Afican Pioneer and his Family Richard Thomas Hall 1823-1889 (1990)

The History of the Henwoods – Their First One Hundred Years 1856-1956 (Durban: The Firm 1956)

Rev. J.C. Harris: Refugees and Relief (London 1901)

Bernard C. Hollowood: Cornish Engineers (Holmans 1951)

Yvonne Miller: Acutts in Africa

Cornish & Other British Newspapers & Journals

The Cambornian

The Cornishman

The Cornish Post & Mining News

The Cornubian & Redruth Times

The Cornish Telegraph

Cornish World

Cornish Worldwide

Hampshire Telegraph & Sussex Chronicle

History Today

History of the Twentieth Century

Illustrated London News

Journal of the Trevithick Society

Mining Journal, Railway & Commercial Gazette

The Observer

The Royal Cornwall Gazette

The Times

The West Briton

The Western Daily Mercury

The Western Morning News

Southern African Newspapers & Journals

Cape Argus

Cape Times

Daily Independent

Diamond Fields Advertiser

Diamond Fields Herald

Diamond Fields News

Diamond Fields Times

Eastern Province Herald

Gold Fields Mercury – Pilgrims Rest

Gold Fields News & Barberton Herald

Grahamstown Journal

Indian Opinion

Journal of South African Studies

Kimberley Advertiser

Kimberley Illustrated

Krugersdorp Standard

Krugersdorp Times

Natalia

Natal Mercury

Natal Witness

News of the Camp

The North Western Press

Personality

Potchefstroom Budget

Potchefstroom Herald

The Rand Daily Mail

The Roodepoort Mail, Florida & Mariasburg News

The Star

The Settler

The South African Mines, Commerce & Industries Journal

The South African Mining Journal

Standard & Diggers News

Standard Transvaal Mining Chronicle

Standard & West Rand Review

Sunday Times (Johannesburg)

The Transvaal Argus & Potchefstroom Gazette

Transvaal Leader

INDEX

The index includes references to the Foreword, Preface and Introduction but not the Notes. References to illustrations are shown in bold type.

Ingogo Hill 43
Isandlwana 36, 38

James, Arthur H 84, 296
James, William 57, 58
Jameson, L.S. **68**, 135, 137, 138, 140, 141, 142, 143
    Prime Minister, Cape Colony 184, 208
Jameson Raid 135, 137-146
Johannesburg **79**
    1913 strike 245
    administration 96
    during Boer War (1899-1902) 174, 175, 176
    after Boer War 195, 196
    early days 91, 99
    hospitals 97, 103
    hotels 93, **94**, 95
    Jubilee celebrations 296, 297
    law enforcement 97-99, 109, 143, 144
    life of miners 108-110, 123, 271
    newspapers 96, 97
    public health 99-101
    share market 109, 110
    social gatherings 93, 94, 106, 109, 110, 258, 265, 276
    see also Cornish Associations: Rand
    stores 91, **92, 93, 94,** 95, 128, **128, 244**

Johns, J. Harry 122, 139, 149, 227, 297
    Consulting Engineer 239
    and labour 198, 205
    mine manager 87, 89
    rock drilling 238
Joubert, Petrus Jacobus (Piet) 46
    Boer War (1880) 41, 42, 43, 44
    Boer War (1899-1902) 151, 152

Khama, Chief of Bamangwato tribe 73
Kimberley 59, 61, 180, 295
    Annual Cornish Dinners 67-69, 267, 268, 270
    communication 59
    Cornish residents 69, 70
    early days 53
    Siege 153, 156-158
    see also Cornish Associations: Kimberley; diamond
    mines: Kimberley
Kimberley School of Mines 61
Kitchener, Lord 154, 155, 158, 163, 168
Kitto, Thomas Collingwood 59, 78, 234, 236, 284, 285
Kitto family 10
Kowie River 2, 3
Kruger, Johannes Paulus (Paul) 42, 46, 96, 97, 98, 163, 174,
    182, 183
    Jameson Raid 135, 136, 138, 142
    Krugersdorp 98
    Uitlanders 146, 147
Krugersdorp 97-99, 143, 293-294

Labour Bureau (Rand) 272, 273
Labour Importation Ordinance, Transvaal 201, 207
Lacy, George 82, 83, 84
Ladysmith, Siege of 153, 154, 156, 160
Laings Nek 43, 44
Langalibalele Rebellion 20, 22
language v, 21, 212, 311, 315

Lanyon, Owen 40, 42, 43, 45
law enforcement 72, 142, 163
    Rand 97-99, 109, 143, 144
Lawn, James Gunson 61, 296
Lawson, Wilfred 199
Levington-Vincent, Anna 259, 276
Liberal Party (Britain) 41, 42, 129-131, 165, 166, 167, 213
libraries 109, 284
Limpopo River 19
Liskeard 166, 298
Lloyd George, David 165, 166
lung disease *see* phthisis
Lyle, John Vacy 33, **33**, 34, 35

MacArthur, J.S. 84
MacArthur-Forrest process 84, *86*
Mafeking 70, 72, 160, 161
Majuba Hill 44
Mandela, Nelson 313
Mann, Tom 242, 243
manufacturing 124-127
marriage 105106
Mathews, Tom 197, 242, 243, 244, **247**, 248, 296
    1907 strike 232, 234, 236, 237
    1913 strike 245, 246, 247, 248
    Chinese labour 205, 206, 207
    phthisis 205, 236, 242, 244
May, Llewellyn *see* Tossel, Frederick de Witt (Llewellyn
    May)
mayors 291, 293, 294
Melvill, Teignmouth 36-38, **37**
Methodism 10, 95, 109, 145, 290, 313
    see also churches; religion
Methuen, Lord 153, 154
Michell, Lewis 46, **68**, 183, 184
    Boer War (1899-1902) 169
    Chinese labour 204, 205
    and Rhodes 54
    Standard Bank 46, 47, 184
    Transvaal self-government 231
Milner, Alfred 146, 147, 177, 178, 195, 201
Mine Managers' Association, Witwatersrand 87, 88
miners
    character 57, 58
    first Cornish settlers 7
    life in Johannesburg 108-110, 123, 271
    migrant labourers 107, 108, 310
Miners' Association (Rand) 197, 205, 206, 231, 236, 238, 239,
    242
Miners' Phthisis Acts 243, 244, 250
mines in Cornwall 117, 118, 121-123, 216, 217, 288, 311
    Basset 55, 122, 288
    benefits from South Africa 90, 91
    Botallack 55, 63, 288
    Chacewater Railway 286
    Dolcoath 121, 122, 288, 291, 295
    East Pool & Agar 121, 122, 291, 295
    Geevor 216, 291, 295, 311
    Levant 55, 56, 63, 122, 209, 287-289, 291, 295
    South Crofty 61, 121, 289, 291, 295, 311
    South Francis 57
    St Just Amalgamated 63
    Tincroft and Cooks Kitchen 121, 289

safety fuse **126,** 127, 280
saffron cake 315
Sand River Convention 31
Sekhukhune, Chief of Pedi tribe 31, 32, 33, 40
share market 109, 110
Shepstone, Theophilus 21-23, *33,* 33-35, 39, 40
Silati River Gold Mining Company 129, 130
silicosis *see* phthisis
Smith-Dorrien, Horace 38, 153, 158
Smuts, Jan 168, 249, 297, 298, 311
    and Indian rights 299-301
    and strikes 245, 246
social gatherings 111, 275, 276, 293, 294
    Annual Cornish Dinners, Kimberley 67-69, 267, 268, 270
    Christmas celebrations 106, 110, 154, 176, 258, 265
    Cornish Fair 276
    Good Friday Picnic 273
    Johannesburg 93, 94, 106, 109, 110, 276
    Pretoria 44, 110-111
South Africa, Union of 243
South African Republic 31, 34, 42
Spion Kop 155, 156
sport *see* cricket; horse-racing; rugby; wrestling
St Just 57, 6266, 148, 164, 171, 172, 209
St Stithians College 285, 286, **286**
Standard Bank of South Africa 45-47, 78, 99
Strauss, Arthur 131, 141, 165-168, 199
strikes
    1907: 231, 232, 234-238, 247
    1911: 243
    1913: 245, 246
    1914: 246, 247
    1922: 249, 250
Stuttaford & Co. 7, 59, 93, **94**
Stuttaford, Samson Rickard 7, 59, 93, 281
sugar industry, Natal 16, 17, 18

telephones 99
Thomas brothers 79
Tickell, W.G. 271, 272, **274**, 275
Tiddy, Frederick J. 284
    Boer War (1899-1902) 142, 149
    Chinese labour 195, 196, 215
    Cornish miners 108, 109
    politics 214, 216, 231
tin mining 148
    Australia XIII
    Cornwall 117, 121-123, 193, 216, 217, 288-291, 294, 295, 311 *see also* mines in Cornwall
    Malaya XIII, 122, 193, 194
Transvaal 237
Tossel, Frederick de Witt (Llewellyn May) 71, 72
    during Boer War (1899-1902) 173, 174
    on Rand 97-99, **98**, 143, 144
Trades Union 284
transport business 47, 48
Transvaal 31, 33, 34, 35, 45, 163
Transvaal Argus 41, 45
Transvaal Mining Argus 96
Tredrea, Thomas Bond **60,** 61
Tredrea, William James **60,** 61
Tregarthen, William Coulson 294

Trembath, James Farquharson 284
Tremeer, Charles Arthur Claud 96, 136, 137
Trewick, 242
Triggs, James 263, 264
Triumvirate 42, 44, 45, 46
Tucker, Joseph 146, 199, 200, 202, 227, 228, 240

Uitlanders 135, 137, 138, 142, 145, 146
    enfranchisement 136, 147, 148, 150
    see also Reform Committee
University of Cape Town 281
University of Witwatersrand 61

Veldt Tragedy 281
Voortrekkers 13
Vriedendorp explosion 144, 145
Vryburg 70, 71, 72
Vyvyan, Courtney 161

Wearne, W G. **292,** 293
West of England Association, Cape Town 269
Wevell Brothers 127, 128
whims 52, 53
White Labour League 201
Whitford, John 88
Wilkinson, Bishop 77
William Hosken & Co. 128, **128**
Williams, James 129, 130
Wolseley, Sir Garnet 39, 40, 45
women 105-106, 110
    during Boer War (1899-1902) 157, 168, 169, 177, 178, 182
    Cornish Association on the Rand 274, 275
    in Cornwall 110, 119-121
    Siege of Kimberley 157, 158
    social gatherings 275, 276
Wood, Henry Evelyn 38-40, 44, 45, 47
Woods, Donald 2
World War I 286, 287
wrestling 10, 69, 263-265, **264**

Young, Henry Arthur 272, 277

Zulu language 21
Zulu War 36-39